INTERNATIONAL BUSINESS

Operating in the Global Economy

INTERNATIONAL BUSINESS

Operating in the Global Economy

JAMES K. WEEKLY
The University of Toledo
RAJ AGGARWAL
The University of Toledo

The Dryden Press
Chicago   New York   Philadelphia   San Francisco   Montreal   Toronto   London
Sydney   Tokyo   Mexico City   Rio de Janeiro   Madrid

Acquisitions Editor: Mary Fischer
Project Editor: Nancy Shanahan
Design Supervisor: Jeanne Calabrese
Production Manager: Mary Jarvis
Permissions Editor: Doris Milligan
Director of Editing, Design, and Production: Jane Perkins

Text Designer: Jan Chappel
Copy Editor: Joseph Pomerance
Indexer: Ann Tomchek
Compositor: Waldman Graphics
Text Type: 10/12 Palatino

Library of Congress Cataloging-in-Publication Data

Weekly, James K., 1933-
 International business.

 Includes index.
 1. International economic relations. 2. Commerce.
3. International finance. 4. International business
enterprises. 5. Export marketing. I. Aggarwal, Raj.
II. Title.
HF1411.W377 1987   658′.049   86-11678
ISBN 0-03-063556-X

Printed in the United States of America
789-038-98765432

Address orders:
111 Fifth Avenue
New York, NY 10003

Address editorial correspondence:
One Salt Creek Lane
Hinsdale, IL 60521

The Dryden Press
Holt, Rinehart and Winston
Saunders College Publishing

Cover Illustration: Jim Rabon/Image Electronic, Atlanta, GA.
Endsheet Source: © Copyright by Rand McNally & Company, R.L. 86-S-45.

With great affection to our wives, Marlyn and Karen,
and our children, Mark, Sean, and Sonia

The Dryden Press Series in Management

Arthur G. Bedeian, Consulting Editor

Preface

The post–World War II era has been marked by momentous developments in international economic conditions and in the scope and character of business operations. Economic growth, increasing affluence,
and the population explosion have generated enormous demands for
capital and consumer goods throughout the world, while rapid technological progress has greatly reduced the cost and increased the speed
with which products and productive resources can be transferred from
country to country to satisfy such demands. Technological innovation
has also brought about the introduction of a multitude of new and
complex products, thereby creating unprecedented opportunities for nations to specialize in production and to trade with one another. Substantial strides have also been made in reducing tariffs and other legal
impediments to the international movement of goods, services, people,
and information.

These and other developments have led to a vast increase in international trade. Perhaps more importantly, they have induced thousands
of firms to undertake business operations outside their home countries
as a means of securing overseas markets, acquiring needed resources,
and lowering their costs of production. Most of·this international direct
investment, which entails the transfer of capital, technology, and managerial skills across national boundaries, has been carried out by **multinational corporations**, giant business enterprises that operate on a
worldwide scale.

The growth of international trade and investment and the emergence
of multinational corporations have resulted in more efficient utilization
of resources and thus have contributed significantly to economic progress
and increased prosperity for the people of the world. However, these
developments have also given rise to serious problems. Nations and
groups of nations have often argued bitterly over trade policies and the
division of the economic benefits of trade. Multinational companies have
been severely criticized for engaging in exploitative behavior and for
ignoring the economic interests or infringing the political sovereignty
of both their home and host countries. As the economies of the nations

of the world become more tightly intertwined and interdependent, the economic health of those nations has likewise become more dependent on external forces, and their industries and workers have become highly vulnerable to foreign competition. Meanwhile, economic competition among nations has steadily intensified, as many of the developing countries have established new manufacturing sectors and begun competing with the more established manufacturing sectors of the industrialized nations for export markets.

These changes in the world economy have created myriad challenges for business firms and their managers. Those companies that have "gone international" have had to learn to cope with widely varying and unfamiliar economic, political, and cultural conditions in their far-flung markets, as well as with differing national laws and attitudes toward business, fluctuating currency values, and disparities in the state of technology and the availability of support facilities. Even companies that have not ventured into overseas production or marketing have frequently found themselves faced with strong foreign competition or increased dependence on foreign suppliers, so that they too have become part of a worldwide production system and marketplace.

This text examines the developments noted above and analyzes the manifold effects they are having on the conduct of business and the tasks and responsibilities of business managers. The principal theses underlying the book and its orientation are that business henceforth will be largely **international** in nature and will be carried on within an integrated **global economy**. Therefore, anyone involved in or preparing for a managerial career must comprehend and be trained to deal with those realities and their ramifications.

As an introductory text, this book is not intended to fulfill such needs totally. Rather, its aims are to help students gain a basic understanding of the forces that are shaping the emerging global economy and an appreciation of how these developments are likely to affect their companies and themselves in their future managerial roles. These aims are pursued consistently throughout the book. It explores major trends in world trade and investment, economic relationships among nations and associated problems, and the principal institutions involved in facilitating and regulating international business and economic activity. Furthermore, this text also explains how and why those developments, relationships, and institutions are linked to the decisions of business firms, and analyzes the problems with which such firms must contend when they are operating in the dynamic international economic environment.

This text is designed for use in undergraduate courses in international business, although it can also be used effectively in introductory or survey courses at the graduate level. It covers key concepts in the field of international business, as well as crucial developments affecting the international business environment, and treats these topics succinctly and in a way that makes them both understandable and thought-provoking to students who may be encountering these subjects for the first time.

The concepts presented in the text are illustrated through examples drawn from current international economic issues or from the actual experiences of business firms. A short case is presented at the end of each chapter, which gives students an opportunity to analyze controversial international economic policy questions or international management problems. Each chapter also includes a list of objectives, a concise summary of the major facts and ideas presented, and a set of questions for review or discussion.

A comprehensive *Instructor's Manual* accompanies this text. It contains for each chapter: teaching objectives, teaching suggestions for the instructor, answers to the end-of-chapter questions for review or discussion, multiple choice questions, and a solution for the end-of-chapter case.

We are indebted to many persons for their contributions to the preparation of this book. Professor Richard Farmer of Indiana University and Professor John Ryans of Kent State University gave us much encouragement and useful advice in the critical early stages of our endeavor, and Professor Ryans also served as one of the reviewers of our manuscripts. Others who reviewed various drafts of the manuscript and provided us with perceptive and helpful critiques are Glenn Boseman (American College), S. Tamer Cavusgil (Bradley University), Victor E. Childers (Indiana University), Bill Davidson (University of Southern California), R. Peter DeWitt (University of Central Florida), Andrew C. Gross (Cleveland State University), Phillip D. Grub (George Washington University), A. G. Kefalas (University of Georgia), Lee C. Nehrt (The Ohio State University), Cynthia Spanhel (University of Texas, Austin), Dennis R. Vanden Bloomen (University of Wisconsin, Stout), and Heidi Vernon-Wortzel (Northeastern University). We also wish to thank Susan Andrews, Gail Stolarski, Sandra Whitman, Katie DeHaven, and Paula Gerrick for their excellent work in typing the manuscripts.

James K. Weekly
Raj Aggarwal
Toledo, Ohio

Dr. James K. Weekly is a professor of International Business and Director of the International Business Institute at the University of Toledo. He received his D.B.A., M.B.A., and B.S. degrees from Indiana University with a major in International Business and supporting fields of economics, finance, business-government relations, and Latin American studies.

In addition to the University of Toledo, Dr. Weekly has taught in the Department of Business and Economics at Macalester College, St. Paul, Minnesota. In addition to his teaching activities at the University of Toledo, Dr. Weekly has been Associate Dean of the College of Business Administration, Acting Dean of the College, and Chairman of the Department of Marketing.

Dr. Weekly's major research interests are in the fields of international business and finance, and he has published numerous articles in professional journals including *The Journal of Common Market Studies*, the *Nebraska Journal of Economics and Business*, *MSU Business Topics*, *Inter-American Economic Affairs*, and *Business and Society*. He has received a number of government and private fellowships and grants for field research in Latin American countries and has served as a consultant in international marketing and export market development of business firms and professional organizations.

Dr. Raj Aggarwal is Professor of Finance and International Business and Chairman of the Finance Department at the University of Toledo. He received his M.B.A. in Operations Management and a D.B.A. in Corporate Finance and International Business.

In addition to the University of Toledo, Dr. Aggarwal has taught graduate courses in finance and accounting, international business, and business policy at the University of Michigan, University of South Carolina, Seton Hall, Kent State, and Indiana University. His business experience includes projects in Strategic Planning, Acquisition Analysis, International Accounting, and Budgeting and Evaluation for International Operations for major corporations. He has conducted numerous seminars for senior executives and has addressed many business groups.

Dr. Aggarwal has published over sixty scholarly papers in refereed journals and five books including *The Literature of International Business Finance* (Praeger, 1984), *The Management of Foreign Exchange* (Arno Press, 1981), *Financial Policies for the Multinational Company* (Praeger, 1976), and *Management Science* (Holden-Day, 1978). He has been a recipient of many research grants and awards, including a *Senior Fulbright Research Fellowship*, and is a member of editorial and review boards of a number of scholarly journals, including the *Journal of International Business Studies.*

He has held many appointed or elected positions in professional and academic organizations such as the Financial Management Association, American Accounting Association, and the Academy of International Business. He is also a member of professional groups such as the Finance Executives Institute. He has been the chairperson for the midwest and program chairman for the annual midwest meetings of the Academy of International Business since 1982 and has been elected Vice President for 1986–88.

Contents

Part 1

THE GLOBAL ECONOMY *17*

Part 2

INTERNATIONAL BUSINESS THEORIES AND POLICIES *101*

Part 3
THE INTERNATIONAL FINANCIAL SYSTEM   *215*

Part 4
MULTINATIONAL BUSINESS ENTERPRISES   *307*

Chapter 16
Multinational Financial Management   393

Appendix
Acronyms and Initials   417

Chapter 1

INTRODUCTION: THE NATURE AND DIMENSIONS OF INTERNATIONAL BUSINESS

Chapter Objectives

- *To define international business and describe its distinguishing characteristics and challenges*
- *To identify and describe the different types of international business activities*
- *To show how international business has grown in recent years*
- *To explain how the subject of international business is studied in colleges and universities and how it will be approached and organized in this book*

International business consists of business activities that are conducted across national boundaries. Such activities generally involve the transfer of resources, goods, or services from nation to nation. International trade, for example, involves movements of products or commodities from sellers located in one nation to buyers located in another nation, while international investment involves the transfer of resources, such as capital or technological know-how.

The basic tasks and processes associated with business are much the same whether business is being carried on domestically (within a single nation) or internationally. Business consists essentially of the production and distribution of products or services and the financing of such activities, and each of these main business functions can be divided into several subfunctions. The nature of these functions and their relationship to one another will not be altered in any fundamental way when business is being transacted across national borders. It is very likely, however, that the business firm will experience greater difficulty in performing these tasks effectively and will encounter more risk in connection with their performance when it is operating internationally.

The heightened difficulty and risk associated with international business operations are primarily attributable to forces and conditions external to the business firm itself. Environmental factors impact the way in which a business firm operates and its success in making profits. This, of course, is the case wherever the firm is doing business. But the external forces with which the firm must contend are apt to be considerably more diverse and volatile when it ventures beyond the borders of its home nation. Similarly, the managers of the firm will usually be less familiar with many of these foreign environmental elements and will lack experience in dealing with them.

The environmental conditions affecting international business may be economic, political, or cultural in nature. In the economic realm, business firms operating internationally encounter sharp differences in levels of development, resource supplies, and consumer purchasing power from country to country. These firms must also contend with disparities in the state of technology, the skills and discipline of workers, and the availability of energy, transportation systems, and other facilities that are essential to the production and distribution of goods and services.

Business firms are also likely to be subjected to much more governmental supervision and regulation and to experience many more problems of a political character when they are doing business outside their home country. Government officials, as well as the general public in foreign host countries often tend to view international companies as "outsiders" or "intruders" and to harbor deep suspicions regarding the effects that such companies might have upon their economies and their economic independence and sovereignty.

Cultural factors frequently prove even more perplexing and troublesome than economic and political conditions for a firm involved in international business. Culture pervades and influences virtually all aspects of human behavior, interactions, and thought, so that a business enterprise cannot ignore or escape its effects. A company endeavoring to do business on a worldwide scale will confront a myriad of cultures and subcultures, each of which will differ from all the others in significant but often subtle ways.

This cultural mix can affect every facet of an international firm's activities. The demand for its product, the kind of production methods that it can utilize, its relationships with workers, suppliers, customers, and government officials, the acceptability and effectiveness of its advertising and selling efforts, the success of communications and working associations among its managers, and the validity and relevance of its ethical standards and corporate policies are all likely to be determined, to some extent, by how well it recognizes and responds to the varied and dynamic cultural environments in which it is operating.

It is mainly this environmental complexity that sets international business apart from its domestic counterpart. This is also what makes international business especially challenging and exciting to managers.

Types of International Business Operations

A business firm wishing to develop and serve markets outside its home country has a number of different approaches or methods available to it. These sometimes are referred to as "entry strategies," since they constitute alternative means of entering foreign markets. Although a firm might choose to utilize only one of these alternatives for all its international operations, it is not uncommon for a company to be employing several different entry strategies simultaneously in the various foreign countries in which it is doing business. A company might also alter its mode of foreign operations over time, so that the different entry strategies make up a sort of evolutionary path that the firm follows as its international activities expand and mature.

Exporting

A business firm may maintain its production facilities within the territory of its home nation and export its products to foreign countries. Such transfers of goods from the country in which they are produced to markets in other countries is the oldest form of international business in historical terms, and exporting continues to account for a substantial portion of all international business activity.

Exporting provides a means by which a company can market its products abroad with a relatively small outlay of resources and limited risk. This is not to imply that exporting is a simple or risk-free process. On the contrary, it entails numerous problems, emanating from the physical distances separating sellers and buyers, a multiplicity of governmental regulations, the complications of dealing in foreign currencies and extending credit to foreign customers, longer and more complex channels of distribution, and cultural differences among the customers and markets being served. However, it is possible for a firm to engage in exporting without making an extensive and permanent commitment of its own capital, personnel, and other resources to the international marketing effort and without incurring many of the risks that would be encountered if those resources were transferred into the foreign market territory. It is for this reason that exporting is frequently looked upon as a comparatively safe and flexible entry strategy.

The view of exporting described above is particularly applicable to **indirect exporting.** Indirect exporting is characterized by the extensive use of export marketing middlemen that are not owned or managed by the firm producing the product being exported. These independent middlemen may buy the product outright for subsequent resale or may act as sales agents for the producing firm under a contractual agreement. The marketing facilities and services that such middlemen can provide, together with their contacts and experience, often make it practical for companies that otherwise could not mount and sustain an export operation to have their products marketed internationally. Relying upon these external marketing intermediaries does, of course, reduce the manufacturer's ability to control the way in which its product is distributed abroad and may reduce or totally eliminate opportunities for the producing firm to have contact with the final users of its product. But such disadvantages of indirect exporting frequently are outweighed by the advantages of a "ready-made" exporting organization, especially if the firm is entering foreign markets for the first time or is expecting to sell abroad only on occasion.

The company that becomes involved in exporting on a permanent basis and on a fairly large scale may decide to develop its own export marketing organization and operate its own distribution facilities. This approach is referred to as **direct exporting.** The line between direct and indirect exporting is not always clear, inasmuch as the distribution channels which a firm uses for its exporting operations could be a combination of its own facilities and those provided by independent middlemen. As a matter of managerial orientation and emphasis, however, a shift from indirect to direct exporting means that the producing firm assumes principal responsibility for the distribution of its product abroad. This permits the manufacturer to more fully control the marketing process, but typically requires substantial outlays of capital funds to acquire and maintain distribution facilities as well as the commitment of considerable managerial time and effort to the exporting program.

Licensing

In licensing arrangements, one business firm (the licensor) makes certain resources or "inputs" available to another business firm (the licensee). The availability of those inputs makes it possible for the licensee to produce and market a product or service similar to that which the licensor has been producing. Licensing constitutes a type of foreign market entry strategy when the two companies involved are located in different countries. The licensing arrangement gives the licensor an opportunity to participate in a limited and indirect way in the production and sale of products outside its home country.

Intangible inputs, such as technology, managerial skills, or patent and trademark rights, frequently form the principal basis of international licensing agreements. An American company might, for example, provide technological or managerial know-how to assist a foreign firm in manufacturing an improved product or reducing its production costs. Or the American firm might permit the foreign licensee to manufacture a patented product or use a registered trademark, which it would otherwise be legally prohibited from doing. In these instances, the American company would be drawing upon the accumulated knowledge and experience of its personnel, its past efforts in research and development, or the favorable image associated with its trademark or brand name for the benefit of the overseas licensee.

Franchising is a form of licensing that has spread rapidly throughout the world in recent years. In international franchising agreements, the franchisor provides its foreign franchisees with a package of materials and services. This may include equipment, products or product ingredients, trademark or tradename rights, managerial advice, and a standardized operating or marketing "system." The layout of the physical facilities that the franchisees will use to produce and market the product or service involved may be a part of that standard system.

Some of the best-known and most successful international franchisors have been the fast-food chains. Kentucky Fried Chicken, Burger King, and Wendy's outlets can now be found in almost every large city in the world, and the story is often told of the Japanese child visiting Los Angeles who excitedly pointed out to his parents that "they have McDonald's in America, too!" Hotel chains, such as Holiday Inns and Ramada Inns, and car-rental companies, such as Hertz and Avis, are other examples of firms that have become heavily involved in international franchising.

International licensing affords attractive opportunities for business firms, inasmuch as it enables them to realize additional revenues, in the form of fees or royalties, for information or assistance that they can provide at very little out-of-pocket cost to themselves. This view of international licensing as a low-cost and low-risk means of extending the firm's return on past investment or already-available assets has made it a very appealing entry strategy.

However, licensing as a foreign market entry strategy is not without its disadvantages and dangers. Since the licensor is restricting its involvement in the foreign business venture to the provision of certain inputs, it follows that its share of the revenues and profits generated by that venture will likewise be restricted. Moreover, the licensor, should it subsequently wish to undertake more extensive and direct operations in the foreign market area, may find that it has, in effect, created competition for itself in the person of its licensee. Licensors have also encountered considerable difficulty in preventing the misuse or unauthorized transfer of patents or trademarks and in ensuring the maintenance of quality and service standards by foreign licensees. As with indirect exporting, licensing offers a business firm relatively easy and inexpensive access to international markets, but it also sets constraints upon the firm's participation in and control over the development of those markets.

Foreign Production

A business firm located in one country may acquire facilities that enable it to produce a product or render a business service within the territory of another country. The acquisition of such foreign production capability usually occurs through **direct investment** by the firm. An essential element in direct investment is the investor's involvement in the management of the productive assets, and direct investment is distinguished from other types of foreign investment by reference to this element of managerial control.

Box 1.1

International Licensing Successes and Setbacks

The Shanghai Bureau of Instruments and Communications has opened a television picture tube plant as part of the Chinese government's effort to make television accessible to more Chinese. The tubes will not carry a made-in-U.S.A. label, but they will exist only because of Corning Glass Company of Corning, New York. The Shanghai venture is the first carried out by Corning Engineering, a subsidiary that was formed in 1981 to market Corning technology throughout the world. In addition to the picture tube contract, the new subsidiary is offering processes for fusing glass, making glass tubing, and high-temperature glass melting to foreign companies.

The license of an operator of McDonald's restaurants in France was revoked by a Chicago judge after testimony that conditions were "filthy" at a dozen Paris outlets that he owns. McDonald's Corporation had charged that the Paris operations did not meet company standards for quality, service, and cleanliness. McDonald's is temporarily withdrawing from the Paris market and relinquishing its growing Paris royalties "in order to preserve its hard-earned reputation." The owner of the Paris outlets was ordered to remove McDonald's signs, equipment, and other trademark material.

Source: "Secrets for Sale," *Sales and Marketing Management* (February 6, 1984): 13; "McDonald's Operator in Paris Loses License over Conditions," *The Blade*, September 10, 1982, 14.

There are a number of ways in which a company headquartered in one country might establish production facilities in other countries, and there also are varying degrees to which such a company may be involved in the management of those facilities. A decision on the part of a company's management to undertake foreign production might be carried out by building and equipping a factory in an overseas location. In this situation, the company would be creating a production facility that did not previously exist. Alternatively, the company might attain the capability to produce abroad by acquiring an existing production facility, for example, by buying a factory that previously was owned and operated by someone else. The company's participation in the ownership and management of such production facilities may be partial or total, which is to say that it might have total ownership and therefore complete control, or it might share ownership and control with other investors. The choice between a **wholly owned foreign affiliate** and a **joint venture** with others is not always left entirely to the discretion of the investing company, since many countries now have laws that prohibit complete foreign ownership of economic enterprises operating in their territories.

Foreign production offers a business firm the basic and important element of proximity to its intended overseas market. This closeness to the market may give rise to substantial cost savings by shortening distribution channels and reducing storage and transportation costs, but the heightened awareness of economic, cultural, and political conditions that comes from being "on the scene" in the foreign market and the related ability to respond quickly to changes in those conditions may be equally important considerations. In addition to these merits of market proximity, companies have often found that locating their producing units in foreign areas has enabled them to secure labor or materials at lower costs than would have been possible in their own country, and that this, in turn, has permitted them to produce and sell at a competitive price, not only in the foreign country, but also in their home market.

While the advantages described above undoubtedly account for much of the massive expansion of foreign direct investment by private business firms that has been going on since the end of World War II, such investment has also been undertaken on numerous occasions as a defensive measure. A great many companies have deemed it necessary to invest abroad in order to maintain a market position that they initially developed through exporting or in order to establish a foothold in a growing foreign market. Acquiring the ability to produce within the foreign market territory has allowed such companies to avoid taxes or other restrictions applicable to exports or has otherwise helped them to cope with competitive pressures.

It should be apparent that foreign production normally entails a considerably greater commitment to the foreign market on the part of the firm than either exporting or licensing. The company that undertakes direct investment abroad is using its capital funds or other resources to acquire real productive assets that will be exposed to the risks that emanate from that country's economic and political environment. In most instances, such direct investment also means that managerial and technical personnel from the investing firm will be assigned to reside and work in the foreign country and will likewise be confronted with a variety of unusual problems and risks. These can occasionally reach extreme proportions, as, for example, in those cases of American managers who become targets for kidnapping or assassination by political terrorists. But more often these expatriate personnel must be prepared to cope with the more mundane but nevertheless complicated task of living and operating a business enterprise in an unfamiliar environment, which differs in innumerable obvious or subtle ways from that to which they are accustomed.

Exporting, licensing, and foreign production comprise the fundamental alternative means through which a firm is able to conduct business in or with foreign countries. However, a number of variations or modifications of these basic entry strategies have been devised and utilized by business firms. One of these variations is the **turnkey project,** in which manufacturing plants or other types of production facilities are constructed and equipped by a firm or group of firms with the intention of turning them over to new owners when they are ready for operation. Turnkey arrangements have become more common in recent years, as countries in the developing Third World and in the communist areas have adopted this method of acquiring production units built and equipped by American or other Western firms without accepting a permanent Western presence in their economies.

Management contracts constitute another variant from the basic foreign market entry strategies. Under such contracts, a business firm will assign some of its managers to assist a firm in another country and to train its personnel to assume managerial positions. These arrangements generally are for a limited period of time, and the managerial assistance may be associated with some specific project or activity or may be more general in scope.

Both management contracts and turnkey projects can be viewed as ways of "unbundling" the resources that historically have been supplied and transferred as a package in foreign direct investment ventures. When a firm undertakes a turnkey project, it is agreeing to provide capital goods and technology without ongoing managerial involvement, whereas in management contracts, the firm is supplying managerial expertise without simultaneously supplying capital goods or other inputs. This unbundling may be viewed as advantageous by both parties in such international arrangements, since it permits the recipient firm (and the country in which it is located) to acquire only those inputs from abroad which are most needed, while allowing the firm supplying such inputs to specialize in what it can do best and to limit its risk exposure. The rapid pace of economic development and change around the world, together with shifting political relationships and growing nationalistic feelings, have increased the need for flexibility and adaptability on the part of business firms wishing to operate internationally, and these variant forms of foreign operations represent just one aspect of this ongoing process of adaptation to a dynamic international business environment.

Growth of International Business Operations

The difficulties and risks that were described in the first section of this chapter have by no means deterred business firms from undertaking international operations. These operations have expanded immensely over the past three decades. Many firms have become **multinational corporations,** which are business enterprises that own and manage **affiliates** located in several different countries and conduct business on a worldwide scale.[1]

U.S. companies have played a major role in this "internationalization" of business, although non-U.S. companies are also extensively involved in foreign operations. Indeed, in recent years such companies, notably those from Western Europe and Japan, have been expanding internationally at a pace that has seriously challenged the predominance of American firms in the global business system.

Measuring the exact extent of international business activity is complicated somewhat by scarcity and lack of comparability of data. Nevertheless, enough quantitative information is available to yield an understanding of the scope of international business operations and an appreciation of how rapidly they have been growing. The following brief survey will consider both the worldwide dimensions of international business activity and those pertaining to U.S. companies specifically.

This survey can begin with export statistics, which are more readily available and generally regarded as more accurate than those relating to the other forms of international business operations described in the preceding section. National governments endeavor to keep careful track of goods moving into and out of their territories for purposes of taxing and regulating such activities, and a number of international organizations also accumulate and disseminate comprehensive data on exports in connection with their efforts to expand and liberalize international trade.

World exports have grown very substantially during the post–World War II era. The dollar value of merchandise exports for the world as a whole reached nearly $2 trillion in 1984, compared with only about $50 billion in 1948. It should be pointed out that these are current dollar figures, which means that a part of the apparent growth of exports is the result of inflationary increases in the prices of the goods involved. However, even when such price effects are taken into account, the volume of products and commodities marketed internationally via the export route is enormous and has been expanding at a very impressive rate.

Export sales by U.S. companies have likewise grown significantly during this period. The dollar value of U.S. merchandise exports was $220 billion in 1984, compared with just under $20 billion in 1960. U.S. exports have been increasing not only in absolute terms, but also in relation to the total output of the American economy. Thus, while export

---

[1]Multinational corporations are described more precisely and discussed more fully in chapters 13 and 14.

sales accounted for just under 6 percent of all goods produced in the United States in 1960, that figure grew to over 16 percent by 1982.[2] This clearly indicates that American companies are looking more toward foreign countries as markets for the goods which they are producing within the United States.

Measures of the volume of foreign production are more difficult to compile than data on exports, since only a small number of countries have attempted to systematically record the amount of output produced abroad by business firms headquartered in their national territories. The U.S. government has been ahead of most other national governments in maintaining such records, and the most accurate data available on foreign production therefore relate to American companies.

One of the most comprehensive sources of information pertaining to foreign production by American business firms is a study carried out by the U.S. Department of Commerce, which surveyed the foreign direct investment of those firms in 1977. This survey found that approximately 3,500 American companies had direct investments in nearly 25,000 overseas affiliates. Those affiliates had total assets of more than $800 billion, employed more than 7 million people, and the sales (or gross operating revenues) of the nonbanking affiliates in this group totaled $846 billion for the year 1977.[3] Such statistics often are difficult to place in perspective, but one way to highlight the immensity of these foreign operations by U.S. companies is to point out that the value of the annual output of their overseas affiliates exceeded the gross national product of all the nations of the world, other than the United States itself and the Soviet Union.

Statistics on foreign production per se are not available on a year-by-year basis. In order to ascertain how such production has expanded over time, it therefore is necessary to examine a related indicator that is reported annually. This indicator is the **book value** of foreign direct investment (FDI), which measures the amount of capital funds that firms have invested in overseas affiliates. Inasmuch as there is presumed to be a direct and fairly stable relationship between this capital base and the output which it helps to create, increases in FDI are indicative of the growth of foreign production itself.

Figure 1.1 shows how the book value of foreign direct investment, both in total and by American firms, has risen during recent years. The world total grew from about $66 billion in 1960 to $546 billion in 1981, while the share accounted for by U.S. firms increased from $32 billion to $226 billion over the same period. The growth rate of U.S. direct investment abroad averaged slightly less than 10 percent per annum

---

[2]"Trends in United States Foreign Trade," *Economic Road Maps* (New York: The Conference Board, 1983), 1.

[3]Bureau of Economic Analysis, U.S. Department of Commerce, "1977 Benchmark Survey of U.S. Direct Investment Abroad," *Survey of Current Business* (April 1981): 29–37.

Figure 1.1   Foreign Direct Investment (Book Value—Selected Years)

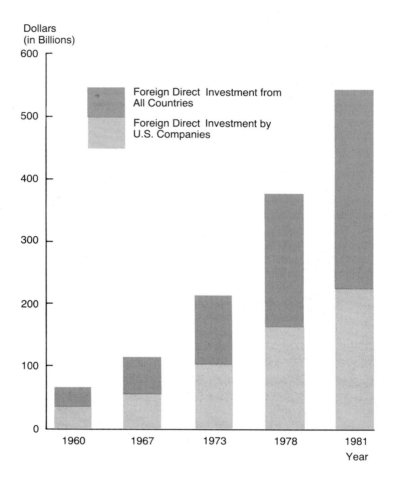

Source: U.S. Department of Commerce, *International Direct Investment: Global Trends and The U.S. Role* (Washington, D.C.: U.S. Department of Commerce, 1984), p 45.

during those years. That rate of increase exceeded the average annual growth of private investment by American firms in the U.S. economy itself by a considerable margin, which means that those firms were expanding their overseas production capacity more rapidly than their productive capacity within the United States.

The third basic form of international business operations, international licensing, must also be measured in a somewhat roundabout manner due to the lack of consistent quantitative data on the actual number of such licensing arrangements. With respect to overseas licensing agreements involving American companies, the statistic that has been gathered and reported on a regular basis is the income that those companies have realized from such arrangements. This income includes fees and royalties received as payment for the intangible properties (including copyrights, trademarks, patents, formulas, designs, franchises, and managerial assistance) that the U.S. licensors have made available to foreign licensees. Prior to 1967, those payments were reported only if they came from foreign affiliates of U.S. companies, that is to say, only when the parent company in the United States was providing intangible resources to a foreign company in which it had an ownership interest. After 1967, the U.S. Department of Commerce began reporting fees and royalties received from both affiliated and nonaffiliated foreign licensors.

What these data reveal is a very substantial increase in licensing income over the past two decades. Fees and royalties received by American licensors grew from less than $1 billion/year in the early 1960s to $7.6 billion for the year 1982. Of that $7.6 billion total, approximately $6.0 billion, or about 80 percent, came from affiliated foreign companies, with the remaining 20 percent being accounted for by payments to U.S. firms from foreign licensees in which they held no ownership share.[4] It is apparent from this breakdown of licensing income that international licensing agreements are closely intertwined with the foreign direct investments of America's corporations.

Even though this brief survey of the quantitative dimensions of international business has had to rely upon some indirect measures and has been restricted to the U.S. experience in some instances, the picture that it imparts is clear and striking. It marks the past three decades as a period in which business became much more global in character, as the international operations of both American and foreign companies expanded at a rapid pace and reached vast proportions.

In the case of U.S. firms, setting these measures of international business activity next to one another points up another important development. This is that foreign production has become the dominant form of such activity. At the present time, the value of output and sales resulting from such overseas production far exceeds the value of exports from the United States. This has not always been the case, for exporting and importing were virtually the only type of international business carried on by American commercial enterprises during much of the nation's early history, and it was not until around 1950 that foreign production by U.S. companies began to outstrip export sales. Although both exports and foreign production have grown enormously since that date, the higher average growth rate of the latter type of operation has

[4]Bureau of Economic Analysis, U.S. Department of Commerce, "U.S. International Transactions, 1983," *Survey of Current Business* (March 1984): 49; "U.S. International Transactions in Royalties and Fees, 1967–78," *Survey of Current Business* (January 1980): 29–30.

resulted in its current preponderance in the international business activities of American firms.

The Study of International Business

The evolution of international business as a field of study in institutions of higher education is very closely linked to the developments described and quantified in the preceding section. Prior to the 1960s, the study of international business in American colleges and universities was limited to a few scattered courses, which usually dealt either with the economic theory of international trade or with the "nuts and bolts" of exporting and importing. But the vast expansion of international operations by U.S. corporations, which began in earnest shortly after World War II and steadily gained momentum thereafter, eventually made these educational institutions aware of a need to respond to the broadened concerns of a business sector whose interests had become global in scope. A substantial number of collegiate schools of business in the U.S. began offering courses in international business during the 1960s, while a smaller group initiated international majors or fields of specialization. Involvement in international business education has continued to increase since that time, and a recent study of some 300 American business schools revealed that 80 percent of the schools surveyed offered some courses in international business.[5]

The objectives of academic programs in international business are not exactly the same among all these U.S. business schools. Some of them have stressed preparation for careers in international management as the principal goal of their programs, while others have emphasized the "broadening" influence of international courses or course materials. The schools in the second group have concluded that the effects of the growing foreign involvement of U.S. business will not be limited to the men and women who actually staff international positions, but will permeate the entire management structure and operating mode of the international firm or even the total business system.

Objectives and Plan of This Book

This book supports that broader view of international business education. It is designed for use in introductory courses in international business, and it has the following major objectives: (1) to make students aware of the expanding scope and significance of international business operations, (2) to familiarize students with the principal features of the

---

[5]Robert Grosse and Gerald W. Perritt, eds., *International Business Curricula: A Global Survey* (Waco, TX: Academy of International Business, 1981), 186.

international economy, (3) to explain how the U.S. economy, particular American industries, and individual business firms interact with or are affected by the international economy, (4) to point out the unique nature of international business and to identify the extraordinary risks, challenges, and problems that business enterprises and their managers encounter when operating across national boundaries or within foreign countries, (5) to describe and illustrate the application of managerial strategies and methodologies for dealing with those extraordinary circumstances and constraints.

The objectives and orientation indicated above are reflected in the organization and contents of this book. This introductory chapter has provided a definition and brief description of international business operations, as well as some perspective on their significance and growth. Following this introduction, Part One of this text, The Global Economy, examines the global business environment and the structure and dynamics of the world economy. This examination covers the important developments in international trade and investment during the post–World War II period, the current pattern of economic relationships that has emerged as a result of those developments, and the institutions that have played a significant part in fashioning and directing the course of the international economy. In this section (as well as in other parts of the book) special attention is accorded to the role of the United States in the situation and events being portrayed and to the impact of those events upon the U.S. economy and upon the present and prospective international operations of American business firms.

Part Two of this text, International Business Theories and Policies, deals with the causes and consequences of international economic transactions. This section draws upon the mainstream theories of international trade and international investment to explain the basis and effects of such transactions. In addition to analyzing foreign trade and investment in theoretical terms, this portion of the text considers the influence of government in order to demonstrate how political interests, expressed through government policies and actions, can affect the nature and outcome of international economic ventures. The U.S. case again receives particular consideration, as the section includes a review and assessment of recent and current U.S. international economic policies.

Part Three of the text, The International Financial System, concentrates upon the monetary dimensions of the world economy and the financial aspects of international economic transactions. This monetary sphere is accorded separate coverage in recognition of its status as a singularly important and, at the same time, "mysterious" element in the international business environment. This section encompasses such subjects as international monetary arrangements, balance of payments, foreign exchange, and financial markets. These are dealt with via a systems approach, that is, they are treated as integrated components (or manifestations) of a financing mechanism whose principal function is to facilitate trade and investment. In keeping with this concept, a definite effort is made to point out both the linkages within this financial mechanism and the manner in which it supports international business activities.

Parts One, Two, and Three of the text provide an overview of the international economy and of the fundamental economic and political institutions and forces at work within it. In Part Four, Multinational Business Enterprises, attention is shifted toward the business firm operating within the international economy. The characteristics, operating methods, economic effects, and political controversies that have come to be associated with multinational corporations are examined and evaluated. The main thrust of this section is to explore the ways in which business enterprise is apt to be affected by foreign operations and interactions with the diversity and dynamics of the global environment.

This final section of the text (chapters 14–16) also considers international business at the operational or managerial level. A functional division of the managerial process will be used to allow for identification of the most pervasive and significant problems that emerge in various functional areas of business as an outgrowth of foreign or international operations and to provide a framework for outlining strategic responses to such problems. This is not intended to constitute an in-depth treatment of the intricacies of international management, but rather an overview with sufficient detail to permit the student to grasp the managerial implications of conducting business internationally.

Summary

1. International business consists of business activities that are conducted across national boundaries. Such activities generally involve the transfer of resources, goods, or services from nation to nation.
2. Although the basic tasks and processes associated with business are the same whether business is being carried on domestically or internationally, a business firm is likely to experience greater difficulty and risk in performing these tasks when it is operating internationally.
3. The heightened difficulty and risk associated with international business are primarily attributable to environmental factors, which may be economic, political, or cultural in character.
4. Despite the problems of doing business internationally, the overseas operations of business firms have expanded immensely during the past three decades.
5. A business firm wishing to develop and serve markets outside its home country has a number of different approaches available. The principal alternative "entry strategies" are exporting, licensing, and foreign production.
6. All forms of international business activity have grown substan-

tially in the post–World War II period. The most rapid expansion has occurred in foreign production, which has become the dominant type of international business activity for U.S. companies.

7.   Collegiate schools of business in the United States have responded to the great expansion of international business operations by increasing their offerings of international business courses.

Questions for Review or Discussion

1.   Discuss why international business operations are likely to be more difficult and risky for a firm than domestic operations.

2.   Compare direct and indirect exporting in terms of such considerations as cost, control, and contact with customers in overseas markets.

3.   Indicate some of the major attractions of international licensing arrangements, as well as the potential problems or risks associated with such arrangements.

4.   Compare the advantages and disadvantages of exporting with those of foreign production from the perspective of a business firm attempting to decide which of these two foreign market entry strategies it should undertake.

Part 1

THE GLOBAL ECONOMY

Chapter 2

THE INTERNATIONAL BUSINESS ENVIRONMENT

Chapter Objectives

- *To highlight the diverse character of the international environment and to indicate how that environmental diversity affects international business*
- *To explain how and why the countries of the world have come to be categorized into major groups on the basis of their economic status and the nature of their economic systems*
- *To point out that international business firms face different types of problems and opportunities in each of those economic groups and to show how such firms have reacted to those differing problems and opportunities*
- *To explain the nature and basis of political risk as it relates to international business operations and to describe the principal strategies that international companies have utilized to avoid or reduce political risk*
- *To consider and illustrate the many complex ways in which culture and cultural dissimilarities can affect a firm that is doing business in several countries and to emphasize the need for cultural sensitivity and adaptability on the part of such firms*

Chapter 1 of this text stressed the idea that the fundamental distinction between doing business internationally and doing business domestically arises out of the environment within which the various functions which comprise the business process are being carried on. A business firm's decision to "go international" involves much more than an expansion of the geographic territory in which it will operate. It also entails a movement into new economic, political, and cultural milieus. Furthermore, the ability of a firm's managers to recognize environmental differences, comprehend their implications, and adapt their products and operating methods to the demands of the environment will usually determine the ultimate success or failure of that firm's international initiative.

This chapter will present an overview of the international business environment. In deference to the magnificent heterogeneity of the societies and nations of the world, it will not aim toward either complete or in-depth coverage. Rather, it will attempt to point out some of the basic and general features that set certain groups of nations and their people apart from others and to indicate how those differences can affect the conduct of business. For purposes of manageability, this survey will concentrate upon the economic, political, and cultural aspects of the international business environment, in that order. These societal elements are always intermingled and interacting with each other, however, so that a complete separation is neither practical nor realistic.

The Economic Environment

Economics has to do with the use of resources to satisfy people's material wants and needs, and the economic life of every nation revolves around the production, distribution, and consumption of "want-satisfying" goods and services. Beyond this elemental similarity, however, there are striking differences throughout the world in the types of economic activities in which people and nations are engaged, the way in which those activities are organized and directed, and the methods and technologies that are employed. There are also pronounced dissimilarities in the efficiency of production and in the amount of economic output that is available for distribution and consumption.

Such variations in the nature of economic activity, the form of economic organization, and the amount of goods and services produced and consumed by different populations have been used extensively as the bases for applying descriptive labels to the countries of the world and dividing them into separate categories. One of the most widely used and enduring of these categorizations has been the division between the "developed" countries and the "developing" countries.[1] The criterion that traditionally has been emphasized in drawing this distinction is per capita gross national product (GNP), which is the value of the goods and services produced by a nation divided by its population. It has thus been tantamount to a distinction between rich nations and poor nations, and it has carried with it all the emotional baggage and tensions which perceptions of unequal divisions of income and wealth can elicit.

Although this developed country/developing country dichotomy may have been a reasonably accurate and serviceable characterization of the

---

[1]Many different designations have been applied to these two groups of countries. The developing countries are also frequently referred to as less-developed countries (LDCs), nonindustrialized countries, or, collectively, as "the Third World," whereas the developed countries are sometimes called the industrialized countries or "the First World." The fact that most of the developing countries are located in the Southern Hemisphere (i.e., in Africa, Asia, and Latin America) while the majority of the developed countries are in the Northern Hemisphere has also led to the use of the terms "South" and "North," respectively, to refer to the two groups.

world at one time, the changes that have taken place in recent years have made it overly simplistic. The economic situations of countries in the developing group have become much more disparate, as some members of that group benefited tremendously from the rapid increases in petroleum prices during the 1970s while others had their economic progress stunted by that same phenomenon. Meanwhile, certain of the developing countries have been able to create strong, export-oriented manufacturing industries, which has raised them to a higher economic status as "newly industrialized countries."[2]

The developed countries have also split into separate blocs, largely as a consequence of differences in their political ideologies that have led them to organize and administer their economies in fundamentally different ways. While the United States, the Western European countries, and Japan have essentially adhered to the capitalistic, private enterprise course (albeit with considerable variation in the extent to which their governments have participated in the ownership and management of economic enterprises), the USSR and the Eastern European nations have followed the communist model of central economic planning and rigid state control of economic activity.

These changes and cleavages have induced those international organizations that are concerned with global economic relationships and conditions to devise classification schemes that more closely reflect the economic (and political) diversity that characterizes the contemporary world. The nations of the world now are commonly divided into several groups and subgroups, and a number of economic and social welfare indicators (such as literacy rates and life expectancy) are taken into account in assessing the relative economic positions of countries in worldwide rankings. The data in Table 2.1, taken from a report by the World Bank, provide a good illustration of this approach. In compiling and presenting these data, the World Bank has used categories that point up differences in the economic systems and major economic activities of the countries included, as well as grouping them by income (per capita GNP) levels.

Table 2.1 provides significant insights into the international economic environment. First, it reveals the large disparities in per capita national product and income that continue to exist around the world. The countries in the low-income group, taken together, recorded an average per capita income of only $260 in 1983, compared with averages of $11,060 for the industrial market economies and $12,370 for the high-income oil exporters. Since some of the low-income countries are among the largest in the world in terms of population, about one-half of the world's people live in this group of nations which collectively produce less than one-tenth of the total world output of goods and services.[3]

---

[2]These developments are discussed more extensively in Chapter 3.

[3]The World Bank, *World Development Report, 1985,* (New York: Oxford University Press, 1985), 148–149.

Table 2.1   Economic Status of Countries of the World–1983

Country	GNP Per Capita (U.S. dollars)	Distribution of Gross Domestic Product (percent)		
		Agriculture	Industry	Services
Low-income economies				
Ethiopia	120	48	16	36
Bangladesh	130	47	13	40
Mali	160	46	11	43
Nepal	160	59	14	27
Zaire	170	36	20	44
Bukrina	180	41	19	40
Burma	180	48	13	39
Malawi	210	—*	—	—
Uganda	220	—	—	—
Burundi	240	58	16	26
Niger	240	33	31	37
Tanzania	240	52	15	33
Somalia	250	50	11	39
India	260	36	26	38
Rwanda	270	—	—	—
Central African Rep.	280	37	21	42
Togo	280	22	28	50
Benin	290	40	14	47
China	300	37	45	18
Guinea	300	38	23	39
Haiti	300	—	—	—
Ghana	310	53	7	40
Madagascar	310	41	15	44
Sierra Leone	330	32	20	48
Sri Lanka	330	27	26	47
Kenya	340	33	20	46
Pakistan	390	27	27	46
Sudan	400	34	15	51
Afghanistan	—	—	—	—
Bhutan	—	—	—	—
Chad	—	—	—	—
Kampuchea	—	—	—	—
Laos	—	—	—	—
Mozambique	—	—	—	—
Viet Nam	—	—	—	—
Middle-income economies				
Senegal	440	21	26	54
Lesotho	460	23	22	55
Liberia	480	36	26	38
Mauitania	480	34	21	45
Bolivia	510	23	26	52
Yemen, PDR†	520	—	—	—
Yemen Arab Rep.	550	21	17	62
Indonesia	560	26	39	35
Zambia	580	14	38	48
Honduras	670	27	26	47
Egypt	700	20	33	47

Country	GNP Per Capita (U.S. dollars)	Distribution of Gross Domestic Product (percent)		
		Agriculture	Industry	Services
El Salvador	710	20	21	59
Ivory Coast	710	27	24	50
Zimbabwe	740	11	32	57
Morocco	760	17	32	51
Papua New Guinea	760	—	—	—
Philippines	760	22	36	42
Nigeria	770	26	34	40
Cameroon	820	24	32	45
Thailand	820	23	27	50
Nicaragua	880	22	32	47
Costa Rica	1,020	23	27	50
Peru	1,040	8	41	51
Guatemala	1,120	—	—	—
Congo, People's Rep.	1,230	7	55	38
Turkey	1,240	19	33	48
Tunisia	1,290	14	36	50
Jamaica	1,300	7	34	60
Dominican Rep.	1,370	17	29	55
Paraguay	1,410	26	26	48
Ecuador	1,420	14	40	46
Colombia	1,430	20	28	51
Angola	—	—	—	—
Cuba	—	—	—	—
Korea, Dem. Rep.	—	—	—	—
Lebanon	—	—	—	—
Mongolia	—		—	—
Jordan	1,640	8	31	61
Syria	1,760	19	25	55
Malaysia	1,860	21	35	44
Chile	1,870	10	36	55
Brazil	1,880	12	35	53
Korea, Rep. of	2,010	14	39	47
Argentina	2,070	12	39	49
Panama	2,120	—	—	—
Portugal	2,230	8	40	51
Mexico	2,240	8	40	52
Algeria	2,320	6	54	40
South Africa	2,490	—	—	—
Uruguay	2,490	12	28	60
Yugoslavia	2,570	—	—	—
Venezuela	3,840	7	40	53
Greece	3,920	17	29	53
Israel	5,370	6	27	67
Hong Kong	6,000	1	30	69
Singapore	6,620	1	37	62
Trinidad and Tobago	6,850	—	—	—
Iran	—	—	—	—
Iraq	—	—	—	—

Table 2.1   **continued**

Country	GNP Per Capita (U.S. dollars)	Distribution of Gross Domestic Product (percent)		
		Agriculture	Industry	Services
High-income oil exporters				
Oman	6,250	—	—	—
Libya	8,480	2	64	34
Saudi Arabia	12,230	2	66	32
Kuwait	17,880	1	61	38
United Arab Emirates	22,870	1	65	34
Industrial market economies				
Spain	4,780	—	—	—
Ireland	5,000	—	—	—
Italy	6,400	6	40	54
New Zealand	7,730	8	33	59
Belgium	9,150	2	35	63
United Kingdom	9,200	2	32	66
Austria	9,250	4	39	58
Netherlands	9,890	4	33	63
Japan	10,120	4	42	55
France	10,500	—	—	—
Finland	10,740	7	33	60
Germany, Fed. Rep.	11,430	2	46	52
Australia	11,490	—	—	—
Denmark	11,570	4	23	72
Canada	12,310	3	29	68
Sweden	12,470	3	31	66
Norway	14,020	4	42	55
United States	14,110	2	32	66
Switzerland	16,290	—	—	—
East European nonmarket economies				
Hungary	2,150	19	42	39
Albania	—	—	—	—
Bulgaria	—	—	—	—
Czechoslovakia	—	—	—	—
German Dem. Rep.	—	—	—	—
Poland	—	—	—	—
Romania	—	—	—	—
USSR	—	—	—	—

*Dashes indicate that data are not available for that country.

†PDR: People's Democratic Republic.

Source: From *World Development Report, 1983*, pp. 148–152, Copyright © 1983 by The International Bank for Reconstruction and Development/The World Bank. Reprinted by permission of Oxford University Press, Inc.

Table 2.1 also shows how the composition of economic activity varies among the world's nations, grouped according to type of economy. One salient point is the large share of total economic output that comes from the agricultural sector in the lower-income countries. Agriculture accounted for 37 percent of gross domestic product for the low-income nations as a whole and 15 percent for the middle-income group, as opposed to just 3 percent for the industrial market economies.

This apparent correlation between heavy involvement in agriculture and low national income is part of the explanation for a persistent inclination in the developing countries to equate economic development with a shift from agricultural to industrial production. But the real problem is not dependence upon agriculture so much as the woefully low level of productivity of the agricultural activity in the developing nations. Some simple but compelling evidence of this is found in the fact that it took fully *73 percent* of the labor force in the low-income countries to produce the 37 percent of total output consisting of agricultural goods.[4] Many developing nations have recognized this problem in recent years and have begun to devote more attention and resources to improving agricultural productivity.

Mention was made previously of how the sharp rise in petroleum prices during the 1970s effectively created some new class distinctions within the ranks of the developing countries. The oil-exporting nations, notably the members of the Organization of Petroleum Exporting Countries (OPEC), realized greatly increased revenues through the higher world market prices that they instigated, and thus experienced a rapid jump in per capita income. This was most pronounced in those OPEC countries with relatively small populations, and Table 2.1 points this out by placing five of these countries (Libya, Saudi Arabia, Kuwait, Oman and the United Arab Emirates) in a special category of high-income oil exporters. The other OPEC countries either could not produce as much oil as these five countries or had much larger economies and populations to absorb their mounting revenues, so that they did not register such dramatic increases in income on a per capita basis. Nevertheless, all of the oil-producing nations enhanced their wealth considerably during OPEC's heyday, and consequently assumed a position of greater prominence and power in the world economy.[5]

A final point worth noting with regard to Table 2.1 is the separation of the "industrial market economies" from the "East European non-market economies." These categories reflect the political and ideological schism in the developed countries that was alluded to previously. The industrial market economies (which are also referred to often as "the Western nations" or simply "the West") maintain economic systems within which decisions relating to the use of resources for the production of goods and services are made primarily by privately owned busi-

---

[4]Ibid., p. 214.

[5]The history of OPEC and its impact upon the international economy are covered in greater depth in Chapter 9.

ness firms in response to the market forces of demand and supply. In contrast, the East European countries with nonmarket economies (which are also referred to variously as "the Eastern nations," "the East," or "the communist bloc") maintain economic systems that are characterized by virtually complete public ownership of resources and production facilities and by extensive governmental direction and control of economic activity. This entails the use of long-range (usually 5-year) economic plans that are formulated and implemented by centralized government bodies in place of market-based economic decision making—hence the term "nonmarket" economy.

Each broad grouping of nations according to type of economy presents a separate and distinct set of market opportunities and problems for international business firms. While it is not feasible to uncover and analyze all these distinctions here, a few general observations related to these groups of countries will emphasize the diversity of economic conditions that international companies face around the world.

The Industrial Market Economies

The Western industrialized nations generally have been looked upon by international firms as the most accessible and promising market area. The relatively high and evenly distributed income levels of the people of these economically advanced nations have created strong and stable demands for a wide variety of products and services, and their well-developed transportation, communication, and marketing facilities have provided the necessary support structure for servicing such demands.

The great majority of international business firms have their home base in one of these countries, and they have shown a marked preference for confining their foreign ventures to this same group of nations, especially in the early phases of their international expansion. While this proclivity is undoubtedly attributable in part to the enticing marketing prospects offered by the affluent populations of these countries, the urge to stay within a circle of nations that have comparable economic systems, industrial structures, labor forces, and production technologies also has been an important factor.

But the same conditions that have made the industrial economies such attractive markets and operating locales for international firms have also brought about intense competition for market shares. This competitive rivalry, together with the prolonged slowdown in economic activity and growth that afflicted almost all the Western nations during the late 1970s and early 1980s, have made it increasingly difficult for international companies to operate profitably, and has even led some of them to withdraw from these markets.

The Oil Exporting Nations

The newfound wealth that the oil exporting countries began acquiring in the 1970s excited the interest of many international companies. However, the markets in these countries proved to be much narrower and more elusive than the mass markets in the Western industrialized nations. In some cases, the oil revenues have never "trickled down" to large segments of the population, so that the demand for foreign goods has come almost entirely from a small, elite segment of society. In other instances, the governments have devoted much of their oil proceeds to large-scale developmental projects or to public works and services, which have generated a need for capital goods and for construction, educational, and health-related services but have not stimulated broad-based demands for consumer products. Thus, while the oil boom prompted many more international firms to explore the markets of the oil exporting nations, these countries have by no means become a lucrative market in which profit bonanzas are easily attained. Moreover, the leveling-off of petroleum prices that started at the end of the 1970s has made the prospects of developing permanent and profitable market positions in these nations even more speculative.

The Developing Countries

The attitudes of international companies toward the rest of the developing countries (those outside the oil exporting group) can probably best be described as cautiously ambivalent. On the one hand, these countries already contain a majority of the world's population, and their rate of population growth is substantially higher than that of other parts of the world. Based on sheer numbers of prospective customers, they therefore constitute an immense market which so far has been only lightly penetrated by international firms. On the other hand, the purchasing power of the masses of people remains very low, and the educational, logistical, and distributional problems that have to be overcome in order to market new products and services to these masses are formidable. Moreover, such problems are often compounded by public attitudes and government policies that militate against foreign products and businesses, particularly those associated with the Western nations.

The difficulties of tapping the large but still-incipient markets of the developing countries are reflected in the past and current posture of international companies vis-à-vis this group of nations. Although a fair number of such companies have had long and successful business experiences in the developing regions, they are a definite minority. The more prevalent situation has been for international firms to concentrate their attention and activities elsewhere and either avoid the developing countries entirely or relegate them to a minor role in their global business operations. Evidence of this can be found in the aggregate trends in world trade and investment over the past few decades. Those trends (which will be examined more thoroughly in Chapters 3 and 4) show that, on the whole, international companies have increased their operations in the developing nations to a lesser extent as compared to the rest of the world, with the result that the developing countries' proportional share of total world trade and investment has declined over time.

Box 2.1

Feeding the Hungry Chinese

"It's like being a child in a candy store," says James L. Dutt, chairman of Beatrice Co. The candy store is China, a market with one billion consumers. And big U.S. food companies such as Beatrice are moving fast to get some of the goodies.

Eager to obtain state-of-the-art technology while catering to growing consumer demand, Beijing is welcoming U.S. food companies. It has approved joint ventures with General Foods Corp. to produce coffee and possibly Tang, an orange-flavored drink, and with H.J. Heinz Co. to produce baby food. Beatrice and Del Monte Corp. have just opened plants in China. Still, the payoff will be a long time coming. "We won't start to see a market of scale until after the year 2000," conceded John F. Manfredi, director of international relations at General Foods.

Source: "Why Beijing is Hungry for U.S. Food Companies," *Business Week*, December 24, 1984, 43.

There are some indications that this situation is changing, however, and that the potential markets represented by the burgeoning populations of the developing nations, combined with the growing competition in other world markets, will eventually cause international companies to substantially step up their activities in these nations. More of these firms have been transferring their manufacturing operations from the developed to the developing countries in an effort to reduce their costs of production and thereby retain their competitive position in their established markets. The recent improvement in political relationships between the Western nations and the People's Republic of China has also engendered a surge of interest among international firms in the long-term opportunities for doing business with that vast country. It is quite possible, therefore, that the developing nations will figure much more prominently in the worldwide production and marketing strategies of international companies in the future.

The Eastern Nonmarket Economies

The Eastern communist countries have presented yet another special set of market conditions to international business firms. But the peculiarities and problems of this market are rooted more in politics than in levels of income or stages of economic development. This is illustrated by the fact that it has only been within the past 15 years or so that international companies have given any serious consideration to this group of countries as viable markets and investment locales. Prior to this time, political antagonism between these nations and the West practically ruled out the possibility of doing business. The Eastern countries were also clinging to the idea that becoming economically dependent upon the capitalist countries would be dangerous to their security and were therefore attempting to achieve and sustain a high degree of economic self-sufficiency.

These obstacles were reduced substantially in the 1970s, as political tensions eased and the leaders of the communist nations displayed heightened interest in expanding trade and other economic relationships with the West. That interest was focused mainly upon products embodying the most advanced technology, but a movement in the Eastern nations to upgrade the economic status of their populations also led to increased demand for Western-style consumer goods.

During this so-called "period of detente," a number of international companies initiated exporting, licensing, and direct investment ventures with the Eastern communist nations, and many of these have endured even though East–West political relations began to deteriorate again in the early 1980s. However, establishing and maintaining such ventures has required that international companies learn and accept some strikingly different ways of doing business.

These differences are primarily due to the pervasive involvement of the government in the business systems of the Eastern European nations. International trade, for example, is under complete government control and is organized and conducted as a national monopoly. This means that foreign firms wishing to make export sales to one of these nations, or desiring to purchase imports from that nation, ordinarily cannot deal directly with the actual end-user or producer of the products involved. Rather, they must deal with the official agency (these agencies are usually called foreign trade organizations or FTOs) that has responsibility for arranging and approving exports or imports.

Unfortunately, these FTOs do not follow the same business principles and "rules of the game" to which Western companies are accustomed. Since each FTO has exclusive control over the buying and selling of the products under its jurisdiction, it is not susceptible to competitive pressures that affect the companies with which it may be dealing. Moreover, an FTO may not be greatly concerned with costs or profits in making business arrangements, but may be guided instead by the dictates of the national economic plan or by the current political or foreign policy aims of its national government. All of this means that international companies that are interested in exporting to, or importing from, the Eastern communist bloc nations must learn to negotiate within an unfamiliar framework, in which the normal considerations of production costs, competition, and profit margins may not be compelling or even applicable.

Foreign direct investments in the Eastern nations are also affected by their economic ideology. These nations have been eager to obtain the equipment, technology, and managerial skills that Western international firms are able to supply in connection with their direct investment projects. At the same time, however, the Eastern countries have been ideologically opposed to having production facilities in their territories owned and operated by Western privately owned, profit-oriented companies.

This dilemma has been resolved in many instances through what are termed "coproduction arrangements." While the exact form of such arrangements can vary, the general procedure is for an international firm to build and equip a factory or other production facility in an Eastern nation and to provide continuing technical and managerial assistance. However, the production facilities are owned by the government of the country in which they are located, with the international firm frequently receiving a portion of the output as payment for its contribution. This allows the communist governments to avoid both private ownership and the appearance of being involved in the capitalistic practice of making and sharing "profits." On a more pragmatic level, this method of paying international companies for their resources and expertise also enables the communist governments to conserve their often-scarce holdings of Western currencies; in addition, it effectively forces the international companies to help find or develop markets for goods being produced in the East.

The foregoing remarks obviously provide only a summary view of the economic systems of the Eastern communist nations and of the kinds of business practices and arrangements that have grown out of those systems. But they serve to point out that international business firms, with their primarily Western backgrounds and private enterprise orientations, have found it necessary to make substantial adjustments—not only in their modes of operation, but also in their business philosophies and policies—in order to do business with these nations. This necessity, combined with the uncertainty that has been created by the on-again, off-again use of trade controls by both the Western and Eastern governments, have kept most of these firms from undertaking strong efforts to establish permanent business ties with the communist bloc.[6] More adventurous firms, however, have decided that the ample resources, productive capacity, and population of this group of nations constitute sufficient reason to cope with the uncertainties and difficulties of establishing such ties. Whether these gradual and limited endeavors will ultimately result in a broad opening of the Eastern group's markets to international companies in general remains to be seen, and also depends heavily upon future developments in East–West political relations.

[6]The use of trade controls for political purposes by the United States and the Eastern European nations is discussed in Chapter 6.

Box 2.2

Marketing U.S. Computers to the Soviets

At Moscow University, where even a good ballpoint pen is a luxury, students find it hard to believe that personal computers are becoming standard gear on U.S. campuses. "It sounds like pure propaganda to me," scoffs an MSU chemistry major.

But Soviet technocrats know better. They are proposing a crash program to close the personal computer gap. If the government can find the money, Soviet schools may soon be shopping for small computers from International Business Machines Corp., Apple Computer, Inc., and European suppliers. The orders could be the biggest purchases from the West since 1979, when the Soviets invaded Afghanistan and trade collapsed.

The way was opened for the sales by the allies' recent decision to ease curbs on high-tech exports to Communist countries. IBM is preparing to apply soon for U.S. permission to sell its personal computer to the Soviet Union. The Soviets could buy up to 10,000 PCs from Western companies.

Source: "U.S. Computers May Enroll in Moscow U.," *Business Week*, February 4, 1985, 44.

The Political Environment

The preceding section was chiefly concerned with the economic dimensions of the international business environment. However, it also indicated how international business can be influenced by politics, specifically the existence of different political ideologies and the consequent establishment of dissimilar economic systems among the nations of the world. This section will examine some additional features of the global political situation and how international business is affected by the attitudes and actions associated with those features.

Political Risk

One useful way to approach this topic is through the concept of **political risk.** International companies have become quite aware of this type of risk, and many of them now devote substantial time and effort to developing effective means of coping with it. A consideration of political risk can therefore uncover those elements of the political environment that are most relevant to the conduct of international business.

Political risk can be defined as the risk of loss of assets, earning power, or managerial control due to events or actions that are politically based or politically motivated. In the case of international companies, political risk typically manifests itself through actions that are taken by the governments of the countries in which those firms are conducting business operations or through events that occur in the host countries.

Such actions and events can differ greatly in their severity and their effects upon the company involved. At the high extreme are acts of violence directed against a firm's properties or employees. Such acts are by no means uncommon, as numerous American firms, for example, have had their overseas properties destroyed by terrorist activities in recent years, and many employees of such firms have been victims of kidnapping or murder. This has forced U.S. companies to formulate special plans and programs to guard against such eventualities and to take extraordinary measures to protect their personnel who are serving in politically sensitive foreign posts.

Government takeovers of the properties of international firms are another manifestation of political risk, somewhat less drastic and dramatic than acts of violence but potentially very costly to the firms experiencing such takeovers. There are various ways in which such takeovers occur, ranging from the sudden outright seizure of a company's facilities by the armed forces or other agents of a host country government to a gradual government encroachment into the management or ownership of those facilities. Another important variant in such takeovers is the compensation that the company receives for its lost properties. Governments have been known to **confiscate** the properties of foreign firms, that is, to take them over without offering any compensation, but the more common approach has been **expropriation,** in which the government takeover is accompanied or followed by some form and amount of reimbursement to the firm.

As with violence, international companies (especially those from the United States) have not been strangers to government takeovers. There have, in fact, been scores of acts of expropriation and confiscation of American business properties overseas during this century, and these have resulted in losses of many billions of dollars. While the incidence of such overt seizures appears to have subsided somewhat in recent years, international companies have been increasingly subjected to demands to relinquish a larger share of ownership and managerial control of their businesses to the governments or nationals of the countries in which those businesses are located. Thus, what is sometimes referred to as "creeping expropriation" continues to confront international firms as part of the political risk syndrome.

Still further down the scale of severity are such governmental actions as discriminatory taxation of foreign-owned firms, legal controls on the prices such firms can charge, restrictions on the ability of these firms to import needed materials or components, refusal to permit transfers of profits out of their country, and demands that the firms employ local workers or managers or utilize specific amounts of domestically produced inputs. This is not to say that all such government measures,

Box 2.3

Political Risk Aftermath:
U.S. Business Claims Against Iran

The January, 1981 agreement that freed American hostages in Iran also provided for the establishment of a U.S.–Iran Claims Tribunal to help in settling U.S. business claims against Iran. Many American companies had been forced to abandon their operations in Iran after Ayatollah Khomeini's revolutionaries seized power in 1979.

U.S. companies which have recently announced settlements with Iran include DuPont, which will receive $42 million; GTE Corp., for $18 million; and Xerox, for $7 million. Iran has set aside $1 billion for the payment of arbitrated claims and has agreed to replenish the fund if it falls below $500 million. So far, about $300 million has been paid to settle about 140 of the nearly 4,000 claims which have been filed. Those claims total more than $5 billion.

The Claims Tribunal consists of three chambers, each manned by three arbitrators, one American, one Iranian, and one from a third country. The Tribunal's headquarters in The Netherlands is probably the only place in the world where loyal subjects of Ayatollah Khomeini and U.S. citizens currently work side by side. American secretaries in Western attire intermingle with Iranian women untouched by makeup and wearing black chadors and dresses that cover all but the head and hands. The Iranian men don't wear neckties, which to them are a symbol of Western culture.

which now are commonplace in many parts of the world, are politically motivated. They often represent a calculated effort by the government to overcome an economic problem or to increase the benefits that a host country is realizing from the presence of foreign business enterprises. But such actions are also frequently taken by governments as a means of exerting their authority over international firms operating in their territories or to "punish" such firms for behavior that the governments consider unacceptable; thus, such actions fall within the boundaries set by our definition of political risk. The problems that an international company experiences as a consequence of these kinds of government

actions may not be as obvious or extensive as those resulting from violence or takeovers, but they nevertheless are capable of seriously eroding a company's profitability or its managerial discretion and flexibility.

Counteracting Political Risk

The dangers and potential losses connected with political risk have
prompted international companies to devise and undertake countermeasures designed to avoid such risk or reduce its detrimental effects.
These countermeasures usually include continuing assessments of what
is often termed the "political climate" in countries in which a company
is operating or contemplating future operations. Many of the larger
international firms have assigned their own personnel to carry on such
investigations, but there are also a number of organizations that now
specialize in preparing political risk reports and forecasts that they make
available to international firms through a subscription arrangement. These
reports typically rate the various countries of the world on the basis of
some composite, quantitative indicator of political risk and then provide
more detailed analyses of the conditions or events that have been considered in arriving at that rating.

   Assessments of this sort can assist international firms in deciding
whether to invest in particular foreign countries or whether existing
operations in those countries should be expanded or reduced. They can
also help the companies decide which type of business operation might
be most appropriate in relation to the degree of political risk indicated
for those countries. A company might, for example, choose an exporting
or licensing strategy for a country that showed a high level of political
risk, rather than investing in production facilities that would be vulnerable to expropriation or other unfavorable actions by the government
of that country.

   International firms have utilized many other methods in attempting
to counteract political risk. Some of the more widely used of these are
listed and described below.

Joint Ventures.   In a joint venture, ownership of a business establishment located in a foreign country is shared with nationals of that country. Such arrangements offer the advantages of overcoming the image
of external domination of business enterprises, having the local investors as "allies," and reducing the amount of capital or other assets which
the international firm itself has exposed to political risk. The chief disadvantage is the need to share control with the local partners, but international companies have found ways to mitigate this disadvantage or
have determined that the offsetting benefits make such a sacrifice of
total control worthwhile.

Linkages.   Developing linkages with local suppliers or dependent industries entails efforts on the part of the international firm to procure

as much of raw materials, component parts, or other inputs that it uses in its operations from suppliers in the country in which those operations are being performed. In addition to such "backward linkages" to the host country's economy, a firm may also develop "forward linkages" by supporting the establishment of locally owned enterprises that utilize its products as inputs to their own production processes or participate in the marketing of those products. The creation of these linkages can forestall political problems by giving host-country nationals a vested interest in the continuation of the international firm's activities.

Prearranged Disinvestment or Domestication.   An international firm may enter into an agreement with the government of a host country to relinquish ownership and/or managerial control of its facilities in that country within a set period of time. This allows host-country nationals to gradually assume responsibility for operating those facilities while retaining the managerial and technical assistance provided by the international firm, and it gives the firm a definite timetable within which it has the opportunity to recoup its investment in the enterprise and earn a reasonable return on that investment.

Home Government Support.   International firms frequently have been able to persuade their own home governments to defend their interests in disputes with the governments of foreign countries in which the firms have operations. The home country government may use the threat of economic reprisals or its influence in international organizations or diplomatic circles as means of pressuring a foreign government to settle such disputes. A home country government may also provide more tangible support in the form of political risk insurance programs—the United States, for example, offers American firms the opportunity to purchase insurance from a government agency (the Overseas Private Investment Corporation) that compensates those firms for any losses which they sustain on their overseas investments as a result of political problems.

This listing does not include all of the basic techniques and strategies that international companies have used to protect themselves against political risk, much less the manifold variations of those techniques that individual companies have devised to fit their specific situations and needs. It nevertheless gives an indication of how seriously such companies have regarded political risk and of how it has played a role in formulating—and, in many instances, altering—their plans and operating policies.

Basis of Political Risk

What are the conditions that underlie and engender political risk? This question relates to the central subject of this chapter, for these conditions are part of the totality of forces and circumstances that comprise the contemporary international business environment.

Economic Ideology.   One of the major conditions that gives rise to political risk is the presence of political groups that are philosophically opposed to the private ownership of economic enterprises. Such groups have attained dominance in many nations of the world, so that private enterprise has been either prohibited entirely or relegated to a minor and limited position in the economy. This is the sort of situation that prevails in the Eastern nonmarket economies, where, as indicated earlier, international companies wanting to do business have been required to enter into arrangements that eliminate (or at least disguise) the element of private ownership.

As a practical matter, however, nations such as those of the Eastern bloc are apt to be less troublesome in terms of political risk than countries in other parts of the world. Since the governments of countries such as the Eastern bloc nations are avowedly communist, international companies are (or should be) fully aware of the rules under which they are permitted to operate. The companies thus can gauge the political situation with a fair degree of certainty and can make investment and policy decisions accordingly.

But there are many other countries in which official attitudes toward private business have been much more equivocal and fluid, and this raises the level of uncertainty with which international firms must contend. Often such shifting views are encountered in countries with relatively brief histories of political independence and are part of the search for a coherent and cohesive political philosophy. Countries such as India and Sri Lanka in Asia and many sub-Saharan African nations fit into this category, as these countries have displayed ambivalent and frequently changing attitudes toward private enterprise during the course of their postcolonial movement toward nationhood.

In other instances, sharp swings in a nation's tolerance for private ownership have come about as a result of changes in the government in power, many of which have occurred abruptly and through extralegal means. The Castro revolution in Cuba in the late 1950s, the election of a socialist government in Chile in 1970, and the overthrow of the Shah in Iran in 1979 are all examples of dramatic governmental changes that resulted in serious political difficulties for international business firms operating in those nations.

Nationalism.   A second significant source of political risk for international companies is **nationalism.** Nationalism, in its broadest and most positive sense, is simply an emotional attachment and loyalty to one's own nation. But nationalistic feelings can become so intense that they bring about a rejection of everything foreign, including foreign involvement in a nation's economy. This kind of militant economic nationalism has been on the rise throughout the world over the past quarter-century, and it has been the basis of many of the political conflicts between international firms and host-country governments. These conflicts have been most pronounced in the developing countries, where foreign-owned businesses continue to be viewed with distrust and associated with "neocolonialist" efforts to dominate and exploit the economies of those countries. But a nationalistic disenchantment with foreign investment has also become prominent in such economically advanced and politically sophisticated areas as Western Europe, Canada, and Australia. These nations have become deeply concerned with what they regard as excessive control of their national economies by foreign-owned international corporations and have adopted policies designed to limit the amount of foreign investment and to subject it to closer supervision by their governments.

Intergovernmental Relations.   Political relationships between national governments constitute a third source of political risk for international business firms. It is not at all uncommon for such firms to be caught in the middle of intergovernmental disputes or power plays and to experience adverse consequences. The long-standing Arab–Israeli conflict provides one illustration of this, as a large number of international companies have been banned from doing business with the Arab nations because of the ties that they or their home governments have had with Israel. The succession of government takeovers of the properties and operations of the international petroleum companies that occurred in the Middle East and North Africa during the 1970s were also linked to that conflict.

Another illustration can be found in the political relationship between the United States and the Soviet Union. U.S.-based international companies have had their business activities disrupted by the ups and downs in that relationship on numerous occasions. One interesting recent incidence of such disruption was the U.S. government's prohibition of sales by American firms and their foreign subsidiaries of equipment and materials to be used by the Soviets in the construction of a giant pipeline to transport natural gas into Western Europe. That prohibition, which was imposed by the U.S. government in response to the Soviet Union's involvement in renewed political repression in Poland, not only caused the American companies to lose substantial sales, but also got them into trouble with the Western European governments that wanted the pipeline project to go forward.

Political Instability.   Still another frequently cited basis of political risk is "political instability." This is an imprecise term, which can be applied to anything from revolutions or civil disorders to normal but frequent changes in government personnel. Notwithstanding this definitional imprecision, political instability is a legitimate concern of international companies insofar as it disrupts the continuity and predictability of government policies or behavior toward their operations. International firms have demonstrated their capability to do business effectively and profitably in countries with political systems ranging from right-wing dictatorships through socialistic and capitalistic democracies to authoritarian communist regimes. However, sudden, drastic change can make any of these countries or systems politically risky. Thus, it is not just the diversity of the international political environment, but also the dynamics of that environment, that poses a constant challenge to international business firms.

The Cultural Environment

Culture is an extremely broad concept. It encompasses all the learned and shared modes of behavior and ways of thinking of the members of a society, as well as their knowledge, beliefs, and values. It also includes a society's legal and social institutions, and its art, music, and other forms of aesthetic expression.

The pervasiveness of culture and its influence on how people live and what they believe makes it absolutely imperative that business firms comprehend its significance and learn to deal with it effectively. Indeed, such firms are themselves products of culture, as evidenced by the fact that their organizational forms, management philosophies and styles, internal personnel relationships, and primary objectives vary substantially from one country or society to another. But business firms also interact continuously with the other members of the cultures that surround them—including workers and other resource-suppliers, the government officials who oversee their activities in the interests of the society-at-large, and the consumers of their products and services—and their success is fundamentally dependent upon the positive outcome of those interactions. Since the attitudes and work-habits of employees, the principles that guide government officials, and the tastes and preferences of consumers are all culturally determined, businesses must be closely attuned to culture if they are to survive and prosper.

Cultural Problems of International Firms

As with the other facets of the business environment, the problems and perplexities associated with the cultural aspect tend to multiply when a firm begins to operate internationally. Although the boundaries of different societies and their cultures seldom conform exactly to national boundaries, the fact remains that a firm doing business in several nations will encounter much greater cultural diversity than a firm operating in only one country. Some of the ramifications of this are illustrated in Figure 2.1, which portrays the interactions between an international firm and its various cultural environments.

The upper portion of Figure 2.1 shows the firm's interactions with the main entities and groups that are part of its domestic market and its native culture. These include the owners of the resources (i.e., labor time and effort, financial and real capital, natural resources and other material inputs) that the firm must acquire in order to produce its prod-

Figure 2.1   Cultural Interactions of an International Firm

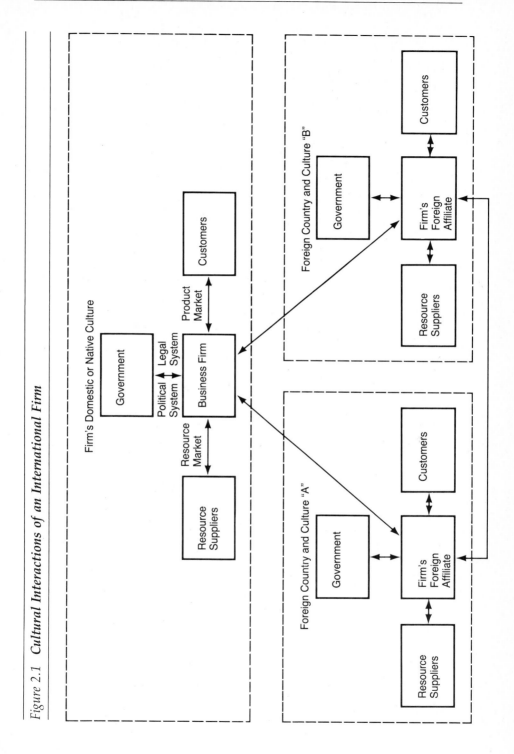

ucts, the consumers of those products, and governmental units and agencies. The firm interacts with these groups in a host of ways—communicating information and ideas, negotiating, buying, selling, delivering products or services, and receiving payment, to name just a few. All these activities are carried on within frameworks (resource markets, product markets, political and legal systems) that are outgrowths of the prevailing culture and in ways that are dictated by the accepted rules, norms, and values of that culture. Thus, a firm is deeply involved in and strongly influenced by cultural factors, even when it is only operating within its own home country.

The lower portion of Figure 2.1 is intended to point out how much more extensive and complicated such cultural interactions can become if the firm is operating in several countries, each of which is presumed to have a distinct culture.[7] In the first place, this requires the firm, through its foreign affiliates, to carry on the same basic types of relationships and activities in other countries that it carries on at home, but to adjust and adapt them to the separate and dissimilar cultural environments of those countries. Second, the firm will be engaged in numerous activities and relationships that transcend the boundaries of those separate cultures. These cross-cultural transactions involve transfers of resources (including people) and products between the firm and its foreign affiliates and among those affiliates. They also involve communication—of data, technological know-how, advertising or other promotional messages, and managerial directives—across those cultural boundaries. Inasmuch as this entails the use of written or spoken language or other symbols to convey information and ideas, there is an ever-present potential for misunderstandings or misinterpretations due to language differences and other variations in the cultural backgrounds of those participating in these various communications processes.

International companies can also experience difficulties as a result of their impact upon the cultures of the countries in which they conduct business. Whenever such companies introduce new products, technologies, or business methods into those countries, they are acting as agents of cultural change. Whereas the companies may regard their intrusions into foreign cultures as benign or beneficial, such views are not always shared by the people or governments of host countries. Groups in several countries (France and Japan being notable examples) have, in fact, displayed strong resentment toward what they consider to be a debasing of their cultures through the materialistic values implanted by international business firms.

Such cultural problems confronting international firms are far from easy to resolve. In the first place, dealing with such problems requires a high level of both cultural awareness and cultural empathy on the part of managers. Not only must they be able to recognize cultural differences and interpret their implications, but they must also be ap-

---

[7]Figure 2.1 depicts a firm with operations and affiliates in only two foreign countries. Most international companies actually operate in many more foreign locations.

Box 2.4

Banks' Interest Charges Clash with Islamic Culture

As part of a move to "Islamize" the country's banking system, the government of Sudan has ordered all banks operating in the country to stop paying or charging interest. Muslim law forbids interest payments; instead, banks are expected to invest their clients' funds and share profits or losses with them. The Sudanese government's action will affect 27 banks, including nine foreign banks operating in that country.

Source: "Sudan Moves to 'Islamize' Banks by Barring Interest," *The Wall Street Journal*, December 12, 1984, 32.

---

preciative of those differences and be willing to make allowances for them. While these are admirable capabilities and qualities, they probably are no more common among international managers than they are among people in general. Such managers are apt to share the normal human tendency to make judgments and decisions on the basis of one's own cultural background and frame of reference. They can also be subject to ethnocentrism, which is a tendency to regard one's own culture as superior and thus to downgrade the values and behavior patterns of other cultures.

Second, the task of analyzing the possible effects of diverse cultural factors on business operations and deciding what to do about those effects can be almost overwhelming, even if a firm and its managers are sensitive to such cultural diversity. The very broadness and ubiquity of culture, that is, its presence in virtually everything that people do or think, accounts for much of this difficulty. In addition, the influence of culture on behavior is often quite subtle and intricate, so that recognition of the overt features of a foreign culture does not necessarily lead to sound predictions as to how members of that culture will behave in particular situations or how they will respond to specific stimuli. There is therefore no assurance that cultural sensitivity can be translated into appropriate business policies and practices.

Finally, an international firm must give very careful consideration to how adjustments to cultural differences might affect the profitability of its operations. Making alterations in products or business methods can be very costly, and the anticipated benefits of such alterations may not justify the added costs. A fair number of international companies have decided that it is better to offer the same products for sale and standardize their methods of doing business in all their foreign markets rather than trying to comprehend and adapt to the cultural heterogeneity of those markets.[8]

Responses to Cultural Problems

Most international companies have concluded, however, that cultural differences cannot be safely ignored. This lesson frequently has been learned through adverse experiences, including advertising campaigns, new product introductions, or other business ventures in foreign markets that were unsuccessful because sufficient consideration was not given to cultural factors.[9]

These companies have adopted a number of different approaches to the cultural problems. One of these involves the greater use of foreign nationals in the design and implementation of business programs for their countries. This reliance upon natives of the foreign cultures in which the firm is doing business can be accomplished either through the decentralization of managerial responsibility within the international firm so as to give the managers of foreign affiliates more control over operations in their respective countries, or through the use of foreign nationals in a consulting capacity. Another approach entails more culturally oriented training and indoctrination for managers and their families from the firm's home country who are being assigned to foreign positions. Some companies have extended this approach to include sensitivity to the foreign country's culture as a criterion for selecting individuals to be given international assignments, although business experience and managerial or technical skills still tend to have greater weight in such selections.

The programs and policies described above do not offer a complete solution to the exceedingly complex cultural problems to which international firms and their managers are invariably and continuously exposed. However, they do indicate an awareness of the importance of culture and an acceptance of the need to understand and conform to the varying norms and values of the societies in which the firms are doing business. Such awareness and adaptability are vital elements for success in dealing with the international cultural environment.

Summary

1.   Doing business internationally entails a movement into new and diverse economic, political, and cultural settings, and a firm's ability to recognize and adapt to these environmental differences

---

[8]This "standardization versus adaptation" issue is discussed in more depth in Chapter 15.

[9]For a very comprehensive and interesting chronicle of such unsuccessful ventures, see David A. Ricks, *Big Business Blunders: Mistakes in Multinational Marketing* (Homewood, IL: Dow Jones-Irwin, 1983).

will usually determine the success or failure of its international initiative.

2.   A firm will encounter great differences around the world in the types of economic activities in which people are engaged, the way in which those activities are organized and controlled, and the production methods being employed.

3.   The countries of the world have traditionally been categorized as "developed" or "developing," chiefly on the basis of differences in the wealth and income of their people. In recent times, however, these categories have been expanded and refined to recognize the increasing economic diversity among countries and regions.

4.   International business firms face very different kinds of market opportunities and problems in the various groups of countries that comprise the world economy. The majority of such firms have their origins in the Western industrialized economies, and they have shown a marked preference for investing and operating within that group of nations.

5.   The Eastern nonmarket economies have presented a special set of problems for international companies, resulting from both political obstacles and their unique methods of conducting business.

6.   Companies doing business internationally are vulnerable to political risk, which manifests itself mainly through actions that are taken by the governments of the countries in which those firms are operating. Such risks and actions often are the result of opposition to private enterprise, economic nationalism, political instability, or political friction between national governments.

7.   A company that is operating in several countries confronts the difficult task of adapting to the cultural differences that exist among those countries; such a firm must also carry out cross-cultural transactions.

8.   Dealing effectively with cultural differences requires a high level of cultural awareness and empathy on the part of international firms and their managers, as well as a willingness to adjust products and operating methods to conform to the local cultural environment.

Questions for Review or Discussion

1.   What are the principal characteristics that distinguish the "developed" countries from the "developing" countries?

2.   Identify the major groups of countries that comprise the world economy and explain the basis for dividing the nations of the world into these subdivisions.

3.   Describe the unique market opportunities and problems that international companies face with respect to: (1) the non-oil-

exporting developing countries; (2) the Eastern nonmarket economies.

4.   Define *political risk* and indicate some of the specific political dangers and problems that international firms have experienced.
5.   What strategies have international firms utilized to avoid or reduce political risk?
6.   How can political relationships between governments result in political risk for international companies? Give some examples.
7.   Why does an international business firm face greater cultural problems than a firm operating within a single country?
8.   What is meant by the reference to international companies as "agents of cultural change"?
9.   How does the concept of cross-cultural communications relate to the activities of international business firms?

Case

Ok Tedi Mining, Limited

In late February 1985, the government of Papua New Guinea (PNG) finally ordered the huge Ok Tedi (pronounced owk teddy) mine closed until further notice. The PNG government and the foreign owners of the mine had failed to resolve their differences with regard to how the mine should be run and the government felt that this extreme step was necessary to protect the interests of its citizens.

According to the PNG government, the owners had done nothing to mine copper in addition to the gold they were already mining, in spite of the terms of their concession that called for copper production along with that of gold, a higher-profit metal. The PNG government also charged that the company had not taken adequate steps to protect the environment and to guard against damage to the health of the villagers that was caused by the mine.

For the mine owners, this action by the PNG government was another of the numerous setbacks they had suffered since they had taken over the mine from the PNG government after Kennecott abandoned the project in 1975. The Ok Tedi gold and copper mine was owned and operated by a consortium jointly headed by Broken Hill Proprietary (BHP) of Australia and the Amoco Minerals division of Standard Oil of Indiana, each with 30 percent ownership. A West German group owned another 20 percent while the remaining 20 percent was held by the PNG government.

The mine seemed to be a good proposition for everybody concerned. Papua New Guinea was a newly independent but underdeveloped country that needed foreign technology to develop its mineral resources. The mine would bring economic development to this region, which was rich in natural resources but was also remote, desolate, and poor. The minerals seemed easily available. All the company had to do was bulldoze Mt. Fublian, a 6,000-foot-high mountain of copper capped by a crown of gold (actually 70 percent of the gold is mixed in with the copper ore). The consortium was quickly put together in an optimistic period of rapidly rising metals prices. The company had little time to do detailed engineering studies and did not purchase any insurance against political risk. The partners all had extensive experience operating in developing countries and planned to subcontract major construction to a unit of the giant and widely experienced Bechtel Corp.

However, things started to go wrong very quickly, leading to massive cost-overruns, and the mine owners are currently disputing with Bechtel about outstanding payments. The mountain being mined is believed to be the haunt of *megalim* or evil spirits according to local tribes. These days the Western engineers no longer laugh at that belief!

In the Star Mountains, the site of the mine, annual rainfall averages 24 feet, and it rains 320 days a year, making this one of the wettest places on earth. However, no sooner had the Ok Tedi owners started bringing heavy equipment upriver by barge than the rain stopped and for 5 months everything had to be airlifted to the site. When the rains did return, they did so with a vengeance and roads and other equipment were washed away.

In 1984, when work on the tailings dam was started and excavations nearly completed, 50 million tons of soft black mud suddenly slid down the hillside and obliterated the site, raising the cost of the dam to $350 million from an estimated $50 million. In order to start gold mining temporarily before completion of the tailings dam, the company tried a chemical method of neutralizing waste. Within the first 2 months, two accidents released untreated cyanide. Alarmed villagers found dead fish and crocodiles and the government became concerned about the villagers' health.

The local village tribes are ambivalent about the mine. When they first agreed to the mine, they never envisioned the details involved in mining the copper and gold. They never imagined that they would see a new town of 3,000 new and strange people or so many machines and new roads. The company tries to be sensitive to the natives' culture. For example, it used a helicopter to catch a rare pig that had to be sacrificed so that a bridge could pass close to an ancestral burial ground. Some tribesmen now wear Western-style clothes rather than feather quills through their noses and the traditional penis-guards.

The company has trained many tribesmen to be heavy equipment operators and some are even computer operators. Modern medicine brought in by the company has worked miracle cures and the company runs a popular school for children. However, a village elder, who sent his three sons to the school and was proud that the eldest had reached the fourth grade, is considering taking them out since he is convinced

that his son (who contracted malaria and died) was bewitched by someone jealous of his achievements. The company suspects that the villagers' concerns about the effects of the mine may have been a factor
contributing to its current difficulties with the government.

The mine owners have already spent over $1 billion to develop the
mine in spite of drastically reduced and falling prices for both gold and
copper. While the mine was producing half a million dollars of gold
daily when it was ordered to cease operating, the PNG government
wanted it to produce some copper as well. The owners contend that
they can not afford any additional expenses until metal prices show
some recovery. The PNG government, on the other hand, wants the
company to build processing lines for copper, hydroelectric facilities,
and a permanent dam to contain the mine's tailings. The owners contend that these facilities will cost an additional $800 million which they
currently can not afford.

The PNG government, through its minister of energy and minerals,
Francis Pusal, proposed that the company could resume gold production if it agreed to proceed with the construction of the permanent
tailings waste dam and one copper production line at this time. Construction of a second copper line and additional hydropower facilities
could wait for an economic viability study at the end of 1986.

Should the company agree to this proposal?

Sources: Geraldine Brooks, "Giant Mining Project in Papua New Guinea is Beset with
Calamities," The Wall Street Journal, April 24, 1985; "Papua New Guinea Sets Conditions
for Mine to Stay Open," The Wall Street Journal, February 13, 1985, p. 35; and "Papua
Reports Mine Owners Accept Proposal," The Wall Street Journal, March 4, 1985, p. 30.

Chapter 3

INTERNATIONAL TRADE: PATTERNS AND PROBLEMS

Chapter Objectives:

- *To illustrate and explain the rapid expansion of international trade during the post–World War II era*
- *To outline the fundamental changes that have occurred in international trade patterns over that period*
- *To analyze major contemporary problems in international trade and to describe and evaluate proposed solutions to those problems*
- *To describe the current international trade position of the United States and the difficulties the United States is experiencing in its international trade*
- *To identify the principal causes of the U.S. trade deficit and to consider the implications of that deficit in relation to the American economy*

International trade consists of the exchange of goods and services among individuals and organizations that are residents of different nations. As noted earlier, trade constitutes the oldest form of international business, as people and commercial enterprises have exchanged goods and services across political boundaries ever since such boundaries were established.

The fundamental reason for conducting trade has always been the expectation of mutual economic benefits to the parties involved in such exchange, and economic theory has certified the potential for such benefits for nations that trade with one another. Despite its demonstrated advantages, however, international trade has been fraught with problems and frictions, and quarrels over trade have often led to military hostilities among nations. Thus, although international trade has made a significant contribution to economic progress and welfare, it has also been a cause of controversy and conflict. These opposing tendencies associated with international trade are as much in evidence today as they have been throughout history.

This chapter will examine the current status and prevailing pattern of international trade, as well as the principal developments that have taken place over the past several years. Attention will also be given to the major trade problems and disputes in which the world's nations are currently embroiled and to the possible future effects of those problems. Our main purposes will be to point out the growing importance of international trade in the economies of the nations of the world and to indicate how trade among countries can affect their economic situations and relationships.

Magnitude and Growth of World Trade

International trade involves purchases and sales of both tangible goods (merchandise) and intangible services. Service transactions now account for approximately one-quarter of all international trade, and available evidence indicates that such transactions have been growing at a faster rate than merchandise trade in recent years.[1] However, the services component of world trade encompasses a variety of heterogeneous items and activities—including banking, insurance, and other financial operations, transportation and travel-related services, foreign investment income, fees and royalties from licensing arrangements, and military expenditures—and it has proved very difficult to compile complete and accurate data on these activities and the international financial flows associated with them. For this reason, most studies and surveys of international trade concentrate upon the merchandise component, and the information and analyses presented in this section will follow that approach.

Trade among the nations of the world has expanded greatly over the past 35 years. The flourishing of trade during the post–World War II era stands in sharp contrast to the 1930s and 1940s, when international trade was stifled by the Great Depression and the Second World War.

Total world merchandise exports, valued in U.S. dollars, increased steadily from a level of $50 billion in 1948 to nearly $2 trillion in 1980. Measured in current dollars, the value of exports doubled in the 1950s, almost tripled in the 1960s, and registered a sixfold increase in the 1970s. This growth in trade was interrupted by the severe economic recession that gripped the entire world during the early 1980s, but the expansion of trade resumed in 1984.

There is a difficulty connected with the use of current dollars as the measuring rod for export growth, in that it conceals the impact of increases in the prices of the goods involved on the total values being compared over time (or, expressed another way, the use of current

---

[1]"International Trade in Services: A Growing Force in the World Economy" in *World Business Perspectives No. 75* (New York: The Conference Board, 1983), 1.

dollars masks decreases in the purchasing power of the dollars being used as the unit of measurement). This distorting effect of such price changes was especially pronounced during the 1970s, when there was a rapid increase in the prices of petroleum and several other products and commodities that figure prominently in world trade.

When world export statistics are adjusted to take account of the price changes noted above, the rate of growth of trade is more moderate but still quite substantial. There has been a tenfold increrase in this price-adjusted volume of trade over the past quarter-century, and annual rates of growth averaged 8.5 percent through the 1960s and 4.0 percent through the 1970s.

One noteworthy feature of the growth of international trade over the period being considered is that it has consistently outpaced the growth of world production (Table 3.1). In other words, commerce among the nations of the world has expanded to a greater extent than could be expected or explained by the expansion of the economic output of those nations. This comparison of trade and output growth rates confirms the observations made previously regarding the increasing relative importance of international (versus purely domestic) business activity and the increasing economic interdependence of nations, inasmuch as it shows that economic transactions across national boundaries have been expanding more rapidly than production within those nations and that the world's countries have become progressively more dependent upon each other as markets and sources of supply.

The causes of this trend toward more extensive involvement in international trade are worth exploring, since such a shift in the balance between domestically oriented and internationally oriented economic

Table 3.1   *Growth of World Exports and Production*
(Average Annual Percentage Changes in Volume)

World Commodity Output	1963–1973	1973–1983
All commodities	6.0	2.0
Agriculture	2.5	2.0
Mining	5.5	0.5
Manufacturing	7.0	2.5
World Exports		
Total	8.5	3.0
Agricultural products	4.0	3.5
Minerals	7.0	−2.5
Manufactures	11.0	4.5

Source: *International Trade,* 1983–1984 (Geneva: General Agreement on Tariffs and Trade, 1983), 2.

activity may affect the lives and economic status of virtually all people in the world. As countries find their economies becoming more closely intertwined with the rest of the world, their governments must pay more attention to international concerns and issues in setting national economic policies; business firms and their employees encounter new marketing challenges and opportunities but may also face intensified competition; and individuals benefit from a wider array of available products but may also discover that the stability of their jobs, their incomes, and the prices they must pay for goods become increasingly dependent upon international events.

The vigorous expansion of international trade since the end of World War II is attributable to a number of developments and circumstances that have come together to stimulate and support such commercial activity. Among the more obvious and important of these factors are technological progress, demographic trends, economic growth, and improved political relationships among nations.

Technological Progress

The world has experienced a technological explosion during the past four decades, as new products and improved production processes have been developed at a pace and in a variety unprecedented in history. This surge of innovations has had profound effects, both directly and indirectly, upon trade among nations. First and foremost, the vast multitude of new products that have come into being and the increasing complexity of such products have provided opportunities for more **specialization** in production, which forms a principal basis for international trade. Technological changes have also resulted in greatly improved transportation facilities and services, which has made it more feasible and less costly for goods to be moved physically from country to country. Giant strides have also been made in communications technology, which have helped to spread awareness and knowledge of different products and consumer life-styles throughout the world, while also making it possible for business firms to communicate easily and quickly with customers and affiliates all around the globe.

Demographic Trends

Over the past several decades, the number of people in the world has been growing so rapidly as to cause widespread concern. The world's population, which was approximately 2.5 billion in 1950, reached 4.7 billion in 1983 and is expected to climb to 6.5 billion by the end of this century. Such rapid population growth raises serious questions as to the adequacy of the world's economic resources and productive capacity to provide for so many people, and this problem is compounded by the fact that the recent and projected increases in population have been and will continue to be concentrated in the poorer, less-developed countries which have the least potential for achieving output increases commensurate with their population growth. While the annual rate of population increase in the wealthier, more economically advanced nations of the world averaged about 1 percent between 1950 and 1980, the growth rate was more than double that in the developing countries. As a consequence, the proportion of the world's people living in these poorer nations increased from about 45 percent in 1950 to 53 percent in 1980. Moreover, since a large part of the population of the developing countries now is made up of young people who will soon reach child-producing age, this shift in the distribution of the world's people will become even more pronounced in the future.

These population trends and the problems they pose are critical international issues, but our purpose here is to consider how such demographic developments have been related to the growth of world trade in the post–World War II period. Some of those relationships are fairly obvious and straightforward. Simple logic would lead one to expect that the tremendous increases in population that have occurred over this time would have created a demand for all kinds of economic goods, and the fact that the population increases have not been evenly spread among countries would imply shifting international demand patterns that would generate trade opportunities. A good example of this effect is the case of food—the volume of world trade in foodstuffs has expanded greatly in recent years, partly as a result of the inability of many nations to increase their domestic food production sufficiently to keep pace with the nutritional needs of their burgeoning populations.

Uneven population growth exerts another, more subtle effect upon international trade by changing the resource "mix" in various nations. This concept will be explored in more depth in Chapter 5 of this text, which deals with the theory of international trade, but the basic idea is simply that nations whose populations (and labor forces) are increasing more rapidly than the world norm can eventually realize competitive advantages in producing goods that are "labor intensive," that is, goods that require large amounts of labor time for their production. By the same token, countries with lagging rates of population growth may find it advantageous over time to import more of the labor-intensive products that they need, while switching their own production toward goods that make greater use of capital or other resources. When viewed in this light, it is not surprising that some of the developing countries that have experienced rapid population growth have begun to penetrate foreign markets with labor-intensive manufactured products or that a large proportion of such exports are going to the more developed nations that have lower rates of population increase.

Economic Growth

The overall growth of economic output and the resulting improvement in incomes and living standards that have been realized in much of the world comprise another set of causes of the post–World War II buildup in international trade. Despite recurring recessions and the continuing prevalence of severe poverty in many regions, the past three-and-a-half decades have been a time of relative prosperity and economic advancement for the world as a whole. As was the case with population growth, this economic uptrend has generated a strong effective demand for consumer goods and for the industrial materials and capital equipment needed to produce them, and the fact that the economic expansion has not occurred at exactly the same time or at the same pace everywhere around the globe has brought about geographic and temporal shifts in relative demand that have, in turn, stimulated international trade. In addition to this kind of direct stimulus to trade, post–World War II prosperity has raised more and more of the world's people to a level of affluence at which they become aware of and desirous of the wider variety of products that are available through trade with foreign countries.

Improved Political Relationships

Both the willingness and the ability of residents of different nations to carry on trade are heavily dependent upon the political relationships that those nations and their respective governments have with one another. Obviously, nations that are at war are unlikely to be simultaneously engaged in trade with their adversaries, but trade can also be forestalled by political animosities that fall short of military hostilities. Many national governments (including that of the United States) currently prohibit or strictly limit trade with other countries for political reasons.

Although a large number of such prohibitions and limitations still are in effect, the post–World War II era has, on the whole, been characterized by cooperative international efforts to reduce governmentally imposed barriers to trade. These efforts were launched immediately after the Second World War, as part of a broad program of economic reconstruction and development that had been formulated by the U.S. and its allies while that conflict was still in progress. The leaders of these nations had foreseen the need for bold measures to revitalize the international economy which had been battered first by the Great Depression and then by World War II, and the expansion of trade was viewed as an important means of achieving such a revitalization.

One significant manifestation of that viewpoint was the adoption in 1947 of the **General Agreement on Tariffs and Trade (GATT)**. This agreement originally was negotiated by 23 countries, but 90 countries now are contracting parties to the agreement. Both the agreement itself and the permanent organization that has been set up to implement it are basically directed toward the encouragement and support of international trade, and the major approaches that have been initiated to attain those ends include regular rounds of negotiations among the contracting parties aimed at mutual reductions of tariffs and other trade restrictions, common rules of conduct that nations are to abide by in their commercial dealings, and a general requirement that each of the contracting parties must accord all the others fair and impartial (non-discriminatory) treatment in setting and applying trade controls.

As a result of GATT and a variety of other multilateral negotiations and agreements, there has been a gradual but substantial dismantling of the maze of governmental restrictions on trade that existed during the 1930s and 1940s. This unquestionably has contributed much to the growth of trade, but the underlying commitment on the part of a majority of the world's nations to establish and maintain more harmonious and peaceful relationships has been of equal or greater importance in creating the sort of international political climate in which business firms from those nations can freely and profitably trade with one another.

This brief review of the technological, demographic, economic, and political changes that have transpired over the past few decades is not intended to comprise a complete explanation of why international trade has expanded in magnitude and assumed greater importance in the economies of many nations. It does, however, help to make the point that this widening and deepening of trade is an outgrowth of several fundamental developments that collectively have created both the necessity and the opportunity for increased economic interaction among the countries of the world. Inasmuch as those developments have by no means run their full course, it is only reasonable to expect that international trade will continue to grow in volume and importance.

Composition and Direction of Trade

As the volume of international trade has grown over time, some basic changes have taken place in the composition and direction of such trade. These changes, which are interrelated to a considerable degree, are significant both because they are indicative of shifting patterns of world market demand for different products and commodities and because they are linked to many of the problems and much of the dissension which have emerged over trade issues.

With regard to its *composition,* world merchandise trade is usually divided into the following three categories: (1) agricultural products, which includes human and animal foods and agricultural raw materials; (2) minerals, which includes ores, fuels, and nonferrous metals; (3) manufactures, which includes a wide variety of products that have undergone some processing or fabricating. The goods that comprise the first two of these categories sometimes are referred to collectively as **primary products,** a term that denotes goods that have undergone little or no processing prior to their entry into trade channels.

Table 3.2   World Trade by Major Commodity Groups 1963–1982
(Percentage Shares)

	1963	1982
Agricultural products	29	15
Minerals	17	27
Manufactures	53	57

Source: *International Trade, 1982–1983* (Geneva: General Agreement on Tariffs and Trade, 1983), Appendix Table A1.

As Table 3.2 shows, the relative importance of each of these three categories of goods in international trade has changed over time. Trade in manufactured goods accounts for well over one-half of total trade, and has continued to increase proportionally over the past 20 years. Trade in minerals has likewise been rising, but much of that increase is attributable to the rapid rise in the prices of fuels, notably petroleum and natural gas, that has occurred since 1973. Meanwhile, the share of trade accounted for by agricultural products declined from 29 to 15 percent between 1963 and 1982. These percentage changes reveal a long-term shift toward manufactured goods and away from primary products in the mix of goods that are traded internationally. As will be noted presently, this shift is of critical importance, inasmuch as it has a direct bearing on the controversial issue of the extent to which different nations and groups of nations have shared in the benefits of expanding world trade.

The *direction* of world trade has undergone alterations over time that are related to the changes in the composition of trade noted above. Since there are more than one hundred countries engaged in trade, it would be very complicated and not particularly fruitful to chart and study the direction of trade flows on a country-by-country basis. Analyses of the direction of trade therefore generally deal with movements of goods among major geographic regions of the world or among groups of countries that can be classified together in some meaningful way. As explained in Chapter 2, it has become common practice to group the countries of the world into the following categories: (1) The Western industrial countries, sometimes referred to as the "First World." This group includes the nations of Western Europe and North America, plus Japan, Australia, New Zealand, and South Africa. These are nations that have attained a relatively high level of economic development and that emphasize a capitalistic or private enterprise approach to organizing and carrying on economic activities. (2) The Eastern countries or the "Second World," which includes the Soviet Union, the communist countries of Eastern Europe, Asia, and Cuba. The common distinguish-

Table 3.3   *World Exports by Major Areas, 1983 (Percentage Shares)*

World	100.0	
Industrial countries	63.0	
Developing countries	25.0	
Oil-exporting		10.0
Non-oil-exporting		15.0
Eastern trading area	11.0	

Source: International Monetary Fund, *IMF Survey* (June 4, 1984): 165.

ing feature of these countries is their adherence to government ownership and central planning in their economic systems. (3) The developing countries or the "Third World," which takes in the multitude of mostly poor and less-developed nations. The share of total world trade associated with each of these groups of countries is shown in Table 3.3.

It is well to note that the criteria used to divide the world into these country groupings are not clear-cut or precisely measurable, and each of the groups includes countries that differ from one another in many ways. However, the countries in each group exhibit sufficient similarities with respect to their economic circumstances and their trade positions to make the classification scheme a useful frame of reference for examining the directional pattern of world trade and the effects of changes that have been taking place in that pattern.

The most striking feature of the pattern of world trade is the predominance of the Western industrial countries. This group, made up of some 25 nations which together contain about one-fifth of the world's people, has for many years accounted for roughly two-thirds of total world exports. Moreover, around 70 percent of the exports of the countries within this group go to other industrialized countries. Thus, we find a high concentration of trade in what, in numerical terms, is a small portion of the world's area and population. However, this group includes most of the countries that have reached an advanced stage of economic development, and these countries produce a share of total world output that is quite comparable to their share of world trade. While there is a logic to this dual concentration of wealth and involvement in trade, it nevertheless constitutes a source of concern and tension in international relations.

The figures in Table 3.3 help to point out other significant features of the direction of trade. They show that the countries making up the Eastern bloc account for only 11 percent of world exports, a figure that seems quite low in view of the fact that this group of countries accounts for 30 percent of the people of the world and includes the world's second largest national economy, that of the Soviet Union. This low level of participation in international trade is often explained in terms of history and politics, particularly the tendencies of the communist rulers of postrevolutionary Russia to strive for economic self-sufficiency as a means of securing their country and its communistic system from external economic pressures or military threats. Those autarkic tendencies guided the international trade policies and actions of the USSR and its satellite countries for many years, and it was not until the 1970s that those nations began to substantially expand their trade with the West.

The position of the developing Third World countries in the scheme of international trade is a complex and troublesome issue, and only its outlines can be discerned from the statistics on the direction of trade. However, these statistics do reveal that this group of more than one hundred countries with one-half of the world's population generated only 25 percent of world exports in 1983. Even that low figure does not accurately portray the limited extent to which much of the Third World participates in international trade or partakes of its benefits, since a small number of developing countries—notably the oil-exporting nations and a few others that have successfully created strong export-oriented manufacturing sectors—are responsible for a substantial portion of total Third World exports. Meanwhile, the great majority of the developing nations see their share of international markets as meager and steadily diminishing. This perception and the situation that underlies it constitute one of the principal problems in the realm of international trade. Those problems will be explored in the following section, beginning with the case of the Third World.

Major International Trade Problems
The Trade Situation of the Developing Countries

The Third World's trade problems have both a long-term and a short-term dimension. The crux of the long-term problem is a declining share of total world exports. As mentioned above, the countries of the Third World, with the important exception of the oil-exporting nations, account for a relatively small percentage of world exports. But even more troubling to these countries than their limited share of export revenues is the downtrend in that share. In 1948, the exports of the non-oil-exporting developing countries (NOEDCs) constituted 26 percent of all world exports, but by 1983 that share had fallen to 15 percent.

The most serious consequence of that downtrend has been the inability of the developing countries to pay for the imports they desperately need. Those countries have become caught in a double bind: they must import more consumer goods to satisfy the expanding needs and rising expectations of their rapidly growing populations, and more industrial materials and capital goods in order to develop their weak and backward economies, but they cannot afford to import more as long as their export earnings are stagnant or declining. Thus, the immediate and pressing economic needs of the NOEDCs are not being met and their aspirations for economic betterment are being stymied. Government leaders and economists in these countries lay much of the blame for this situation on the deterioration of the export position.

The causes of this decline in the export performance of the developing countries are complex and have been the subject of extensive study and much debate. The NOEDCs themselves regard their heavy involvement in the production of primary products as the key to this problem. In 1982, primary products made up 58 percent of the exports of the NOEDCs, whereas, in contrast, such products constituted only 25 percent of the exports of the industrial countries. The NOEDCs see the world economic picture as one in which the industrialized countries continue to dominate world trade in manufactured products, which has been the fastest growing component of total trade, while the developing nations continue to be relegated to the task they were assigned under the colonial system, that of providing raw materials and agricultural commodities for the world market.

While there may be no intrinsic disadvantage in supplying primary products, the NOEDCs feel that it has become disadvantageous as a result of unfavorable demand and price trends. Trade in nonfuel primary products has been falling over time as a share of total trade, an indication that international demand for such goods has not kept pace with the increased demand for manufactured products. These divergent rates of growth in demand have been attributed to many factors, including low income elasticities of demand for agricultural commodities, the development of synthetic substitutes for many natural raw materials, technological advances that have enabled manufacturers to economize on the use of such raw materials, and the rapid expansion of agricultural output in the developed countries due in part to government subsidies in their domestic agricultural sectors. Whether and to what extent each of these factors has actually affected the demand for primary product exports from the NOEDCs are questions that still have not been resolved despite much investigation and heated arguments among economic experts and government leaders. Definitive answers to those questions cannot be provided here. However, regardless of the exact nature of its causes, the lagging growth of demand for primary products has frustrated the efforts of the NOEDCs to expand their export sales.

There is another facet of this demand situation, which has to do with prices or, more precisely, with **terms of trade**. When economists speak of the terms of trade of a country (or group of countries) they are referring to the ratio of export prices to import prices. Therefore, an increase or improvement in the terms of trade would mean that the prices of the country's exports were rising relative to the prices it was paying for imports, while a decrease or worsening of the terms of trade would mean that the prices it was realizing for its exports were declining in comparison to what it was paying for imported goods. While the concept of terms of trade is important both for analytical studies and as a real determinant of how much a country benefits from international trade, the ratio of export to import prices is very difficult to calculate in practice, since it usually involves computations of price movements for a large number of imported and exported goods. Also, in attempting to measure changes in a country's terms of trade, the results obviously will be influenced by the time period selected and by the goods included in the measurement.

Such complications notwithstanding, leaders of the NOEDCs have repeatedly voiced their conviction that their countries' terms of trade have tended to worsen over time as the world market prices of manufactured goods generally have risen more than the prices of primary commodities. The explanation that has been advanced for this tendency includes the differential rates of change in demand for the two categories of goods that was discussed above, but reference also has been made to the greater ability of producers of manufactured products in the developed countries to control the prices at which their output is offered for sale due to the lack of effective competition in their industries.

The short-term dimension of the NOEDC's trade problem is associated with the **instability** of world market prices of primary products. Those prices have been subject to more frequent and wider fluctuations than have the prices of manufactured products, and such fluctuations can result in substantial changes in the export revenues of the developing countries within relatively short spans of time. The impact that this price volatility has upon the total export earnings and the entire domestic economies of the NOEDCs is heightened by the fact that many of those countries are heavily dependent upon the production and sale of only one or a very few goods. It is not unusual for a single mineral or agricultural commodity, such as coffee, sugar, copper, tin, or bananas, to account for more than half of the total export earnings of a developing country, and government tax revenues and employment and profits in the private sector may likewise be tied closely to foreign sales of that commodity. In such situations, a sharp rise or fall in the international price of the commodity can disrupt the normal course of economic activity, and frequent price changes may make it difficult for the country to engage in long-range economic planning or undertake investment projects that require stable funding over a long time period.

The developing countries tend to attribute such adversities to conditions and forces that are largely beyond their control. As mentioned previously, they often regard their dependence upon world market demand for primary products as a vestige of the colonial system that existed during the latter half of the nineteenth century and the first half of the twentieth century. Under that system, the economic activities that were established in the colonized developing countries consisted mainly of plantation agriculture and the extraction of minerals, and the output of those activities were shipped as raw materials to the industrialized "mother countries." Such an arrangement made the economies of the developing countries highly vulnerable to changes in the demand for primary commodities associated with business cycles in the industrialized nations and also left them with very little ability to regulate the supply of such commodities.

Although the colonial system disintegrated after World War II as virtually all the developing countries won their political independence, there is a strong feeling among the NOEDC countries that they are still in the unfavorable economic position they occupied under the colonial system. Thus, their inability to maintain stable prices for their primary product exports and the extensive adverse effects that fluctuations in those prices can exert upon their domestic economies are viewed as evidence of their continuing economic dependency and vulnerability.

The New International Economic Order

How have the developing countries responded to the international trade problems described above and to their perceptions of the root causes of those problems? Their response began to take shape as early as the 1950s, when a number of economists contributed to the formulation of a theoretical doctrine which analyzed the trade difficulties of the developing nations and argued that such difficulties were severely retarding the economic progress of those countries.[2] This doctrine, which gained widespread acceptance among Third World leaders, provided both the impetus and the framework for a set of proposals that a large group of the developing countries put forth as an action program for overcoming obstacles to their economic growth.

This program was introduced at the first United Nations Conference on Trade and Development (UNCTAD) in 1964, and the developing countries subsequently continued to press the industrialized countries to accept and implement the proposals it contained. In 1974, the United Nations General Assembly adopted a resolution formally entitled the "Program of Action on the Establishment of a New International Economic Order," which advocated several major international measures to improve the position of the developing countries in the international economic system and thus to assist their developmental efforts.

The call for a **New International Economic Order (NIEO)** has generated a great deal of controversy among national governments and in international organizations. While the developing countries regard the NIEO as a much-needed and long-overdue plan for correcting the imbalances in the international economy that have perpetuated their economic backwardness, the industrialized countries tend to view it with

---

[2]The economist who was most influential in formulating this doctrine was Dr. Paul Prebisch, who, at that time, was associated with the United Nations Economic Commission for Latin America (ECLA).

considerable suspicion as a device for transferring economic wealth and power from the First World to the Third World. As a consequence of these differing views, there has been only gradual and partial acceptance and implementation of the proposals contained in the NIEO. But even these tentative steps are highly significant, inasmuch as they already are changing from long-established policies and practices in international trade and could ultimately alter the international competitive situation and the global distribution of economic output and wealth in profound ways.

Some of the more important and controversial of the NIEO proposals have to do with international commodity agreements, compensatory financing arrangements, and preferential tariff treatment.

International Commodity Agreements.   International commodity agreements are agreements among producing and consuming countries that are aimed at stabilizing the prices of primary products. Some agreements of this sort have been in existence for many years, but the NIEO advocates strengthening of such arrangements and applying them to a broader list of raw materials traded internationally. From the perspective of the developing countries, these agreements would have the desirable effect of guaranteeing them more stable export earnings by reducing fluctuations in the prices of the primary products that make up a large portion of their exports. However, the industrialized nations have voiced numerous reservations with regard to the practicability of attempts to regulate the prices of commodities which are produced and marketed in massive volumes and to the desirability of substituting price-fixing arrangements for a competitive market mechanism in which prices presumably are determined by demand and supply conditions. They are concerned, moreover, with potential costs and funding, inasmuch as many of the proposed agreements would entail the purchase and storage of commodities whenever output exceeded current demand. Such "buffer stock" arrangements could become very expensive, and the industrialized countries feel that they would bear the bulk of those expenses.

Compensatory Financing Arrangements.   Compensatory financing arrangements are also aimed at reducing the adverse effects of fluctuations in export prices and revenues. They are designed to provide loans or other forms of external financing to developing countries on an automatic or guaranteed basis to offset declines in their export earnings due to downturns in primary product prices. Such arrangements would protect the import purchasing power of the developing countries, but they would also require the wealthier, industrialized countries to make a more-or-less unconditional commitment of funds for that purpose.

Preferential Tariff Treatment.   Preferential tariff treatment applies to manufactured goods exported by the developing countries. This proposal calls for the industrialized nations to reduce or eliminate the taxes (duties) that they levy on manufactured products imported from the developing countries, while maintaining such duties on comparable products coming into their markets from other industrialized countries. This supposedly would give new manufacturing enterprises in the Third World a competitive edge in selling part of their output abroad and would thereby support the establishment and growth of such enterprises.

Several of the developed countries have adopted a version of this proposal, but this so-called "Generalized System of Preferences" contains a number of limitations as to products and duration and also includes an escape clause that allows an industrialized country to reinstitute duties if increased imports from the developing countries threaten serious economic injury to its own domestic producers. Such limitations reflect the reluctance with which the First World nations have embraced the concept of tariff preferences. They sometimes justify that reluctance on the grounds that preferential tariffs conflict with the tradition of nondiscriminatory treatment of imports from all foreign suppliers, but their fear of intensified import competition may constitute the more pragmatic reason.

The International Debt Problem

The chronic inability of the developing countries to earn sufficient export revenues to pay for their import needs has led those countries to borrow heavily from external sources. The principal sources of loans to the developing countries traditionally have been official international financial institutions, such as the International Monetary Fund and the World Bank, and foreign governments.[3] In recent years, however, private commercial banks in the Western industrialized nations have become deeply involved in such lending activities.

The incidence and amount of external borrowing by the developing countries increased enormously during the late 1970s and early 1980s. That increase was the result of a number of developments in the world economy. One such development was the rapid escalation of petroleum prices during 1979 and 1980, which added greatly to the import bills of those developing countries that must import oil. A second important causal factor was the onset of an exceptionally severe recession, which, among its many adverse consequences, resulted in a sharp cutback in the industrial countries' imports of industrial raw materials and other primary products from the developing nations. This "double whammy" of higher import costs and falling export earnings caused the trade imbalance (i.e., the excess of import expenditures relative to export receipts) of the NOEDCs to rise from $38 billion in 1977 to $109 billion in 1981.

---

[3]The International Monetary Fund (IMF) and the World Bank are discussed more fully in Chapters 10 and 11.

As the developing countries accelerated their borrowing to finance those growing trade imbalances and to fund developmental projects, their external debts mounted precipitously. Figure 3.1 traces that increase in external debt, which had grown to more than $800 billion by the end of 1984. That indebtedness was highly concentrated within the developing country group, as almost half of the total was owed by just seven countries, and four Latin American nations (Argentina, Brazil, Mexico, and Venezuela) accounted for $270 billion, or about one-third of the debt outstanding.

Figure 3.1 **External Debt of the Developing Countries**

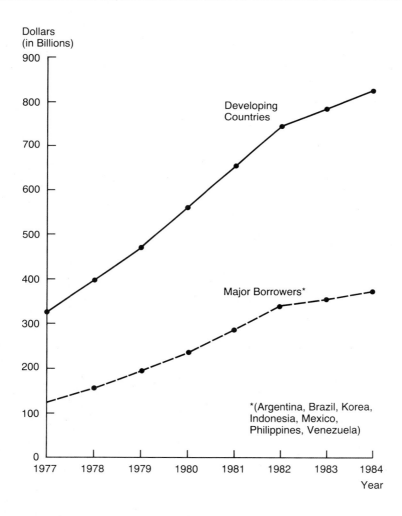

While this debt has been a serious problem for the NOEDCs in general, it has been especially troublesome for those Latin American nations and the other major borrowers. The size of their debts, combined with the historically high rates of interest that prevailed throughout the first half of the 1980s, have made it exceedingly difficult for those countries to pay the interest due to foreign lenders, much less repay the principal amounts of their loans. The so-called **debt service ratio**, which indicates what proportion of total export receipts must be used to make interest and amortization payments on external debts, rose from 15 to 22 percent between 1977 and 1984 for the developing countries collectively, and from 17 to 55 percent for the major borrowers. This meant that those main debtor nations would have to devote more than one-half of all the revenues that they realized from exports of goods and services just to meet the current interest obligations on their foreign debts.

This debt burden created a near-crisis situation during 1982 and 1983, as several of the debtor nations, notably Brazil, Mexico, and Argentina, found it next to impossible to make their scheduled payments. Actual defaults were averted through rescheduling and refinancing agreements worked out between those nations and their governmental and private creditors. However, the debtor countries were required to curtail their imports drastically and to initiate internal austerity programs. Those measures were designed to curb both foreign and domestic spending, so as to reduce the need for further borrowing and make the servicing of the existing debt more manageable.

Although the cooperative efforts of the governments, international financial organizations, and commercial banks that were directly concerned with the debt situation kept it from turning into a full-blown international financial crisis, the debt nevertheless has had many unfavorable repercussions. The developing nations, especially the major borrowers, have been forced to postpone investment outlays, cut government expenditures, and hold down the already-meager incomes and consumption levels of their populations. Those contractionary actions have, in turn, had deleterious effects upon other countries. The United States, for example, experienced a substantial decline in its export sales to Latin America during the early 1980s, which resulted in losses of thousands of jobs in the United States. Meanwhile, a number of financial institutions in Western Europe and the United States, including some of the giants of the commercial banking industry, found themselves saddled with massive amounts of questionable loans and had to take extraordinary steps to keep from writing off those loans as uncollectible and thereby sustaining heavy losses.

The international debt problem has by no means disappeared or been resolved. The developing countries still face the painful prospect of transferring scarce and much-needed capital funds abroad for many years in payments on their debts, and those capital outflows will undoubtedly detract from their domestic developmental efforts. In the meantime, the governmental and private lenders in the industrialized nations will be obligated to accept delays in repayment and perhaps lower returns on their loans than they would realize under more normal circumstances. Those nations are also obligated to keep their own economies expanding and to open their markets to goods from the developing countries, since it is only through expanded exports that the Third World nations can hope to earn the wherewithal to deal with their debt burdens.

This need for more open markets in the First World countries presents a particularly perplexing challenge, in view of the strong competitive pressures that already exist in the international trade sphere. That competitive situation constitutes another major trade problem, which will now be examined.

International Competition

An intense competitive struggle for export markets has been taking place around the globe for the past several years. It may seem somewhat paradoxical to discuss competition as a trade problem, inasmuch as competition traditionally has been regarded as beneficial in promoting productive efficiency and in preventing sellers from unfairly exploiting their customers. While this concept of competiton as a benevolent force remains valid in a fundamental, long-term sense, it is also true that competition can have very harmful and disruptive shorter-term effects upon workers, business firms, or entire industries. It is also the case that such effects often are viewed with particular dismay and distaste when the competition is coming from outside the country in which the affected industries are located.

This international brand of competition has been increasing steadily in intensity over the past several years, especially in markets for manufactured goods. The heating up of competition can be traced to those developments (discussed earlier in this chapter in Magnitude and Growth of World Trade) that have liberalized and stimulated world trade, but it also results from an enormous worldwide expansion of productive capacity in the manufactured-goods industries. That expansion initially took place in the United States, Western Europe, and Japan and involved such product lines as automobiles, basic metals, and chemicals. All those products are highly capital intensive, which means that large investments in fixed assets are required to produce them and high levels of output (and sales) are then needed to attain economies of scale by spreading those investment costs. The buildup of production capability in these industries thus has led to a fierce competitive scramble, as the companies involved have invaded one another's home territory in search of markets.

More recently, this competitive battle has been joined by business firms from some of the more advanced developing countries. As noted earlier, several such countries, including Hong Kong, South Korea, India, Brazil, Mexico, Yugoslavia, and Argentina, have developed sizeable manufacturing sectors and have begun to export very substantial quan-

Box 3.1

The Koreans Are Coming

Hyundai Motor Co. of South Korea has set its sights on the U.S. auto market. Hyundai captured 11 percent of Canada's auto import business in 1984, its first year of sales in Canada, and it has said that Canada is a test market for entry into the U.S. market by 1986. The company recently opened a new plant in South Korea to meet expected U.S. demand. That plant raises its annual production capacity to 400,000 to 450,000 cars. Hyundai built around 150,000 cars in 1983.

Hyundai's competitors in Canada have been urging the Canadian government to apply import duties to the Korean-made cars. As an auto maker from a less-developed country, Hyundai currently can import cars into Canada free of duty, whereas Japanese and other foreign car manufacturers are required to pay tariffs equal to 10.5 percent of the value of the vehicles.

Source: Peggy Berkowitz, "Hyundai Motor Took 11% of 1984 Market of Canada Imports," *The Wall Street Journal* (January 10, 1984), 8.

tities of goods to the rest of the world. The exports of these newly industrialized developing countries have been concentrated in a few product lines, notably textiles, clothing, consumer electronics, and electrical machinery, and their competitive impact consequently tends to be very heavy in a few specific sectors of the economies of the importing countries. Since these products generally fall in the labor-intensive category, their importation also tends to create serious unemployment problems in those economic sectors.

This intensification of international competition unfortunately has occurred during a period of time in which the economies of most of the countries of the world have performed rather poorly and in which economic activity and growth have been unusually slow. At such times, the people and governments of individual nations become especially concerned with the threat that foreign competition may pose to domestic jobs and to the health of domestic companies and industries, and such concerns are likely to outweigh any realization or appreciation of the favorable aspects of international trade. Strong pressures for restricting imports in order to preserve jobs and protect local firms from this competitive threat invariably emerge and gain widespread support during these periods. This is the current world situation, and it is a very delicate and dangerous one inasmuch as import restrictions initiated by one or a few countries might easily touch off a wave of retaliatory measures that could thoroughly stifle trade and other forms of international commercial activity.

This chapter began by pointing out that international trade offers many significant economic benefits to the nations that engage in it, but that the conduct of trade has always been beset by problems and tensions. This section has described some of the main problems that afflict international trade at the present time and that may, if left unresolved, undermine the spirit of economic cooperation that has helped to make the past three-and-a-half decades a period of prosperity and progress in the world economy. The final section of this chapter will consider the position of the United States in this promising but troubled international trade scene.

The U.S. International Trade Position

Extent of U.S. Trade

For much of this century, the United States has been the world's largest trading nation, and the value of its exports and imports still exceeds that of any other single country. However, several nations, notably Japan and West Germany, have been challenging this lead by expanding their exports at a more rapid rate than the United States. American exports now account for around 11 percent of the world's total, compared with 18 percent in 1960.

The first-place position that the U.S. has held in volume of trade is a reflection of the dominant size of its economy compared to those of all other nations. That is to say, the United States exports and imports more than any country largely because it produces and consumes much more than any other country. When the extent of U.S. trade is measured in an alternative way, by relating it to the total output of the American economy, a different picture emerges. The data in Table 3.4 point out that this *ratio* of U.S. exports to its gross domestic output (GDP) is quite low by comparison with the same ratios for other countries. This ratio, which economists sometimes refer to in more technical language as the **average propensity to export**, is a crude but useful indicator of the extent to which a nation is involved in or dependent upon trade with the rest of the world. The export/GDP ratio basically reveals what portion of the output produced by a country is sold in foreign markets, while its companion ratio of imports to GDP (the **average propensity to import**) provides an indication of the importance of foreign sources of supply to the country's economy. Changes that occur in these ratios over time are also of interest, since they help to reveal whether the nation's interaction and ties with the rest of the world are becoming more or less significant in relation to its overall level of economic activity.

Table 3.4   **Ratio of Exports to Gross Domestic Product**
(Selected Countries—1981)

Country	Exports as Percentage of GDP
Belgium	58.0
Netherlands	49.1
South Korea	32.3
Venezuela	32.0
Switzerland	29.0
South Africa	25.6
West Germany	25.6
Canada	25.4
Sweden	25.2
Italy	21.6
United Kingdom	21.0
France	18.6
Australia	13.5
Japan	13.5
Mexico	8.4
United States	8.1
Brazil	7.8
India	5.2

Source: International Monetary Fund, *International Financial Statistics, Supplement on Trade Statistics* (Washington, D.C.: International Monetary Fund, 1982), 54.

There are many reasons why these ratios of trade to national output for the United States have historically been smaller than for most other countries, but the most basic cause can be found in the size and richness of the U.S. domestic economy. America's national territory is among the largest in the world in terms of area, and that territory has been abundantly endowed with fertile agricultural land and natural resources. This rich land has become the home of more than 230 million people, making the United States the world's fourth largest country in population. Moreover, the United States has become the wealthiest and most productive nation in the world in economic terms, and thus America's people have attained a level of individual affluence that is matched by only a handful of other countries.

America's limited dependence upon trade with other nations is a corollary of these demographic, territorial, and economic characteristics. The plentitude of its own resources made it possible for the United States to develop economically without relying upon foreign sources of raw materials, while its population, which has constantly expanded by immigration as well as by natural increase, has provided both the labor force to produce a wide range of goods and a mass market for these goods. Thus, the United States, without deliberately planning to do so, evolved as a largely self-sufficient and self-contained national economy.

Box 3.2

Growing U.S. Dependence on Foreign Markets

A study by The Conference Board, based primarily upon data from the U.S. Department of Commerce, has shown that U.S. manufacturing is becoming more dependent upon exports for its growth. The study shows that nearly 80 percent of all new manufacturing jobs created in the U.S. between 1977 and 1980 were linked to exports. The Conference Board report said that a total of 4.7 million U.S. jobs were related to the export of manufactured products in 1980.

Meanwhile, American companies are placing more emphasis upon exports than they did in earlier years. U.S. exports rose rapidly during the 1970s, and U.S. companies that have become export-oriented are now hanging tough in the face of the strong dollar, which handicaps their ability to sell in foreign markets.

Source: "U.S. Manufacturing Increases Dependency on Exports for Growth," *The Wall Street Journal* (August 11, 1982), 24; "U.S. Increases Its Exports, Despite Problems," *The Wall Street Journal* (June 11, 1985), 6.

As was noted previously, this economic independence has been diminishing over recent years, as evidenced by a gradual upward movement in the ratios of U.S. exports and imports to its national product. This opening of the American economy to the rest of the world has to some degree been forced upon the United States by developments such as the depletion of its domestic supplies of certain natural resources. The United States now depends almost entirely upon foreign sources for a multitude of essential minerals and metals, including manganese, chromium, cobalt, tin, nickel, bauxite, and industrial diamonds. Many American business firms have also found it increasingly necessary to look toward foreign countries as outlets for their products, as stronger competition and market saturation have reduced their ability to expand sales at home. However, in a more positive vein, the expansion of America's participation in international trade can be seen as part of that worldwide trend toward greater economic interdependence that was cited earlier in this chapter and as indicative of American leadership in the progressive developments that underlie this trend.

The U.S. Balance of Trade

The aspect of America's international trade position that has received most attention and caused the greatest consternation in the past few years is the relationship between exports and imports or the **balance of trade.** Whenever the value of a nation's exports exceeds that of its imports for a given time period, the nation is said to be experiencing a **surplus** or **positive** balance of trade. Conversely, if imports exceed exports in value, the trade balance is described as a **deficit** or **negative** balance. Historically, there has been a tendency to view surplus trade balances as inherently "favorable" and deficit balances as "unfavorable," but this legacy of the old mercantilist economic doctrine is overly simplistic, inasmuch as the favorableness or unfavorableness of any particular export–import balance depends upon the overall economic circumstances of the country experiencing it. A temporary deficit in the balance of trade might, for example, be a favorable condition if it were the result of a country's importing capital goods to develop productive new industrial enterprises.

With regard to the U.S. balance of trade, the most striking development has been the shift from a long-standing surplus balance to what has become a chronic and substantial deficit. That shift began to show up in the late 1960s after an almost uninterrupted succession of annual surpluses going back to the turn of the century, but the trade accounts did not actually register a deficit balance until 1971. Since that year— with the exception of 1975, when a deep recession in the United States led to a sharp but temporary curtailment of imports—trade deficits have prevailed and have reached very sizeable proportions (Table 3.5).

Table 3.5 **U.S. Balance of Merchandise Trade (Millions of Dollars)**

Year	Exports	Imports	Trade Balance (Deficit)
1960–1964 avg.	21,662	16,260	5,402
1965–1969 avg.	31,295	28,533	2,762
1970	42,469	39,866	2,603
1971	43,319	45,579	(2,260)
1972	49,381	55,797	(6,416)
1973	71,410	70,499	911
1974	98,306	103,649	(5,343)
1975	107,088	98,041	9,047
1976	114,745	124,051	(9,306)
1977	120,186	151,689	(31,503)
1978	142,054	175,813	(33,759)
1979	184,473	211,819	(27,346)
1980	223,966	249,308	(25,342)
1981	237,019	265,086	(28,067)
1982	211,217	247,606	(36,389)
1983	200,203	260,753	(60,550)
1984	220,343	327,778	(107,435)

Source: Federal Reserve Bank of St. Louis, *International Economic Conditions,* annual edition (St. Louis, 1985), 4.

U.S. trade deficits have raised serious concerns for a number of reasons. In the first place, deficits of such duration and magnitude can have very undesirable effects upon the economy of the nation experiencing them. The most immediate and apparent of those effects is usually reduced employment of domestic workers, as goods produced abroad displace those produced by the nation's own firms and labor force. If such displacement is extensive and continues over a long period of time, entire domestic industries may be eliminated. Chronic trade deficits can also retard investment spending and the economic growth that such spending normally promotes, to the extent that investors are discouraged by import competition and declining demand for domestically produced goods.

Although such developments may yield economic benefits in the long run, insofar as they lead to greater production efficiency on a worldwide basis, they are apt to be highly unsettling and injurious in the short run. Several American industries and large numbers of American workers have experienced those painful effects of import competition and the trade deficit over the past decade. Table 3.6 shows how employment has fallen in some of those industries as imports have increased as a proportion of U.S. consumption of their products and the trade deficit associated with those industries has risen.

Underlying Causes of the Deficit.   A second reason for concern over the negative imbalances in the U.S. trade accounts has to do with the idea that those deficits may actually constitute *symptoms* of other, more

Table 3.6   Effects of Trade Deficits and Import Penetration on Selected U.S. Industries

Industry	Production Employees (Thousands of Workers)		Trade Deficit (Millions of Dollars)		Imports (Percent of U.S. Consumption)	
	1979	1983	1979	1983	1979	1983
Automobiles	764	571	$11,061	$19,203	22.0	26.0
Communications equipment	347	321	3,218	7,474	29.5	41.1
Iron and steel	380	211	6,076	4,924	15.2	20.5
Lumber and wood products	654	547	818	969	24.9	29.5
Metalworking and machine tools	271	193	143	344	23.0	32.5
Paper and paper products	536	495	1,564	1,324	13.0	12.6
Textiles and apparel	1,888	1,625	3,581	9,025	32.6	45.5

Source: Manufacturers Hanover Economic Report (December 1984): 1.Reprinted by permission.

basic weaknesses in the U.S. economy. To use a medical analogy, the deficits are like the headaches or fever that may be symptomatic of a serious illness or bodily disorder. Inasmuch as the "patient" involved here is the economic system on which all Americans depend for their livelihood, this idea merits consideration.

What sorts of weaknesses or "disorders" in the American economy are the trade deficits signaling? Among those that have been discerned are a growing dependence upon foreign sources of essential raw materials, poor performance in productivity, a loss of leadership in technology, and inadequate investment for capital formation.

It is quite clear that America's growing dependence upon foreign sources of several raw materials, together with rapid increases in the prices of those commodities, have contributed to the succession of trade deficits. This is best illustrated by the case of petroleum. U.S. oil imports roughly doubled in volume between 1970 and 1980, but, due to the sharp price increases imposed by the Organization of Petroleum Exporting Countries (OPEC) during that decade, the annual cost of U.S. oil imports rose from less than $3 billion in 1970 to nearly $80 billion by 1980. Although both the amount and the price per barrel of U.S. petroleum imports have declined since reaching that peak in 1980, the "oil deficit" has accounted for a significant share of the overall negative balance in U.S. trade.

The underlying problem that the U.S. oil deficit reveals is that America has become progressively more vulnerable to external forces that could disrupt its supply of essential raw materials or drive their prices so high as to impose onerous costs upon American consumers and industries. This vulnerability, and its potential adverse economic consequences, were brought home to U.S. businesses and consumers by the severe disruptions associated with the oil and gasoline "crises" of 1973–1974 and 1978–1979, when supplies of imported petroleum were sharply curtailed as a result of political upheavals and hostilities in the Middle East. The fear has been expressed by many in the United States that those occurrences were only modest demonstrations of the extent to which America's economic health, and even its political power and independence, have become hostages to foreign events or to the decisions of foreign governments.

Other weaknesses in the U.S. economy, such as declining productivity, lagging technological innovation, and inadequate capital investment, can be considered together since they are closely interrelated and have a common causal linkage to trade deficits. Each of these problems has been widely noted and thoroughly analyzed elsewhere, and no attempt will be made to document their existence or probe their causes here. It is sufficient for our present purposes to point out that any one of these negative developments is capable of eroding the competitive position of the industry or industries involved, since it will ultimately result in higher production costs, higher product prices, deteriorating product quality, or all of these factors.

Whenever such deleterious developments interact and pervade a large part of a nation's economy, as they did in the United States during the late 1970s, that nation's ability to compete with foreign producers, either internationally or in its own home market, will invariably suffer. A continuing and growing trade deficit thus serves as a warning symptom of the economic debility that will inevitably overtake any country that fails to improve the productivity of its human and nonhuman resources, develop new technology, and expand and modernize its stock of capital. It is imperative for the economic future of the United States that such symptoms not be ignored.

The Strong (Overvalued) Dollar.   While the problems of the American economy identified above had much to do with the emergence of deficits in the U.S. trade balance during the 1970s, another phenomenon has been responsible for perpetuating and enlarging those deficits in recent years. The value of the U.S. dollar, relative to the currencies of other countries, began climbing steeply in 1980. The so-called **trade-weighted value** of the dollar, which is a weighted average of the dollar's price in relation to several other national currencies, rose by over 60 percent between early 1980 and the end of 1984.

The principal direct cause of that increase in the dollar's value was an upsurge of foreign investment in the U.S. economy and in dollar-denominated securities. Those investments created a strong demand for dollars and pushed up their prices in the foreign exchange markets.

The growth of foreign investment stemmed from a number of related conditions. As a consequence of tight monetary policies and the federal government's need to borrow heavily to finance its huge budget deficits, U.S. interest rates were unusually high through the early 1980s, both by historical standards and in comparison with those prevailing in other countries. That interest rate differential, combined with a perception of the United States as politically stable, economically prosperous, and relatively inflation free, apparently convinced foreign investors that America offered greater risk-adjusted yields on their investible funds than could be realized elsewhere in the world.

The inflows of capital from abroad helped to finance both the government budget deficit and capital formation by U.S. private business firms. However, the investment-fueled escalation in the dollar's value, by markedly reducing the effective cost of foreign goods to American buyers, brought a flood of imports of both industrial and consumer goods into the United States. In the meantime, American manufacturers found it increasingly difficult to sell their products overseas, as the lofty price of the dollar made their products uncompetitively expensive in foreign markets. The U.S. trade balance therefore worsened steadily as the dollar progressively strengthened in the foreign exchange markets.

It may be somewhat confusing to attribute a nation's troubles in the trade sector to a "strong" currency. This confusion may be due to the terminology employed. It has become common parlance to refer to a currency that has been appreciating in value relative to other currencies as "strengthening" or "strong," which implies that a higher exchange value is better than a lower value. This is not always the case, since a strong currency is likely to have a detrimental impact upon portions of a nation's economy, notably those industries and workers that are exposed to import competition or that are dependent upon export markets.

It is less ambiguous to describe a currency as **overvalued,** rather than "strong," although the term overvalued (and its converse, undervalued) can also sometimes mean different things to different people. Broadly speaking, a currency is overvalued if the price at which it trades for other currencies in the foreign exchange market exceeds its real purchasing power relative to those of the other currencies. To take a very simple example, if it cost $20 in the United States to buy exactly the same mix and quantity of goods that could be purchased for £10 sterling in Great Britain, then the relative value of the two currencies, based upon their real purchasing power, would be $2 = £1 sterling.

To continue the example, it is quite conceivable that the **exchange rate** between these two currencies, that is, the price at which they would trade for one another in the foreign exchange market, could differ from that purchasing power relationship. The exchange rate might, for instance, be $1.50 = £1 sterling. At that rate, the dollar would be overvalued, since its exchange market value exceeds its purchasing power relative to the pound.

Whenever the currency of a particular country becomes overvalued, the residents of that country will find it beneficial to substitute imports for domestically produced goods. In terms of the example given above, Americans would be able to acquire more real goods by buying British pounds for their (overvalued) dollars and then buying goods from Great Britain with those pounds. By the same token, overvaluation discourages foreign purchases of the export products of the country with the overvalued currency, by making these products more expensive to foreign purchasers than they otherwise would be. Again, in terms of the above example, British residents would not be interested in importing American goods so long as the dollar remained overvalued, since they could acquire goods more cheaply at home.[4]

This description of an overvalued currency and its effects upon imports and exports is applicable to the dollar and the U.S. trade situation in the first half of the 1980s. The dollar's foreign exchange market value escalated during that period as a consequence of the investment-based demand for dollars on the part of foreign business firms, individuals, and governments, and this escalation engendered a great increase in U.S. imports while American exports declined.

---

[4]The effects of overvaluation or undervaluation of currencies are discussed in a more formal manner in Chapter 5, which deals with the theory of international trade.

Box 3.3

Bayer: Why the High Dollar is No Headache

Executives at Bayer, West Germany's biggest chemical company, are counting up their profits. "We couldn't be happier with the high dollar," says Klaus Schlede, Bayer's corporate finance director, "The dollar is knocking out our U.S. competitors in foreign markets. It forces U.S. chemical producers to compete abroad with one hand tied behind their back." The result: record sales for Bayer that have more than doubled earnings over 1983. This is generating cash to help support its planned expansion in pharmaceuticals, particularly in the U.S.

Source: "Bayer: Why the High Dollar is No Headache," *Business Week* (October 24, 1984), 53.

These developments serve to emphasize the interconnections among currency values, international capital movements, trade balances, and internal economic conditions, as well as the dilemmas that can arise when a nation such as the United States employs economic policies that are out of harmony with those of other countries. In this instance, the tight monetary and loose fiscal policies of the United States created both a need for foreign capital and an interest rate structure that attracted such capital. But the resulting international capital flows triggered exchange rate changes that wreaked havoc with America's foreign trade and the competitive status of many of its industries. This situation provides convincing evidence of the economic interdependence that now exists between the United States and the rest of the world, and of the need for that interdependence to be taken into account in making economic decisions.

Summary

1.   International trade consists of the exchange of economic goods among individuals or organizations that are residents of different nations or nation-states.

2.   The fundamental reason for international trade is the expectation of mutual benefits to the parties involved. However, despite its demonstrated benefits, international trade has historically been fraught with problems and frictions and has been a cause of controversy among nations.

3.   International trade has expanded greatly since the end of World War II, both in absolute terms and in relation to world output. This vigorous expansion of trade is attributable to rapid technological progress, demographic trends, economic growth, and an improved political climate.

4.   Both the composition and the direction of trade have undergone some significant changes over the past three decades. Trade in manufactured goods and fuels has grown more rapidly than trade in agricultural products and minerals. Trade among the more economically advanced countries has also increased more rapidly than trade among other country groupings.

5.   Some of the major problems in international trade are the relatively slow growth and instability of exports of the non-oil-producing developing countries, the resultant external debts of those countries, and the greatly intensified worldwide competition in manufactured goods.

6.   The trade problems of the developing countries have led them to call for some fundamental changes in international trade policies and practices. Those proposed changes constitute what is termed the "New International Economic Order."

7.   The United States is the world's largest single trading nation in terms of the absolute volume of its exports and imports, although international trade accounts for a smaller proportion of its overall economic activity than is the case for most other countries.

8.   The United States has experienced a sharp change in its balance of trade in recent years, from a historic surplus position to a substantial trade deficit. This shift is regarded by some as symptomatic of certain fundamental problems in the U.S. economy.

9.   The deficit in the U.S. balance of trade has been perpetuated and enlarged in recent years by the overvaluation of the U.S. dollar.

Questions for Review or Discussion

1.   Indicate and explain the major reasons for the rapid expansion of international trade during the post–World War II period.

2.   What basic changes have been occurring with regard to the composition and direction of international trade? What are the implications of these changes?

3.   What are the long-term and short-term trade problems of the non-oil-producing developing countries? How do these relate to the debt burdens of those countries?

4.   What are the major proposals included in the New International Economic Order? Explain how the adoption of those proposals might affect the economies of the more industrialized countries such as the United States.

5. Explain the principal causes and consequences of the international debt problem.
6. What are the major causes of the greatly intensified international competition in manufactured goods? What implications does this new competition have for the American economy?
7. What changes have taken place in the international trade position of the United States in recent years? How do those changes relate to conditions within the U.S. economy?
8. What does *overvaluation* (or undervaluation) of a currency mean? How do overvaluation and undervaluation effect exports and imports?

Case

The "Four Tigers" Move Upstream

In 1960, Japanese products were thought of in the West as poorly made, and Panasonic, Sony, or Toyota were hardly known outside Japan. A quarter-century later, most U.S. consumers consider these brand names and other Japanese products to have standards of quality as good as— if not better than—comparable products produced in the West.

South Korea, Taiwan, Hong Kong, and Singapore, collectively known as the "Four Tigers," exported $93 billion in goods to the United States in 1984, mostly in the form of private-label production for U.S. companies like Sears, IBM, and Mattel. Now these four countries would like to widen profit margins, reduce vulnerability to protectionism, and obtain other benefits of establishing their own brand names in the United States. However, in doing so, they will be competing against some established Japanese and U.S. companies.

Most companies from "Four Tigers" are small compared to their competition in the United States which limits their resources for developing expensive U.S. promotion and distribution channels. Only South Korea has an internal market large enough to test consumer products. Companies from the other three nations do not have this key advantage that Japanese companies possess, due to the latter firms' ability to compete fiercely in their domestic market of over 100 million consumers and refine their products there before introducing them to the U.S. market. Consequently, companies from the "Four Tigers" have faced many problems in developing their brands in the United States.

Taiwan's Fulet Electronic Industrial Co. has annual sales of only $40 million, yet the firm planned for $50 million in 1984 U.S. sales of its Proton brand of high-fidelity equipment and televisions which it introduced to America in 1982. Fulet actually achieved sales amounting to only one-half of its projected goal. On the other hand, Taiwan's Pro-

Kennex brand of rackets has captured 15 to 20 percent of the market for high-quality tennis rackets. Despite worldwide sales of only $40 million, the manufacturers of Pro-Kennex rackets are planning to spend $3 million on advertising in 1985. South Korea's Samsung is fast establishing a name for itself as the "sensible" alternative to high-priced Japanese and U.S. televisions.

Because of the difficulty of developing their own brand names, some companies from the "Four Tigers" are buying established brand-name products. Hong Kong's Universal International bought out British toy car maker Matchbox; Universal's U.S. sales are expected to be $110 million in 1985. Similarly, Hong Kong's largest camera maker, Haking, took over the Ansco brand from GAF. Murjani Industries of Hong Kong expects to sell $250 million of their Gloria Vanderbilt jeans and other products in 1985.

What do these examples illustrate about the evolving nature of global trade patterns? Can companies from other developing countries learn anything from the experiences of the firms from Hong Kong and the three other "tigers"? If so, what?

Sources: "The 'Four Tigers' Start Clawing at Upscale Markets," *Business Week,* July 22, 1985, pp. 136–142; and Raj Aggarwal, "As New Japans Rise, U.S. Must Innovate," *The Toledo Blade,* (Toledo), January 25, 1985, p. 27.

Chapter 4

INTERNATIONAL DIRECT INVESTMENT TRENDS

Chapter Objectives:

- *To explain the nature of international investment and the various forms and methods it takes*
- *To trace the growth of international investment and the principal trends in the direction and composition of that investment over the past three decades*
- *To describe the role that U.S. companies have played in international investment and to show how changes in the world economy and political situation have affected the international investment behavior of those companies*
- *To analyze the causes and consequences of the recent dramatic expansion of foreign direct investment in the United States*

International (or foreign) investment occurs when individuals, business firms, or government bodies that are residents of one country acquire assets in another country. This may also be thought of as the acquisition by residents of one nation of **financial claims** on foreign residents, since the investors presumably will realize financial returns from the assets in which they are investing. Foreign investments may be **long-term** or **short-term**, depending upon the maturity of the financial claim involved, or, stated somewhat differently, the length of time the investor is expected to hold the asset. Financial claims that mature in less than 1 year or are collectible on demand are regarded as short term, whereas those with maturity periods of more than 1 year or those with no specified maturity (e.g., common stocks representing shares of ownership in a corporation) are classed as long term.

Long-term foreign investment is categorized as either **direct** investment or portfolio investment, with the distinguishing criterion being **managerial control**. In direct investment, the investor exercises some degree of managerial control over the assets acquired, while in portfolio

investment the investor's concern and involvement are limited to realizing income from the investment or a capital gain (or loss) from changes
in the value of the assets. The distinction between portfolio and direct
investment may be difficult to draw, since it is not always clear at what
point a holder of foreign assets may begin to assume a managerial role
or what share of ownership of an enterprise is required to exert managerial control.[1] But the intent of the investor with respect to participation in management is usually apparent from the size or nature of
the investment. Thus, when a company builds production facilities in
a foreign country or buys a substantial share of the voting stock or real
assets of a foreign firm, it is generally safe to assume that the investing
company intends to become involved in managing the production facilities. On the other hand, investment in debt-type securities, such as
bonds or commercial paper, or the purchase of a small amount of the
common stock of a foreign company ordinarily would not enable the
investor to take part in managing the enterprise that issues those securities.

Attention in this chapter will be concentrated upon one component
of international investment, long-term direct investment by business
firms. As was noted in Chapter 1, such investment has become the
principal foundation of modern international business operations. Although the bulk of international investment was of the portfolio type
prior to the Second World War, direct investment has surged to the
forefront in the postwar period as thousands of business firms have
acquired factories, warehouses, mines, retail outlets, hotels, office buildings, and a variety of other business establishments outside their native
countries. The acquisition of these productive assets has helped to trans-
form such firms into international enterprises, capable of producing and
distributing goods or offering business services in many parts of the
world.

Alternative Methods of Investing Abroad

Before examining the quantitative dimensions of this upsurge in international direct investment, it is important to recognize the alternative
means by which such investment has been accomplished. There are a
variety of ways in which business firms can obtain managerial control
over productive assets located in other countries, and these alternatives

---

[1]The U.S. Department of Commerce, which is the U.S. government agency chiefly responsible for reporting on American investment abroad, includes under direct investment
any situation in which a U.S. investor (defined to include an associated group of investors)
owns 10 percent or more of a foreign business enterprise. This figure is an arbitrary one,
however, inasmuch as managerial control might be effectuated with less than 10 percent
ownership in some instances and might require a greater share in other cases.

may have quite different effects upon the financial positions of the firms themselves and upon the economies of the countries involved.

Perhaps the simplest way to illustrate the various possible approaches to foreign direct investment is by considering a hypothetical example of an American manufacturing company that wishes to operate a factory in another country. Several options might be available to such a company including: (1) it could use funds raised in the United States to purchase partial or full ownership of a factory already operating in the foreign country; (2) it could use funds raised in the United States to pay for the construction and equipping of a new factory in the foreign country. Both of these options entail an **international capital transfer**, that is, the company would be transferring capital funds (money) from the United States to pay for the purchase or the construction of the foreign factory. Such international capital transfers are a principal means of effectuating foreign direct investments, but they do not exhaust the possibilities. The American company might also consider: (3) borrowing money (e.g., from banks or through the sale of bonds) in the foreign country to buy or build the factory that it wishes to operate there; or (4) investing earnings from other affiliated business enterprises that it might have in the foreign country in the new factory. In these cases, no international movement of capital funds would be necessary, as the financing for the factory would come from the foreign country in which it was being located. Still another feasible option would be for the U.S. firm to: (5) trade some intangible resource, such as technology, patent rights, or managerial assistance, for a share of ownership in a foreign company that possessed or could acquire the kind of factory sought by the American firm. Such a transaction would also obviate the need to transfer money per se from one country to another.

All of the foreign direct investment methodologies described in the hypothetical example above have actually been utilized by business firms during the post–World War II expansion of international direct investment. The following section will consider the magnitude and some of the major trends associated with that expansion.

Global Trends in Direct Investment

Tracking the incidence and growth of foreign direct investment for the world as a whole is a difficult exercise. Many countries do not gather data on such investments on a regular basis, and much of the information that is reported regularly covers only those direct investments that are financed through international capital transfers. Nevertheless, sufficient information has been assembled to permit one to perceive the broad dimensions and to identify the more significant trends in foreign direct investment.

The available data reveal that foreign direct investment by business firms has grown substantially during the past quarter-century, both in absolute terms and in comparison with other measures of economic activity. A study by the International Trade Administration (ITA) of the U.S. Department of Commerce estimated that international direct investment increased at an average rate of 10.6 percent/year between 1960 and 1981. Those continuing annual increases brought the value of international direct investment to approximately $547 billion by the end of 1981, which represents an eightfold increase over the 1960 figure of $66 billion.[2]

Sources of International Direct Investment

Some interesting and noteworthy changes have been taking place over time in the *sources* of international direct investments. The great bulk of such investment continues to come from business firms based in the developed nations of the First World. There has been a significant increase in recent years in the incidence of overseas investment by companies from the developing countries, but the volume of investment by those so-called "Third World multinationals" is still quite small compared with that emanating from the industrialized nations.

Business firms headquartered in the United States clearly led the expansion of overseas direct investment activity through the 1950s and most of the 1960s. Outflows of direct investment capital from the United States accounted for over 60 percent of the world total of such capital movements prior to 1967, and U.S. firms held approximately one-half of the worldwide stock of foreign direct investment by the end of that year. British firms were a distant second in foreign direct investment activity, accounting for some 9 percent of pre-1967 capital outflows and holding 17 percent of the stock of direct investment by year-end 1967.[3]

The reasons for the preponderance of American firms in the early stage of the postwar upswing in international direct investment are not difficult to uncover. That was a time in which the U.S. economy and the American dollar were manifestly stronger than the economies and currencies of the other industrialized nations. American corporations therefore had the wherewithal to launch and finance overseas expansion, while their European and Japanese counterparts still were preoccupied with rebuilding their productive capability sufficiently to satisfy consumer demand in their own countries. The Americans also were leading in the development and application of new industrial technology and were able to turn that technological edge into a competitive advantage in their penetration of foreign markets. These conditions sup-

[2]International Trade Administration, *International Direct Investment: Global Trends and the U.S. Role* (Washington, D.C.: U.S. Department of Commerce, 1984), 6.

[3]Organization for Economic Cooperation and Development, *International Investment and Multinational Enterprise: Recent International Direct Investment Trends* (Paris: OECD, 1981), 39–40.

ported and stimulated a buildup of U.S. direct investment abroad which quickly outstripped the foreign investment activities and holdings of other countries.

But the balance of economic power between the U.S. and the other industrialized nations shifted perceptibly after the mid-1960s. The Western European and Japanese business sectors had fully recovered from the destructive effects of World War II by that time and had regained their economic vitality. Business firms from those countries began moving aggressively into international markets, and American corporations found themselves facing greatly intensified competition, both in exporting and in the foreign direct investment/foreign production sphere.

The extent of the changes that have transpired between the earlier and later stages of the postwar era with regard to the sources of international direct investment can be discerned from the data in Tables 4.1 and 4.2. These data, which show the distribution of the stock of international direct investment and the origins of direct investment capital outflows, trace the decline of American preeminence or (to describe the transition in a more positive manner) the more even distribution that has evolved in the national origins of international direct investment.

Table 4.1   Stock Value of International Direct Investment Classified by Country of Origin, 1960 and 1981

Country of Origin	Billions of Dollars		Percentage of World Total	
	1960	1981	1960	1981
United States	31.9	226.4	48.5	41.5
United Kingdom	10.8	65.5	16.4	12.0
West Germany	0.8	45.5	1.2	8.3
Japan	0.5	37.0	0.8	6.8
Switzerland	2.0	36.4	3.0	6.7
Netherlands	7.0	32.4	10.6	5.9
Canada	2.5	25.6	3.8	4.7
France	4.1	24.5	6.2	4.5
Sweden	0.4	7.9	0.6	1.5
Belgium–Luxembourg	1.3	6.4	2.0	1.2
Italy	1.1	5.9	1.7	1.1
South Africa	—	5.4	—	1.0
Australia	0.2	2.5	0.3	0.5
Other developed countries	2.5	6.6	3.8	1.2
Developing countries	0.7	17.6	1.1	3.2
World total	65.8	545.6	100.0	100.0

Source: International Trade Administration, *International Direct Investment: Global Trends and the U.S. Role* (Washington, D.C.: U.S. Department of Commerce, 1984), 45.

Table 4.2   **Origin of Outward Direct Investment Flows**

Country or Country Group	Outward Direct Investment Flows (Percentage of World Total)	
	1965–1969	1980–1981
United States	65.2	28.0
Europe	29.3	48.6
Canada	2.0	9.7
Japan	1.8	7.6
Other developed countries	0.9	1.3
Developing countries	0.2	4.8

Source: International Trade Administration, *International Direct Investment: Global Trends and the U.S. Role* (Washington, D.C.: U.S. Department of Commerce, 1984), 46.

Recipients of International Direct Investment

Some significant patterns and trends can also be discerned in relation to the *destination* of international direct investments. One of these has to do with the proportion of such investment going into the Third World countries. This tends to be a closely watched statistic, mainly because of the presumption (widely but not universally held) that foreign direct investment can greatly assist these poorer countries to progress economically by providing them with part of the capital, technology, and managerial skills they require in order to modernize their economies and expand their economic output.

The actual record of foreign direct investment during the postwar period has not been encouraging to those who believe that such investment could be a key contributor to economic progress in the Third World. As noted previously, the major portion of that investment has come from the developed nations, and its usual destination has been other developed nations rather than the Third World. Less than one-third of the total stock of international direct investment was located in the developing countries in 1967, and that portion declined to 27 percent by 1980. Although the annual growth rate of direct investment in the developing countries has been increasing somewhat in recent years, much of this upturn has been in the export-oriented manufacturing sectors of a few of the newly industrializing developing countries referred to in Chapter 3; or in financial enterprises that have been established mainly for tax avoidance purposes. Meanwhile, the majority of the developing countries are continuing to fare poorly in the global distribution of direct investment, despite their large and rapidly increasing populations and their collective importance as sources of raw materials.[4]

Perhaps the most notable recent change in the destination of international investment flows has been the dramatic upsurge in foreign direct investment in the United States. Prior to the 1970s, both the stock of foreign direct investment in the U.S. economy and annual additions to that stock were quite modest in amount. However, this situation has changed markedly since the early 1970s, as foreign business firms and foreign governments have rapidly expanded their holdings of agricultural land, urban real estate, financial institutions, and industrial enterprises in the United States. Average annual inflows of foreign capital for direct investment in the United States increased from less than $1 billion in the 1960s to well over $10 billion by the early 1980s, and the value of foreign direct investments in the United States rose from $21 billion in 1973 to $135 billion by 1983. On a worldwide basis, the United States was receiving between 35 and 40 percent of total international direct investment during the early 1980s, compared with only 2 to 3 percent in the 1960s.[5]

The causes of this sharp upturn in foreign direct investment in the United States are of sufficient interest to warrant investigating them in greater depth. It is more informative, however, to consider this development in combination with the record of overseas direct investment by American business firms. Such a juxtaposition can help reveal how and to what extent the circumstances that have prompted American firms to invest abroad correspond to those that have brought the recent influx of foreign investors to the United States.

Foreign Direct Investment by U.S. Business Firms
Dimensions of U.S. Foreign Direct Investment

Several of the more significant facts and figures relating to foreign direct investment by American businesses have been discussed previously and need only be summarized here. These data show that U.S. firms launched a strong thrust into foreign production operations soon after the close of the Second World War and have sustained that movement to the present time. The book value of the overseas business enterprises owned and managed by American companies increased at an average rate of 10 percent annually over this period, going from just under $12 billion in 1950 to $233 billion by the end of 1984. It is also worth reiterating that the number and magnitude of foreign direct investment ventures by American firms have overshadowed those of companies based in

---

[4]*Ibid.*, pp. 14–19.

[5]International Trade Administration, *International Direct Investment*, 47; "Foreign Direct Investment in the United States in 1983," *Survey of Current Business* (October 1984): 26.

other countries. Although the degree of American dominance in this arena has lately been reduced, the United States still ranks first among all countries as a source of direct investment capital and accounts for over 40 percent of all such investment around the world.

A number of interesting changes have taken place over the past 30 years in both the geographic distribution and the industry composition of U.S. foreign direct investments. With respect to geographic distribution, there has been a marked change in the allocation of American investments between the developing and developed countries. In 1950, U.S. direct investments were almost equally divided between these two categories of countries, whereas by 1983 three-fourths of U.S. investments were located in the developed nations while the share of the developing countries had fallen to one-fourth.[6]

In terms of industry composition, that is, the kinds of economic activity in which American firms have invested, the most noticeable trend has been the increasing emphasis upon manufacturing activities. Manufacturing accounted for 40 percent of all U.S. overseas direct investment in 1983, compared with 32 percent in 1950. Over this same period, the share of U.S. investment in petroleum-related activities fell from 29 to 27 percent, while the proportion invested in "other industries" also declined. Table 4.3 provides a breakdown of U.S. foreign direct investments by geographic location and type of economic activity as of year-end 1983.

Motives for U.S. Foreign Direct Investment

These statistics provide some useful clues to the conditions and considerations that have motivated American business firms to invest abroad and to how those motivating factors have altered over time. In exploring this subject further, it will be necessary to deal in broad generalizations, since the specific foreign investment decisions that have been made by each American firm undoubtedly have involved a complex combination of considerations, many of which presumably apply only to that firm.

One way to understand the multitude of diverse motives for foreign investment is to group these motives together in a few categories. Using such an approach, business firms can be characterized (in terms of their reasons for investing abroad) as: (1) resource motivated—here the principal reason for investing overseas is to establish or maintain control over supplies of material inputs the firm needs to carry on its business operations; (2) market motivated—here the firm is mainly concerned with gaining access to a foreign market or protecting an already established market position; (3) efficiency motivated—firms in this category

[6]Obie G. Whichard, "Trends in the U.S. Direct Investment Position Abroad, 1950–1979," *Survey of Current Business* (February 1981): 39; "U.S. Direct Investment Abroad in 1983," *Survey of Current Business* (August 1984): 18.

Table 4.3   **U.S. Direct Investment Abroad Classified by Economic Activity and Geographic Location, 1983**

Economic Activity	Billions of Dollars	Percentage of Total
Manufacturing	$ 90.1	39.9
Petroleum	59.8	26.5
Mining	6.7	3.0
Trade	28.5	12.6
Banking	11.5	5.0
Finance (except banking, insurance, and real estate)	17.2	7.6
All other	12.2	5.4
Total	226.1	100.0
Geographic Location		
Canada	$ 47.5	21.0
Europe	102.5	45.4
Japan	8.1	3.6
Australia, New Zealand, South Africa	11.5	5.1
Latin America	29.5	13.1
Africa	5.2	2.3
Middle East	3.0	1.3
Asia and Pacific	13.3	5.9
Unallocated	5.6	2.4

Source: "U.S. Direct Investment Abroad in 1983," *Survey of Current Business* (August 1984): 29.

invest abroad as a way of reducing the costs of doing business. Potential savings in labor costs or transportation costs are frequently cited inducements for companies seeking such cost reductions via foreign production.

As is the case with most classification schemes that attempt to reduce the complex realities of human or organizational behavior to a few generalizations, the categories set forth above are neither all-encompassing nor mutually exclusive. It is quite possible that many American companies have invested overseas for reasons that do not fit neatly into any of these categories or for multiple reasons that fall into more than one category. Nevertheless, these motivational generalities, when placed into the context of changing international political and economic conditions, offer some plausible explanations for the major historical trends that were previously noted in the geographic and industry allocation of U.S. foreign direct investment.

Thus, the distribution of overseas investment by American business for several years after the end of World War II exhibited a strong element

Box 4.1

Ford Invests in Auto Manufacturing Facilities in Mexico

Ford Motor Co.'s plan to build a $500 million plant in Mexico to build small cars for the U.S. market is another example of auto makers increasingly moving abroad to take advantage of very low labor costs.

High labor costs in the U.S. have made domestic cars expensive for American consumers. Although Ford says the venture is the result of a Mexican decree that in effect forces auto makers there to build new plants, the labor cost of less than $3 an hour in Mexico—compared with $23 for U.S. assembly-line workers—no doubt has played a major role in Ford's decision. But the United Auto Workers Union doesn't like it.

Source: "Ford Plans Reflect Auto Makers' Move Abroad to Cut Costs," *The Wall Street Journal* (January 11, 1984), 3. Reprinted by permission of *The Wall Street Journal*, © Dow Jones & Company, Inc. 1984. All Rights Reserved.

of resource motivation, as a large part of the capital invested abroad by American firms through the mid-1950s went into the developing countries for the extraction of petroleum and mineral raw materials. That distributional pattern was consistent with a growing concern on the part of American business and the U.S. government with dwindling domestic supplies of many essential raw materials, a concern that was increased by contemporary studies that documented the problem of diminishing availability of natural resources in the United States. It was also consistent with the general condition of the industrialized countries outside the United States at that time. Almost all of these countries were struggling to restore their war-torn economies and raise the consumption levels of their people above bare subsistence, and they did not then offer American investors either attractive markets or significant opportunities for establishing efficient production facilities.

The international economic and political scene began changing markedly by the 1960s, and these changes brought different motivations for foreign investment. Chief among such changes was the renewed economic vitality and prosperity of the Western European countries. The vigorous economic expansion occurring in those nations attracted the attention of American firms and affected their foreign direct investment decisions via motivation for both new markets and new production facilities. The combination of increasing incomes and rising consumer expectations was elevating the level of effective demand at a more rapid rate in Europe than in the United States, and numerous American companies initiated or expanded direct investments in the Western European countries in a bid to capture a share of that demand. But the resurgence of those economies also represented a growing competitive challenge to American firms, to which many of them responded by investing abroad in a quest for savings in production or transportation costs.

Another important element in the scenario described above was the economic integration movement that was launched in Western Europe in the late 1950s and progressed rapidly during the 1960s. This movement will be examined in detail in Chapter 9, but its relevance to the present topic can be indicated by noting that European economic integration—that is, the progressive joining together of the economies of the Western European nations—represented both a "carrot" and a "stick" in relation to the foreign investment calculations of American companies. The carrot was the attraction of the large single market for mass-produced manufactured goods that was being created through the integration process, while the stick was the threat that American companies that had been exporting such goods to Western Europe might be shut out of that market by the uniform import taxes that the Europeans were adopting. Such taxes would have the effect of raising the costs (and prices) of imported American products relative to European-produced goods that were free of such import taxes. Here again, the market and production efficiency motivations prompted many American companies to invest in production facilities in Western Europe in order to tap the newly integrated regional market and to avoid the adverse cost impact of this region's common external tariff. U.S. direct investment in manufacturing facilities in Western Europe increased by 16 percent annually in the 10 years following the formal beginning of the European economic integration program, and this rapid growth rate accounts for the overall shift toward manufacturing operations located in the more developed countries that has been one of the basic trends in U.S. foreign direct investment.[7]

At least two other sets of factors need to be taken into account in explaining those investment trends. One factor is political. The foreign investment decisions of business firms are highly sensitive to political conditions and events, since managers are well aware that their ability to operate business enterprises profitably in foreign countries and the risks attendant upon such operations depend to a great extent upon the actions of the host-country government.

Broadly speaking, one could describe the political climate as having been quite favorable for U.S. overseas investment during the first two decades following World War II. The American government viewed such investment as an important supplement to its efforts to assist in

---

[7]*Ibid.*, p. 48.

the economic reconstruction and development of friendly foreign nations and actively encouraged American companies to undertake direct investment ventures. The national governments of most foreign countries were also eager to welcome American firms that could bring badly needed capital, managerial skills, and modern technology to their economies. Direct investment by American firms was considerably bolstered by this favorable political situation and by the variety of incentives—in the form of tax advantages, direct financial assistance, and guarantees against takeovers of business assets—that were being proffered by the U.S. government and the governments of foreign host countries.

Unfortunately, this happy state of affairs was not perpetual. By the late 1960s, American companies were encountering a more hostile political environment and increasing governmental resistance to their foreign investment plans and projects. A strong spirit of economic nationalism had emerged in the the Third World countries that had won political independence and were attempting to gain greater control over their domestic economies. This nationalistic fervor sometimes led to complete government takeovers of foreign-owned firms via acts of expropriation or nationalization, but it more often manifested through increased governmental regulation of the operations of such firms.

It is not possible to isolate and quantify the exact effect that this changing political atmosphere had upon U.S. foreign direct investment. However, in numerous instances politically inspired actions against American firms by foreign governments led to the withdrawal of U.S. investments from the countries involved, and one may reasonably connect the decline in U.S. direct investment in the developing countries—particularly such regions as Latin America, the Middle East, and North Africa—to the increasingly antagonistic attitudes and heightened political problems that many American companies experienced in these areas from the mid-1960s onward.

The other set of circumstances that has influenced the course of American direct investment lies in the monetary domain and has to do with the international status and value of the U.S. dollar. From the end of the Second World War through the 1960s, the dollar was a stable and relatively "strong" or highly valued currency. This was due in part to its role as an international reserve currency, which gave rise to a foreign demand for dollars to hold as a liquid and easily convertible asset, and in part to the heavy demand for American products and services, which created a need for dollars to pay for such goods. The stability and high value of the American currency enabled U.S. business firms to invest abroad (i.e., to purchase real assets in foreign countries) on favorable terms and thereby served as a significant stimulus to the expansion of such investment. The strength of the dollar proved not to be permanent, however, and the diminution of its value during the 1970s played an important part in altering the direction of international capital flows. This point will be considered again in the following section, which considers recent developments in foreign direct investment in the United

States and compares the causative factors involved there with those that
have prompted and fashioned American direct investment abroad.

Foreign Direct Investment in the United States

Dimensions of Foreign Direct Investment in the United States

By the end of 1983, the book value of foreign direct investments in the
United States had reached $135 billion dollars, compared with the ap-
proximately $226 billion book value of American direct investments in
foreign countries. Thus, the amount of foreign direct investment in the
U.S. economy, when measured in these terms, is still substantially less
than the amount of overseas investment by American companies. The
industry composition of foreign direct investment in the United States
shown in Table 4.4 does not vary greatly from that of U.S. investments

*Table 4.4   Foreign Direct Investment in the United States Classified
by Economic Activity and Country of Origin, 1983*

Economic Activity	Billions of Dollars		Percentage of Total	
Manufacturing	$ 47.7		35.3	
Petroleum	18.5		13.7	
Trade	25.2		18.6	
Finance	11.2		8.3	
Insurance	8.3		6.1	
Real estate	13.8		10.2	
Mining	1.9		1.4	
Other	8.7		6.4	
Total	135.3		100.0	
Country or Region of Origin				
Canada	11.1		8.2	
Europe	92.5		68.4	
United Kingdom		32.5		24.0
Netherlands		28.8		21.3
West Germany		10.5		7.8
Switzerland		7.1		5.2
France		6.0		4.4
Japan	11.1		8.2	
Latin America	14.4		10.6	
Middle East	4.4		3.3	
Rest of world	1.8		1.3	

Source: "Foreign Direct Investment in the United States in 1983," *Survey of Current Business*
(October 1984): 38.

overseas. In both cases, manufacturing constitutes the largest investment sector, accounting for 37 percent of foreign direct investment in the United States and 42 percent of U.S. direct investment abroad, and the petroleum industry holds an important position in both investment schemes.

Table 4.4 also identifies the source of foreign direct investments in the U.S. economy, that is, the country or region of residence of the investors. As these data indicate, the Western European countries constitute the principal source, accounting for about two-thirds of the total, followed by Canada and Japan. Approximately 85 percent of foreign direct investment in the United States comes from these developed nations. The remaining 15 percent comes from developing regions, chiefly Latin America and the Middle Eastern oil-producing nations.

Reference was made in the section Recipients of International Direct Investment, above, to the recent sharp increase in foreign direct investment in the United States, which was described as one of the major shifts in the pattern of global direct investment. That increase became noticeable around 1973 and has accelerated since then. The annual rate of growth of such investment averaged 24 percent between 1977 and 1982, compared with annual growth rates averaging only 6 to 7 percent in the late 1960s. The causes and possible consequences of this development have received a great deal of attention, and it is instructive to examine them, both for additional insights into the causative factors underlying international direct investments and as a means of emphasizing and clarifying the duality of America's position—as principal investing country and now also the principal host country—in the worldwide direct investment network.

Causes of the Growth of Foreign Direct Investments in the United States

Virtually all studies of the rapid growth of foreign direct investment in the United States between 1973 and 1980 stress the decline in the value of the dollar as a key causative factor. As mentioned earlier, the U.S. dollar was generally regarded as a strong currency throughout the 1950s and 1960s, and its international value was maintained and kept reasonably stable by the U.S. government's commitment to sell gold for dollars at a fixed price. However, for reasons that will be investigated thoroughly in Chapter 12, this situation changed drastically in the 1970s. The dollar was officially devalued in 1971 and again in 1973, and the price of the dollar subsequently fell even further in relation to other major national currencies to reach an unprecedented low in late 1978.

The fall in the dollar's value affected foreign direct investment flows in several ways. Its most obvious and direct effect was to make it "cheaper" for foreign companies, individuals, and governments to invest in the United States by lowering the effective price of dollar-denominated American securities and real assets. These foreign residents found that they could acquire more dollars in exchange for their national currencies and could therefore purchase the stocks and bonds issued by American corporations, as well as land, buildings, capital equipment, and other tangible assets, at more attractive prices.

The declining value of the dollar also stimulated foreign investment in the United States in less direct and more subtle ways. Many foreign companies that had established a market position in the United States through exporting realized that the production cost and resultant product price advantages that enabled them to compete effectively in the American market were being eroded by the rising price of their currencies in relation to the dollar. A good example of this process is the automaker Volkswagen. This West German company, which had very successfully exported its automobiles to the United States through the 1960s and early 1970s, decided in 1976 to establish manufacturing facilities in the United States. This decision was prompted by Volkswagen's declining share of the U.S. automobile market, which in turn was attributed in large part to the fact that the value of the West German deutsche mark has risen so much relative to the dollar that Volkswagens built in West Germany could no longer compete on a price basis with American-built compact cars. Volkswagen's management concluded that they would have to undertake manufacturing in the United States, thereby reducing the deutsche mark content of their cars and increasing the dollar content, in order to restore their price competitiveness.[8] The same set of conditions and the same line of reasoning led numerous other non-American companies to develop production facilities in the United States through direct investment.

Political considerations have also played an important part in bringing greater numbers of foreign investors to the United States since the early 1970s. Many of those investors have been attracted by their image of the United States as a safe haven for private investment capital. This image arises out of the political stability of the United States and its continuing basic commitment to the principles of private enterprise, a commitment that foreign investors and business leaders apparently contrast with the "leftward" or socialistic drift they feel has been occurring in many other parts of the world.

The influence of politics on foreign investment in the United States has also extended into the sphere of government controls. Here again a kind of "push/pull" or "carrot and stick" effect seems to have been operating. On the one hand, the United States has consistently advocated and maintained a nonrestrictive "open door" posture toward foreign direct investment, even while most other national governments have been tightening their regulation of foreign investors operating in or wishing to enter their countries. Foreign direct investors, therefore, have found it rather easy to comply with the modest requirements im-

---

[8]"Why VW Must Build Autos in the U.S.," *Business Week* (February 16, 1976), 46–51.

posed upon them by the American government and have encountered a comfortable regulatory environment. On the other hand, the adverse effects of rising imports have led many American business and labor leaders to call for more governmental protection against what they describe as "unfair" foreign competition, and these pleas have generated considerable U.S. government support for legal restrictions on imports.

The net effect of these contrary U.S. government attitudes toward foreign direct investment and imports has been to "push" foreign companies supplying the American market out of their exporting operations and "pull" them into production ventures inside the United States. The large Japanese automobile manufacturing companies provide a prime example of this process. Imports of Japanese cars into the United States increased tremendously during the late 1970s and early 1980s. That upsurge greatly reduced the profitability of America's automobile companies and raised the unemployment level among U.S. autoworkers to historic highs. The U.S. government responded to the resulting demands for protection against the import competition by convincing the Japanese government to impose temporary limits upon exports to the U.S. by the Japanese automobile companies.

Faced with those limitations and the possibility of even more stringent legal restrictions on their future exports to the American market, several of those Japanese companies established production facilities within the United States. Honda and Nissan built new manufacturing plants in Ohio and Tennessee, respectively, while Mazda took over an idle Ford Motor Company plant in Michigan and Toyota entered into a joint venture with General Motors (GM) to build cars in a GM facility in California.

While all the above factors have contributed to the multitude of foreign direct investors coming to the United States over the past 10 years, probably the most fundamental and important magnet for those investors has been the large and prosperous American economy itself. Even after the post–1980 uptrend in the value of the dollar eliminated the investment incentive that the weakened dollar had provided throughout the late 1970s, the American economy continued to attract foreign companies that had a scale of operations and resource base of sufficient size to permit them to operate effectively in the vast American marketplace.

Another closely related attraction of the U.S. economy is the access it offers to up-to-date technology and management skills. Several studies have determined that the opportunity to assimilate technological and managerial know-how ranks very high among the reasons given by foreign business executives for undertaking direct investment in the United States.[9] This finding also helps to explain why many of those executives and the companies that they represent have exhibited a dis-

---

[9]Riad Ajami and David A. Ricks, "Motives for Non-American Firms Investing in the United States," *Journal of International Business Studies* (Winter 1981): 25–34.

Box 4.2

Upsurge in European Direct Investments in the United States

An agreement under which Nestle S.A. of Switzerland will buy the Carnation Co. of Los Angeles is just another instance of surging European interest in U.S. acquisitions, according to investment bankers and other takeover specialists. Foreign acquisitions of U.S. companies increased 26 percent in the first quarter of 1984 from a year earlier, and the increase doesn't show any signs of slowing.

European executives and investment bankers are referring to the U.S. as "a capitalist haven," and are pointing up the attractiveness of its "free enterprise dynamics" and the lure of U.S. technology. The U.S. economy has also been growing at more than double the average rate in Europe. European companies and managers apparently are hoping that their U.S. acquisitions will result in some of that rapid U.S. growth rubbing off on them.

Source: Peter Truell, "European Firms on Buying Spree in U.S.," *The Wall Street Journal* (September 6, 1984), 28.

---

tinct preference for buying into existing American businesses rather than setting up brand-new enterprises on their own. By acquiring total or partial ownership of such businesses, foreign investors are obtaining a package that includes technology and managerial expertise, as well as an already established position in the American market.

The Changing U.S. Direct Investment Position

One of the more interesting aspects of the U.S. experience with international direct investment has to do with the alteration that has taken place over time in the country's position vis-à-vis the rest of the world. This alteration is the result of the conspicuous changes in the sources and direction of international direct investment capital flows which began around 1970. Up to that time, such flows had predominantly been *outward* from the United States, but several other nations then emerged as significant sources of direct investment capital and the United States began to record substantial *inward* movements of capital targeted toward its own economy. The term **reverse investment** is frequently used in reference to this phenomenon, to denote the turnaround in the direction of international direct investment in relation to the United States.

Reverse investment has greatly affected the role the United States plays in the global direct investment scene. This was alluded to earlier, when mention was made of the duality of America's direct investment position. The nation's business firms have long been the major suppliers of direct investment capital to the rest of the world, and Americans have therefore tended to view direct investment mainly from a supplier or "home country" perspective. However, reverse investment has given the United States the new additional role of principal recipient of foreign capital and has thereby forced America to also look at direct investment from a "host country" perspective.

This situation has given rise to considerable ambivalence in American attitudes toward foreign direct investment. As long as the United States was primarily a capital-exporting nation, it was both practical from a business standpoint and consistent with private enterprise ideology for the American business and political communities to support the concept of free international capital movements and to argue against governmental regulation of foreign investment. However, the accelerated inflow of foreign capital into the United States in recent years has generated a great deal of apprehension over the prospect of excessive foreign involvement in the American economy, and that apprehension has been expressed through demands for more governmental supervision and legal limitations on foreign direct investment in this country. American policymakers have therefore found themselves facing a troublesome philosophical dilemma, which requires them to reconcile the imposition of more government controls on foreign investors in the United States with their traditional opposition to such controls being placed on U.S. investments abroad.

This dilemma has been aggravated by the lack of a clear concensus as to the exact nature and extent of the threat that increased foreign direct investment poses to the United States. Indeed, there are many businesspeople and government officials in America who—far from regarding such investment as undesirable or threatening—look upon it as a job- and income-creating boon to local and regional economies and who actively encourage foreign firms to establish operations in the United States. Meanwhile, even those who are wary of foreign direct investment often have difficulty in precisely defining or articulating its potential detrimental effects and therefore fall back upon the general premise that foreign-owned economic enterprises are apt to make decisions that are not consistent with America's national interests or the needs of the geographic locales in which they are operating.

Despite such ambiguity and ambivalence, however, government regulation of foreign direct investment has become more stringent in some sectors of the U.S. economy. The American banking industry, by persuasively arguing that foreign-owned commercial banks enjoyed greater operating freedom in the United States than their domestically owned counterparts, convinced Congress of the need to extend America's banking laws to cover foreign banks. The International Banking Act, adopted in

1978, brought foreign banks in this country fully within the jurisdiction of U.S. regulatory law. Legal limitations on foreign investors have also been extended to the agricultural sector, as states have passed laws to restrict foreign ownership of agricultural land. Although foreign citizens still own less than 1 percent of the total agricultural acreage in the United States, American farmers have contended that increased foreign purchases of such acreage constitute a menace to the family-owned farm and a danger of misuse of the land by absentee owners.

In terms of an overall national policy toward foreign investment, all the U.S. government has done to date is to set up an interagency group known as the Committee on Foreign Investment in the United States (CFIUS). This group was initially charged with analyzing trends in foreign investment, consulting with foreign governments wishing to invest in the United States, reviewing investments with possible major implications for U.S. national interests, and considering proposals for regulating investments. In keeping with the historically open and liberal posture of the United States toward foreign investment, the CFIUS has maintained a low profile and has limited its activities to monitoring foreign investments in this country. However, members of Congress have urged that the Committee take a more active role in determining whether specific foreign investment projects are desirable from the U.S. point of view, and blocking those that are deemed undesirable.

The differences of opinion in government circles as to the appropriate functions of CFIUS are evidence of the perplexity that continues to characterize American attitudes toward and responses to foreign direct investment. Such perplexity is really not surprising, since it is extremely difficult to measure or predict the total effect that either foreign direct investment in general or particular investment projects will exert upon the country in which such investment is undertaken. In addition, there exists a long and still-unresolved controversy regarding the net benefits or adversities resulting from international direct investment. The basis of this controversy was summarized succinctly but eloquently by one respected economist who stated that "foreign private investment shares to a very high degree the ambiguity of most human inventions and institutions; it has considerable potential for both good and evil."[10] This matter will be delved into more deeply in Chapters 8 and 13, when foreign direct investment is considered from a theoretical and policy standpoint.

[10]Albert O. Hirschman, "How to Divest in Latin America and Why" in *Essays in International Finance* (Princeton, NJ: International Finance Section, Princeton University, 1969), 3.

Summary

1. International investment occurs when individuals, business firms, or government bodies that are residents of one country acquire assets in another country or financial claims on foreign residents.
2. International investment is categorized as short-term or long-term on the basis of the maturity of the financial claim, and as either direct or portfolio investment on the basis of the acquisition of managerial control by the investor.
3. Foreign direct investment can be effected in a number of ways, some of which involve international transfers of capital funds.
4. International direct investment has grown substantially in the period since the end of World War II. The major portion of this investment has been undertaken by business firms headquartered in the Western industrialized countries, notably the United States.
5. Since the early 1970s, there has been a very pronounced increase in direct investment in the American economy by foreign investors.
6. Foreign direct investment by American companies has increased steadily over the past three decades. There has been a marked change in the geographic and industry distribution of that investment during this period, with more investment going into manufacturing enterprises in the industrialized countries.
7. The rapid buildup of foreign direct investment in the United States during the past decade has been attributed to changes in the value of the dollar, political considerations, and the large and relatively prosperous American economy.
8. The United States has had to rethink its policies toward foreign direct investment as it has become an important host country for such investment.

Questions for Review or Discussion

1. Describe the difference between foreign direct investment and foreign portfolio investment.
2. What have been the major trends in international direct investment since 1950?
3. Describe and indicate the causes of the significant changes that have occurred in U.S. overseas direct investment patterns during the post–World War II era.
4. What developments or conditions account for the sharp rise in foreign direct investment in the American economy that has taken place in the past decade?
5. Should increased foreign direct investment in the United States

be regarded as "good" or "bad" for this country? Give reasons to support your position.

6.   Should the U.S. government establish new policies relating to foreign investment in this country? If so, what should its major policies be?

Case

Toyota Motor Co.

Toyota Motor Co. was considering establishing an automobile manufacturing plant (200,000 units/year) in the United States in early 1985. It had already established a joint venture in California with General Motors (GM) to produce the "Nova" car for the Chevrolet division and had also decided to locate a smaller (50,000 units/year) plant in Canada.

With this decision, Toyota would be joining a number of other Asian manufacturers who have announced plans to locate auto plants in the United States or Canada. Canada and America are considered one market because of a trade agreement between the two countries that allows duty-free movement of autos across the border if more than 50 percent of the auto's value was added in North America.

Honda already has a plant (130,000 units/year) in Ohio, Nissan is building one (150,000 units/year) in Tennessee, and Mazda is planning one (240,000 units/year) in Michigan. Furthermore, Mitsubishi just announced the location of a joint-venture plant (180,000 units/year) with Chrysler in Illinois. In addition, Korea's Hyundai, and fellow Japanese companies Honda and Suzuki have also announced plans for establishing automobile manufacturing plants in Canada.

Toyota and other Japanese automakers are establishing plants in North America primarily to protect the markets they have built and served so far through exports. Protectionist sentiment is strong in North America and the Japanese automakers face the strong possibility of heightened trade barriers.

Hyundai of Korea is already the leading importer of automobiles in Canada since it is given preferential treatment there, as Korea is still considered by Canada to be a developing country. In the United States, Toyota sells more cars than any other foreign automotive company.

Foreign investment in automobile plants is a relatively new activity for Toyota and other Japanese industrial firms. Toyota has worked hard to become the lowest-cost car producer in Japan, and one reason for its success may be the fact that all of its automobile production in Japan is concentrated in Toyota City, along with its three hundred suppliers. Eight of its ten factories are in Toyota City, while the other two are 40 miles away in Nagoya. In contrast, its rival, Nissan, has plants in Italy, Mexico, Great Britain, and Spain in addition to its manufacturing facilities in Japan.

The Toyota Motor Company, controlled by the wealthy Toyoda family, is the world's third largest automotive company and the Toyota group accounts for about 3 percent of Japan's GNP. It commands an impressive 42 percent of the car market in Japan and 8.1 percent of the global car market (GM has 19.9% share of the global market). Some observers believe that Toyota, with its lead as a low-cost producer and 1985 capital spending of $1.4 billion and a cash hoard of over $5 billion, is determined to increase its share of the global market to 10 percent or 12 percent. In addition, Toyota and the other Japanese automakers plan to switch to a product mix emphasizing higher margin, and more high-quality and luxury automobiles, especially since they face competition at the low end from Korean and emerging Taiwanese automakers. As one strategy, the design departments of Toyota and other Japanese automobile firms are borrowing technology and ideas from the aerospace industry.

Toyota's investment in the United States would be a part of a global shift in the pattern of foreign direct investment (FDI). Until recently, the United States was the major source of outward FDI. In recent years, however, U.S. FDI has begun to slow down (2 percent and 3 percent increases in 1983 and 1984, respectively), while FDI into the United States has begun to increase rapidly (10 percent and 16 percent increases in 1983 and 1984, respectively). Concurrently, Japanese FDI has begun to increase globally (14 percent increase in 1984), especially since Japan can use its surplus in foreign trade profits to fund its FDI. After the United States, the largest targets for Japanese FDI have been Indonesia and the Peoples Republic of China. While U.S. FDI is slowing down and Japanese FDI is becoming more significant, FDI from some developing countries like Korea, Hong Kong, Singapore, Brazil, and India is just beginning.

Does Toyota have good business reasons for going along with these economic trends and investing in an automobile plant in the United States?

Sources: "Toyota's Fast Lane," *Business Week,* November 4, 1985, pp. 42–46; "Toyota Charges Up," *Far Eastern Economic Review,* August 8, 1985, pp. 63–64; "Why a 'Little Detroit Could Rise in Tennessee," *Business Week,* August 12, 1985, p. 21; Ashley Ford, "A Wish Come True," *Far Eastern Economic Review,* October 12, 1985, p. 81; "Asian Auto Makers Find a Back Door to the U.S. Market," *Business Week,* December 9, 1985, pp. 52–53; "Another Turn of The Wheel: A Survey of the World's Motor Industry," *The Economist,* March 2, 1985, pp. S1–S22.

Part 2

INTERNATIONAL BUSINESS THEORIES AND POLICIES

Chapter 5

THE THEORY OF
INTERNATIONAL TRADE

Chapter Objectives

- *To provide an understanding of why international trade takes place and of the economic benefits resulting from such trade*
- *To identify the conditions that are necessary in order for mutually beneficial trade to occur between nations*
- *To demonstrate how specialization in production activities among nations and the trade resulting from that specialization lead to increased efficiency in the use of resources and increased availability of products and commodities*
- *To explain why certain nations specialize in producing products or commodities*
- *To show how international trade and international transfers of productive resources are interrelated*
- *To present some contemporary versions of the traditional theory of international trade and illustrate how these constitute refinements of the insights and explanations provided by traditional trade theory, rather than fundamental revisions of that theory*

Chapter 3 of this text was devoted to an examination of the dimensions of international trade and major developments in trade flows and worldwide trading relationships. It traced the remarkable expansion of international trade over the past few decades and identified the major economic, political, and demographic conditions that stimulated and supported that expansion. However, the fundamental and critical question of *why* international trade takes place and the equally important issue of the *effects* of such trade have not yet been considered. An understanding of these fundamentals is obviously essential for anyone participating or preparing to participate directly in international commerce, either as a businessperson or as a government policy-maker, and this circle of participants is widening steadily as such commerce assumes increasing importance in world economic activities. In addition, comprehension of the causes and consequences of international trade is also necessary for anyone who wishes to make informed choices in what has become a tightly knit global economic system.

In a quest for an undertanding of the basics of international trade, one can draw upon observations and ideas that have been recorded and formulated over several centuries. Economic thinkers have given attention to trade among nations ever since it began, and their collective insights have developed through continuous synthesis and refinement into a comprehensive and highly sophisticated body of theory. This chapter will not attempt to fathom the depths and intricacies of this body of theory, but will instead extract those central concepts that explain the reasons for and the results of international trade.

One should be mindful in this undertaking that the theory of international trade, like the rest of economic theory, makes extensive use of assumptions and abstractions. These are not rejections of reality, but rather means of reducing the enormous diversity and complexity of real-world conditions to mentally manageable models. Such theoretical models help to identify and verify the more relevant and important causal factors and relationships in economic behavior and thereby make it possible not only to explain, but also to predict such behavior.

A good example of the usefulness of theoretical abstraction is found in the notion of "international trade" itself. Traditional trade theory has been couched in terms of trade between *nations* when, in actuality, most trade takes place between individuals or business organizations. Economists are, of course, fully aware of this. However, the impracticability of dealing with the multitude of specific circumstances and motives that might have led each and every one of those individuals and organizations into trading transactions has forced the theorists to simplify and generalize. Thus, when reference is made in economic theory to trade between nations, this is usually an abstraction that stands for trade between (or among) all the businesspeople and firms that are residents of those nations. Other abstractions and simplifying assumptions that have been utilized in formulating the theory of international trade will be pointed out as they are encountered.

The Economic Basis of International Trade

Price Differences

The question of *why nations trade* provides a good starting place for exploring the basis and effects of international trade. This question directs the inquiry toward the economic conditions that make it "profitable" or mutually beneficial for residents of different countries to exchange goods with one another. The prospect of *mutual* benefit is, of course, crucial to the conduct of trade, since it is deemed unlikely that either individuals or business firms would voluntarily engage in foreign trade unless they expected to improve their economic situation by doing so.

If that proposition is generalized to the national level, it can be asserted that trade would take place between two nations when and if underlying conditions are such that both nations could be economically better off by trading with one another than by not trading.

The "underlying conditions" with the most immediate bearing here are the *prices of goods* in the two countries. It is the existence of *different prices* for the same or similar goods in the two countries that constitutes a reason for them to engage in trade. If these price differences are such that consumers in each country can obtain a good more cheaply by importing it from the other country than by buying a comparable domestically produced good, these consumers could make themselves better off economically (i.e., they could acquire the same amount of the good for a lesser outlay or more of the good for the same outlay) by entering into trade. In reality, consumers normally would "enter into trade" only as partakers of goods that had been imported by business firms. But the intermediation of the firms does not alter the premise that price differentials induce trade, since the firms would view those differentials as opportunities to realize profits by importing and reselling the lower-priced foreign product.

Although price differences are the proximate cause of international trade, reference to these differences actually provides only a superficial explanation of why such trade occurs. To get to the root of this matter, it is necessary to consider how and why the price differentials came to be. Since the prices at which products are offered for sale are directly tied to the *costs of producing* those products, it follows that observed differences in prices between two nations are largely attributable to differences in the costs of production of the goods involved. These costs represent payments for the resources or factors of production utilized in creating such goods, including a return to the owners and managers of the economic enterprises that organized and carried out the production process. When such renowned political economists as Adam Smith, David Ricardo, and John Stuart Mill were laying the foundations of the classical theory of international trade almost two hundred years ago, they classified resources into the three categories of land (natural resources), labor, and capital. The definition and classification of resources have since been expanded and refined, but modern trade theory continues to emphasize resource-linked cost differences as the fundamental basis for trade between countries.

Absolute Cost Differences

The most readily apparent situation in which cost differences (and the resulting price differences) would engender trade between two countries is the case of **off-setting absolute cost differences.** *Absolute* cost differences are revealed when the cost of the products under consideration is expressed in some common unit of measurement, such as money or resource inputs. The complications associated with national currencies and exchange rates can be avoided at this juncture by expressing absolute costs in terms of resource inputs, and demonstrating how off-setting differences in such costs would make it beneficial for two countries to trade with one another. This can be demonstrated by utilizing a two-country, two-product model and setting aside the costs that would be incurred in physically transporting products from one country to another. As noted previously, such simplifying assumptions highlight the essential elements of the trading situation.

Since the resources required for production are used to measure the cost of the two products in the two countries, tribute can be paid to the classical economists and their "labor theory of value" by utilizing man-days of labor to express those costs. As long as it is understood that these man-days of labor really represent some given "bundle" of inputs that could be combined to produce the two goods, this does no damage to the credibility or applicability of the model.

Let us postulate that 1 man-day of labor is capable of producing the following amounts of either corn or shoes in the United States and in France:

	Output Per Man-day	
	United States	France
Bushels of corn	or 6	or 2
Pairs of shoes	10	12

What has been set forth in this example is a case of *off-setting absolute cost differences*. The United States has an absolute cost advantage in producing corn, since it can produce six bushels per man-day while France can produce only two bushels, whereas France enjoys a cost advantage in shoes, being able to produce 12 pairs per man-day compared with 10 in the United States. Such a situation forms a clear and obvious basis for mutually beneficial trade between the two nations. The source and magnitude of those potential benefits can easily be uncovered by adopting the additional (and very plausible) assumptions that the residents of both these countries wish to consume some of both products and that each of the countries has some finite amount of labor (let us say 100 man-days) to devote to the acquisition of the two products.

France and the United States have two alternatives available for acquiring the corn and shoes that their residents demand. One alternative would be for each country to produce both products, perhaps by splitting its available labor evenly between the two. That approach would allow the United States to produce 300 bushels of corn (6 bushels per man-day times 50 man-days) and 500 pairs of shoes (10 pairs per man-day times 50 man-days), while France could produce 100 bushels of corn (2 bushels per man-day times 50 man-days) and 600 pairs of shoes (12 pairs per man-day times 50 man-days). The total combined output of the two products in the two countries would thus be 400 bushels of corn and 1,100 pairs of shoes.

The other alternative would be for each country to **specialize** in producing one of the two products by devoting all its available labor to that product and then to acquire the second product by *trading* with the other country. If this approach were chosen, and each of the two countries devoted its entire labor supply to producing the product in which it possessed the absolute cost advantage, the total combined output of the two products in the two countries would be 600 bushels of corn produced by the United States (six bushels per man-day times 100 man-days) and 1,200 pairs of shoes produced by France (12 pairs per man-day times 100 man-days). This illustrates the potential **gains from specialization,** which is the incremental output of economic goods that can be garnered from a fixed amount of resources by the simple act of applying those resources to producing the good(s) they can produce most efficiently. In this situation, the gains from specialization consist of the two hundred additional bushels of corn and one hundred additional pairs of shoes that the two countries can acquire by specializing rather than by having each country produce both products.

In order for consumers in both France and the United States to enjoy the gains from specialization and fulfill their demand for both corn and shoes, it will, of course, be necessary for the two nations to trade with one another. The United States will have to offer some of its corn in exchange for French-produced shoes. It is through such exchange that the gains from specialization become available to the people of the two countries as **gains from trade,** that is, an additional quantity of goods available to satisfy their consumption needs.

To substantiate the availability of the gains from trade, let us suppose that France and the United States each decide to retain one-half of what they have produced for domestic consumption and offer the remaining one-half to secure the other product. The United States would keep three hundred bushels of corn and offer the other three hundred to France in exchange for shoes, while France would retain six hundred pairs of shoes and offer to trade the remaining six hundred pairs. Let us further suppose, for the moment, that the two goods were exchanged for one another at a ratio that exactly matched the relative cost of producing them. Since it requires twice as many man-days to produce a bushel of corn as it does to produce a pair of shoes, that ratio of exchange would be one bushel of corn for two pairs of shoes. The magnitude of the gains from trade can now be indicated by comparing the amount of the two products that each country could acquire through specialization and trade with the maximum amount that it could acquire through strictly domestic production. This comparison is shown on page 108.

Both countries clearly would benefit from specialization and trade in this instance, as each then could acquire a larger combined amount of the two products than it could obtain through strictly domestic production of both goods.

		Corn	Shoes
France	using 100 man-days of labor split evenly in domestic production between corn and shoes could produce:	100 bushels	600 pairs
United States	using 100 man-days of labor split evenly in domestic production between corn and shoes could produce:	300 bushels	500 pairs
France	using 100 man-days of labor to specialize in production of shoes and then trading 2 pairs of shoes for 1 bushel of corn could acquire:	300 bushels	600 pairs
United States	using 100 man-days of labor to specialize in production of corn and then trading 1 bushel of corn for 2 pairs of shoes could acquire:	300 bushels	600 pairs

Division of the Gains from Specialization and Trade

In presenting the above example, an important issue was momentarily sidestepped. This has to do with the **division of the gains,** that is, how the additional output that resulted from specialization will be divided between the two countries. A division was arrived at in the illustration by merely "supposing" that the two products would be exchanged for one another at a ratio that exactly reflected their relative production cost. That is not an unreasonable supposition, but it constitutes only one of a range of possible ratios at which the two goods might be traded for one another. Since the actual exchange ratio, which can be referred to as the **barter terms of trade,** is the immediate determinant of how much each country benefits from a trading arrangement, it is worthwhile to consider the derivation of these terms of trade a bit further.

Trade theory cannot reveal precisely what the barter terms of trade between two products will be, since those terms would depend upon the specific set of circumstances attendant in each trading situation. However, trade theory does point out that the barter terms of trade must lie within a range that is circumscribed by the internal or domestic costs of producing the two products in each of the two countries.

The rationale supporting this assertion is fairly easy to discern. Inasmuch as neither country would be willing to engage in trade unless it could enhance its economic well-being by doing so, the barter terms of trade could not be such as to make a product more costly to acquire by trading than through domestic production. Given the cost ratios specified in the preceding example, the United States obviously would not be willing to offer more than six bushels of corn for ten pairs of shoes in trade with France, since it could obtain ten additional pairs of shoes through domestic production by transferring resources out of corn production, and the opportunity cost (the "sacrifice" of corn production) needed to acquire those additional shoes would be six bushels of corn. France, for its part, would be unwilling to offer more than 12 pairs of shoes for two bushels of corn in trade, inasmuch as its internal cost structure is such that it could produce another two bushels of corn domestically at an opportunity cost of 12 pairs of shoes. The limits of the barter terms of trade therefore are set by the internal cost ratios of the two products.

Traditional international trade theory further asserts that, within the limits established by the internal cost ratios of each country, the barter terms of trade will be determined by **reciprocal demand,** which refers to the relative intensity and elasticity of each country's demand for the product being produced by the other country.[1] Thus, if the U.S. demand for French shoes exceeds the French demand for corn from the United States, the barter terms of trade will tend to be more favorable for the French (and vice versa). This theoretical conclusion is consistent with what common sense would lead one to expect—that whenever consumers (in this case, residents of a particular country) have a strong or increasing desire for a foreign-made product, they must be prepared to give more for it than would consumers with a lesser demand.

Comparative Cost Differences

Thus far, the examination of the basis and effects of international trade has been dealing with off-setting differences in absolute costs. It is reasonably easy to perceive the potential for mutually beneficial trade between countries when such cost differences exist. An intuitive grasp and acceptance of such potential becomes a bit more strained, however, when the possibility is raised that one country might be able to produce virtually all economic goods more cheaply (i.e., at a lower absolute cost) than another country. This is by no means a far-fetched possibility, for the real world is characterized by great divergences in levels of economic development among nations and is therefore replete with examples of countries that would appear to be capable of outproducing their prospective trading partners across a very wide range of products.

The critical question that emerges here is whether trade can be profitably carried on in such a situation. Trade theory answers this question affirmatively and substantiates that answer by reference to **comparative costs.**

Comparative cost is an expression of the costs or value of one product in relation to another product. When David Ricardo introduced this concept into international trade theory in the early 1800s, he couched it in terms of his labor theory of value and accordingly used the relative

[1]John Stuart Mill, *Principles of Political Economy* (London: Longmans, Green, 1926; originally published 1848).

labor content of different products to set their comparative values.[2] Other economists subsequently improved upon Ricardo's formulation by pointing out that the relative costs and values of different goods are not determined solely by labor input, but by the total package of resources used to produce each of them. Thus, **opportunity cost**—which stresses the fact that using resources to produce any particular product entails the sacrifice of some other product(s) that those same resources might have produced—has emerged as the modern version of comparative cost.

However, the substitution of opportunity cost for Ricardo's labor content has in no wise altered the fundamental principles he elucidated or invalidated the conclusions he drew. Those principles and conclusions, which comprise the **doctrine of comparative advantage,** make it clear that two nations can profitably trade with one another when one is more efficient than the other in all branches of production. This is so because comparative cost differences constitute the only necessary basis for mutually beneficial trade, and such differences can (and almost inevitably will) exist even when one country has an absolute cost advantage in all products under consideration.

To provide proof of these assertions, our hard-working model need only be modified slightly. The assumption relating to France's shoe-producing capabilities can be changed to portray a situation in which the United States has an absolute cost advantage in both products. It can then be demonstrated that specialization and trade could still improve the economic position of the residents of both nations.

| | Output Per Man-day | |
	United States	France
Bushels of corn	*or* 6	*or* 2
Pairs of shoes	10	8

Notice that the revised model shows the United States as being able to produce more corn or more shoes with the same resource input than France is able to produce. Therefore, the absolute cost of producing both products is less in the United States than in France. However, while the United States has an absolute cost advantage in both products, it has a comparative cost advantage in only one of them, namely corn. A quick and easy way to discern this is by calculating the extent of America's absolute advantage in each product to determine where that advantage is greatest. This shows that the United States has a 3:1 advantage over France in corn production (it can produce three times as many bushels as France with the same resources) but only a 1.25:1

---

[2]David Ricardo, *Principles of Political Economy and Taxation* (London: J.M. Dent & Sons, 1960; originally published 1817).

advantage in shoe production (it can produce 1¼ times as many pairs as France with the same resources). This procedure correctly identifies the product in which the United States has a comparative advantage (as well as the one in which it has a comparative disadvantage), but may not clearly indicate why this is so or exactly how that identification is derived from the concept of comparative cost.

A somewhat more laborious but perhaps more enlightening path to the same conclusion involves calculating the comparative cost of each product in each country, remembering that comparative cost is the cost of one product (e.g., corn) stated in terms of the amount of the other product (e.g., shoes) that must be sacrificed to obtain it. Following this path, one finds that:

1. In the United States, one bushel of corn costs 1⅔ pairs of shoes, *whereas* in France, one bushel of corn costs four pairs of shoes, *therefore*, the United States has a comparative cost advantage in corn production.

2. In the United States, one pair of shoes costs ⅗ bushels of corn, *whereas* in France, one pair of shoes costs ¼ bushels of corn, *therefore*, France has a comparative cost advantage in shoe production.

The cost relationships that have been elucidated in detail above are actually axiomatic. Once the presence of different internal cost ratios in two countries has been established (either by assumption or by observation of actual conditions), it is certain that each country will have a comparative cost advantage (and a comparative cost disadvantage) in one of the two products. This follows from the fact that the cost of each product is being measured in terms of the other product, which means that if one country can produce one of the products more cheaply, the other country will necessarily be able to produce the other product more cheaply. However, this axiom is the crux of both the theory and the practice of international trade, because it reveals an almost limitless potential for countries to profit from trading with one another. Given the extremely high probability that different countries will not have exactly identical internal cost ratios, the prospects for mutually beneficial trade are likewise extremely high. The same two-country model can be used yet again to verify the availability of gains from trade whenever comparative costs (or internal cost ratios) differ.

Such verification can be accomplished through a fairly simple thought process. Consider first what it would cost the residents of the United States to obtain an additional one hundred pairs of shoes by producing them domestically. With a fixed amount of resources available, the United States would have to shift some of those resources out of corn production in order to produce the additional one hundred pairs, and the U.S. corn/shoe cost ratio indicates that the United States would incur an opportunity cost (a sacrifice of corn production) of 60 bushels of corn. Since the cost of the shoes obtained in this way is 60 bushels of corn, it follows that the United States could better its economic situation if it could otherwise acquire more than 100 pairs of shoes for 60 bushels of corn (or pay less than 60 bushels for 100 pairs).

Turning now to France while maintaining the same numerical parameters, it can be ascertained that the French would have to sacrifice 240 pairs of shoes in order to acquire an additional 60 bushels of corn through domestic production. France therefore could better its economic situation if it could otherwise acquire 60 bushels for any amount of shoes less than 240 pairs. This establishes a range of barter terms of trade (bounded, not coincidentally, by the internal cost ratios of the two products in the two countries) within which both nations would gain economically by trading with one another. The exact barter terms would depend upon reciprocal demand, but the specification of those exact terms is not crucial to the conclusion that is being pursued. The objective was to prove that trade can be advantageous to two countries even though one of them is absolutely more efficient than the other in all relevant lines of production, and the outcome of the illustration fulfills that purpose. It shows that the United States could improve its economic situation by concentrating on the production of corn, the product in which it has a comparative cost advantage, and exchanging part of its corn output for shoes. France could likewise better itself economically by specializing in producing shoes, the product in which it has a comparative cost advantage, and trading part of its output for American corn.

It may be refreshing and reassuring to pause here long enough to indicate that the scenario that has just been considered and the conclusions that were drawn are neither terribly profound nor unique to the realm of international trade. On the contrary, the doctrine of comparative advantage is based upon principles with which everyone is intuitively familiar and it advocates a type of economic behavior in which almost everyone regularly engages. Reduced to its fundamentals, the doctrine points out that it is economically advantageous for nations—or individuals—to concentrate upon what they can do "best of all," even if they might be able to do several things better than their fellows.

This lesson is frequently brought home by drawing an analogy between two nations and two individuals. Just as one of the two nations may be more efficient than the other in producing each of two products (as in the model which has been used above), so may one of the individuals be more skilled and efficient than the other in two lines of work. One might, for example, imagine an excellent dentist who is also an excellent typist in relation to a second person who is a good typist but has no training or skill in dentistry. What both common sense and the theory of comparative advantage would indicate is that the dentist would be well advised to hire the second individual to do whatever typing was required in his business and to spend all his working hours practicing dentistry. That arrangement would not only permit the dentist to maximize his earnings, but would also provide gainful employment for the person with lesser skills in both activities. The "magic formula" in this example is the same one that the doctrine of comparative advantage applies to nations, namely, that specialization or division of labor can benefit everyone who participates, even though some of the participants may be capable of performing all the relevant tasks better than the other participants. The key element required to make this formula work is "unequal superiority"; so long as those nations (or individuals) that are "better" or "superior" are not equally better in every task, there are gains for all to be had from specializing and trading.

The Causes of Cost Differences

Although the preceding section emphasized the role of cost differences—especially, comparative cost differences—as the fundamental basis for trade among nations, it did not consider why such differences exist. The theory of international trade again provides a generalized but trenchant and plausible explanation for these trade-creating cost differentials. Two Swedish economists, Eli Hecksher and Bertil Ohlin, are credited with developing this explanation and making it one of the principal building blocks of trade theory.[3] Hecksher and Ohlin emphasized variations in the combinations of resources found in different regions—what they termed different *productive factor endowments*—as the root cause of division of labor (specialization) and trade among those regions.

Some of these variations in resource availability among nations or regions are readily apparent and quite pronounced. Natural resources provide good examples of this, in that climatic conditions obviously vary greater from one part of the world to the other, as does the existence of mineral deposits, fertile land, forests, and freshwater supplies. Other differences in factor endowments may be more subtle and are often the result of long-term trends and economic development strategies rather than "accidents of nature." Thus, certain nations over time have developed a more highly skilled labor force, or a larger stock of capital, or more advanced industrial technology than other countries.

Regardless of their source, such differences in the mix of factors of production give rise to the comparative cost differences that, in turn, generate specialization and trade. Here again, there are numerous situations in which this linkage can be readily perceived. It is easy to see, for instance, that those nations whose territories hold accessible deposits of copper or iron ore will have a definite and virtually infinite cost advantage in producing those minerals relative to countries that have no such deposits. By the same reckoning, countries that are located in the tropics will enjoy an obvious cost advantage over their temperate-zone counterparts in the production of bananas, coffee, or pineapples. This is not to say that such commodities could not conceivably be pro-

[3]Eli Hecksher, "The Effect of Foreign Trade on the Distribution of Income," *Economist Tidskrift XXI* (1919):497–512; Bertil Ohlin, *Interregional and International Trade* (Cambridge, MA: Harvard University Press, 1933).

duced in the temperate zone countries, but the cost of doing so by artificially duplicating the required resource inputs—notably soil and temperature conditions—that are naturally available in the tropics would make such efforts highly impractical.

The examples used above are somewhat extreme, but they are nevertheless consistent with the basic premises of the Hecksher–Ohlin theory. One of those premises is that the extent to which a particular factor of production is available in a nation or region will directly affect the price of that factor (i.e., the return that is necessary to draw it into the production process). If, for example, a given nation is abundantly endowed with a certain resource (say unskilled labor), the price of that resource (the average wage rate) would ordinarily be lower than in a nation with a *relatively* smaller labor force.

It is important to stress the word "relatively" here, because it is not only (or even primarily) the absolute amount of a resource available that determines its price, but also the supply of that resource *in relation to* the supply of other resources. Thus, a country might have a very large labor force measured in absolute number of workers. But if it also possessed a very large stock of capital, so that its *ratio of labor to capital* was lower than in other countries, its average wage rate might well be above those of the countries with smaller labor forces but higher labor/capital ratios.

Let us refer to a hypothetical case of two countries, say Taiwan and West Germany, to clarify this idea. Consider two resource inputs, labor and capital, and assume the following supplies available in the two countries:

	Units of Labor (Workers)	Units of Capital
Taiwan	10 million	1 million
West Germany	50 million	25 million

West Germany has a much larger population and therefore a much larger labor force than Taiwan. But it also has accumulated a stock of capital that exceeds that of Taiwan by an even greater proportional amount than does its labor force, so that the labor/capital ratio in West Germany is 2:1 while Taiwan has a labor/capital ratio of 10:1. In comparing these two countries, West Germany would therefore be correctly designated a labor-scarce (or capital-abundant) country and Taiwan a labor-abundant (or capital-scarce) country, because those designations are denoting the **resource mix** within each country. By extension, the price of labor could also be expected to be lower in Taiwan than in West Germany and the price of capital to be lower in West Germany than in Taiwan.

Since the total cost of producing any good is the sum of the prices of all the resources used in its production, it is clear that differences in the relative availability of various resources in different nations will directly affect production costs within those nations. Moreover, because differ-

Cartoon A   *(The Wizard of ID)*

Source: By permission of Johnny Hart and News America Syndicate.

ent products can best be produced with particular combinations of resources, it is these national differences in resource availability that give individual nations a cost advantage in certain products. The example of West Germany and Taiwan was used above to indicate how the greater availability of labor in Taiwan would result in the price of labor being lower there than in West Germany. This example can be expanded by asserting that Taiwan should therefore have a comparative cost advantage vis-à-vis West Germany in those products that require a great deal of labor to produce, whereas West Germany would find its cost advantage in products that utilized less labor but more capital. The accompanying cartoon provides a humorous commentary on this concept.

Although the foregoing example and line of reasoning admittedly bypass a number of ancillary questions and complicating factors, they nevertheless bring out the key points and conclusions expounded by Hecksher and Ohlin. These economists pointed out that the differing national endowments of productive resources will result in different resource prices and costs of production among countries, and that a nation's cost advantage for trading purposes will lie in products that "contain" relatively large inputs of the resource(s) with which that nation is relatively well endowed. The product composition of a nation's exports, as well as of its imports, will therefore be determined by the composition of its domestic supply of factors of production.

The Substitutability of Trade and Factor Movements

There is an important corollary to these conclusions, which has to do with the relationship between international trade and international movements of factors of production. That relationship is one of mutual substitutability, which is to say that international trade, that is, the transfer of products between nations, can act as a substitute for the international transfer of resources, and vice versa.

Further reference to the hypothetical situation of Taiwan and West Germany will disclose this substitutability. It was noted that Taiwan's abundance of labor would tend to hold down the price of that factor of production and thereby prompt Taiwan to specialize in and export labor-intensive products. In this instance, Taiwan is indirectly transferring some of its labor to West Germany "embodied in" the export goods. Meanwhile, West Germany, with its relative abundance of capital, will be indirectly transferring that resource to Taiwan, likewise embodied in capital-intensive products.

Most of the early trade theorists, including Hecksher and Ohlin, viewed productive resources as being largely immobile between countries. There is considerable rationale for such a view, especially with regard to such resources as land, climate, and mineral deposits which cannot in any practical sense be moved physically from country to country. Other resources, including labor, capital, and technology, are not character-ized by such physical fixity, but their intentional mobility is nevertheless likely to be impeded by a variety of economic, political, or cultural con-straints. If one were to ponder, for example, why Taiwanese workers confronted with low wages and uncertain job prospects in their own nation do not migrate en masse to West Germany where labor is scarce and wages are high, numerous factors—including the unaffordability of transportation, immigration laws, and reluctance to confront an unfa-miliar cultural milieu—could provide an answer.

Although the recognition of these limitations on resource mobility helps to highlight the role of trade as a substitute for international factor movements, one should not lose sight of the fact that such limitations are neither complete nor immutable. Labor, capital, and technology can and do move between countries, and there may well be situations or periods of time in which transferring these resources across national boundaries is easier or more profitable or otherwise preferable to trans-ferring products. Chapters 1 through 4 of this text contained numerous references to how changing circumstances have led to shifts between trade and foreign investment as the preferred form of international com-mercial activity, and these shifts are indicative of the *mutual* substitut-ability of international trade and international factor movements.

Money and Exchange Rates

Up to this point, this exposition of the principles governing international trade has largely ignored the role of money. This simplification presum-ably has made it easier to follow the main thread of international trade theory. In reality, however, trading activities generally involve the use of money as a facilitating medium of exchange. Monetary variables therefore can influence trading decisions and relationships, although taking money into consideration does not change the basic causes and effects of trade.

Earlier in this chapter, it was stated that trade between two countries would be undertaken in response to differences in the prices of goods. This reference to price differences between two nations provides an opportunity to call attention to an elementary but very important fact about international price comparisons, which is that those comparisons must take account not only of the price of the good(s) in each country expressed in that country's currency, but also the **exchange rate,** which is the price of each country's currency in terms of the other country's currency. In trying to compare the price of a bushel of corn produced in the United States to the price of a bushel of corn produced in France, it is necessary first to find out the price of U.S. corn in dollars and the price of French corn in francs and then the price of the dollar in francs. This also means, of course, that shifts in product price relationships between countries can result from either domestic price changes or changes in the exchange rate; for example, a bushel of American corn could become cheaper in France because its dollar price had fallen in the United States or because the price of the dollar had fallen relative to the franc (or both).

While it is true that business firms that carry on international trade base their exporting and importing decisions on price comparisons, this fact does not alter the conclusions set forth previously regarding the necessary basis for trade and the ascertainment of what products a nation would produce for trading purposes. It has already been demonstrated that both the opportunity for mutually beneficial trade between nations and the product composition of that trade would be determined by the relationship between their domestic cost of production ratios. These ratios will remain the same whether costs are measured in resource inputs (as has been done in our models) or in money terms, and the use of money prices will therefore not change the outcome of any analysis of trading capabilities.

This can be demonstrated by restating the France–United States model postulated earlier, in which costs were expressed in terms of a standard measure of resource inputs (man-days of labor):

	Output Per Man-day			
	United States		**France**	
Bushels of corn	*or*	6	*or*	2
Pairs of shoes		10		8

Here the internal cost ratios were 1 corn:1⅔ shoes in the United States and 1 corn:4 shoes in France. It was shown that those differing internal cost ratios would make it profitable for the two countries to specialize and trade, with the United States exporting corn and France exporting shoes.

It should be apparent that, so long as the monetary value of the standard bundle of resource inputs is the same throughout each country, these internal cost ratios would not be affected by expressing them monetarily. If, for example, the average rate (i.e., the monetary value of our standard measure of resources) were 20 dollars per man-day in the United States and 50 francs per man-day in France, the above model could equally well be presented in this form:

	Cost/Price Per Unit	
	United States	France
Corn	$3.33/bushel	fr25/bushel
Shoes	$2.00/pair	fr6.25/pair

Note that a bushel of corn in the U.S. still has a price that is equivalent to that of 1⅔ pairs of shoes, and a bushel of corn in France continues to be worth 4 pairs of shoes. It is these dissimilar internal cost/price ratios that constitute the only requisite condition for trade between the two countries, and the pricing of the products in the domestic currency of each country has left that condition intact.

But the use of domestic currency prices appears to have raised another troublesome question. It was pointed out previously that international price comparisons could only be made through reference to the exchange rate between the relevant national currencies. Is it not possible, then, that the dissimilar internal cost ratios that should engender trade might be masked or offset by the exchange rate? If, for instance, the dollar–franc exchange rate applicable in the above situation were $0.50 = 1 franc (or 2 francs = 1 dollar), it would seem that no trade could occur between the U.S. and France since (even disregarding transportation costs) U.S. residents would have to pay more dollars to acquire either product from France than to produce it domestically. France would have a strong incentive to trade at such a price, but the United States would be unwilling to enter into trade.

Such a situation is by no means uncommon in the real world, where governmental manipulation or other forces may bring about exchange rates that are inconsistent with underlying cost/price relationships. At the exchange rate of $0.50 in the above example, the franc would be *overvalued,* which is to say the price of the franc in relation to the dollar is higher than is justified by the relationship between the domestic price levels of the two countries. (This assumed exchange rate could just as well be described as one that *undervalues* the U.S. dollar, since, if one of two currencies being considered is overvalued, the other must be undervalued.)

The likely effects of this overvaluation of the franc on prospects for trade between the two countries have already been mentioned. The overvaluation would generate a strong demand in France for imports of U.S. goods, since imported American products would be cheaper than comparable French-produced goods. The effective price to French buyers of a bushel of U.S. corn would be only 6.66 francs compared with 25 francs for corn grown in France, while the effective price of U.S. shoes would be 4 francs compared with 6.25 francs for French-made shoes. This heavy French demand for American goods would give rise to an equally heavy demand for U.S. dollars to pay for the imports from the United States.

However, Americans would have no desire to purchase French products at this exchange rate, as French corn would command an effective price of $12.50/bushel in the U.S. and French shoes a price of $3.13/pair, both of which exceed the price of the comparable U.S. products. Thus, there would be no demand for francs on the part of U.S. residents and no willingness to offer dollars in exchange for the French currency.

In a free foreign exchange market (i.e., one in which there is no governmental interference with the setting of exchange rates), the demand imbalances indicated above would bring about a change in the exchange rate. The excessive demand for dollars on the part of French residents would result in a greater number of francs being offered for each dollar. The relative values of the two currencies consequently would shift in favor of the dollar until a new exchange rate was established at which two-way trade could occur.

The important insights to be gleaned from the foregoing explanation and illustrative examples are that the exchange rate constitutes a critical link between the production cost/price levels existing in different countries and that the exchange rate therefore can conceivably either accurately mirror or distort the real relationship between those cost/price levels. However, if exchange rates are allowed to fluctuate freely in response to market demand and supply forces, they will tend to function in support of trade by effectively translating existing differences in the relative costs and prices of goods within different countries (i.e., differences in the internal cost/price ratios) into absolute price differentials that would make it attractive and advantageous for each country to import from the other.

Some Refinements of Trade Theory

The body of trade theory that has been examined thus far is a venerable one, developed by economists who observed and proposed theories many decades ago. Although the passing of time has not discredited the fundamental merits or worth of their ideas, changing economic conditions have reduced the appropriateness of many of their assumptions and the comprehensiveness of their theoretical framework. This has created the need for refining and updating that framework, a need that has been answered through the individual and collective efforts of contemporary economists. This section will consider a few of the more significant of these modern contributions to the theory of international trade.

A considerable part of the refining that has taken place has been prompted by perceived inconsistencies or shortcomings relating to the Hecksher–Ohlin theory. That theory states that a nation's comparative cost advantage will be determined by its domestic factor (resource) supply, and dictates that a nation will specialize in and export tho: od- ucts that make greatest use of the productive factor(s) with wl (in relative terms) most abundantly endowed.

The Leontief Paradox

This theory has been called into question on several counts these indictments resulted from a study done by Wassily L renowned economist who subsequently received the Nobel Pri nomics.[4] Through a detailed investigation of U.S. internatio: Leontief found that U.S. exports were more labor intensiv capital intensive) than import-substitutes produced in the Uni This finding was exactly the reverse of what the Hecksher–Ol would have predicted for a capital-abundant country such as States, and it was accordingly dubbed the "Leontief parado:

Leontief's results spawned a host of additional studie potheses, too numerous (and often too inconclusive) to revi tique thoroughly here. But a significant insight which came efforts was that the Hecksher–Ohlin theory probably had causes of trade between countries too narrowly. One as narrowness was the categorization of resources into pre: mogeneous groups. Such a categorization failed to take fu the many qualitative variations that can exist within a partic group, for example, variations in the level of skill and workers. Indeed, some of the more plausible explanatic advanced to resolve the Leontief paradox centered aroun the United States actually held a comparative advantage i labor. Inasmuch as the development of such a skilled lab investment in education and training—that is, the creati capital"—these explanations not only stressed greater sources within each of the traditional categories, but a distinctions that had traditionally been made between those ca

Another aspect of the narrowness of the Hecksher–Ohlin formulation was its assumption that particular products would be produced in much the same way everywhere in the world. In other words, the combination of resources used to produce a given product (which economists call the production-function) would not vary from country to country. Such an assumption clearly supports the conclusion that each country will have a comparative cost advantage in those goods that require large

---

[4]Wassily Leontief, "Domestic Production and Foreign Trade: The American Capital Position Re-examined" in *Readings in International Economics,* ed. R. E. Caves and Harry C. Johnson (Homewood, IL, Richard D. Irwin, 1968), 503–527.

inputs of the factor that is plentiful in that country—if, for instance, cotton cloth could only be produced by a production process that required large amounts of labor, then labor-abundant countries would invariably have and maintain a comparative advantage in cotton cloth. The fact is, however, that production-functions for given products can and do differ considerably from one locale to another and even from one producing firm to another. Those variations are largely attributable to differences in **technology,** which can be thought of in simplest terms as *knowledge* applicable to production. Once technology is recognized as an important element in the production process, it follows that differences in levels of technology between countries can be a source of comparative cost differences at least equal in importance to differences in the availability of other resources. It also follows that technological innovation, that is, progress in developing new products or discovering and implementing better production methods, can continuously alter existing patterns of comparative cost advantage among nations. The United States again provided a good case in point to show the relevance of this refinement of trade theory, as the composition of U.S. exports indicated that this country's comparative advantage lay to a great extent in high-technology products, which was consistent with America's position of technological leadership.

The Product Life Cycle Model

The concept of a technology-based comparative advantage forms part of the foundation for what has become a widely-known addendum to trade theory, the **product life cycle (PLC) model.** The central idea in this concept is that new products will pass through fairly distinct stages of buyer acceptance and sales following their introduction to the market. Those stages usually are designated as (1) introduction, (2) growth, (3) maturity, and (4) decline, and they are portrayed graphically in Figure 5.1.

The PLC formulation has long been an important analytical and decision-making tool in marketing management, where awareness of this cycle has helped companies to make judgments relating to product development and the appropriate mix of promotional, pricing, and distributional strategies. However, the model has also proved useful in explaining and predicting why and when manufacturing industries (and, by extension, the nations in which those industries are located) will become involved in international operations.[5] The model actually deals with both *exporting* and *foreign investment* decisions and behavior, therefore reference will be made to it again in discussions of the various theories of foreign investment in Chapter 8.

[5]Raymond Vernon, "International Investment and International Trade in the Product Cycle," *Quarterly Journal of Economics* LXXX (May 1966):190–207; Louis T. Wells, Jr., "A Product Life Cycle for International Trade?" *Journal of Marketing* 32 (July 1968):1–6.

Figure 5.1   **The Product Life Cycle**

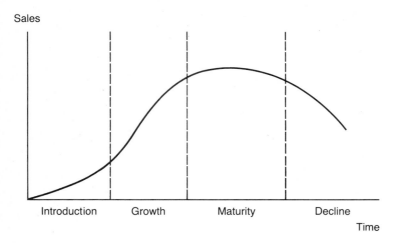

Briefly summarized, the PLC model postulates that new products will most likely originate in an affluent, economically advanced country such as the United States, where there is both strong potential demand and the wherewithal to support research and development endeavors. The firm that introduces a new product will initially enjoy a virtual monopoly position in its home market, and should therefore experience rapid increases in sales, as indicated in Figure 5.1 by the steep upslope of the sales curve in the introductory and growth stages. Until its product is well into the growth stage, the lack of price competition and the desire to test and perfect the product will induce the firm to concentrate mainly upon its domestic market; in the latter part of this stage, however, the attainment of scale economies in production will encourage the firm to export the product, especially to other advanced countries with similar demand and purchasing power conditions. Although this point is not always emphasized in presentations of the model, the firm may also regard such export ventures as a means of "stretching out" the upward-sloping segments of the product's sales curve, by introducing the product into overseas markets in which competition and market saturation have not yet emerged to dampen its sales potential.

According to the PLC model, exporting continues to be profitable so long as the production-cost savings emanating from scale economies and access to the needed technology exceed the costs of transportation abroad and import duties. However eventually the foreign markets will become large enough and the technology for producing the product so widely disseminated that the firm will be under heavy pressure to undertake overseas production in order to stave off local competitors in its export markets. The firm may then undertake direct investment in those advanced countries to which it had been exporting and may thereby successfully defend those markets for a time. However, as the production of the product becomes more and more standardized and the number of producers steadily increases, the firm that pioneered the product may find itself in a serious competitive battle, even in its own domestic market. Ultimately, most of the output of the product may come from the developing countries, where low labor costs would become the decisive factor in determining where production facilities are located.

Although the PLC model is not without its limitations, its explanatory and predictive usefulness has been borne out by numerous empirical investigations and historical case studies of the international expansion paths of several industries. The model therefore constitutes a significant modern extension of trade theory, which, among its other contributions, reaffirms and clarifies the linkages between international trade and international direct investment.

Income and Internal Demand

Another important and incisive addition that has been made to the theory of international trade emphasizes the influences of demand and purchasing power in the determination of trading relationships. This modification of trade theory, like the others that have been reviewed, grew out of observed inconsistencies between actual trading behavior and the situation that traditional trade theory would have predicted. The actual situation, in this instance, was that the majority of world trade was taking place among countries with similar economic structures and resource bases—namely, the industrialized First World countries—whereas the logic of the Hecksher–Ohlin formulation of the theory of comparative advantage points in the opposite direction, that is, toward more trade among countries with *dissimilar* economies and resource endowments.

A theoretical resolution of that inconsistency was formulated by Staffan Lindner.[6] Lindner drew a distinction between trade in primary commodities and trade in manufactured goods and asserted that trade in the former, which are natural resource intensive, can be explained by differences in national factor endowments, whereas trade in the latter depends more upon other conditions. Those conditions include **established demand (consumer preference) patterns** within countries that, in turn, result mainly from **income levels.**

Lindner argued that products were not likely to be manufactured for export unless there was first a demand for them at home, since business firms or entrepreneurs would be incapable of visualizing a foreign de-

[6]Staffan Lindner, *An Essay on Trade and Transformation* (New York: John Wiley & Sons, 1961).

mand for a product with which they were unfamiliar or would be unwilling to incur the cost of developing or designing products solely for foreign markets. Thus, business firms (and countries) would tend to export products closely akin to those that were being produced or imported for domestic consumption, and the nature and range of such products would be a reflection of the income-based preferences of indigenous consumers.

This line of reasoning leads to the conclusion that the greatest potential for trade in manufactured goods will be found among countries with similar income structures, inasmuch as the business sectors of those countries will have acquired the experience and productive capacity needed to satisfy foreign demands that correspond closely to demands in their home markets. This does not imply, of course, that these countries will all produce and export *exactly* the same products, since some product differentiation is essential for trade. But it does mean that specialization and trade can flourish among countries that are much alike in terms of economic development, composition of economic output, and consumer characteristics. By contributing this insight, Lindner moved the theory of international trade closer to the reality of present-day economic circumstances and substantially enhanced its explanatory and predictive powers.

A Recapitulation

The search for answers to some very basic questions relating to international trade has led to a rather lengthy examination of international trade theory. The intricate depths of that theory have purposely been avoided, but answers to the queries that were raised at the beginning of this chapter have nonetheless been found. The causes of international trade were found to be price and cost differentials which are themselves the consequences of dissimilar resource endowments. This chapter has also explained how money and exchange rates enter into trading decisions and relationships, and has considered some of the more important contemporary supplements to trade theory. This has emphasized that the theory of international trade is continuously evolving in response to new information and insights and to changing world economic conditions.

Perhaps the most significant conclusion that has emerged from this discussion is that the residents of the various nations of the world can reap significant economic benefits from engaging in trade with one another. The willingness and ability to carry on trade makes it feasible for the residents of different countries to specialize in the economic activities they are best equipped to pursue, and such specialization results in higher levels of productivity and thus in a greater output of economic goods and services. Stated another way, international trade can contribute greatly to the attainment of economic efficiency, which can be defined as maximization of the output from a given stock of resources. Applied to the world economy as a whole, this means that the amount of material goods available for consumption—and therefore the economic welfare of the people of the world—can be markedly enhanced by unrestrained international trade. This is an idea that the majority of economists have accepted and promoted for more than two centuries, but one that national governments have often been unwilling to embrace in the formulation and implementation of their economic policies. The reasons for this will be considered in Chapter 6, which is devoted to government regulation of international trade.

Summary

1.   International trade is based upon the prospect of mutual economic benefits to the trading nations.
2.   International differences in the prices of goods are the proximate reason for trade to take place. Such price differences are themselves the consequence of differences in costs of production.
3.   The most obvious situation in which cost differences could engender mutually beneficial trade between two countries is the case of off-setting absolute cost differences. In such circumstances, total output of goods could be increased if each country specialized in producing that product in which it had an absolute cost advantage, and exchanging the two products would give each country some economic gains from trade.
4.   Two countries could also benefit from specializing and trading with one another even if one country had an absolute cost advantage in producing both of two products. This is possible as long as there are differences in the comparative costs of the two products in the two countries.
5.   Traditional international trade theory emphasizes the existence of different resource endowments among nations as the principal basis for differences in costs of production. The Hecksher–Ohlin theory states that a nation will have a comparative cost advantage in those goods that utilize relatively large amounts of the resource(s) with which that nation is abundantly supplied.
6.   Taking money and exchange rates into account does not alter the basic causes or effects of international trade, although governmental manipulation of exchange rates can lead to trade patterns that differ from those that would prevail if exchange rates were completely responsive to demand and supply forces.
7.   Changing economic conditions and new insights have led over time to several refinements of the traditional theory of international trade. While these refinements have served to update and expand that theory, its fundamental ideas and conclusions have remained intact.

Questions for Review or Discussion

1.   Explain the difference between absolute costs and comparative costs.
2.   Define and give an illustration of the gains from specialization and the gains from trade.
3.   What determines how the gains from trade will be divided between two trading nations?
4.   Explain the doctrine of comparative advantage in terms of two individuals who have different skills or talents.
5.   Explain precisely what economists mean when they describe a country as "labor-abundant." Relate such a description to the doctrine of comparative advantage.
6.   "International trade and international movements of factors of production can be regarded as substitutes for one another." Explain.
7.   Indicate what is meant by "overvaluation" of a currency and explain what effect such overvaluation would have upon exports and imports.
8.   What is the "Leontief paradox"?
9.   Explain how the product life cycle model and the Lindner model have contributed to our understanding of the causes of international trade.

Case

The Evolving Plastics Industry

In early 1985, a major new producer of polyethylene entered the market. By the end of the year, this new producer, Saudia Arabia Basic Industries Corporation (SABIC), with its huge petrochemical complex located in the modern industrial city of Jubail on Saudi Arabia's Persian Gulf coast, is expected to represent 5 percent of the world's total global polyethylene productive capacity. SABIC's new 4.5 million tons/year capacity is being added to an industry already suffering from overcapacity.

About 60 percent of the investment in SABIC is being financed with low-interest loans from the Saudi Arabian government. Furthermore, SABIC will be using natural gas feedstock, most of which is currently being wasted (flared), and therefore its raw material costs are likely to be well below feedstock cost of plastics plants elsewhere in the world. Thus, SABIC is expected to manufacture polyethylene at a lower cost than any other current producer.

The SABIC plants have been built as joint ventures with and using technical assistance from the following firms: Exxon, Shell Oil, Celanese, Texas Eastern, Mobil, and Mitsubishi. These partners have been given the opportunity of marketing worldwide the low-cost Saudi Arabian polyethylene production.

Polyethylene producers in Europe and Japan suffer from excess capacity and higher feedstock prices, and are threatened by SABIC's productive capacity and ability to sell in their markets. In 1984, prior to SABIC's arrival on the scene, polyethylene prices had already declined 30% in Western Europe. SABIC is already setting up a U.S. sales office, and Shell has contracted to supply Union Carbide in the United States with polyethylene made in Jubail. However, SABIC's impact on the domestic U.S. polyethylene industry is likely to be minimal. U.S. companies have access to low-cost feedstock and place greater emphasis on polypropelyne production. SABIC, on the other hand, faces large transportation costs to North America. However, SABIC is likely to cut into U.S. exports of polyethylene ($3.5 billion in 1984), resulting in greater domestic competition. Overall, for the U.S. petrochemical industry as a whole, the International Trade Commission forecasts a change from a current $8 billion trade surplus to a trade deficit of about $4 billion by 1990.

Observers of the plastics industry point to the fact that polyethylene is now becoming a commodity business. U.S. companies are finding it difficult to compete in this industry just as a few years ago they found it hard to compete in the manufacture of polyvinyl chloride (PVC). Formosa Plastics of Taiwan is now the world's largest producer of PVC, having bought up failing firms and money-losing PVC plants all over the globe, including some in the United States. These observers believe that in order to survive the shakeout in the polyethylene industry, U.S. companies must move away from commodity petrochemicals, streamline their operations, and move downstream into specialty chemicals that require a higher level of technology and more geographic closeness to markets. Others, however, contend that the United States should not give up without a fight, especially since U.S. antidumping laws can be used to keep the government-subsidized SABIC products out of America. However, the Saudis imported $20 billion of U.S.-made goods in 1984, while their petrochemical exports to the United States are unlikely to exceed $3 billion.

How is the plastics industry evolving? What is the best strategy for U.S. producers of polyethylene?

Source: David Fairlamb, "Saudi Petrochemicals: How Big a Threat?" *Dun's Business Month,* February 1985, pp. 66–69; and "Saudis, Europeans Argue over Import Issues," *Chemical and Engineering News,* April 1, 1985, p. 14.

Chapter 6

GOVERNMENT REGULATION OF INTERNATIONAL TRADE

Chapter Objectives

- *To identify the principal motives that cause national governments to limit and regulate international trade*
- *To describe the different methods that governments employ to control international trade*
- *To analyze and compare the effectiveness and the economic consequences of those alternative methods of regulating international trade*
- *To explain how and why the types of trade controls used by national governments have changed over time, especially the shift from tariffs to nontariff barriers as the predominant means of regulating trade*

Reference was made at the close of Chapter 5 to a long-standing and perplexing dichotomy between the conclusions of the theory of international trade and the character of national policies regarding foreign trade. International trade theory has stressed the substantial benefits to be gained from national production specialization and trade between nations. Those benefits accrue through **economic efficiency,** which means maximizing the productivity of available resources to realize the largest output that can feasibly be obtained from them using a given level of technology. International trade furthers the attainment of worldwide economic efficiency by making it possible for each nation to specialize in the economic activities it is best able to perform.

The dichotomy mentioned above manifests itself in the strong inclination of national governments to set up barriers to foreign trade, and even to prohibit such trade altogether. Governmental policies have often been directed at restricting international trade.

What is the explanation for the prevalence of trade policies that are contrary to the teachings of trade theory? One possible explanation is that those who determine national policies either do not understand or do not accept the lessons of the trade theorists. There may be some merit in this explanation but it is too simplistic to constitute a complete solution to the question. It is unlikely that the failings of political leaders could be responsible for such a prevalent policy orientation. We must look elsewhere for the answer to the contradiction between trade theory's advocacy of free trade and the restriction of trade by national governments.

The key lies in recognizing that economic efficiency is only one among many national goals. National governments usually are seeking to achieve several goals simultaneously, and their attempts to achieve these goals may lead them to adopt measures that conflict with free trade or to reject the concept of free trade altogether. This thesis of conflicting national goals will be explored in the first part of this chapter, Objectives of Trade Regulation, which discusses the major purposes of government regulation of trade. The following section, Methods of Regulating Trade, discusses the most important of these methods and their economic effects.

Objectives of Trade Regulation

National Security

Certain fundamental goals of national governments lie outside the sphere of economics, although economic actions may be used to attain them. A prime example of this is **national security,** which refers to the preservation of the nation as a sovereign and independent political entity. Most countries are striving either to attain or maintain this condition of political autonomy, and this strongly influences their internationl economic policies.

Governments may perceive a conflict between maintaining national security and allowing uncontrolled trade with other countries. Indeed, this potential may be regarded as inherent and virtually inescapable, since (as Chapter 5 indicated) international trade grows out of and intensifies **national specialization** in productive activity. While such specialization can yield immense economic benefits, it also leads inexorably toward greater **economic interdependency,** as each nation foregoes domestic production of some goods in order to concentrate on producing those in which it holds a comparative advantage. In an ideal political environment of peace and goodwill among nations, such interdependency would be quite acceptable. However, in our imperfect political world, it is reasonable for national leaders to conclude that the dependency resulting from trade can make their country vulnerable to external economic pressures or hostile political acts.

Nations may become overly dependent on foreign sources of raw materials or products. Having those supplies cut off in times of war or other political disturbances is a threat that has preoccupied government

Box 6.1

Shoe Imports Threaten U.S. Defense

Defense experts, long preoccupied with debates over Cruise missiles and space-based weapons, are beginning to hear about a new weakness in the nation's defenses: shoes.

The U.S. shoe industry is trying to convince Congress that growing reliance on imported footwear is "jeopardizing the national security of the U.S." The headline on a recent industry press release cautioned, "Military Might Go Barefoot in Case of War."

The industry began pushing the national security argument after the U.S. International Trade Commission rejected its petition for relief from imports, which make up 60 percent of the U.S. market. The shoemakers now hope they can persuade Congress to enact import quotas.

Source: Art Pine, "Footwear Industry Tells Congress 'Shoe Gap' Threatens U.S. Defense," *The Wall Street Journal* (August 24, 1984), 19. Reprinted by permission of *The Wall Street Journal,* © Dow Jones & Company, Inc. 1984. All Rights Reserved.

leaders (as well as many economists, including some staunch advocates of free trade) for centuries. There is much historical evidence to reinforce such concerns. This threat became very real for the United States during the Second World War, when enemy actions severely curtailed this country's access to many imported raw materials. The United States was forced to ration scarce materials and launch a massive effort to develop new sources of these scarce materials or to develop synthetic substitutes. The United States faced the same threat again in a more moderate form when some Organization of Petroleum Exporting Countries (OPEC) nations used the "oil weapon" in an attempt to manipulate American policies and relationships in the Middle East.

Efforts to guard against such a danger repeatedly appear in national policies toward foreign trade, generally as restrictions on imports of specific materials or products. The ostensible intent of such restrictions is to create or maintain a domestic capability to produce the commodities or products involved or usable substitutes for them and thereby to reduce the nation's vulnerability to supply interruptions.

Although reason and experience may justify some of these precautionary restrictions on trade, national security considerations have frequently been used as a pretense for imposing trade controls that have only a remote connection with such security. Thus, the problem with the national security argument (as well as with other arguments for trade restraints that will be examined presently) is not that it is invalid, but that it is too often misused to rationalize trade restrictions that actually have less defensible aims.

In addition to serving as a justification for limiting imports of foreign goods, national security concerns have also prompted national governments to place controls on exports. Most of the world's major trading countries, including the United States, currently enforce extensive and stringent legal restrictions on sales of goods to other countries. Many of these restrictions are based upon the nature of the product involved. Goods directly associated with military activities are always prime candidates for export controls, but bans also are frequently extended to nonmilitary items. Restrictions may also be directed toward specific foreign countries, and a national government may prohibit its residents from exporting products of any kind to those countries.

One major rationale for such export restrictions is to prevent hostile foreign countries from obtaining products that might enhance their military capabilities. This is often interpreted broadly to include goods that might contribute to the hostile country's military capability indirectly by strengthening the nation's economy. The national security argument occasionally is stretched even further, to cover export limitations that are intended to "punish" a foreign country for actions that the exporting country deems politically harmful to its own national interests. The United States can again be used to exemplify the application of such reasoning, since it has maintained tight controls on exports of strategic goods to the communist countries ever since the "Cold War" period of the late 1940s, and has more recently imposed some additional specific restrictions on exports to the Soviet Union as a way of expressing disapproval of Soviet actions in Afghanistan and Poland. But the United States is by no means the only country that engages in such practices, as restrictions or total embargos of exports are a widely used device for waging "economic warfare."

Protectionism

The term *protectionism* may be defined in a number of different ways. It will be used here to refer to the adoption or retention of trade restrictions for the purpose of protecting the economic well-being of particular groups of individuals or business organizations within a nation.

The thesis that is being considered here is that national governments control foreign trade because free trade would conflict with other national interests; protectionism is adequately explained by this thesis. Indeed, the issue of free trade, or, more precisely, the issue of "freeing" or "liberalizing" trade by reducing existing trade controls, almost always places national governments in a difficult dilemma. On the one hand, a government may be well aware of the probable benefits—lower prices, a greater variety of available products, increased exporting opportunities—that it could gain from freer trade with other countries. On the other hand, however, the government is likely to realize that the removal of import barriers would expose certain segments of the national economy to more intense competition. The dilemma confronting the government is whether to accept the prospect of economic injury to certain groups, notably the workers and investors in those domestic industries that would bear the brunt of the new foreign competition, in order to gain the benefits of trade for the country as a whole.

National government leaders have wrestled with this dilemma for a long time, and they have not found consistent advice or wholly workable solutions in the solutions proposed by economists. Since the issue involved goes beyond the realm of descriptive or "positive" economics and deals with policy choices affecting the welfare of various economic groups, the prescriptions offered by different economists have often reflected their own ideological leanings.

One seemingly "scientific" and unbiased conceptual approach to the issue holds that a nation should reduce or eliminate trade controls if the overall economic benefits of doing so are expected to exceed the economic costs (injuries) that would be imposed upon particular groups. The reasoning here is that the total benefits would be sufficient to compensate those who had sustained injury and still leave some net economic gains for the public at large. Unfortunately, this concept is difficult to apply in reality due to the problem of measuring the anticipated costs and benefits and developing transfer mechanisms to adequately compensate those who experience economic losses as a result of the removal of trade restrictions.[1]

Since protectionism results in economic gains to some and losses to others, it has historically been a controversial political issue. It is not surprising that whenever this issue is fought out in the political arena, the outcome usually favors those who advocate the adoption or continuation of national controls on foreign trade. One reason for this is that the economic benefits of freer trade tend to be widely dispersed, whereas the injury that might result from freer trade tends to be much more concentrated. To clarify these tendencies and their political implications, let us consider the probable distribution of the economic gains and losses that would result from a (hypothetical) decision on the part of the U.S. government to eliminate all import controls on clothing.

Who would benefit from such a decision? Presumably, the entire "American consuming public" might experience some benefits through the availability of lower-priced wearing apparel and a larger selection of such apparel from which to choose. But, how much would such benefits be worth to each American consumer or family? It seems un-

---

[1]This concept forms part of the basis of the so-called "trade adjustment assistance" programs that have been implemented by several nations during the past two decades. The U.S. trade adjustment assistance program will be examined in the section on U.S. Trade Policies Since 1930 in Chapter 7.

likely that the average American household would save more than a few hundred dollars per year, at the very most, by purchasing cheaper imported clothing. Thus, in this example, the economic gains from freer trade are broadly distributed and relatively modest for each beneficiary.

Who would bear the adverse consequences of such a decision? It seems reasonable to expect that the adverse effects of increased foreign competition would fall most heavily and directly upon the American clothing manufacturing industry, that is, the firms and workers producing wearing apparel, and might spread to firms and workers linked to that industry as suppliers or distributors. While concentrated in their scope, these effects could be quite onerous, possibly entailing job losses for workers, reduced returns to investors, or bankruptcies and plant closings in the affected industries.

Since those experiencing these economic difficulties are linked by occupation and possibly by geographic location, and since they might be seriously affected by the elimination of import controls, they might undertake organized political action directed at reversing the government's action. By contrast, there would be little if any cohesion among the masses of consumers who might have benefited from the removal of the clothing import controls, and little likelihood that they would be aware of, much less excited about, the modest savings that they might have realized.

The point of this hypothetical example is that protectionism has a natural and often vocal political constituency among those who see their livelihood threatened by foreign competition, whereas free trade is supported primarily as an ideal by those who are cognizant of its generalized, long-term advantages. In the rough-and-tumble political arena, where elected officials are responsive to immediate pressures and special interests, the odds usually are with the advocates of protectionism. This helps to explain the endurance of protectionist trade policies, especially limitations on imports, even though the economic welfare of the general public might be advanced through freer international trade.

Domestic Full Employment

Another national goal that frequently causes governments to impose restrictions on imports is **domestic full employment.** The link between this goal and regulation of trade is similar to that involved in protectionism, since both involve the notion of defending jobs at home against threats posed by foreign competition. However, as noted above, protectionist motives usually relate to particular industries or sectors of a country's economy, while attaining or maintaining full employment is a broad objective related to the national economy as a whole.

"Full employment" is an elusive objective even with respect to its definition and measurement. There is no uniformity of opinion among national governments, governmental officials, economists, or other observers as to exactly what constitutes full employment, and opinions relating to this question also are inclined to change over time. In the United States, for instance, the consensus once was that a 4 percent rate of unemployment was indicative of full-employment conditions, since it was felt that this proportion of the labor force might be between jobs at any given time even when employment opportunities were plentiful. More recently, however, the slow growth of the economy and the changing composition of the labor force have caused many observers of U.S. labor market conditions to redefine full employment as coinciding with an unemployment rate greater than 4 percent.

Despite these definitional problems, full employment unquestionably has been a high-priority goal of national governments for the past 40 years. The United States actually embodied this in law in the Employment Act of 1946, which made it the responsibility of the American government to help maintain a high level of employment. Although not all national governments have formally legislated their commitment to full employment, creating and maintaining domestic jobs is a universal goal.

The possibility of a conflict between domestic full employment and unrestricted trade with the rest of the world is a concept that can be deceptive in its apparent obviousness and validity. The idea can assert itself appealingly whenever a nation is experiencing a high rate of unemployment while simultaneously importing goods from foreign countries. In such a situation, curtailing imports through government controls may appear to be a "quick fix" for the unemployment problem, since this presumably would shift domestic demand from imported goods (produced by foreign labor) to domestically produced substitutes and thereby create more jobs at home. A government struggling with stubborn unemployment may be sorely tempted toward this course of action and is likely to find considerable support among the unemployed and the population at large.

However, there is a significant flaw in this formula for relieving unemployment. A nation's attempt to generate employment in import-substitution industries by reducing imports may be accompanied by corresponding losses of jobs in sectors of the economy connected to exports. Any country is apt to find it difficult to cut imports through direct governmental controls without also experiencing a reduction in export sales. This repercussive effect may result from **retaliation** by foreign governments for the restrictions that have been imposed upon their products. If, for example, the United States were to put limits on imports from other countries as a means of expanding domestic employment opportunities, there is a strong likelihood that its trading partners would retaliate by placing their own controls on U.S. goods coming into their territories. The probability of such countermeasures would be especially high if the trading partners were also facing unemployment problems at home, since this would make them particularly resistant to

"Relax—It's Just to Keep HIM Out"

Source: Reprinted with permission of John Trever, Albuquerque Journal.

U.S. efforts to alleviate its job shortage by reducing purchases of their goods. The accompanying cartoon points out the fact that curtailing imports also entails limiting exports.

Even if there were no direct retaliation, the United States might still find its export markets shrinking as a consequence of exchange rate changes brought about by its use of import controls. As the United States began importing less, American residents would be offering fewer dollars in exchange for foreign currencies (since their demand for those currencies would be reduced). The exchange value of the dollar would therefore tend to rise, which would make it more expensive for foreign buyers to acquire American products. U.S. producers would then find it more difficult to sell abroad, and this could force them to cut back output and lay off workers. Jobs would thus be lost in export-dependent industries in the United States, even though foreign governments had not deliberately sought to curtail imports of American-made products.

In addition to the prospective futility of attempts to get a *net* increase in domestic employment by curbing imports, such attempts may have other undesirable effects. One of these would be a forced reallocation of resources within the economy, which is apt to be disruptive while it is occurring and inefficient when it has been effectuated. As noted above, import restrictions designed to raise the level of domestic employment frequently result instead in trading-off existing jobs in export-related industries for new jobs in import-substitution industries. This process is likely to prove difficult and wasteful, since it entails installing new production facilities and training workers to produce goods to replace imports at the same time that established productive capacities and experienced workers are being idled in other sectors of the economy. Furthermore, the reallocation process would be misdirected from the standpoint of overall economic efficiency, as it would reduce production in industries with a proven comparative cost advantage while increasing production in industries that must be insulated from import competition in order to survive.

Despite all these potential pitfalls, national governments still may deem it politically expedient to shut out imported goods as a remedy for unemployment, and, given the right circumstances, employment gains might result. However, trade controls are, at best, an uncertain and economically inefficient means of creating job opportunities, and nations that resort to such measures in periods of widespread unemployment always run the risk of touching off a mutually destructive series of retaliatory measures. Wisdom therefore dictates that governments should rely mainly on other courses of action to assure domestic full employment.

Economic Development

It is probably safe to assume that every nation of the world wishes to further develop its economy so as to increase output and productivity. But **economic development** has become a matter of special urgency for the Third World countries that are struggling to feed, clothe, and shelter their burgeoning populations. It also is evident that, for those countries, development typically implies something other than simply producing more of what they already are producing. The poverty and chronic economic difficulties associated with these nations' historical role as producers of agricultural commodities and mineral raw materials have led them to embrace industrialization as the key to economic progress. Thus, they seek not only to expand their economies, but also to diversify their economic activities and output through the establishment of new industrial enterprises.

Economists have long recognized that the traditional theory of international trade does not reflect such developmental aspirations. The doctrine of comparative advantage, which is the cornerstone of traditional trade theory, is a *static* doctrine, which applies to a given set of existing economic conditions. It shows how a fixed stock of economic resources, distributed among the nations of the world in a particular manner, can be used more efficiently. But it does not deal with how that stock of resources can be made to grow, nor with the controversial issue of

whether the historically determined distribution of the world's resources and the resultant pattern of productive activity are either optimal or "fair."

These limitations have caused many of the intellectual and political
leaders of the Third World countries to reject the free-trade policy prescriptions derived from traditional trade theory on the grounds that
such prescriptions serve to legitimatize and perpetuate what they regard
as an undesirable status quo in the global economy. They perceive an
inherent conflict between free trade and their efforts to improve their
economic status through national economic development programs, and
they advocate governmental controls on foreign trade as an essential
component of those programs.

This conflict between unfettered international trade and domestic economic development is not new. Rather, it constitutes a modern-day
manifestation of a venerable idea known as the **infant industry** argument.[2] This argument justifies imposing restrictions on international
trade by asserting that young industries must be shielded from foreign
competition until they attain a scale of operations and a technological
and managerial maturity that enable them to hold their own in the
competitive marketplace. The Third World countries have found this
argument applicable to their economic circumstances and objectives,
since they are striving to develop new industries which—in the absence
of protective controls on imports—might by highly vulnerable to competition from established industries located in more economically advanced nations.

Although the infant industry argument is most closely associated with
the restrictive trade policies of the Third World countries, it also turns
up in the trade and developmental strategies of some of the First World
nations. Japan is frequently cited (and criticized) as a classic example of
a nation that has effectively utilized import controls as a means of stim-
ulating and supporting the growth of new industries, and many have
urged that the United States implement similar measures in order to
develop modern high-technology industries to replace or supplement
its declining "smokestack" industries.

The durability and widespread acceptance of the infant industry argument are testimonials to its commonsense appeal and theoretical co-
gency. Nevertheless, there are obvious problems and substantial risks
connected with its practical application or use in formulating national
economic policy.

---

[2]With regard to the long history of the infant industry argument, it is interesting to note
that Alexander Hamilton used this argument in his *Report on Manufactures*, written in
1791, to support American tariffs on manufactured goods: Samuel McKee, Jr. (ed.), *Alexander Hamilton, Papers on Public Credit, Commerce and Finance* (New York: Columbia University Press, 1934), pp. 204–205. A broader and more sophisticated version of the argument
is found in a work by Frederich List, first published in 1841, entitled *The National System
of Political Economy* (New York: Longmans, Green & Co., 1904).

In the first place, a nation may find it hard to determine which, if any, new industries or economic endeavors have enough real growth potential to merit protection from foreign competition. Such a determination would require extremely thorough analyses of a multitude of factors, including the availability and costs of resources, technological and engineering feasibility, geographic advantages, and market demand, and these analyses would necessarily involve some inherently problematic long-term forecasts.

Mistakes in this analytical process could prove costly, since the granting of infant industry protection status constitutes a substantial commitment on the part of the nation. The curtailment of competing imported goods effectively forces the people of the nation to subsidize the fledgling domestic industry by buying its higher priced goods; these consumer subsidies are frequently supplemented by direct governmental aid, including capital funds from the national treasury.

Once a nation and its government have made such a commitment, it may prove virtually impossible from a political standpoint to withdraw what was intended to be temporary aid and protection from the industry involved. If it turns out that the industry cannot attain a level of output and efficiency that makes it truly competitive, then continuing protection may be granted in order to "cover up" the erroneous predictions of success and the associated investment of resources. Even if the industry should eventually become competitively viable, it may exert considerable pressure to retain its comfortable protected position.

Thus, the difficulties of predicting economic viability, together with the realities of human nature and politics, create a high probability that many infant industries will never "grow up," and historical experience lends credence to that probability. The adoption of the infant industry concept—or, in broader terms, the application of restrictions on international trade—must therefore be viewed as a risky means of furthering economic development, which may result instead in a wasteful misallocation of the developing nation's scarce resources.

Balance of Payments Equilibrium

It has become a widespread practice for national governments to interfere with the free flow of international trade in order to influence the volume of their nations' imports and exports. These nations often are attempting to maintain or restore what they consider to be an acceptable relationship between their international receipts and payments—a relationship termed **balance of payments equilibrium**—and they may regard that objective as unattainable in the absence of direct governmental involvement. This perceived conflict between free trade and balance of payments equilibrium will merely be noted here as an important addition to the list of reasons for government regulation of trade. Chapter 12 of this text will deal with the balance of payments.

This examination of governmental restraints on international trade was not intended to be exhaustive. A complete listing of the arguments that have been advanced in support of such restraints would be lengthy indeed. It would include many notions of questionable validity which nevertheless have enjoyed considerable popular support, as well as some profound theoretical rationales advanced by economists but never actually adopted (or perhaps never fully understood) by governmental officials. We have examined arguments that fall between these two extremes. They combine at least a modicum of conceptual soundness with applicability to real economic problems, and therefore are most commonly cited in support of trade controls.

Methods of Regulating Trade

Political officials and economists have shown much ingenuity in devising methods for manipulating the volume, direction, and composition of international trade, and many types of trade controls have emerged in the several centuries during which nations have regulated trade among themselves. These methods differ greatly, not only in their form and manner of application, but also in the nature and severity of their effects upon trade. This section will consider those methods categorized as either **tariffs** or as **nontariff barriers**. International trade can also be regulated via governmental controls on the price and availability of foreign currencies, but investigation of that methodology will be deferred to Chapter 11, which deals with foreign exchange.

Tariffs

Tariffs are taxes (frequently referred to as customs duties) that are levied on goods as they cross the borders of a nation. The term *tariff* may also be applied to the entire schedule of such duties listed on a product-by-product basis. Duties may be levied either on imports (i.e., goods entering the nation) or on exports (goods outbound from the nation) or both, although some countries, notably the United States, do not tax exports.

Duties that are set and calculated as a percentage of the value of the product being taxed (e.g., 20 percent of the invoice price) are called **ad valorem duties,** whereas duties set on the basis of physical quantity of the product (e.g., $1.00/unit or $30.00/ton) are termed **specific duties.** Although the choice between these two options often may be dictated by administrative convenience, it also is apparent that an ad valorem duty will provide a more consistent level of protection when prices are rising over time, since a specific duty will automatically become smaller in proportion to the increasing monetary value of the product on which it is levied.

Tariffs are generally levied for one of two purposes, either to provide revenue for the government of the tariff-levying country or to protect industries in that country from foreign competition.[3] In the nineteenth century, import tariffs provided a substantial proportion of the total tax revenues of a great many national treasuries, including that of the United States. During this century, however, the rising expenditures of national governments in the industrialized countries have far outstripped the revenue-generating capacity of import duties, so that such duties have dwindled in relative significance as sources of funds for these governments. But many of the developing countries continue to rely heavily upon tariffs for revenue purposes, partly because importing and exporting often comprise a large component of the overall economic activity in those countries, but also because their governments find import and export duties easier to collect than other types of taxes.

Inasmuch as the major countries that account for the bulk of world trade currently employ tariffs mainly for protective reasons, this discussion will concentrate upon the economic effects of these protective import duties. The discussion will also be limited to the more immediate and obvious effects, since it would be very difficult to identify all of the conceivable "ripple effects" of a tax placed on imported products.

Economic Effects of Protective Tariffs.   In examining the economic impact of protective tariffs, it is worthwhile to first consider the *intended* effects of such tariffs and then to point out that those intended effects may not always be realized. When a national government levies a protective duty on a particular imported product, the intent is to make that product more expensive for domestic buyers and thereby to persuade those buyers to purchase less of it. The corollary intent is, of course, to induce those same buyers to shift their purchases to domestically produced goods as substitutes for the imported product. Such a shift in demand is expected to benefit domestic producers by enabling them to increase the quanity of their output and sales, or the prices they charge, or both.

It should be apparent that the *rate* at which the duty is set will exert an influence in this demand-diverting endeavor. Generally speaking, the higher the duty rate (in relation to the price of the imported product) the greater the likelihood that customers will turn to domestic substitutes. A duty rate that is less than the price differential that exists between the imported good and domestic substitutes will offer partial protection to the domestic producers, but complete protection from import competition would require a duty rate that exceeded that differential.

---

[3]These two purposes are not mutually exclusive, since an import duty which has been imposed as a means of raising revenue may also have a protective effect, and a protective tariff (unless the duty rate is set so high as to completely curtail imports) can yield some revenue for the government.

While the calculation of the duty rate and the determination of the resultant degree of protection that rate affords might appear to be fairly simple exercises, they can be quite complicated. This is especially true of situations in which a nation imposes import duties on finished manufactured products but permits raw or semifinished materials that go into the making of those products to be imported duty free. In such instances, the duty rate specified for a finished product (often called the **nominal rate**) actually applies only to the portion of that product's selling price which results from the manufacturing or finishing process, and the **effective rate** applicable to that portion will be higher than the nominal rate. To clarify this through an example, let us assume that the United States maintains a 15 percent ad valorem import duty on finished woolen cloth which carries an invoice price of $4.00/yard, but has no import duty on raw wool. Here the nominal duty rate on the woolen cloth is 15 percent. However, if we further assume that one-half of the $4.00/yard price of that cloth represents the cost of the raw wool that it contains and the remaining one-half represents the cost of the manufacturing process that turns the raw wool into cloth, then the $0.60 tax on each yard of woolen cloth imported (15 percent of $4.00) turns out to be a 30 percent effective rate of duty on the $2.00 of value added by the manufacturing process.

This distinction between nominal and effective tariff rates has important real-world implications, and has become a subject of contention in international trading relationships. As the above example indicates, even a seemingly low nominal duty on finished products can actually constitute a much higher rate on the value added by manufacturing and can therefore give domestic manufacturers substantial protection against foreign competitors. Spokespersons for the Third World countries that are attempting to develop new export-oriented manufacturing industries have recognized this possibility and have criticized the industrialized countries for retaining high effective rates of duty on imported manufactured goods.

Returning now to the economic effects of protective tariffs, let us consider why the intended effects outlined above might not be fully realized. Whether or not a protective tariff accomplishes its mission by curbing imports and increasing sales of domestically produced substitutes is contingent upon several circumstances. First, the duty must raise the price of the imported product in the tariff-levying country. At first glance, such a price increase would seem to be inevitable, since the duty is a sum of money that importers must pay to their government and that presumably will get added to the price at which that product is resold. It is by no means certain, however, that the price of the product will be increased by the amount of the duty, or even that it will rise at all. There is always the possibility that the duty will be wholly or partially *absorbed* by either the importer or the foreign producer(s) of the product, rather than being passed along to other buyers in the distribution chain. If, for example, a country placed a duty of $1.00/unit on a product that previously had carried an import price of $5.00/unit, the foreign producers could absorb all of that duty by reducing their price to $4.00 or could absorb part of it by setting a new price somewhere between $4.00 and $4.99.

There are no hard and fast rules for determining when or if an import duty will be absorbed. However, it is reasonable to expect that producers would be more likely to absorb some or all of such a duty if they feel that the demand for their product in the tariff-levying country is *elastic,* that is, if they think that buyers would react strongly to an increase in the price of the product via a more-than-proportional reduction in the amount that they were willing to purchase. The producers' inclination to absorb the tariff would also depend on how such an action would affect their profit margins, as well as on their perceptions regarding the importance of the market in the tariff-levying country and the availability of alternative markets for their output. Since these supply and demand factors vary greatly from one situation to the next, it is impossible to make any valid general prediction as to whether or to what extent import duties will raise the prices of the products on which they are levied.

A second element of uncertainty affecting the economic effect of import tariffs relates to how consumers in the tariff-levying country will respond to tariff-induced increases in the prices of imported goods. It was noted above that the producers' feelings with regard to this responsiveness (the elasticity of demand) might influence their willingness to absorb an import duty. However, the actual elasticity of demand will further determine the extent to which any price increase that does result from a duty will decrease sales of the product involved. Demand for an imported product could well be so **inelastic** that an import duty would exert only a negligible effect upon its sales in the tariff-levying country. If consumers in that country want the imported product badly enough and markedly prefer it to domestically-produced substitutes, then an import tariff may fail to dislodge that product from its market position even though its price has been forced upward.

The possibility that market forces will sometimes circumvent the intended protective effects of import tariffs may be frustrating for domestic industries that are seeking protection and for national governments that are trying to provide it. But this may be something of a blessing for the consuming public, since a tariff that succeeds in insulating domestic producers from foreign competition generally forces consumers either to pay higher prices for imported goods than they otherwise would, or to turn to less-desirable substitutes, or some combination of the two. It also lowers economic efficiency by shifting demand in such a way as to reduce the output and sales of more efficient foreign producers while increasing the output and sales of the less-efficient domestic producers.

As was noted in Objectives of Trade Regulation, above, there may be overriding national concerns or pressing needs that justify the occasional use of protective tariffs. However, tariffs are a risky and costly means of supporting home industries or dealing with other internal economic problems, and the nation that uses them unwisely or indiscriminately also runs the risk of retaliation against its exports by other nations. Indeed, "tariff wars" among nations in the past have had a very destructive impact upon overall international trade and hence upon the health and prosperity of virtually all national economies, and the prospect of a repetition of such an unhappy scenario can never be totally dismissed.

Nontariff Barriers: Quantity Limits

Tariffs are the oldest and best-known method by which national governments attempt to regulate international trade. However, during the past half-century in particular, governments have devised and utilized numerous other methods. These **nontariff barriers** have taken on increasing significance within the regulatory framework, partly as a consequence of multilateral negotiations and agreements that have reduced the power and prominence of tariffs.

Nontariff barriers include any government policy or practice that has a direct effect upon international trade. These effects more often are thought of in terms of impeding imports (hence the word "barrier"), but the category also takes in subsidies or other measures that governments may use to promote exporting from their countries. One of the major types of nontariff barrier is the **quota,** which is a quantitative limit on imports or exports. Import quotas will be considered first, followed by a brief look at quotas on exports.

Import Quotas.   An *import quota* specifies the maximum amount of a product which can legally be brought into a country during some time period. This amount usually is expressed in physical units, but often it represents some percentage share of the market for the product in the country that is imposing the quota. As a hypothetical example, the U.S. government might establish an import quota of so many million barrels of petroleum per year in order to hold U.S. consumption of (and dependence upon) imported oil to a tolerable proportion of the total consumption.

Historically, quotas designed to limit imports usually have been imposed and enforced unilaterally by the importing country. A quota set in this manner might specify the total which could be imported without specifying which foreign countries or producers would be allowed to supply that amount. This would be a **global** or **unallocated** quota, and foreign exporters could fill such a quota on a first-come, first-served basis. Alternatively, import quotas can be **allocated** among different foreign suppliers or supplying countries, or among importers in the country imposing the quota.

Box 6.2

Reduction in Nicaragua's Share of U.S. Sugar Imports

The Reagan Administration cut by almost 90 percent the amount of sugar that Nicaragua can sell in the United States.

Nicaragua, which normally sends almost its entire sugar crop to the United States, will be permitted to sell this country only 6,000 tons in the year that begins October 1, 1983. Its original quota was 58,800 tons.

The United States has accused Nicaragua of secretly supporting rebels trying to overthrow the American-backed government in El Salvador.

White House spokesman Larry Speakes said the sugar quota taken from Nicaragua would be distributed among Honduras, Costa Rica, and El Salvador.

Source: "Nicaragua Sugar Quota Allowed for U.S. Is Cut by 90 Percent," *The Blade* (May 11, 1983), 12. Reprinted with permission of The Associated Press.

The manner in which an import quota is allocated can be a very important issue, since the quota tends to elevate the price of the product involved in the importing country, thereby making it very lucrative for suppliers or importers to have a share in filling the quota. Because the privilege of sharing in a quota can be a valuable prize, government officials have often been inclined to dispense these privileges so as to reward their friends. The American government has not been immune from this practice. For instance, the United States has maintained a quota on the importation of sugar for many years and has periodically reallocated shares in that quota among the various producing nations in accordance with changing political relationships between each of those nations and the United States.

A different approach to quota-setting has come to the fore in recent years, in which quotas have been negotiated between the governments of exporting and importing countries. The quantitative limitations on trade resulting from such negotiations are referred to as **voluntary quotas** or **orderly marketing agreements.** These terms are euphemistic, in that they imply that the supplier countries have willingly "volunteered" to restrain exports. In actuality, the supplier countries often are pressured by the importing countries into setting limits on their exports and subsequently enforcing such limits. The lever used to exert this pressure

Box 6.3

Quotas or Tariffs?

The U.S. International Trade Commission (ITC) has ruled that imports of unwrought copper are injuring U.S. copper producers and has given President Reagan the choice of imposing quotas or increasing tariffs as a means of aiding the U.S. industry.

A spokesman for the 11 U.S. copper producers that petitioned the ITC for relief from import competition said that the industry prefers quotas because they could "shelter us from a flood of imports at the next economic downturn."

The five-cent-a-pound additional tariff proposed by two members of the ITC probably would provide little help for the depressed industry, as it would only raise the cost of imported copper to 68 to 71 cents a pound. That would still be well below the average U.S. production cost of 82 cents per pound.

Source: "ITC Is Divided on How to Aid Copper Industry," *The Wall Street Journal* (June 28, 1984), 12.

typically is the threat that, in the absence of voluntary self-restraint by the exporters, the importing nations might unilaterally impose even more stringent import controls. The United States has been active in initiating this kind of arrangement for regulating imports. Over the past 10 years, the U.S. government has prodded foreign nations to enter into orderly marketing agreements applying to such major product categories as textiles, steel, shoes, televisions, and automobiles.

Differing Effects of Quotas and Tariffs.   Regardless of how import quotas are established and administered, their proximate aim almost always is to protect domestic producers against foreign competition. As in the case of tariffs, this protective aim may be linked to some broader national objective, such as full employment or national defense. But, while tariffs and quotas have much the same purposes, there are important differences in their economic effects.

One of these differences has to do with the certainty of the protection provided. It was shown above how the intended protective effects of import duties are susceptible to being reduced or offset by market forces. Quotas are much more inflexible in this regard, since there is very little that either producers or consumers can do (at least legally) to overcome the restrictions that a government has established through an import quota. Whereas it is possible for exporters to deter the intended demand-depressing effects of an import duty levied on their product by absorbing part or all of that duty, they have no comparable means available for maintaining sales volume above the level prescribed by a quota. Similarly, consumers in a country that has set a quota on an imported product are unable to purchase any more of that product than the quota allows, regardless of the intensity of their demand or their willingness to pay a higher price.

The certainty that quotas will actually hold imports to a targeted level makes them attractive to governments or interest groups that are seeking quick and sure reductions of imports. Quotas therefore tend to be favored over tariffs whenever the need for controlling imports is regarded as urgent or imperative, as, for example, when a country is experiencing severe balance of payments problems or when a major domestic industry is being battered by foreign competitors. However, these same features of certainty and inflexibility that are associated with quotas make them repugnant to advocates of freer international trade. As a consequence, international negotiations and agreements directed toward the liberalization of trade often have given particular attention to circumscribing the use of quotas as a means of regulating imports.

A second difference between quotas and tariffs relates to the disposition of the revenues they generate. In the case of a tariff, the money raised by taxing imports is collected by the government of the importing country and becomes a part of the total revenues flowing into the public treasury. The revenue effects of quotas are less overt, however, and the disposition of those revenues is also less clear-cut or predictable.

An import quota generates revenues by bringing about a difference between the price the affected product commands with the quota in force and the price it would command without the quota. Inasmuch as a quota usually is set so as to reduce the amount of the product being supplied by imports, it generally could be expected to push up the price of that product (or of substitute products) in the importing country. This higher price, in turn, gives sellers an opportunity to realize higher revenues than they would have realized without the quota.

It is not easy to determine exactly which sellers would receive these additional revenues. They could go to foreign producers or exporters of the product or to importers in the country that imposed the quota or, conceivably, to someone else in the distribution channels, depending upon the relative market power of these organizations or upon how the quota was allocated. But it is clear that quotas differ from tariffs in that the incremental revenues they yield tend to go to private business firms, rather than public treasuries, unless steps are taken by government to alter this outcome. Since these incremental revenues can amount to many millions of dollars in some instances, national governments have been sensitive to this tendency and have frequently devised elaborate procedures for recouping these revenues or for preventing import quotas from unduly enriching particular firms or individuals.[4]

Export Quotas.   Our consideration of quotas has thus far concentrated upon their use in regulating imports, but national governments also make extensive use of quantitative limits on exports. These **export quotas** may be imposed for any number of reasons. One purpose for which they are commonly used is to prevent military goods or other strategic products from being acquired by unfriendly foreign nations. This was discussed earlier in connection with the national security rationale for trade controls, and it was noted then that the tensions and hostilities that continue to pervade the international political scene have spawned a complex mass of such controls.

There are many instances in which the politically motivated use of export quotas has been carried to the point of forbidding any exports to particular foreign nations. Such complete restrictions are sometimes referred to as **embargos,** and the American government's prohibition of trade with Cuba, which has been in force since the early 1960s, is an example of such an embargo. Another comprehensive form of trade restriction is the **boycott,** which involves an agreement among several nations to partially or totally curtail exports to some specific foreign country; a contemporary example of this is the Arab boycott of Israel.[5]

Export quotas are also employed in connection with **international commodity agreements.** These agreements, which were discussed briefly in Chapter 3, are designed to stabilize the prices of foodstuffs and raw materials, and such stabilization efforts often entail limitations upon the amounts of the commodity that each producing country can export during a given time period. The basic aims of these export quotas are, of course, to regulate the total supply of the commodity involved that is being offered for sale in the world market so as to prevent sharp price fluctuations and to keep the average price level higher than it would be in the absence of supply controls. Commodities that are currently covered by international agreements include tin, sugar, coffee, rubber, wheat, and cocoa. As noted in Chapter 3, the developing Third World countries have been pushing for the extension of such agreements to other commodities, but they have encountered resistance from some of the developed nations which have expressed reservations regarding the practicability, effectiveness, and costliness of such arrangements.

Still another purpose for which export quotas are sometimes utilized is to preserve the available supply of some product or commodity for domestic use. Scarcity of a good resulting from production shortfalls or

---

[4]One such procedure involves the "auctioning" of quota shares to importers. The importers bid for licenses that permit them to import a certain amount of the product involved and pay the government for those licenses.

[5]See Dan S. Chill, *The Arab Boycott of Israel* (New York: Praeger, 1976).

sudden increases in demand may induce a government to set limits on exports to help ensure that domestic needs will have priority over sales to foreign countries.

Other Nontariff Barriers

In addition to quantitative restrictions, nontariff barriers include a multitude of other government regulations and practices affecting international trade. Indeed, the number and variety of these regulations and practices are so great that it has been extremely difficult to identify and enumerate all of them and even harder to measure the extent of their influence on trade flows. The task of tracking down these elusive barriers is also complicated by the fact that their impact upon trade may be incidental to some other purpose. A good example of this would be **product standards** that are designed mainly (or ostensibly) to safeguard the environment or the health of consumers, but that can be administered or interpreted so as to discriminate against imported products.

Some other governmental policies or actions that have become notorious through their use in restricting trade are government purchasing regulations, local or domestic content requirements, and subsidies.

Government Purchasing Regulations.   Many nations, as well as states and municipalities, have either formal or informal regulations relating to the purchasing decisions of government agencies that result in preferential treatment being accorded to domestic suppliers vis-à-vis foreign producers. Inasmuch as government purchases have grown rapidly over time and now comprise a substantial portion of total spending for goods and services throughout the world, these regulations have become a significant impediment to free trade and militate against the concept of competition on equal terms.

Domestic Content Requirements.   A growing number of countries now have laws or regulations which make it mandatory that products being marketed in their territories "contain" some specified amount or proportion of domestically supplied inputs. Those inputs may consist of labor applied to making the product or materials used in their production, but, in either case, the intent of the requirement is to limit the importation of goods that have been completely processed or manufactured abroad. Requirements of this sort have been most commonly found in the developing countries, where they have served as a means of forcing foreign exporters or foreign investors to employ more local workers or suppliers. However, similar requirements have recently been adopted or seriously considered by governments of some of the more advanced nations. This includes the United States, where a bill that would apply domestic content requirements to automobiles has been vigorously debated in Congress.

Subsidies. The governments of many nations provide subsidies to particular domestic industries or firms. These subsidies may take the form of direct cash payments, tax reductions, low-interest loans, or technical assistance, and their ostensible purposes typically are to support the development or ensure the survival of industries that are deemed to be important to the nation's economy or security. However, such subsidies are very likely to affect international trade, either by giving the subsidized producers a competitive advantage in export markets or by making it more difficult for foreign producers to compete with them in their home market. Certain subsidy programs, notably those involving governmental assistance which permits exporters to grant low-cost credit to foreign buyers, have become so widespread and such a source of rivalry among nations that the governments of those nations have found it necessary to restrain themselves (and one another) by mutually agreeing to limit the amount of such subsidies.

The list of nontariff barriers could go on and on, but the above examples should suffice to indicate the general nature, intent, and effects of these barriers. It is worth noting again that the tremendous number of such measures in existence, together with their heterogeneity and their propensity to lurk beneath more reputable governmental activities, have rendered them very troublesome to contend with. Despite several international negotiating sessions directed toward reducing or eliminating them, the bulk of these nontariff barriers have remained stubbornly in place and have long since displaced the tariff as the principal obstacle to free international trade.

Summary

1.   Despite the economic efficiency arguments for free international trade, national governments historically have erected and maintained extensive barriers to trade with other countries.

2.   Government restrictions on foreign trade often are due to the pursuit of national objectives that may conflict with free international trade. These objectives include national security, protection for the economic interests of specific groups, domestic full employment, economic development, and balance of payments equilibrium.

3.   A variety of forms of trade controls are utilized by national governments. These are sometimes categorized as either tariffs or nontariff barriers.

4.   Tariffs are taxes levied on goods as they cross the boundaries of a nation. These taxes are levied either as a means of raising revenue or to protect domestic industries against foreign competition.

5.   The intended effects of a protective tariff may be unrealized due

to absorption of the tariff or inelastic demand for the product in the tariff-levying country.

6.   Nontariff barriers to trade include quantitative limits on imports or exports (quotas) and a multitude of other governmental policies or actions that affect such imports or exports.

7.   Quotas generally provide much more certain and inflexible protection from import competition than do tariffs.

8.   Nontariff barriers have become an increasingly significant type of trade restriction as tariffs have been progressively reduced through international negotiations. The great number and variety of these nontariff barriers have made them difficult to deal with through international negotiations.

Questions for Review or Discussion

1.   Explain the supposed conflict between free international trade and national security.

2.   Define "protectionism" and explain the dilemma national governments face with respect to the anticipated costs and benefits associated with the freeing of trade with the rest of the world.

3.   What is the major problem connected with the use of import restrictions as a means of increasing domestic employment?

4.   Explain and evaluate the infant industry argument for trade restrictions.

5.   How does the elasticity of demand for imported products influence the effectiveness of a protective tariff?

6.   Compare and contrast the economic effects of an import quota with those of a tariff on imports.

7.   Explain the difference between the nominal duty rate and the effective duty rate with regard to an import tariff.

8.   Why have nontariff barriers proved to be very difficult to deal with in terms of international negotiations for their reduction or elimination?

Case

Fair or Free Trade with the Japanese?

On July 18, 1853, U.S. Navy Commodore Matthew Perry sailed into Tokyo Bay with a fleet of four American warships armed and ready for action. He demanded (unsuccessfully) that the Japanese government sign an agreement ending more than 200 years or self-imposed isolation from Western trade and contact. Perry returned the following February with even more warships and demanded an answer. Within a few weeks, the Japanese signed a treaty opening two ports to the Americans.

Hoping to accomplish a similar feat, in the spring of 1985 members of the U.S. Congress were introducing bills aimed at slowing or stopping the Japanese penetration of U.S. markets, while the U.S. House and Senate passed nonbinding resolutions urging Japan to open its markets to U.S. goods. The reasons for the lawmaker's ire was a record high U.S. trade deficit of $123 billion ($37 billion with Japan alone) in 1984 and the expiration, with the administration's blessing, of the 1981 "voluntary" import quota on Japanese-made cars. Imported automobiles accounted for a record 30 percent of the U.S. market in July 1985. "Millions of American workers have lost jobs while the Reagan administration and several of its recent predecessors sat idly by, mouthing the rhetoric of free trade," said Representative John Dingell, the Michigan Democrat (as quoted in the April 7, 1985 Detroit *Free Press*). Reflecting the sentiments of a number of his colleagues, he added, "Unless we do something, we can look forward to the substantial decline of the domestic automobile industry and the continued de-industrialization of the United States." Lawmakers in the Senate echo these feelings. "Boekisen" says one Senator. "An eye for an eye" says another. In Japanese or in English, they mean the same thing: trade war.

Economic studies have repeatedly shown that trade restriction rarely benefits a country and during the recent (1981–1984) quota on Japanese automobile imports into the United States, the Japanese raised prices and made more money on fewer cars than in the prequota days. The United States has a strong tradition of supporting free trade and most Americans feel that protectionism can result in higher prices. However, by overwhelming margins, Americans now support measures to restrict imports to save U.S. jobs. For example, in a CBS News/*New York Times* national survey taken May 29–June 2, 1985, 70 percent of the respondents answered affirmatively when asked the question, "Would it be a good idea to put limits on imports of foreign products?" Only 20 percent thought it would be a bad idea (Fig. 6.1).

Critics of Japanese trade practices say that Japan closes its markets to U.S.-made goods while flooding the United States with its products. Almost every lawmaker has a story to support this contention, for example, a U.S. telephone parts supplier who was permitted to sell his product in Japan but was allowed to advertise only in English, or a U.S. spark plug manufacturer who complained that Japanese automobile inspectors would only pass cars with the brand of Japanese spark plugs that were used as original equipment.

The Japanese take the U.S. reaction seriously and are lobbying hard (1984 expenditures of approximately $14 million) to offset the protectionist mood in the United States. They see different reasons for the mounting U.S. trade deficit. They feel that the U.S. dollar has greatly and rapidly increased in value (nearly 50 percent) over the last few years, making U.S. exports very expensive and imports inexpensive.

Figure 6.1   Are Quotas Acceptable?

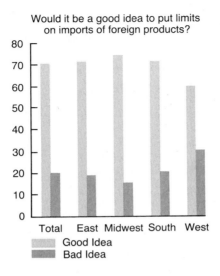

Would it be a good idea to put limits
on imports of foreign products?

Good Idea
Bad Idea

Total   East Midwest South West

Source: CBS News/*New York Times* national survey May 29–June 2, 1985. Reprinted from *Japan Economic Survey* (August 1985): 13.

They also contend that most U.S. manufacturers who are unsuccessful in Japan do not make a long-term commitment to the Japanese market.

Some Americans agree with these Japanese contentions and also argue that the normal American style of doing business is very different from what is needed for success in Japan and often comes across as impatient, overly legalistic, and brusque. They point out that compared to the number of Japanese who are relatively comfortable with the English language and Western culture, very few Americans know the Japanese language or culture. Despite these obstacles, Japanese imports last year (1984) from the United States rose 27 percent in computers, 29 percent in communication equipment, 32 percent in office equipment, and 50 percent in semiconductors, according to the Japanese Embassy in Washington.

Furthermore, the Japanese have invested $14.8 billion in the United States, creating more than 100,000 jobs, with additional investments planned and underway. In addition, the Japanese are also making significant portfolio investments in the United States and are helping to fund the U.S. federal deficit by buying U.S. government securities. The Japanese are also the largest importers of U.S. agricultural products ($5 billion in 1984). Furthermore, the Japanese proclaim that they buy the same amount of American goods as Americans buy of Japanese goods.

Figure 6.2   ***Consumer Spending and United States–Japan Trade***
(in 1984 dollars per person)

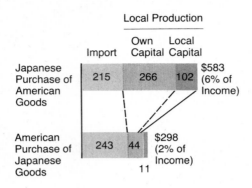

Note: Estimates by McKinsey based on MITI (Ministry of International Trade and Industry) and Commerce Department statistics.

Source: Japan Economic Journal, June 18, 1985, 24.

Figure 6.3   ***Presence of America and Japan in Each Other's***
Marketplace—1984

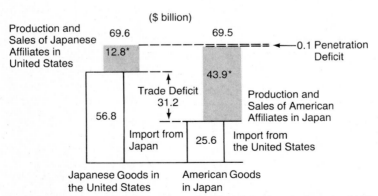

*Portion Represented by Actual Equity Position: Americans in Japan = 31.70
                                            Japanese in the United States = 10.24

This assertion is based on adding American goods made in Japan to American goods made in America and imported by the Japanese, and vice versa (i.e., adding Japanese goods made in America to Japanese goods made in Japan and imported, for the total amount of Japanese goods bought in the United States [Figs. 6.2 and 6.3]).

Should President Reagan support legislation protecting U.S. markets and businesses from Japanese imports? If so, what are the relative merits of quotas versus tariffs and other protective measures available to the U.S. government?

Sources: "Most Americans Support Protectionism," *Japan Economic Survey*, August 1985, p. 13; Eduardo Lachia, "Japanese Are Lobbying Hard in U.S. to Offset Big Protectionist Push," *The Wall Street Journal*, August 23, 1985, pp. 1, 5; Art Pine, "Protectionism Appeals To House and Senate But Faces Big Hurdles," *The Wall Street Journal*, July 31, 1984, pp. 1+; Ken Fireman, "Japanese Remember U.S. Gunboat Diplomacy: Trade Threats Recall Days of U.S. Gunboats," *Detroit Free Press*, April 7, 1985, pp. 1B, 4B; Charles Green, "U.S.-Japan High Noon on Trade," *Detroit Free Press*, April 7, 1985, p. 1B; Hobart Rowen, "Low Point in Japan-Bashing," *The Washington Post*, August 1, 1985, p. A19; and Ellen Hume, "Many Americans Put Blame for Import Ills on Both Japan, U.S.," *The Wall Street Journal*, October 11, 1985, pp. 1, 10.

Chapter 7

INTERNATIONAL TRADE POLICIES: THE ROLE OF THE UNITED STATES

Chapter Objectives

- To trace the historical development of the international trade policies of the United States and to show how this country has influenced the course of international trade policy for the world as a whole
- To describe the background and provisions of the General Agreement on Tariffs and Trade (GATT) and to indicate how it has affected international trade practices and relationships
- To identify and analyze major current issues and controversies in trade policy
- To explain how a failure to resolve those trade issues through international negotiations might jeopardize the continued expansion of international trade and the economic benefits that have resulted from progress in liberalizing trade

As the largest economy and the single biggest exporter and importer among the nations of the world, the United States exerts a considerable effect on the volume and growth of international trade. For the past half-century, the United States has also been a leader in formulating and implementing international agreements relating to the conduct of trade. Thus, the rules and understandings that currently govern international commerce are, to a considerable extent, a reflection of American attitudes regarding the desirability of free trade and appropriate trading procedures and relationships.

This chapter is devoted to an examination of contemporary international trade policies, and will emphasize the role of the United States in fashioning the present global trade regime. The first section will trace the historical development of U.S. trade policies. In order to stay within reasonable limits of time and space, it will only describe the main thrust of those policies and highlight a few of the major legislative acts and multilateral arrangements that are representative of America's viewpoints and influence. In the section Contemporary Trade Policy Issues, there will be a discussion of the more significant and controversial trade problems that have yet to be resolved by international negotiations and agreements.

U.S. International Trade Policies

1930–1950: From Hawley–Smoot to the General Agreement on Tariffs and Trade

The early years of the 1930s witnessed the birth of modern U.S. international trade policy. Those years witnessed a significant turning point in the general orientation of U.S. trade policies, as well as the emergence of American leadership in shaping such policies for the world as a whole. Until that time, the United States had maintained a basically protectionist and inward-looking stance with regard to international trade. It had begun putting high duties on imports shortly after winning its independence, partly for revenue purposes, but also as a means of protecting its developing manufacturing industries from European competition. For the next 150 years, the American tariff continued to serve as a substantial barrier against imports and as a symbol of the nation's inclination to limit its economic ties with the rest of the world.

This protectionist-isolationist philosophy reached its peak in the decade following the First World War, and this was manifested in U.S. trade legislation adopted during that period. In 1930, the U.S. government enacted the Hawley–Smoot Tariff Act, which set import duties at historically high levels and greatly extended the range of products covered by such duties. This blatantly protectionist act, coming at a time when virtually every industrialized country was beginning to experience the downturns in employment and economic activity that signaled the onset of the Great Depression, brought about a wave of retaliatory import restrictions that sharply curtailed world trade and greatly aggravated the worldwide economic crisis.

Within a matter of months after the Hawley–Smoot Tariff was enacted, many American business leaders, government officials, and academic economists were pointing out its serious adverse consequences and calling for changes in the country's trade policies. Those arguments and pleas were heard by the new administration of President Franklin D. Roosevelt, which was searching desperately for ways to counteract the horrendous economic malady that had gripped the nation. In 1934, Congress, prodded by the Roosevelt administration, passed the Reciprocal Trade Agreements (RTA) Act as an amendment to the Hawley–Smoot Tariff Act. The RTA Act was a complex piece of legislation, but its most important provisions empowered the President (i.e., the executive branch of the U.S. government) to undertake negotiations with foreign governments aimed toward the reciprocal reduction of import tariffs. The act also specified that agreements arrived at through such negotiations were to include an **unconditional most-favored-nation (MFN) clause.** The inclusion of such clauses would automatically extend any tariff reductions that the United States either granted or received by bargaining with any one foreign nation to all other nations with which the United States had trade agreements. The MFN provision thus constituted a powerful instrument for spreading the liberalizing effects of tariff reductions beyond the nations that initially and directly negotiated them.

The RTA Act launched the United States on a course directed toward freer trade with the rest of the world. Progress in that direction was interrupted by the outbreak of the Second World War, but, even while that conflict was still going on, U.S. government officials and economists were meeting with their counterparts in other countries to lay plans for the postwar reconstruction and revitalization of the world economy. Those efforts resulted in some dramatic achievements, including the establishment of the International Monetary Fund (IMF) and the International Bank for Reconstruction and Development (the IBRD, which now is commonly called the World Bank). The basic mission of those institutions, both of which began operations in 1946, was to facilitate worldwide economic recovery and growth. The IMF was to concentrate on maintaining a stable international monetary system, while the IBRD was to help provide long-term financing to countries that were endeavoring to rebuild or develop their economies.[1]

The plans and negotiations in which the United States was involved in the latter years of World War II and the immediate postwar period were also concerned with expanding international trade. It was anticipated that another international institution, to be called the International Trade Organization (ITO) would be established to encourage and oversee world trade. The ITO never came into being, but many of the basic principles that were to have governed its activities were brought into effect through the **General Agreement on Tariffs and Trade (GATT).** That agreement was entered into by the United States and several other countries in early 1948, and has since become the main facilitator of international efforts to increase and liberalize trade.

The General Agreement on Tariffs and Trade

The GATT is a unique mixture of several elements. It began as a document that listed the tariff reductions that had been negotiated by 23 nations at a conference held in Geneva, Switzerland in the summer of 1947. More importantly, that document set forth certain rules the con-

---

[1]These international organizations will be treated in greater detail in Chapters 10 and 11.

ferees had agreed to observe in their future commercial dealings with one another. Those rules, with some subsequent additions and amendments, comprise the basic provisions of the GATT.

The most important GATT provisions are: (1) a commitment on the part of each member country (technically referred to as a "contracting party" to the General Agreement) to treat all other member countries in a nondiscriminatory manner with regard to the taxation and regulation of trade. This effectively obligates each GATT member to accord MFN treatment to every other member. Exceptions to this nondiscrimination rule are permitted for countries that have had long-standing preferential trading arrangements with one another and for countries that join together in regional economic integration programs; (2) prohibitions against the use of quantitative controls on trade, except for certain specified purposes or circumstances; (3) an obligation to enter into tariff-cutting negotiations requested by another member country and to maintain all agreed-upon tariff reductions. The intent of these requirements is to ensure that GATT members are willing to bargain in good faith for tariff cuts and to make agreed-upon cuts permanently binding. Exceptions are also permitted here, however, in the form of **escape clauses** which allow a nation to modify or rescind a tariff concession that has resulted in serious economic injury to a domestic industry.

These provisions and the others contained in the General Agreement constitute a kind of free-trade and fair-trade manifesto, through which the contracting parties declare their intent to work toward the elimination of barriers to trade and to behave in an open and impartial manner in their commercial relationships with one another. The agreement also specifies how member nations should proceed to liberalize trade, including specific measures. The GATT thus has great significance as a treatylike document, whose terms have now been accepted by 90 countries which collectively account for approximately 85 percent of total world trade.

In addition to treatylike elements, the GATT also provides an organizational framework for the resolution of differences among nations relating to trade issues, and for the negotiation of trade concessions (i.e., reductions in tariffs or other trade restrictions). An important aspect of this function of the GATT is that concessions negotiated by any of the member countries—including those arrived at by pairs of countries bargaining with each other on a bilateral basis—are automatically extended to all other GATT members through the application of the MFN principle. This both expedites trade negotiations and greatly enlarges the scope of agreements reached, by effectively making all such agreements **multilateral** in their coverage.

The GATT has achieved considerable success as a forum for negotiating reductions in trade barriers. A total of seven major negotiating sessions (known as "rounds" in GATT parlance) have been held by the member countries since the inception of GATT, and the last two of these—the "Kennedy Round," which lasted from 1963 to 1967, and the

"Tokyo Round," which got underway in 1973 and was concluded in 1979—were especially productive. Largely as a consequence of these negotiating rounds and other agreements reached through the GATT, import tariffs on manufactured products have been lowered to such an extent that they no longer constitute a serious impediment to trade. GATT negotiations and agreements have been less successful, however, in dealing with governmental controls affecting trade in agricultural products and in doing away with nontariff barriers to trade.

The GATT has its shortcomings. As was noted above, the GATT is replete with exceptions to its rules and principles. Moreover, the enforceability of those rules and principles is a questionable matter, since the means through which members can be penalized for violating them are cumbersome and vague, and in the last analysis, depend upon the willingness of the member countries to accept penalties or offer redress.

The GATT has also been criticized by Third World countries which have charged it with promoting the interests of the wealthier and more advanced nations and with perpetuating trade policies that do not support the developmental aspirations of the poorer countries. In 1965, an effort was made to respond to these charges and make the GATT more responsive to the needs of the developing countries, when a new section on trade and development was added to the GATT. This section committed the developed countries to opening their markets more fully to exports from the developing countries. This commitment was not unequivocal or binding, however, and the steps that the richer countries have since taken to fulfill it have not convinced the Third World nations that the GATT constitutes an effective means to improve their international trade position.

Despite its weaknesses and the charges leveled at it by critics, the GATT has been a strongly positive force in the international economy, and its existence has unquestionably accelerated the movement toward freer world trade. Inasmuch as the United States was one of the principal architects of the GATT and has continued to be one of its staunchest supporters, U.S. interntional trade policies have been closely linked to the objectives, principles, and procedures that are embodied in the GATT.

U.S. Trade Policies Since 1950

The 1950s witnessed a resurgence of protectionist sentiment in the United States and a backlash against the trade-liberalization orientation represented by the RTA Act. Each time that act came up for Congress for review and extension, amendments were added to it which constricted the president's authority to negotiate further tariff reductions with foreign countries and required the inclusion of escape clauses in whatever trade agreements were negotiated. By the end of the decade, the legislative base for U.S. initiatives in removing trade barriers had been severely eroded.

This transpired at the same time that certain developments in the international economy were making further efforts to liberalize trade more important and urgent. The most significant of these developments was the economic integration movement in Western Europe. In the late 1950s, the Western European nations formed two regional economic unions, the European Economic Community (the EEC, which initially was known as the European Common Market) and the European Free Trade Association (EFTA). The EEC was made up of France, Italy, West Germany, Belgium, The Netherlands, and Luxembourg, while EFTA included the United Kingdom, Norway, Sweden, Denmark, Austria, Switzerland, and Portugal.[2]

As was noted in Chapter 4, the emergence of those economic groupings—especially the EEC, which was the stronger and more tightly integrated of the two—posed a formidable challenge to the United States. The fundamental issue was whether the integrated European countries would turn inward and attempt to form a self-sufficient economic bloc that would be an unfriendly rival to the United States, or whether they would join in cooperative endeavors to expand trade and investment throughout the Free World. That issue was of critical importance to the United States, not only because it wished to maintain its political alliances with the Western European nations in opposition to the spread of communist influence, but also because Western Europe was a major market for U.S. exports and promised to become an even larger and more affluent market as the integration movement progressed.

The United States was therefore in a predicament at the beginning of the 1960s, since its ability to bargain with other nations for mutual reductions of trade barriers had practically vanished just when America needed to discourage Western European nations from protectionism. In an effort to resolve that predicament, the Kennedy administration asked Congress for new trade legislation to replace the virtually defunct RTA Act. Congress responded by passing the **Trade Expansion Act (TEA)** of 1962.

The core of the TEA was the renewed and enlarged authority given the president to reduce U.S. import duties in exchange for reciprocal reductions by other countries. The TEA permitted reductions of up to 50 pecent of those duty rates in general, but it provided for even greater reductions on goods produced primarily by the United States and the EEC countries. This and other provisions of the TEA clearly indicated that the principal aim of the act was to provide a basis for trade agreements between the United States and the EEC.

The TEA also contained some innovative provisions, including the initiation of a **trade adjustment assistance program** in the United States.

---

[2]The European integration movement will be more thoroughly examined in Chapter 9.

The basic idea involved in such a program is that the government should assist domestic firms and workers in adjusting to the intensified competition created by the removal of protective trade barriers, rather than maintaining such barriers and thereby depriving the public of the benefits of freer trade. The TEA ostensibly made such assistance—in the form of technical and financial aid to business firms, and retraining and relocation allowances to workers—available to American companies or employees that were injured by import competition. However, it made the requirements for obtaining such assistance so stringent that U.S. companies and workers found it virtually impossible to qualify.

The passage of the TEA set the stage for another round of multilateral trade negotiations under the auspices of the GATT. Those negotiations, called the **Kennedy Round** in honor of the assassinated American president, involved more than 50 countries and lasted from 1963 until 1967. The principal achievement was a cut of approximately 35 percent in tariffs on industrial products, but a start was also made in attacking nontariff barriers and governmental restraints on trade in agricultural products.

The TEA expired at the same time that the Kennedy Round was concluded in mid-1967, and this left a vacuum in U.S. trade policies that protectionist interests rushed to fill. During the 5 years following the Kennedy Round, the Congress was swamped with lobbyists and legislative bills proposing stricter controls on foreign trade. One of those bills, referred to as the Burke–Hartke bill after its principal Congressional sponsors, called for the establishment of sweeping and stringent restrictions on both imports and foreign direct investment by American companies. Congress gave very serious consideration to the Burke–Hartke bill, but it ultimately failed to pass, due in part to its having become too drastically protectionist for the majority of Congressional members to swallow.

Congress did eventually pass a new trade bill, known simply as the **Trade Act of 1974.** That act seemed to symbolize the ambivalence which members of Congress and other government officials were feeling toward international trade and trade policies at the time. Some of its provisions supported renewed U.S. attempts to liberalize trade. They gave the president the tariff-cutting authority needed to participate in still another round of GATT negotiations and also set up procedures that made it easier for nontariff barriers to be reduced or eliminated. But the act also included many provisions designed to "safeguard" the United States against unfair trade practices by foreign nations and trade agreements or relationships that proved detrimental to this country. The Trade Act of 1974 also loosened the requirements that American industries and workers had to meet in order to obtain relief from the injurious effects of foreign competition. Such relief could come either through the imposition (or reimposition) of controls on imports, or through various types of adjustment assistance.

The negotiating authority contained in the Trade Act of 1974 was the basis for U.S. participation in the seventh round of GATT negotiations. Ninety-nine countries, including several that were not members of the GATT, took part in those negotiations, which were known as the **Tokyo Round.** When the Tokyo Round finally ended in 1979, it had achieved some very substantial results including:

1. Pledges on the part of the industrialized countries to reduce their import tariffs by an average of about one-third. Those reductions were expected to affect approximately $110 billion of trade in industrial goods and $12 billion of trade in agricultural goods.

2. The establishment of codes of conduct to govern the use of nontariff barriers (NTBs) and presumably to lead to their systematic reduction. The adoption of those codes represented the first multilateral agreement on a comprehensive means of curbing the use of NTBs.

3. An agreement that sanctioned the use of preferential trade arrangements to assist the developing countries. Although such preferential arrangements had existed before, they had been regarded as temporary departures from the GATT principles of nondiscrimination and reciprocity. The Tokyo Round agreement recognized that the Third World countries needed more permanent assurances of access to export markets in order to justify and support the development of new industries.

4. Improvements in the procedures through which nations notify and consult with one another regarding contemplated trade policy changes, and in the means available for settling trade disputes.[3]

Notwithstanding its impressive achievements, the Tokyo Round left some crucial trade problems unresolved. The United States, under pressure from its deteriorating trade balance and international competitive position, took the initiative again in the early 1980s and began lobbying for yet another round of multilateral negotiations to address those problems. In preparation for such negotiations, Congress passed an international trade bill known as the **Trade and Tariff Act of 1984,** which President Reagan signed into law in October of that year.

This act extended the participation of the United States in the Generalized System of Preferences (GSP), which grants preferential duty rates for imports from the developing countries. It also authorized the president to negotiate a free trade agreement between the United States and Israel. A chief purpose of the act was to establish the legal basis for future actions, including involvement in GATT negotiations, by means of which the United States could deal with some serious threats to its economic health and to the preservation of harmonious economic and political relationships among the world's nations. These issues will be analyzed briefly in the following section.

[3]"Complex Conclusions of Tokyo Round Add up to Framework for Future Trade," *IMF Survey* (May 7, 1979): 133–137.

Box 7.1

A U.S.–European Food Fight

After the U.S. government recently slapped a 25 to 40 percent increase in duties on pasta imported from the European Economic Community, enraged Community officials countered with a massive tariff hike on American lemons and walnuts. The outbreak of hostilities in this "pasta war" may scuttle U.S. hopes of launching a new round of global trade talks among GATT member nations in 1986. Those talks could cover issues ranging from trade in industrial and agricultural products to services such as banking and insurance.

Whether or not the latest flap scuttles such talks (which the Europeans have not been keen on in the first place), U.S. officials are fed up with what they regard as European intransigence over barriers to U.S. agricultural trade with the Community.

Source: "Pasta Wars Make It Harder to Talk Turkey on Trade," *Business Week* (July 15, 1985), 35.

Contemporary Trade Policy Issues

Agricultural Trade

Agricultural trade is one of the problem areas in international commerce and causes considerable friction among trading nations. A principal root of this problem is the provision by many nations, including the United States, of subsidies and other forms of assistance to their agricultural sectors. The reasons for this special assistance are varied and complex, and will not be presented here. In terms of trade policy, it is significant that agricultural support programs almost invariably necessitate the use of import controls and/or devices to stimulate agricultural exports. A nation that is bolstering the prices its agricultural producers receive for their output cannot simultaneously permit unrestricted importation of agricultural commodities, as this would either undercut the supported prices or require the nation to effectively subsidize foreign agricultural producers as well as its own farmers. It is likely that domestic agriculture price-support programs will result in a larger output of farm products than the nation can consume domestically, thereby tempting the nation to "dump" some of the surplus in foreign markets.

Trade in agricultural goods has thus become a prime target of governmental intervention, and governments have been especially reluctant to dismantle the mechanisms they have used to manipulate such trade. The rounds of trade negotiations that have occurred under the GATT have had only a very modest effect on these mechanisms, and they remain a serious issue of contention in international trade relationships.

The developing countries have long protested the combination of domestic price supports and import limitations maintained by the developed nations, asserting that this artificially stimulates agricultural production within the advanced nations. This is viewed as severely detrimental to the ability of the Third World countries to export their own agricultural commodities.

The developed nations—notably the United States and the EEC members—have also been at odds with each other over this issue. Both the United States and the EEC maintain elaborate agricultural price support programs, which have resulted in massive surpluses in recent years. This has led to accusations between these two economic superpowers regarding each one's utilization of import restrictions and export subsidies to protect its own agricultural sectors, while disposing of excess output in world markets.

Trade in Services

International trade policies historically have been directed almost solely toward merchandise trade. In recent years, however, there has been a rapid increase in international trade in services, which (broadly speaking) occurs whenever services are provided to residents of one country by business firms or individuals that are residents of another country. The types of services that now figure prominently in such trade include: (1) banking and financial services; (2) insurance; (3) transportation of both freight and passengers; (4) construction, engineering, and architectural services; (5) communications-related services, for example, films, recordings, data processing, printing; (6) professional services, for example, health, legal, accounting, and educational services.[4]

The rapid growth of international trade in these areas has raised serious concerns about the need for policies applicable to such transactions. The development of policies through international negotiations poses a formidable challenge, however, due to the large volume and disparate nature of the activities involved, the difficulties of measuring the value or "output" of such activities as a basis for determining acceptable levels of protection or reciprocal concessions, and the lack of precedents to guide such negotiations.

---

[4]"International Trade in Services is Under Study in Various Forums," *IMF Survey* (May 21, 1984): 145 ff.

Moreover, the desirability of setting international rules to govern trade in services has become a subject of controversy. The United States, which is the largest exporter of services to other countries, has been strongly advocating that the nondiscrimination and "free trade" rules of the GATT be extended to cover international service transactions. But the developing countries have resisted such a move, fearing that it would expose their fledgling service industries to overwhelming competition from the United States and other developed nations. As a consequence of these complications and controversy, progress in formulating international accords relative to trade in services is lagging far behind the expansion of such trade.

Countertrade

Countertrade is a broad term applied to trade and other international business transactions that involve **barter,** that is, the exchange of goods for other goods. Although barter was the earliest form of trade, it was almost entirely displaced by the use of money and credit during the past millenium. Barter has made a strong comeback in recent years, however, and it is estimated that countertrade now accounts for as much as 25 to 30 percent of total world trade.

The revival of barter has been attributed mainly to the difficulties that many nations—notably in Eastern Europe and the Third World—have experienced in trying to develop cash markets for their exportable products. Such difficulties have, in turn, made it hard for those countries to accumulate sufficient foreign currency to pay cash for their imports. The solution they have adopted is to insist upon bartering. Foreign firms wishing to sell anything to these countries have been required to accept products in exchange, rather than receiving monetary payments.

This has complicated the jobs of the managers of the supplying firms considerably, as they have had to accept compensation in goods having an uncertain value. They have then had to sell or otherwise dispose of those goods, often without any prior experience in marketing the kinds of products involved. But the fierce competition for international markets has compelled them to engage in barter deals, despite such added complications.

In addition to the problems it has created for business firms and managers, the resurgence of countertrade has been criticized as a dangerous departure from a free and open system of trade among nations. Many countertrade agreements between governments cover a series of transactions extending over several years. The effect of these agreements is to prevent firms from other countries from competing in the markets encompassed by such arrangements. Countertrade agreements may also be used as a device for "dumping," which refers to offering surplus output in foreign markets for less than its domestic market price or cost of production. Most nations have laws to discourage such dump-

Box 7.2

Instances of Countertrade

Counterpurchase: A set of parallel cash sales agreements in which a supplier sells a plant or product and orders unrelated products to offset the cost to the buyer.

Canada is buying McDonnell Douglas F-18 aircraft worth $2.4 billion. In return, the company will help Canada find customers for goods and services worth $2.9 billion.

Yugoslavia requires auto makers to buy Yugoslav goods equal in value to components they ship to Yugoslav auto plants. Fiat buys autos from its Yugoslav Licensee.

Brazil asked bidders on a $130 million space satellite for pledges to export Brazil's goods. Canada's Spar Aerospace won jointly with Hughes Aircraft and will arrange imports of Brazilian products of equal value into Canada.

Iraq is buying frigates worth $1.5 billion from Italy's state-owned Italcantieri. In payment, Italy's state oil company will take Iraqi crude.

Russia is buying construction machinery from Japan's Komatsu and Mitsubishi. The Japanese are taking Siberian timber.

Colombia is asking equipment suppliers to buy its coffee. A Spanish government company did so in return for Colombia's purchase of buses from Spain's ENESA.

Buyback: Under a separate agreement to the sale of a plant, the supplier agrees to purchase part of the plant's output for up to 20 years.

Russia is buying phosphates from Occidental Petroleum. In a $20 billion deal, Oxy helped the Soviets build ammonia plants and is buying part of the output.

China awarded a $500 million contract in Italy's Tecnotrade to expand mines and modernize a railroad. Tecnotrade agreed to buy coal for sale abroad.

Clearing agreement: An exchange of products between two governments to achieve an agreed-on value of trade, tabulated in non-convertible 'clearing account units.'

Russia rationed hard currency for copier imports. So Britain's Rank Xerox is making copiers in India for sale to Moscow under Russia's 'clearing' agreement with India.

Source: "New Restrictions on World Trade," p. 119. Reprinted from the July 19, 1982 issue of *Business Week* by special permission, © 1982 by McGraw-Hill, Inc.

ing, but the absence of stated prices in countertrade deals interferes with the enforcement of those laws. Another criticism of countertrade is that it gives an unwarranted advantage to very large international companies (such as the giant Japanese trading combines) which have the worldwide marketing organizations and experience to handle such dealings.

These criticisms have not yet resulted in any concerted attempts to develop international policies pertaining to countertrade. However, both the U.S. government and the Organization for Economic Cooperation and Development, whose membership includes all the major noncommunist industrialized nations, have registered serious concerns over the spread of countertrade and its potential detrimental effects. It therefore appears highly probable that this "new" approach to trade and trading relationships will be the focus of increasing attention and will ultimately have to be addressed through global trade policy negotiations.

Safeguards

The use of **safeguards** constitutes another contentious issue. This term refers to a variety of measures—such as new, possibly higher import duties or quantitative limits on imports—employed by nations to prevent foreign competition from causing excessive injury to a particular domestic industry. The prerogative of a country to utilize safeguards is recognized in the GATT, but that prerogative is subject to several conditions and was intended to be exercised sparingly. However, the rising tempo of global competition in recent years has caused nations to resort to the use of safeguards more and more frequently. The United States and Western Europe have been particularly prone to adopt safeguards to insulate their aging "smokestack" industries against competition from each other, from the Japanese, and from manufacturing industries located in the newly industrialized developing countries.

There are at least two aspects to the safeguard controversy. First, there is a dispute over "technical" questions, such as what types of safeguard measures are permissible, whether nations can employ those measures selectively (i.e., against imports from one particular foreign source), and what conditions should be fulfilled to justify their imposition or retention. As in the case of agricultural trade, the United States, the EEC nations, and the developing countries all have different views regarding these questions and therefore are at loggerheads over them.

Second, underlying these technical questions are deeper concerns having to do with the extent to which safeguards can be utilized before they become the norm, rather than the exception, and the world's nations begin to backslide into rampant protectionism. Such concerns, which permeate all aspects of international trade policy, have become more widespread and pronounced as the severe economic recession of the late 1970s has persisted into the early 1980s. The general stagnation of economic activity and rising unemployment intensified international competition for stable or shrinking markets and simultaneously made individual nations acutely sensitive to the potentially adverse effects of foreign competition upon their already weakened domestic economies.

In this environment, the survival of the existing international trading system has itself become a critical issue. That system, symbolized by the GATT and by the willingness of most nations to move toward freer trade, is facing as grave a challenge now as any it has encountered since its founding after World War II. Not only are nations increasingly taking advantage of safeguards and like measures incorporated in the GATT in order to reestablish protective barriers against foreign competition, but they also are making greater use of bilateral trade agreements. Such agreements between two nations or two groups of nations may strike a satisfactory compromise between the protective urges of one participant and the marketing drives of the other, but they typically do so at the expense of third countries. In addition, bilateral trade agreements militate against the multilateralism that has characterized the trade liberalization movement.

That movement and the trading system in which it is embodied have served the world economy well, as both world economic output and international trade have expanded at unprecedented rates during the post–World War II era. But the trade liberalization movement and its institutional support system have always been fragile, and their perpetuation has depended upon the goodwill and determination of individual nations. The slackening of the upward trend of economic growth and prosperity that those nations have recently experienced is seriously testing that goodwill and determination, and it remains to be seen whether the United States and its trading partners will continue to participate in international free trade.

Summary

1. The United States has been a leader in efforts to liberalize international trade since the early 1930s, although the U.S. commitment to such trade liberalization has occasionally faltered as import competition has aggravated domestic economic downturns.

2. The General Agreement on Tariffs and Trade was adopted in 1948 as a set of rules to be followed by nations in their commercial relationships. The GATT has also provided a framework and forum for multilateral efforts to reduce restrictions upon international trade.

3. The so-called Tokyo Round of trade negotiations under GATT

auspices, which was concluded in 1979, resulted in a substantial reduction of tariffs and the establishment of codes of conduct to deal with nontariff barriers.

4.   However, the conclusion of the Tokyo Round left several serious international trade issues unresolved. These include agricultural trade, which has been a very complicated problem due to extensive governmental involvement in agricultural production in many countries of the world.

5.   Trade in services has been expanding very rapidly in recent years, and controversy has emerged over the need for international policies to govern such trade.

6.   Countertrade, which involves the bartering of goods for goods, is another rapidly growing and potentially troublesome form of trade that is not covered by multilateral trade policies.

7.   The use of safeguards to prevent foreign competition from injuring domestic producers has been increasing as economic growth has faltered in many parts of the world. Excessive reliance upon such safeguards could undermine the progress that has been made in freeing international trade during the post–World War II era.

Questions for Review or Discussion

1.   Explain why the passage of the Reciprocal Trade Agreement Act in 1934 is regarded as a historic turning point in U.S. international trade policy.

2.   What is the meaning and significance of the unconditional most-favored-nation concept in relation to international trade policy?

3.   What are the major provisions included in the General Agreement on Tariffs and Trade?

4.   How did the formation of the European Economic Community influence U.S. international trade policies?

5.   Explain the underlying philosophy and operation of trade adjustment assistance programs.

6.   Why has trade in agricultural products proved to be a particularly difficult problem in terms of trade relationships among nations and the formulation of international trade policies?

7.   Why is it likely to be more difficult to develop international agreements relating to trade in services than it has been for merchandise trade?

8.   How might countertrade conflict with the ideal of an open and freely competitive international trade system?

9.   Why does the use of safeguards present a threat to the continuation of the movement toward free international trade?

Case

The Semiconductor Industry

John Ricks, the vice-president of international operations for Advanced Microprocessors Inc., of Sunnyvale, California, was considering whether to recommend for or against a proposal to enlarge the firm's Singapore assembly plant. As a diversified producer of a wide range of microchips, American Microprocessors faces a rapidly changing business environment in the semiconductor industry. American Microprocessor owns chip plants in the United States, Singapore, Bangkok, and Mexico and joint-venture chip plants in Korea and India. Its production of semiconductor chips ranges from "commodity" products like 64-k and 256-k memory chips, and 8-, 16-, and 32-bit microprocessor chips, to sophisticated semicustom chips. As a U.S. producer, it faces domestic and, increasingly, international competition in each area.

Historically, the semiconductor industry has grown rapidly, chalking up an average annual sales growth of 20 percent. However, the industry has also suffered from boom–bust cycles that periodically drive many of the weaker firms out of business. Currently, in the fall of 1985, the industry is undergoing another downturn caused by sales of personal microcomputers that are far below projections.

Companies in the semiconductor chip industry can be divided into two categories. The first category of companies includes those that produce chips primarily for use in their own products. U.S. companies like IBM, Motorola, and AT&T, and Japanese companies like NEC, Hitachi, and Fujitsu are examples of such companies. Some of these companies also produce chips for sale to other firms like the companies in the second group. The second group includes companies such as Texas Instruments, Intel, and National Semiconductor. In terms of chips sold to others, the four largest companies (with over $2 billion in 1984 sales) are Texas Instruments, Nippon Electric Company (NEC), Motorola, and Hitachi. They are followed by the four second-largest firms (with 1984 sales of between $1 and $2 billion), Intel, Fujitsu, National Semiconductor, and Matsushita. As these lists show, the Japanese and United States companies dominate the global market for traded chips.

Between them, United States and Japanese companies control over 90 percent of the World's $26 billion (1984) semiconductor chip market. However, the Japanese share has been increasing steadily. In 1978 the U.S. and Japanese shares were 62 percent and 24 percent, respectively; while in 1984 these shares had changed to 50 percent and 40 percent, respectively. This competition is likely to become more intense as major investments made recently by Japanese and Korean companies in chip production lines come onstream and achieve their production levels.

New competition in the low end of the chip business is already coming from some of the developing countries. In 1984, Korea's four big electronic companies, Lucky-Goldstar, Samsung, Hyundai, and Daewoo shipped $1 billion of semiconductor chips and are investing heavily to upgrade and increase their chip capacity. Other countries in South and Southeast Asia, including Taiwan with its United Microelectronics and other corporations, are also stepping up their investments in chip production lines. The Japanese, who currently dominate the memory chip market with an estimated 86 percent of the 256-k chip market and 60 percent of the overall memory chip market in 1985, are likely to bear the brunt of most of this emerging competition. This will increasingly force them to compete more heavily with the United States in the mid or high sectors of the semiconductor chip market, that is, the markets for microprocessor and semicustom chips. The Japanese chip companies continue to invest heavily in research and development (R&D) (20 percent of sales) and in new capital equipment (30 percent of sales). Unlike mostly independent U.S. chip firms, the Japanese chip companies are parts of big, diversified companies with ample financial backing. Driven in part by national goals, the Japanese companies continue to invest heavily in new chip production lines even during industry downturns and are starting up 39 new production lines in 1985 after having started 30 new lines the year before. These new lines employ highly sophisticated flexible manufacturing systems and are designed to quickly shift from making one product to another.

While U.S. companies tend to spend only about 15 percent of sales on product research, because of their entrepreneurial nature, they currently enjoy worldwide leadership in the development and production of newer and more advanced chips. However, several of the smaller U.S. semiconductor companies are being taken over by or are working on joint ventures with Japanese chip companies and the Japanese are also setting up design centers in the United States. This trend toward the global integration of the semiconductor industry is evidenced by the record 47 joint-venture or licensing agreements involving U.S., Japanese, and European firms that have been signed in 1985. A number of industry observers are forecasting that only the top 10 to 15 of the 200 or so semiconductor producers can eventually survive and remain profitable and the others will run out of cash and be "merged or submerged" as they will be unable to keep up with the rapidly changing technology.

Reflecting the intense competition in this industry is the trade war developing between United States and Japanese companies and the current spate of legal actions by U.S. firms against Japanese competition. The United States Semiconductor Trade Association has filed a complaint under section 301 of the 1974 Trade Act to seek government relief from alleged unfair trade practices by the Japanese firms. U.S. firms allege that they are being prevented from achieving a higher market share of the Japanese market in semiconductor chips by various forms of Japanese discrimination against foreign products, while Japanese companies are gaining an increasing share of the United States chip market by dumping their chips in the United States at prices below their production costs.

Reflecting overall trends in manufacturing, labor costs in the semiconductor industry are becoming a smaller portion of overall manufacturing costs. In addition, because of the need to compress increasing numbers of components on a single chip, automation is becoming necessary for an ever-larger segment of this industry. The semiconductor industry in the United States is changing rapidly because of these trends. A number of U.S. companies have now shifted production of chips back to the United States from offshore production in Southeast Asia and elsewhere. Machines can now perform most of the formerly labor intensive work of assembling chips and mounting and wiring circuits less expensively than foreign labor and with fewer flaws. Additional savings result from lower transportation and inventory costs. Furthermore, rapid changes sweeping through the industry make it more important for producers to have assembly plants closer to customers. For example, Schlumberger's Fairchild Camera subsidiary recently moved some of its Southeast Asian production to its automated plant in Portland, Maine. Mostek Corporation has closed its assembly plant with 700 wokers in Kota Bahru, Malaysia, and laid off 600 workers in Penang, while National Semiconductor is phasing out a thousand-worker plant in Seramban, Malaysia. Motorola is also reducing its operations in Malaysia and Thailand. Southeast Asian countries are already feeling the impact of these moves and are planning a shift in their development strategy away from emphasizing hardware manufacture to the development of software.

What factors should John Ricks consider in making his decision regarding the proposed expansion of the Singapore plant? How permanent are these industry trends likely to be and how should he assess their impact on Advanced Microprocessors?

Sources: Steven P. Galante, "U.S. Semiconductor Makers Automate, Cut Chip Production in Southeast Asia," *The Wall Street Journal,* August 21, 1985, p. 26; "Chips: The War of Tomorrow's Worlds," *The Economist,* August 24, 1985, pp. 69–70; Stephen Kreider Yoder, "Japanese Industry Gambles Heavily on Sophisticated Chips," *The Asian Wall Street Journal Weekly,* October 14, 1985, pp. 1, 20; Carl Goldstein, "The Necessity of Invention," *Far Eastern Economic Review,* November 21, 1985: 138–139; Francis Pearce, "Asean Pushes Hard in a Major Bid to Go 'Soft'," *Far Eastern Economic Review,* October 31, 1985: 73–75; "U.S. Chipmakers Get Mean, and Japan Gets Meaner," *Business Week,* September 16, 1985, pp. 126, 130; and Carolyn Sherwood-Call, "The Semiconductor Industry," *FRBSF Weekly Letter,* October 18, 1985, pp. 1–3.

Chapter 8

INTERNATIONAL INVESTMENT THEORIES

Chapter Objectives

- *To point out the basic changes that have occurred in the nature of international investment since the end of the Second World War and how those changes have led to the formulation of new international investment theories*
- *To examine the more prominent contemporary theories of international direct investment and to consider the elements of commonality and dissimilarity among those theories*
- *To analyze the applicability of these theories to actual international investment patterns and to evaluate their contributions to an understanding of international investment behavior and decisions*

As previous chapters have pointed out, the period since the close of the Second World War has seen an enormous expansion of international investment. The movement to acquire production facilities and other economic enterprises in foreign locales was led by American companies, but business firms from the other industrialized nations soon joined the parade into foreign markets. The urge to invest abroad has since spread to several of the more advanced developing countries and even to the state-owned business organizations of the communist nations.

This period has also witnessed many efforts to develop a coherent theoretical explanation for the expansion of international investment. Although economists long ago devised a theory pertaining to transfers of capital among countries, that theory has only limited relevance to the postwar international investment phenomenon. It was formulated in an era in which virtually all international investment was of the portfolio variety, and it therefore could not adequately deal with the shift from portfolio to *direct* investment which was one of the most notable features of that phenomenon.

Portfolio investment, as explained previously, essentially involves the investment of capital funds to acquire financial assets, such as stocks or bonds. Such investments are motivated by the investors' desire to realize interest or other monetary returns from capital funds, and these investors typically take no active part in managing the real assets that the stocks, bonds, or other securities represent. Given those motivations and characteristics, international portfolio investment could be attributed to differences in risk-adjusted interest rates among countries. The traditional theory of international capital flows emphasized such differences as the primary reason for such investment, and went on to relate the interest rate differentials to variations in the availability and productivity of capital among nations.

Direct investment is a much more extensive and complicated undertaking than portfolio investment. It entails the transfer of a "package" of resources—which usually includes technology, managerial skills, and production processes, in addition to capital—into foreign areas. Such investment also entails continuing control over the utilization of those resources, so that the investing firm is actually establishing itself in the foreign environment on a permanent basis. Moreover, each foreign direct investment project that a multinational corporation undertakes becomes an integral part of that corporation's worldwide business operations and of its global profit-maximizing strategy.

The traditional theory of international capital flows proved to be too simple and narrow to fully explain the causes of the postwar upsurge of international direct investment or the behavior of the multinational firms that were carrying it out. This spurred economists and other researchers into a quest for new ideas that could be fashioned into a theory of direct investment by multinational enterprises. That quest is still in progress, as no single, definitive theory has yet won universal acceptance. There are, instead, a number of theories that possess some common elements, but differ in their perspectives and emphases.

This chapter will examine a few better-known theories of international direct investment. These theories will first be categorized on the basis of shared perspectives, and representative examples of each category will then be reviewed. The three categories into which the theories will be grouped are: (1) financial theories, (2) life cycle theories, and (3) market imperfection theories.

Financial Theories

Certain of the theories that have been advanced to explain international investment are based upon well-established tenets and principles of finance. One of these basic tenets is that the worth of any asset is the present value of all future cash flows associated with that asset, discounted at a rate that reflects the riskiness of such flows. A firm can therefore maximize the value of its assets—and thus its own overall value—either by increasing its net future cash flows (by increasing revenues or decreasing costs) or by decreasing the riskiness of those cash flows (safer cash flows will have higher net present values).

In the financial theories of foreign investment, such investment is seen as the result of a firm's seeking the highest rate of return for its capital investments, or the result of its efforts to take advantage of the risk-reducing potential of international diversification. Opportunities for such advantageous international investments are presumed to exist because financial markets in various countries are often isolated from one another and because capital markets are not well developed in many countries.

The traditional theory of international capital flows that was described in the introductory section logically fits into this financial theory category, inasmuch as it considers the prospect of increased future cash flows, in the form of higher interest returns, as the principal motive for foreign investment. Another more recent theory of this type, which emphasizes the risk-reduction potential of international investment, is referred to as **diversification theory.**

Diversification Theory

Diversification theory states that companies invest overseas in order to increase their value by reducing the risks which they face.[1] Such risk reduction is effectuated through diversification, that is, by combining investments whose returns are influenced by different environmental forces. A company is thought to be able to reduce its average risk in that way, since all of its diversified investments would be unlikely to perform poorly at the same time.

A company might accomplish diversification by undertaking investments in several countries, whose economies are dissimilar in structure or in the nature of their output and are not closely tied to one another or to the economy of the company's home country. Those economies presumably would not be subject to simultaneous "ups and downs" in business conditions, so that cyclical reductions in cash flows from investments in some countries would be counterbalanced by stable or increased cash flows from investments in others.

Diversification theory holds that multinational corporations, which operate throughout the world, have much greater opportunities for risk reduction through diversification than comparable domestic companies. Furthermore, since national financial markets are not well integrated and international movements of capital funds are often restricted by government regulations, individual or institutional portfolio investors are also thought unlikely to have the same opportunities as multi-

---

[1]The diversification theory for international investment has been set forth by several authorities. See, for example, Tamir Agmon and Donald Lessard, "Investor Recognition of Corporate International Diversification," *Journal of Finance* (September 1977): 1049–1055; and Alan M. Rugman, *International Diversification and the Multinational Enterprise* (Lexington, MA: Lexington Books, 1979).

Box 8.1

Diversification Via Foreign Direct Investment

A survey of chief executives of 193 companies in 15 Western European countries has revealed that those executives view international diversification through foreign direct investment as essential for the continued growth of their firms. Thirty-two percent of the executives expected that more than half of that growth would come from overseas operations during the next five years.

The survey, conducted by *The Wall Street Journal/Europe*, also showed that the U.S. was clearly the top choice of the Europeans as a site for foreign direct investment. The executives expressed less enthusiasm for diversifying within Europe and most of them said they were wary of diversifying into Asia, the Mideast, and Latin America.

An official of Booz-Allen & Hamilton, Inc., the management consulting organization which assisted in making the survey, stated that "for European companies, diversifying into the U.S. has gone from being appealing to being a necessity."

Source: George Anders, "European Executives Consider U.S. Prime Area for Expansion Abroad, Journal Poll Shows," *The Wall Street Journal* (December 5, 1984), 34.

national corporations to diversify internationally. Multinational firms are therefore regarded as having a unique capability to increase their asset values via international diversification, and the exploitation of that capability is viewed as the central impetus to overseas investments.

Life Cycle Theories

Many studies of foreign direct investment have associated such investment with a particular stage in the evolution of business firms. These studies see involvement in foreign direct investment as part of an ongoing process of organizational development and as a means of satisfying the goal of organizational growth. A firm's movement into this evolutionary stage may be impelled by its having reached a growth ceiling in its domestic market, due to market saturation, competition, or the threat of antitrust actions by government. But the movement might also be triggered by some more specific event, such as the development of a new product.

The **product life cycle theory** is probably the best known and most comprehensive of the theories that take this evolutionary approach.[2] This theory was introduced in Chapter 5, since it encompasses the evolution of a firm's international trading activities, as well as its subsequent venture into foreign production via foreign direct investment. Its application to such investment will now be examined.

The Product Life Cycle Theory

The various stages associated with the product life cycle model were identified in Chapter 5. Reference will be made to those stages again in the following discussion.

Introduction and Growth (New Product) Stage. The product life cycle theory asserts that the development of new products or substantial improvements of existing products will most likely occur in economically advanced countries such as the United States. Those countries are more apt to possess the potential demand, risk capital, technological expertise, and research capabilities needed to support product innovation and the introduction of new products to the market.

It is also likely that production of a new product will initially be concentrated in the country in which that product has been developed. This may allow the firm that has developed the product (which will be referred to hereafter as "the innovating firm") to utilize existing production facilities, rather than having to invest in new facilities to make a product that has not yet passed the test of market demand. Producing close to the market also offers the advantage of fast feedback of information relating to consumer acceptance of the new product and the possible need for design changes or other modifications. Moreover, the new product is likely to exhibit low price elasticity of demand in this introductory stage, due to the absence of competition and its novelty appeal, so that the innovating firm will not have to be greatly concerned with production costs and their effects upon the price at which the product is offered for sale. There is thus little pressure at this time on the innovating firm to seek out production locales in other countries in order to reduce labor or other production costs.

While the bulk of sales of the new product will come from the domestic market in this introduction/growth stage, the innovating firm will also encounter exporting opportunities. Those opportunities will first appear in other advanced countries, where consumer tastes and purchasing power are similar to the country in which the product has been developed. (If the product is assumed to have been developed in

---

[2]The product life cycle theory is most closely associated with Professor Raymond Vernon. A restatement of the theory can be found in Vernon's book, *Storm Over the Multinationals* (Boston, MA: Harvard University Press, 1977).

the United States, the model would predict that export markets would most likely appear first in Western Europe.) By this time, the innovating firm should also be producing at a level at which per-unit costs are being reduced by the realization of scale economies, so that exporting also becomes attractive from an output-volume and cost perspective.

It is in the latter part of this stage that the innovating firm will be compelled to give serious consideration to direct investment abroad. The major force pushing the innovating firm toward that decision will be the advent of competition in its export markets, as local companies in those advanced countries (or perhaps other companies from the innovating firm's home country) have acquired the know-how to duplicate the new product and the export markets have become large enough to support internal production.

Maturity (Mature Product) Stage.   During the mature product stage, the innovating firm will undertake foreign direct investment to establish its own production capability overseas. Those production facilities will be located in the other advanced countries that constituted the innovating firm's former export markets. Those countries will offer markets of sufficient size to allow the attainment of scale economies in production, but the chief reason for locating there will be the innovating firm's desire to protect the market position it had initially gained by exporting. Thus, defensive motives, perhaps including the need to avoid competitive disadvantages resulting from import duties or high transportation costs, will dictate the choice of foreign direct investment sites during this stage.

Decline (Standardized Product) Stage.   The competitive pressures experienced by the innovating firm will continue to intensify, as more imitators begin producing and total productive capacity overtakes the available demand. This competition may be felt not only in foreign markets, but also in the innovating firm's home country. At this juncture, the reduction of production costs becomes imperative, and the search for cost savings may compel the innovating firm to shift the locus of its production into less-developed countries where labor costs, in particular, will be lower. Foreign direct investment may therefore be undertaken in the developing countries, with a part of the output resulting from that investment directed toward the innovating firm's domestic market.

The product life cycle theory has contributed a great deal to furthering our understanding of the reasons for international direct investment. It has also provided useful insights relative to the timing and the geographic location of such investments, and its explanatory and predictive capabilities have been verified by studies of the actual exporting and investment patterns of a number of U.S. industries. However, it gives very heavy emphasis to product influences and defensive motivations, to the exclusion of certain other factors that may underlie the foreign

---

Box 8.2

Shifting Global Production Sites in a Mature Industry

Ford Motor Co. said its Ford Lio Ho Motor Co. joint venture plans to invest $35 million to expand its subcompact car production capacity in Taiwan and export about 30,000 vehicles a year.

Ford declined to say which export markets it had in mind, but didn't rule out the U.S. If Ford brings subcompacts into the U.S., it would be the first Taiwanese-made cars imported into this country.

Other auto makers currently import, or have plans to import, subcompact cars into the U.S. from South Korea and Mexico, where production and labor costs are low.

Source: Damon Darlin and Maria Shao, "Ford Joint Venture Plans to Expand Taiwan Capacity," *The Wall Street Journal* (November 15, 1984), 2. Reprinted by permission of *The Wall Street Journal,* © Dow Jones & Company, Inc. 1984. All Rights Reserved.

---

direct investment decision. Some of those additional factors are addressed by the market imperfection theories of international direct investment, which will be considered next.

Market Imperfection Theories

A number of theoretical works have focused upon market imperfections as the root cause of foreign direct investment by business firms. Those imperfections may have to do with the competitive structure of the market or industry in which a firm is operating. They may also refer to deficiencies in the workings of markets external to the firm. These theories essentially argue that such imperfections make it advantageous, in profit-maximizing terms, for the firms to engage in international direct investment. Two well-known examples of the theories in this category are the **monopolistic advantage theory** and the **internalization theory.**

Monopolistic Advantage Theory

Monopolistic advantage theory centers around the idea that business firms acquire certain capabilities in the course of their evolution and operations in their home market.[3] Those capabilities will then enable them to "out-compete" and earn higher returns than local firms in foreign markets, despite the benefits of market proximity, familiarity, and experience which the local firms ordinarily would enjoy. The capabilities are deemed to result from market imperfections—that is, departures from the purely competitive market structure in which all firms in an industry would produce identical products and have equal access to all factors of production (including managerial and technological know-how)—hence, the reference to *monopolistic* advantages.

The monopolistic advantages can take many forms including:

1. The ability to produce a differentiated product, which other firms cannot duplicate due to lack of knowledge or patent protection.
2. Exclusive control over raw materials or other essential inputs.
3. Economies of scale in production, that is, low unit costs due to large output volume. This advantage may be buttressed by preferential access to capital funds, which allows the firm to accumulate and maintain a large-scale physical plant that would be prohibitively expensive for other firms to duplicate.
4. Superior managerial, organizational, or marketing skills.

Once a firm has gained capabilities or advantages of this sort in its home market, there would be strong incentives to extend them into foreign markets via direct investment. First, such extension might be accomplished at little or no incremental cost, especially when the advantage derives from technology that the firm has already acquired and paid for, or from widespread consumer awareness and acceptance of its products. Second, the capabilities would give the firm a distinct competitive edge in foreign markets, which could translate into high profit margins. Third, a move into new markets abroad might help the firm to preserve, or possibly improve, its position vis-à-vis rivals in its home country.

This last point calls attention to a particular version of the monopolistic advantage theory, which emphasizes the **oligopolistic** nature and behavior of industries and firms that tend to engage most heavily in foreign direct investment. In economics, the term **oligopoly** refers to industries made up of a small number of large and powerful firms. Those industries are further characterized by the existence of barriers to the entry of new firms and by a high degree of interdependence

---

[3]One of the best-known exponents of the monopolistic advantage theory was Professor Stephen H. Hymer. A presentation of this theory appears in Stephen H. Hymer, *The International Operations of National Firms: A Study of Direct Investment* (Cambridge, MA: Harvard University Press, 1976).

among the existing firms. This interdependence factor refers to the imperative need for each firm to take account of the actions and possible reactions of its rivals in the industry in making its own output, pricing, and other business decisions.

The oligopoly version of international direct investment theory associates the advantages underlying such investment with the large size and economic power of oligopolistic firms. It views the acquisition and retention of those advantages as the means through which such firms seek to bar the entry of new competitors to their industry. Thus, foreign direct investment by multinational corporations is seen as a sort of global spreading of the anticompetitive and exploitative activities and proclivities of oligopolistic business organizations.

Some of those proclivities, notably the great importance that each oligopolistic firm supposedly assigns to protecting its share of the market against inroads by its rivals, are also used to explain what has been called the "bandwagon effect" in international direct investment. This relates to the clustering of direct investments in the same foreign locale by firms in the same industry. Oligopoly theory attributes this to an oligopolistic firm's fear that failing to match the efforts of its fellow oligopolists to penetrate and to develop new markets abroad would eventually undermine its competitive strength and status in its industry.

The monopolistic advantage and oligopoly theories also provide explanations for what might be termed **cross-investments,** in which companies that are in the same industry but headquartered in different countries undertake direct investments in each other's home territory. Numerous cases of such cross-investments can be found. Ford and General Motors, for instance, have invested in car manufacturing facilities in Western Europe while Volkswagen, Renault, and other European automakers have invested in facilities in the United States. American and European manufacturers of glass, petroleum exports, tires, chemicals, and electronic products have likewise crossed into one another's domestic or regional markets.

These cross-investments are consistent with the idea that foreign direct investment is predicated upon monopolistic advantages, insofar as those advantages are regarded as **firm-specific,** that is, possessed by individual firms rather than by all members of an industry. It is not unreasonable, for example, to believe that General Motors and Volkswagen could each have some unique advantages, perhaps in technological know-how or product image, that would enable each of them to build and sell small cars successfully in the other's home market. Cross-investments have also been linked to the tendency of oligopolistic firms to counteract any expansionary moves by their industry rivals. Based on this line of reasoning, the European automakers' investments in the United States could be construed as a reaction to expansion of the American manufacturers (their rivals in the "international automobile oligopoly") into Europe.

Internalization Theory

Internalization theory takes a different view of the role of market imperfections in relation to foreign direct investment.[4] It asserts that markets external to the firm often do not provide an efficient means for the firm to profit from the resources and capabilities that it has accumulated. The firm therefore is induced to create an internal market, by establishing (via foreign direct investments) a global network of affiliated enterprises to utilize those resources and capabilities.

The type of resource that best illustrates the potential benefits of such internal market creation is the *knowledge,* usually related to products or production processes, that a firm may accumulate through experience and through its research and development efforts. The firm has two alternative ways to profit from that knowledge. One of those is through external markets, in which the firm might offer its proprietary information, at a price, to other firms or organizations.

However, such external markets may be hard to identify and not well organized. Moreover, it is apt to be quite difficult for the firm to protect its proprietary knowledge against unauthorized disclosure and dissemination once the firm has entered external markets.

The second alternative is for the firm to expand its own organization and operations in order to utilize its knowledge internally. This allows the firm to maintain control over its valuable proprietary information and to collect what economists refer to as the "monopoly rent" that can be realized from the exclusive possession and utilization of such a unique and nonexpandable resource. The organizational expansion might occur within a single nation, but it can also take place across national boundaries and thereby comprise the basis for the formation of multinational corporations.

Internalization theory, like oligopoly theory, provides a plausible explanation for some frequently observed aspects of foreign direct investment and multinational corporate behavior. It sheds light on the reasons for a heavy involvement of "knowledge-intensive" or high-technology companies among the participants in international business, and indicates why those companies may prefer direct investment to licensing as a means of profiting from the technological know-how that they generate. It also serves to explain why most of the recorded international transfers of technology and other intangible resources actually occur as **intrafirm transactions** among multinational parent companies and their overseas affiliates, rather than among unaffiliated businesses. Internalization theory thus constitutes a very important extension of the market imperfection theory of multinational direct investment.

---

[4]Several studies emphasize internalization as a theoretical explanation for direct investment by multinational enterprises; these include: Peter J. Buckley and Mark Casson, *The Future of the Multinational Enterprise* (New York: Holmes & Meier, 1976); and Alan M. Rugman, *Inside the Multinationals* (New York: Columbia University Press, 1981).

Conclusion

The theories presented in this chapter comprise only a sampling of the study and thought that has been devoted to foreign direct investment by multinational business enterprises. Each of these theories, as well as the many others that were not considered in this survey, has added to our store of knowledge and understanding regarding international direct investment. But none of these theories has supplied a complete explanation of the causes of that investment or its historic patterns and permutations.

   This incompleteness is not surprising, given the comparative recentness of the upsurge in direct investment and the multiplicity of motives that play a part in the investment decisions of firms. However, it is important to understand this development, and the decision-making processes that underlie it, in view of the tremendous impact direct investment has had on the economies of individual nations and on international economic and political relationships. These effects, together with governmental policy responses, will be dealt with again in Part Four of this text, which is concerned specifically with multinational corporations.

Summary

1. The enormous expansion of international investment since the close of the Second World War, together with the shift from portfolio to direct investment, have stimulated efforts to develop a coherent theory to explain these phenomena.
2. Direct investment is a more complex activity than portfolio investment, and cannot therefore be satisfactorily explained by the traditional theory of international investment, which dealt with international movements of portfolio capital.
3. No single, definitive theory of direct investment has yet emerged. The theoretical works that have been formulated have many common elements, but differ in their perspectives and emphases.
4. Some theories of direct investment take a financial perspective, and attribute such investment to the efforts of firms to maximize the risk-adjusted returns on their investible funds or to reduce overall risks through international diversification of their investments.
5. Other direct investment theories perceive a firm's engagement in such investment as a stage in the evolution of the firm itself or in the evolution of its products. The product life cycle theory is the best-known of these theories.
6. Still other direct investment theories have emphasized market imperfections as the primary cause of foreign direct investment.

Some versions of these theories regard foreign investment as a means through which firms attempt to extend the profitability of monopolistic advantages they possess.

7.   Another version of the market imperfection approach perceives direct investment as a way for the firm to overcome the inefficiency of external markets by creating an internal market for its resources and capabilities.

Questions for Review and Discussion

1.   Why is foreign direct investment thought to be a more extensive and complex undertaking than foreign portfolio investment?
2.   Explain how a business firm might utilize foreign direct investment to reduce its overall risk.
3.   What are the motivations for foreign direct investment that are emphasized in the product life cycle theory?
4.   How does the product life cycle theory explain the decision of business firms to locate production facilities initially in more economically advanced nations and subsequently in less-developed nations?
5.   What incentives might a firm have to extend the monopolistic advantages that it has gained in its home country into foreign markets?
6.   What explanation does the oligopoly theory of foreign direct investment provide for cross-investments by firms located in different countries?
7.   What is meant by the creation of "an internal market" by multinational business firms? What considerations might motivate a firm to create such a market?

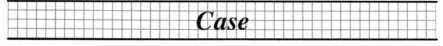

Case

IBM

In March 1984, IBM asked the Mexican government to approve its proposal to establish a 100 percent owned plant in Mexico to produce IBM personal computers (PCs). Until that time, U.S. computer makers with plants in Mexico, such as Apple and Hewlett-Packard, had been limited to a 49 percent ownership.

The proposed Mexican plant, which is small by IBM standards, would give IBM a dominant position in the rapidly growing PC industry in Mexico as well as a strong foothold in Latin America. IBM would invest $6 to $8 million directly in the factory, which is expected to produce

600,000 PCs over the first 5 years (in contrast, 1984 U.S. IBM PC sales are expected to be 1.2 million units). About 92 percent of the output is expected to be exported to non-U.S. markets in Latin America and Asia. The proposed facility will be located in Guadalajara near an existing IBM plant for electric typewriters and mainframe computers.

The current PC market in Mexico totals approximately 15,000 to 20,000 units/year and is divided among 20 companies. Because of low volumes and high use of imported parts, PC prices in Mexico are currently about 40 percent higher than in the United States. It is estimated that up to 50 percent of the Mexican market for PCs is supplied by PCs smuggled in from the United States.

The proposed IBM PC plant is, therefore, expected to significantly upgrade Mexico's PC industry by introducing more advanced technology and by providing additional competition in the local market. However, IBM's initial proposal was rejected by the government because the proposed plant would have used relatively few local parts.

As a result, IBM revised its proposal, agreeing to use 65 percent local parts initially, and to increase the local content to 95 percent eventually. IBM also agreed to spend $40 million on financial and technical help for Mexican suppliers of computer parts. IBM also agreed to manufacture its new PC-AT in Mexico and to hold down prices to within 10 to 15 percent above U.S. retail prices. The Mexican government further sought a pledge from IBM to limit its market share in Mexico. The IBM project is being viewed by many foreign investors as a test of Mexico's stated policy of welcoming 100 percent foreign-owned projects in selected sectors such as high technology and export industries.

Should the Mexican government approve the proposed IBM PC plant? If so, why?

Sources: Steve Frazier, "Mexico to Decide Soon on Whether to Allow Computer Venture 100% Owned by IBM," *The Wall Street Journal,* October 29, 1984, p. 37; Steve Frazier, "Mexico Gambles IBM Will Alter Plans for Factory," *The Wall Street Journal,* January 21, 1985, p. 27; and Steve Frazier, "Plans to Expand Plant in Mexico Revised by IBM," *The Wall Street Journal,* March 11, 1985, p. 33.

Chapter 9

INTERNATIONAL ECONOMIC ALLIANCES

Chapter Objectives

- *To explain the nature and aims of regional economic integration programs*
- *To trace the historical development and worldwide expansion of those integration programs*
- *To identify and analyze the principal economic effects of regional integration, with respect to both participating and nonparticipating countries*
- *To show how the operations and decisions of business firms can be affected by regional economic integration*
- *To describe the character and purposes of the raw material producer cartels that have been formed in recent years*
- *To assess the impact of the raw material producer cartels on the international economy and to identify the conditions that determine the effectiveness of such cartels*

During the past four decades, many nations have entered into economic alliances. These have taken different forms, but the fundamental aim of all of them has been to improve the economic situation of the member nations. Often the countries that have formed such alliances have been relatively small and economically backward, and they have banded together in an effort to overcome those disadvantages and to enhance their power and position in the world economy.

Not all of these unions have been successful or enduring. Several of them have foundered on the rocks of political sovereignty or have been abandoned when hard economic times have prompted their individual members to ignore the rules of unification and fend for themselves. Few if any of them have fulfilled the sometimes grandiose expectations that have attended their formation.

Despite such shortcomings and disappointments, however, the creation of these alliances has been an important development, and they have exerted a significant impact upon the international economy. They have altered global trading relationships and investment patterns and have heavily influenced the domestic economic well-being and the international economic policies of many countries, including the United States.

Two types of international economic alliance will be considered in this chapter. The first part will deal with **regional economic integration.** After defining economic integration, it will look briefly at the history of the integration movement and at the composition and accomplishments of the major regional integration programs. Also, and perhaps most importantly, the economic effects of regional integration will be examined, both with respect to those countries that are directly involved in the integration process and those that are "outsiders." As elsewhere in this text, special attention will be given to the U.S. economy and American business interests.

The second part of the chapter will be concerned with **international cartels,** specifically those made up of raw material producing nations. A number of these organizations have been formed in recent years, and at least one of them, the Organization of Petroleum Exporting Countries (OPEC), has profoundly affected the state of the world economy and the international distribution of wealth.

Regional Economic Integration

Webster's New Twentieth Century Dictionary defines *integration* as the bringing together of parts into a whole and indicates that this usually involves the removal of barriers that have separated those parts. When this is related to international economics, integration can be thought of as the bringing together of economic units that have been separated by barriers resulting from those units belonging to different nations. Stated in more practical terms, economic integration is the joining together of national economies through the reduction or elimination of nationalistic obstacles to trade, investment, or other economic activities.

Levels of Integration

The process of economic integration is both open-ended and reversible, which means that the joining together of national economies can be carried to whatever lengths the participants choose and can also be partially or completely reversed. Bela Balassa has described the lengths to which economic integration can be carried.[1] This categorization is still used to describe and differentiate the various forms of economic integration in the world today. It includes the following levels of integration:

The Free-Trade Area.   The formation of a free-trade area requires each participating nation to remove tariffs, quotas, and other barriers affect-

---

[1]Bela Balassa, *The Theory of Economic Integration* (Homewood, IL: Irwin, 1961), 2.

ing its trade with the other participating nations. However, it allows each participant to decide how it will conduct its trade with nonparticipating countries. The free-trade area is the most limited form of integration, as it applies only to trade in goods or services (and may cover only certain classes of such goods and services) and permits each member country to pursue whatever policies it wishes in terms of its economic relationships with nonmembers.

The Customs Union.   The establishment of a customs union goes one level beyond the free-trade area by requiring the participating nations to adopt common trade policies vis-à-vis nonmember countries. A basic manifestation of this is the **common external tariff** which sets identical duty rates for goods entering any of the member countries from external sources.

The Common Market.   In addition to eliminating barriers to trade among themselves and accepting a single set of policies applicable to external trade, the nations that form a common market also agree to permit capital and labor to move freely within their combined territories. Thus, the common market carries integration an important additional step past the customs union by removing restrictions on the transfer of factors of production across national boundaries.

The Economic Union.   The creation of an economic union entails, in addition to the removal of restrictions on trade and factor movements, the "harmonization" of economic policies. This means that the member countries—each of which previously had devised and implemented its own national policies in such areas as taxation and government spending (fiscal policy), the availability and cost of money and credit (monetary policy), labor and industrial relations (human resources policy), and government regulation of business (industrial policy)—endeavor to pursue identical or at least compatible policies in these and other areas. Such harmonization can be effected either through continuous consultation among the officials responsible for each of those policy areas in each of the member countries, or through the establishment of **supranational agencies** whose policy-making authority supersedes that of the various national agencies. For example, the harmonization of the monetary policies of the member nations of an economic union might be accomplished through close and constant cooperation among the individual central banks of those nations or through the creation of a single central bank that would assume responsibility for monetary policy for the entire group of nations.

It is fairly easy to describe the steps involved in economic integration and to delineate the various levels of integration to which a group of nations might aspire. In the real world, however, the process of economic integration is decidedly difficult and uncertain in its outcome. Moreover, the problems and hazards tend to increase geometrically as integration is carried to higher levels, not only because more economic activities and enterprises are being drawn into and directly affected by the integrative process, but also because each of the member nations is being required to surrender more of its sovereign control over its economic affairs. The potential perils of integration and the reluctance of nations to give up their sovereignty are illustrated by the stunted progress or actual demise of several attempted integration programs and by the painstakingly gradual pace at which even the successful programs have advanced. The following section will briefly review this historical record of success and failure.

History of the Economic Integration Movement

Integration in Western Europe

Although there were some attempts at economic integration prior to World War II, the modern integration movement got under way in earnest a few years after that conflict had ended. The movement began in Western Europe, where it was closely associated with efforts to restore the war-devastated economies of that region's nations. Several of those nations, supported by the United States, formed the Organization for European Economic Cooperation (OEEC) in 1948 as an organizational vehicle for allocating financial aid from the United States and developing a joint economic reconstruction program. Although the OEEC had specific and limited aims, it demonstrated the advantages of coordination and cooperation among the Western European nations and thereby set the stage for more ambitious economic integration programs.

In 1952, six Western European countries established the European Coal and Steel Community (ECSC), a common market arrangement involving coal, steel, and iron ore. That successful experiment helped lead those same countries—West Germany, France, Italy, Belgium, The Netherlands, and Luxembourg—into what has proved to be the most significant venture in economic integration, the formation of the European Economic Community (EEC).

The EEC (also called the European Common Market) was formally launched by the signing of the Treaty of Rome in 1957. That treaty committed the six nations to (1) gradually eliminate all barriers to trade among themselves; (2) develop a common tariff schedule applicable to imports from nonmember countries, (3) remove restrictions on movements of capital and labor within the six-nation group, (4) implement common policies relating to the regulation of industry and the production and marketing of agricultural commodities, (5) create funding mechanisms to assist in the economic development of the six nations as well as certain foreign countries and territories with which they had close economic and political ties, and (6) set up a "social fund" to compensate workers who might experience economic injury due to the integration process.[2] These were very demanding and far-reaching pledges, and the more visionary leaders of the six nations hoped that the fulfillment of such commitments to economic integration eventually would result in the actual political unification of the member countries.

Although the other nations of Western Europe had been involved in the OEEC and related economic integration negotiations, they were reluctant, for a variety of reasons, to take part in such an extensive integration effort as that envisioned in the Treaty of Rome. Seven of these nations joined together in a more loosely knit and limited integration effort by forming the European Free Trade Association (EFTA). The EFTA was formally established in 1960 by the United Kingdom, Norway, Sweden, Denmark, Austria, Portugal, and Switzerland. The split between the so-called inner six EEC members and the outer seven EFTA members continued through the 1960s; however, the United Kingdom and Denmark joined the EEC in 1973 and the remaining members of EFTA have since made arrangements with the EEC that provide for free trade among the countries making up both groups.

Integration Among Developing Countries

While the integration movement was taking shape in Western Europe, the concept of economic integration was also being studied by economists and government officials whose interests and loyalties lay with the developing countries. Those studies, together with the early successes enjoyed by the Western European nations, served to convince the leaders of several developing countries that integration could greatly accelerate their economic development efforts. The first regional economic integration programs among the Third World nations were undertaken in Latin America. The Latin America Free Trade Association (LAFTA), which included most of the South American countries plus Mexico, was formed in 1960; the Central American Common Market (CACM) was created by the Central American nations in 1961.

The effects of economic integration will be examined in detail later in this chapter, with regard to both participating and nonparticipating nations, but it is worth noting here that the anticipated beneficial effects that prompted the developing nations to experiment with economic integration are somewhat different, at least in their order of importance, than those that the more economically advanced European countries were seeking. The latter group of countries was concerned with what economists term the static effects of integration, that is, the greater efficiency in utilizing an already existing stock of resources that can be realized by removing artificial impediments to trade and the mobility of

---

[2]Delbert A. Snider, *Introduction to International Economics* (Homewood, IL: Irwin, 1967), 221.

factors of production. The developing countries, on the other hand, were more concerned with the dynamic effects of integration, which have to do with enlarging the available stock of productive resources and undertaking new types of economic activity. Simply stated, the advanced countries were counting on integration to make their established industries more efficient, whereas the poorer countries were hoping that integration would stimulate investment in new industries.

Progress of the Integration Movement

Since its beginnings in the 1950s and early 1960s, the economic integration movement has become firmly rooted and has spread throughout the world. Of the major industrialized countries, only the United States and Japan have not joined any full-fledged integration program, and even these two countries have considered different integration schemes on several occasions. After taking hold in Latin America, the integration idea captured the imagination of leaders in other developing regions; the vast majority of Third World countries are now or have been part of one or more economic integration projects. The communist countries, which make up the so-called Second World, also have devised their own brand of economic integration under the aegis of a joint economic planning organization known as the Council for Mutual Economic Assistance (CMEA or COMECON). Table 9.1 lists these contemporary regional economic integration programs and their member countries.

Notwithstanding the integration movement's ubiquity and apparent popularity, it has not always progressed easily and smoothly. Furthermore, the accomplishments of some of the regional integration programs have been limited and disappointing.

Of the many integration programs that have been undertaken, the EEC clearly has been the most successful. One major indicator of the success of such programs is the extent to which trade among the member countries (intragroup trade) has increased relative to their trade with the rest of the world. In the case of the EEC, intragroup trade has grown considerably more rapidly, increasing from approximately one-third of total trade when the EEC was formed to one-half of the total trade 20 years later.

The EEC is the only group that has had any real success in moving into the higher stages of integration in which not only trade goods, but also productive factors move freely from country to country. It is also the only group that has achieved any meaningful progress in harmonizing member nations' economic policies, although even the EEC countries have found this progress to be slow and problematic. For example, the EEC's efforts to institute a common agricultural policy (CAP) have been under way since the early 1960s, but its agricultural sector is still beset with serious problems, and agricultural policy issues continue to generate acrimonious disputes among the member countries. The development and implementation of common policies in the fiscal, monetary, transportation, industrial regulation, and energy fields also have

turned out to be painfully slow processes, but the EEC members nevertheless have managed to move gradually ahead in these areas.

In addition to its impressive internal achievements, the EEC has greatly
expanded both its own membership and its associations with nonmem-

Table 9.1 **Regional Economic Integration Programs**

Program	Member Countries
European Economic Community (EEC)	Denmark, United Kingdom, Ireland, The Netherlands, Belgium, Luxembourg, France, West Germany, Italy, Greece
European Free Trade Association (EFTA)	Iceland, Sweden, Norway, Austria, Portugal, Switzerland, Finland (Associate)
Latin American Integration Association (LAIA)*	Bolivia, Brazil, Colombia, Chile, Ecuador, Argentina, Peru, Uruguay, Paraguay, Mexico, Venezuela
Central American Common Market (CACM)	Costa Rica, El Salvador, Guatemala, Honduras, Nicaragua
Caribbean Common Market (CARICOM)	The Bahamas, Belize, Jamaica, Antigua and Barbuda, Montserrat, Dominica, St. Lucia, St. Vincent, Grenada, Barbados, Trinidad and Tobago, Guyana, St. Kitts–Nevis–Anguilla
Andean Common Market (ANCOM)	Colombia, Venezuela, Ecuador, Peru, Bolivia
Association of Southeast Asian Nations (ASEAN)	Thailand, Malaysia, Singapore, Indonesia, Philippines, Brunei
Economic Community of West African States (ECOWAS)	Mauritania, Senegal, Mali, Ivory Coast, Niger, Upper Volta, Benin, The Gambia, Guinea, Ghana, Nigeria, Sierre Leone, Togo, Cape Verde, Guinea–Bissau, Liberia
Council for Mutual Economic Assistance (CMEA or COMECON)	USSR, Hungary, Poland, Romania, Bulgaria, East Germany, Cuba, Czechoslovakia, Mongolia, Vietnam
West African Economic Community	Ivory Coast, Mali, Mauritania, Niger, Senegal, Upper Volta
Arab Common Market	Iraq, Jordan, Libya, Mauritania, Syria, South Yemen

Source: The Europa Yearbook, 1984 (London: Europa Publications, 1984). Reprinted with
permission.

*This program was known as the Latin American Free Trade Association (LAFTA) prior
to 1980.

Box 9.1

European Economic Community Growing Pains

Spain and Portugal's entry into the European Economic Community in 1986 is expected to strengthen Western European unity, but it is also likely to create serious trade difficulties for nonmember countries.

U.S. exports to Spain and Portugal, currently totaling between 3 and 4 billion dollars annually, are in jeopardy, inasmuch as European competitors will eventually gain duty-free entry to the markets of the Iberian countries. U.S. officials are also concerned that the enlargement of the Community may lead to overall increases in the Community's external tariff.

Meanwhile, several North African countries that have developed strong trade ties with Europe face the prospect of losing their European markets. Spain and Portugal produce many of the same products as North Africa, and will be able to displace Tunisian, Moroccan, and Algerian exports of olive oil, wine, fish, textiles, and fresh fruits and vegetables. This would deprive the North African nations of badly-needed hard currency earnings and could potentially throw millions of their citizens out of work.

Source: Steve Mufson, "Admission of Spain and Portugal to EC May Harm North African Economies," *The Wall Street Journal* (December 18, 1984), 36. Gary Putka, "Common Market's Planned Expansion Next Year Could Harm U.S. Exports, Washington Worries," *The Wall Street Journal* (April 16, 1985), 34.

ber countries. The United Kingdom, Ireland, and Denmark joined the original six members of the EEC in 1973, Greece joined in 1980, and Spain and Portugal became full members on January 1, 1986. As mentioned previously, the EEC also has entered into agreements with the remaining EFTA countries that have effectively turned all of Western Europe into a single free-trade area for industrial goods. Furthermore, the EEC has reached outside Western Europe by establishing formal ties with several countries bordering the Mediterranean Ocean and with many developing countries that once had been colonies of the EEC member nations. These ties allow imports from these associated countries to enter the EEC on a preferential or duty-free basis and provide financial and other forms of developmental assistance from the EEC.

Although the differing economic circumstances and different integration objectives of the participants make direct comparisons difficult, it is evident that regional economic integration programs among the developing countries have fared less well than those in Western Europe. In Latin America, for instance, the trade-liberalizing agreements negotiated within the LAFTA have been limited in coverage and riddled with exceptions and escape clauses. Partly out of frustration with the LAFTA's limited accomplishments, five of its member countries entered into a separate "subregional" integration arrangement in 1969, known as the Andean Common Market (ANCOM). Meanwhile, the CACM, which was viewed as one of the world's most promising and progressive integration programs in its early years, had virtually disintegrated by 1980.

Although there are a few exceptions—notably the Association of Southeast Asian Nations (ASEAN), whose members have been enjoying vigorous economic growth in recent years—the regional integration efforts of the developing nations have usually proved unstable and appear not to have contributed significantly to the economic progress of those nations. Some of the reasons for this will be explored in the next section, which deals with both the positive and negative effects associated with economic integration.

The Effects of Economic Integration on Participating Countries

Economic integration has been thoroughly investigated by a multitude of economists, and their combined efforts have yielded a comprehensive theory of integration. That theory identifies the effects that can be expected to result from the decision of a group of nations to integrate their economies. The nature and extent of those effects obviously will vary depending upon the level of integration attained. The total economic impact of forming a customs union will be greater in magnitude than the impact of forming a free-trade area, and this progression continues up the integration ladder.

In analyzing the consequences of integration, economists have drawn a distinction between static and dynamic effects. This distinction (which already has been referred to briefly) recognizes that integration begins at some finite moment in time at which the nations involved already possess an **economic structure,** that is, a stock of resources being utilized in a particular way. The static effects of integration deal with how the integrative process will affect the use pattern or allocation of that given stock of resources. By contrast, analyses of the dynamic effects of integration focus on the possibility that the nation's economic structure itself will be changed, leading to accelerated economic growth and expanded production capabilities. Both outcomes have important social implications, since either a reallocation of existing resources which improves the efficiency of their utilization, or an increase in the quantity of resources being utilized for productive purposes will enhance the nation's economic well-being.

Trade Creation

One of the major beneficial static effects of economic integration is **trade creation.** Since trade creation results from the reduction of tariffs or other protective trade barriers, this effect can be achieved at any level of integration from the free-trade area on up. Economists describe trade creation as the substitution of lower-cost sources of supply for higher-cost sources. In practice, this usually involves the opportunity for consumers in any one of the member countries of an economic union to begin acquiring products from lower-cost (more efficient) producers in other member countries rather than continuing to purchase these products from higher-cost (less-efficient) domestic producers. As a simple hypothetical example, consumers in France, prior to the formation of the EEC, might have been buying French-made toasters, even though the West Germans could produce comparable toasters more cheaply, because France maintained a high protective tariff on imported toasters. The creation of the EEC would result in the elimination of that protective tariff and thereby would permit the French consumers to obtain the lower-priced German toasters.

It should be apparent that this trade creation effect is just the familiar comparative advantage doctrine at work in an economic integration setting. It was shown in Chapter 5 that the freeing of trade benefits consumers by giving them access to products that can be produced more cheaply in foreign countries. However, as explained in Chapter 6, nations have been hesitant to accept free trade on a worldwide basis. Economic integration programs actually represent a limited acceptance of free trade, in which a group of nations—typically nations that are clustered together in a particular geographic region of the world—eliminate trade barriers among themselves and thereby create intraregional trade flows that those barriers previously had prevented.

Trade Diversion

Since barriers are removed only for trade *among* the group of countries and regional integration usually entails the retention of a common external tariff or other barriers to imports from nonparticipating nations, such integration is likely to have a second effect, referred to as **trade diversion.** Trade diversion is defined as the substitution of higher-cost sources of supply for lower-cost sources (the opposite of trade creation).

As a practical matter, trade diversion occurs when buyers in nations that are integrating their economies shift their buying from lower-cost (more efficient) producers located in nonparticipating countries outside the integrated region to higher-cost (less efficient) producers located in another of the countries that is taking part in the integration program. This can be illustrated by returning to the toaster example and amending its initial assumptions somewhat. Add a third country, the United States, to the example and assume this time that West Germany still can produce toasters more cheaply than France, but that the United States can produce them even more cheaply than West Germany. Assume further that France maintains an import duty on toasters to protect its inefficient domestic toaster industry, but that this industry is too small to satisfy the total French demand, so France imports some of the toasters its people wish to purchase. Now, so long as the French import tariff is applied equally to all imported toasters, France will import whatever toasters it is purchasing from abroad from the United States, since it is a lower-cost producer than West Germany. (This illustration ignores transportation costs.)

In this situation, however, when France and West Germany become part of the EEC customs union and thereby eliminate import tariffs between themselves while setting a common tariff on products imported from nonparticipating countries, the effect may well be to shift French purchases away from toasters made in the United States toward those made in West Germany. This would be the outcome if the common external tariff rate applicable to imported toasters were set high enough to make the American appliances more expensive in France than the West German ones.

This is a highly simplified example involving only one product and three countries, but it serves to point out the very real and significant potential for trade diversion that is inherent in regional economic integration programs. Given the actual number of such programs in existence, trade diversion conceivably can affect hundreds of products being traded by scores of countries, and the total value of the trade involved could be immense.

From a theoretical standpoint, trade diversion is regarded as undesirable because it penalizes more efficient producers and supports less efficient ones. It thereby reduces economic efficiency and welfare for the world as a whole. It follows from this that a determination of the net efficiency and welfare effects of a regional integration program would entail an assessment and balancing out of its trade creation and trade diversion effects. If the analysis were limited to these two effects, it could be concluded that the program results in a net gain to the world economy if the trade creation effects outweigh the trade diversion effects and a net loss if trade diversion exceeds trade creation.

Increased Productivity

Another significant static effect that may be realized from regional economic integration is the increased productivity of resources that results from their increased geographic mobility. A regional integration agreement that includes the elimination of nationalistic barriers to the movement of resources can enhance the productivity of labor and capital within the region by encouraging and expediting greater resource mobility.

The EEC provides a good example of how this has actually worked, since the Treaty of Rome provided for the free movement of labor and capital among the EEC member countries and also established some mechanisms to facilitate such movements. One of the most dramatic results of this has been a massive migration of workers from areas of high unemployment in southern Europe into the northern European countries. That migration initially helped alleviate labor shortages in West Germany, Belgium, and France and thereby increased the productivity of both the immigrant workers and the industrial enterprises of the host countries. In recent years, these host countries have experienced some problems related to the cultural and social assimilation of the foreign workers and competition between those immigrant workers and their own citizens for jobs which are no longer plentiful. However, the early successes demonstrated the beneficial effects that can be realized from the resource mobility aspects of a regional economic integration program.

Economies of Scale

It has been noted that the **dynamic effects** of economic integration have to do with the prospects for both enlarging and altering the economies of the participating countries, as well as that such prospects have been particularly significant and appealing to the developing countries of the Third World. The concept of **economies of scale** figures prominently in considerations of the dynamics of regional economic integration. This is a fundamental theoretical and analytic concept in economics, and economists have identified two basic types of scale economies, which they call **internal** and **external.**

Internal Economies.   Changes in production costs that a business firm will experience as it changes its own level of output have to do with **internal economies of scale.** The most important aspect of this relationship is the tendency for the per-unit or average cost of producing goods to decrease as the level of output increases, at least over a sizeable range of output. This tendency constitutes the basic rationale for setting up large, mass production manufacturing plants, which presumably achieve great cost savings by employing mammoth machines (what the economists would call indivisible capital goods) and assembly line operations (which, the economists would say, generate efficiencies by allowing for extensive division and specialization of labor) to turn out vast quantities of products at low unit costs.

This discussion will make no attempt to delve deeply into the manifold implications of internal economies of scale, but will include a few simple observations that indicate the link between these scale economies and regional economic integration. One such observation goes back at least as far as Adam Smith's *Inquiry into the Nature and Causes of the Wealth of Nations,* first published in 1776. In that monumental work,

Smith noted that the division of labor (and thus the opportunity to achieve scale economies in production) is limited by the extent of the market for the output involved.[3]

That profound insight goes a long way toward explaining the appeal of regional economic integration, especially for small and/or economically backward countries that are seeking rapid economic progress and that (as has been pointed out previously) often are inclined to equate such progress with the development of modern industrial enterprises. Many of those countries have become convinced that their individual domestic markets are simply too limited, in terms of population and purchasing power, to support the establishment of manufacturing facilities that could produce enough output to attain the economies of scale necessary for low-cost production. They also have become convinced that their market-size problem could be overcome by joining other similarly situated countries in regional economic unions.

The CACM is an informative case study of this kind of thinking about economic integration and of the integration formula that can result. When the five small countries of Central America (Costa Rica, El Salvador, Guatemala, Honduras, and Nicaragua) formed the CACM in the early 1960s, their principal objective was to encourage and sustain the development of manufacturing industries in what historically had been agrarian economies. Their strategy for accomplishing this included the rapid elimination of barriers to intraregional trade in manufactured products and the imposition of a high uniform tariff on imports of such products from outside the region. This combination was designed to guarantee new or existing manufacturing enterprises operating in Central America a reasonably large market that would be protected from external competition. The hope was that the availability of such a market would not only stimulate investment in industrial facilities, but also would permit those facilities to reach a size at which they could produce on an efficient scale.[4] Other regional integration programs among developing countries have emulated this strategy even though the CACM integration effort subsequently foundered because of a complex set of political and economic problems.

External Economies.   **External economies** refer to cost savings that a particular business firm may realize as a consequence of occurrences outside that firm, including the expansion of the industry or economy of which it is a part. Such expansion might benefit a single firm in a variety of ways that ultimately would show up as a lowering of its costs

---

[3]Adam Smith, *An Inquiry into the Nature and Causes of the Wealth of Nations* (New York: The Modern Library, 1937), 17.

[4]The Central American countries also adopted an "integration industries" plan, which was to provide developmental assistance to selected new industrial enterprises and also insure that such enterprises would be evenly distributed among the CACM member countries.

of production. For instance, the firm might gain access to improved technology or skilled workers that were being developed or trained elsewhere in the growing industry or economy, or it might be able to acquire material inputs at a lower price because more suppliers were emerging.

External economies can be linked to regional economic integration in several ways. First, the merging of previously separated national economies effectively widens the area within which beneficial interactions among firms may occur, as well as the number of potential participants in such interactions. Second, the expanded market size that results from regional integration may result in the establishment of supplier industries that would not otherwise have been viable. For example, a regional economic union might make it feasible for a group of small countries to develop a steel industry, which then could make lower-priced steel available to other firms in those countries. Third, a regional integration program can provide for the development of various kinds of support facilities to assist business firms. Such facilities—which sometimes are referred to broadly as the economic **infrastructure**—can range all the way from an improved transportation network to industrial research centers and regional development banks that help supply technology and capital funds to businesses. Many existing regional economic integration programs include such infrastructure provisions.

Economists have disagreed about the actual significance of these external economies, and since many of the linkages and interactions through which such cost savings are transferred within an industry or economy are quite subtle and therefore difficult to measure, such disagreement is likely to persist. Nevertheless, it seems evident that regional economic integration can substantially enhance the prospect of such externally generated benefits for business firms. This has been a strong selling point for integration, especially among the developing countries.

Competitive Effects

In addition to increasing opportunities to attain scale economies in production, regional economic integration may affect economic structures more directly by altering competitive relationships among business enterprises. A common expectation here is that integration will intensify competition, both by opening previously protected national markets to competitors from other member countries and by fostering the establishment of new firms in various industries. In keeping with the general proposition in economics that more competition is usually better than less competition (because it forces firms to operate with greater efficiency and to be more responsive to the interests of consumers), economists look on this as an important beneficial effect of integration.

There is no complete assurance, however, that regional economic integration will result in increased competition in all economic sectors. Indeed, the larger markets that are created through integration in some instances may lead to a greater concentration of economic power among fewer firms, if large enterprises with the resource capability needed to serve those markets are allowed to discourage or eliminate smaller competitors and subsequently exploit their dominant market positions. This danger has been recognized by the administrative authorities of some regional economic integration programs, and preventative measures have been adopted in those cases.[5]

Effects of Economic Integration on Nonparticipating Countries

Thus far this examination of regional economic integration has concentrated its effects within countries that are taking part in an integration program. Rounding out an understanding of the overall impact of economic integration requires consideration of potential external repercussions. It is important to recognize that countries (such as the United States) can be drastically affected by integration processes in which they are not directly involved. This analysis of the external effects of integration will consider how the regional integration programs that have proliferated in the rest of the world have affected the U.S. economy and the behavior of U.S. business firms.

Trade Diversion

The previous discussion of the trade diversion effect touched upon these topics to some extent. That effect was illustrated by a hypothetical example of how the formation of a customs union such as the EEC could result in the diversion of demand from lower-cost producers outside the union (a U.S. producer in the example) to higher-cost producers inside. Such a result emanates from a form of discrimination that is inherent in a customs union whose member countries eliminate trade barriers among themselves while retaining, or perhaps elevating, barriers against imports from nonmembers.

American managers might not have been familiar with trade diversion as an economic concept when the European economic integration program was being launched in the late 1950s. Many of them nevertheless recognized the possibility that that movement might result in their being shut out of European markets because of their inability to surmount the competitive disadvantage that a high common external tariff would im-

---

[5]For example, the EEC's Treaty of Rome contains specific provisions designed to prevent monopolies or cartels from lessening competition. Not surprisingly, the Western European nations have shown greater concern with the danger of excessive economic concentration than the developing countries, since this latter group of countries has been much more interested in encouraging industrial development than in regulating industry so as to insure competitive efficiency.

pose upon them. This very pragmatic concern caused the U.S. business community and the U.S. government to view the emergence of the EEC with considerable trepidation.

Chapters 4 and 7 noted how both the trade policy decisions of the U.S. government and the business decisions of U.S. companies were strongly influenced by the economic integration of Western Europe in the 1950s and 1960s. Industry in the United States reacted by undertaking more direct investment in Western Europe in order to set up production facilities that would be "inside the EEC tariff wall" and therefore immune to the trade diversion threat. The U.S. government endeavored to persuade the EEC member countries to keep their external tariff low, since the likelihood of trade diversion occurring decreases as the uniform external duty rates are lowered.

The Terms of Trade Effect

Economists have identified a corollary of the trade diversion effect, which has to do with the terms of trade. In Chapter 3, *terms of trade* was defined as the ratio of export prices to import prices. Economists have pointed out that any trade diversion that results from the formation of a customs union may alter the terms of trade between the members of that union and nonmember countries. This follows from the fact that trade diversion is essentially a reduction of demand within a customs union for goods imported from external suppliers (because of the substitution of internally produced goods for those imports). If external suppliers respond to that reduced demand by lowering their prices in an effort to retain their markets inside the customs union, the member countries will realize an improvement in their terms of trade; that is, the prices they were paying for imports will have declined relative to their export prices. Although the exact terms of trade effect that might result from a regional economic integration program is dependent upon the complex interaction of a number of variables, the odds favor an outcome in which the countries participating in that program will benefit at the expense of nonmember countries.

It may appear from this discussion that regional economic integration will invariably have adverse repercussions upon outsiders. This is indeed likely so long as consideration is given only to such static and short-run effects as trade diversion and changing terms of trade. However, the longer-run dynamic effects of regional economic integration must also be considered, and this brightens the prospect that residents of nonparticipating countries will share in the benefits of regional integration programs taking place elsewhere in the world.

Just as "a rising tide raises all ships," the beneficial economic effects that member countries enjoy from integration—because of trade creation, realization of scale economies in production, increased productivity of resources, and economic efficiency induced by intensified competition—are likely to affect the rest of the world.

The Income Effect

One of the principal ways in which this spillover occurs is referred to as the **income effect.** The income effect postulates that the internal economic benefits of integration previously noted will show up as increases in disposable income for residents of the integrating region. To the extent that regional economic integration results in goods being produced more efficiently and in increased investment and employment opportunities, the owners and employees of business firms will be able to reap higher returns, consumers will have access to lower-priced goods, and all of this will enhance the disposable income of those fortunate individuals. Such enhanced income translates directly into increased purchasing power, and it is reasonable to presume that some of the added purchasing power will be used to import goods from nonmember countries. In this way, the intraregional prosperity attributable to economic integration creates demand and employment opportunities outside the region.

Since the income effect and the trade diversion/terms of trade effects work in opposite directions, they must be weighed against one another in attempting to determine whether nonmember countries will be helped or damaged by regional economic integration programs. Such determinations are quite difficult to make in practice, not only because of the problem of measuring these effects, but also because they somehow must be isolated from a host of other events and developments that simultaneously may be altering economic relationships between an integrating region and the outside world.

The Impact of Economic Integration on U.S. Business

Despite the analytic hurdles, there have been a number of studies of the consequences of regional economic integration for nonmember countries. One of the most comprehensive of these traced the effects of European economic integration on U.S. international trade and investment during the decade of the 1960s. That study found that the United States had experienced a net loss of export sales between 1958 and 1970 as a result of the formation of the EEC and the EFTA. It further concluded that new investments by American companies in Western Europe had risen as a consequence of those integration programs.[6]

A more recent investigation likewise found that regional economic integration, especially in Western Europe, had had a negative effect upon U.S. export performance between 1960 and 1980. The combined

---

[6]Lawrence B. Krause, *European Economic Integration and the United States* (Washington, DC): Brookings Institute, 1968), 222–223.

threat of trade diversion and the prospect of larger markets also had induced American firms to step up their direct investment in Western Europe and Central America.[7]

These studies show that U.S. business firms have been affected by regional economic integration and that their decisions have been influenced by the integration movement. The ability of these firms to export to overseas markets has sometimes been impaired by the external tariffs and other measures that member countries have used to protect their own producers. However, regional integration also has created broader markets, which allowed U.S. companies to take advantage of their large-scale manufacturing and mass merchandising capabilities and experience.

Regional economic integration can have many other effects upon the decisions and actions of individual firms. The decision to undertake international operations, the choice of overseas business locations, the selection of target markets, the type of entry strategy used to penetrate those markets, and the tactics needed to deal with competition are only some of the many areas of managerial decision making that have been influenced by regional economic integration programs.

Although the postwar economic integration movement has experienced problems and setbacks, it seems clear that many regional integration programs are here to stay. The world economy therefore will continue to be compartmentalized by such economic alliances for the foreseeable future, and business firms will have to recognize and contend with this condition in planning and conducting their international operations.

International Cartels

Another form of economic alliance that has had a strong impact on the world economy and international business is the **cartel.** Cartels are associations of various producers of a product or commodity. Such associations may differ in their structure and mode of operations, but they are all designed to benefit their members economically and to give them greater control over the markets in which they sell. These purposes generally are pursued through joint limitations upon output, price-fixing agreements, or allocations of sales territories.

Cartels have existed for decades, but in the past they usually have been formed by private manufacturing firms headquartered in the industrialized countries. The cartels that have emerged during the past 20 years or so differ from their historical predecessors. These newer cartels are involved in producing raw materials rather than manufac-

---

[7]Penelope Hartland-Thunberg, *Trading Blocs, U.S. Exports, and World Trade* (Boulder, CO: Westview, 1980), 8–29.

tured goods, and they have been organized by the governments of the countries that produce those commodities, rather than by private companies. Among other things, this means that the aims and decisions of these cartels may be based upon political as well as economic considerations.

The Organization of Petroleum Exporting Countries

The first and unquestionably the most powerful of the new cartels is the Organization of Petroleum Exporting Countries (OPEC), which is made up of 13 oil producing and exporting countries.[8] Although OPEC was actually formed in 1961, it did not become a significant force until the 1970s. The cartel began to achieve some success in pressuring the large international oil companies to raise their prices in the early 1970s, but the real extent of OPEC's power was first demonstrated to the world in 1973. Following the outbreak of a war between Israel and the Arab countries in October of that year, the Arab members of OPEC declared an embargo on oil shipments to the United States, reduced their oil production, and raised the price of their oil from an average of $3.00 per barrel to almost $12.00 per barrel by the end of 1973. More price increases in subsequent years, including an especially sharp rise connected with the disruption of oil supplies that resulted from the revolution in Iran, brought the average price of a barrel of crude petroleum to approximately $34.00 by 1981. Thus, OPEC succeeded in bringing about a ten-fold increase in the world market price of this vital commodity in one decade, and, in doing so, effectuated some major changes in the international economic order as well as in the rate of progress and level of prosperity of many of the world's nations.

The extent to which the OPEC nations were able to alter international trade relationships and expand their own influence in the world economy during the 1970s can be seen in trade statistics. These show that the value of OPEC's exports rose from just $25 billion in 1972 to $294 billion in 1980, while its share of total world exports climbed from less than 7 percent to 15 percent over the same period. Although the OPEC members also began importing more from the rest of the world, such imports did not keep pace with the massive increase in their export revenues. Consequently, their trade surplus, that is, the excess of their export earnings over their expenditures on imports, totaled almost $580 billion between 1972 and 1980 and reached $152 billion in 1980 alone.

Lying behind these unadorned statistics is the reality of an enormous transfer of income and wealth from the countries that import oil to the OPEC nations. That transfer forced a severe curtailment of consumption and investment spending in many of the countries that had to continue

---

[8]OPEC members include Algeria, Ecuador, Gabon, Indonesia, Iraq, Iran, Kuwait, Libya, Nigeria, Qatar, Saudi Arabia, the United Arab Emirates, and Venezuela.

Box 9.2

Difficult Times for OPEC

Oil ministers from members of the Organization of Petroleum Exporting Countries (OPEC) have agreed to adhere to the organization's production quotas but failed to agree on steps to prop up sagging oil prices. The current president of OPEC, Indonesia's oil minister, said that the ministers would meet again soon to consider a proposal to introduce a "floating production ceiling" that would be adjusted periodically to meet changes in the demand for oil. He also said that the ministers had decided "not to quarrel about the price issue now."

Meanwhile, some oil industry analysts indicated that the outcome of the meeting was unlikely to halt the decline in oil prices that has been eating away at OPEC's wealth and influence over the past three-and-a-half years. Most of OPEC's member countries have been selling oil below the organization's official price in an effort to keep their customers during a period of declining demand for petroleum and increased competition from non-OPEC oil producers such as Mexico and Britain.

Source: "OPEC Ministers Vow to Adhere to Quota Policies," *The Blade* (Toledo, OH: July 8, 1985), 1.

importing oil at higher and higher prices, and those rising prices created or aggravated inflationary pressures in the importing countries. What is perhaps most unfortunate is that the heaviest burden of the oil price increases fell upon those developing countries that have no domestic petroleum deposits and that had become dependent upon imported petroleum to meet their domestic consumption needs and fuel their fledgling industrial sectors. Those developing countries had much less capacity to absorb higher petroleum costs than the wealthier, industrialized nations, and therefore found it very difficult to sustain their developmental efforts in the face of steadily mounting bills for imported oil.

The escalation of oil prices during the 1970s also necessitated reductions in energy consumption in the oil importing nations and stimulated the development of alternative energy sources. These effects may ultimately prove to be highly beneficial, but they were very costly and disruptive while they were in progress.

It undoubtedly will take many years for economists to sort out the multitudinous economic effects of OPEC's actions, and the rightness or wrongness of those actions will remain a matter of personal judgment (or perhaps national bias). There is no question, however, that the rapid rise in petroleum prices between 1973 and 1980 placed severe strains on the economies of a great many nations and must bear some of the responsibility for the "stagflation," that is, the combination of sluggish economic activity and inflation, that plagued most of the world during that period.

OPEC has experienced a serious diminution of its economic power and cohesiveness since 1980. The combination of conservation efforts in the oil-consuming nations, the discovery and development of new oil fields outside the OPEC sphere, and a worldwide slowdown in economic growth and activity has brought about a sharp reduction in the demand for OPEC's oil. The cartel's share of total oil production in the noncommunist world dropped to 44 percent in 1984, compared with 67 percent in 1973. The weakening of demand has forced OPEC to make reductions in its official benchmark price for oil and has resulted in many "under-the-table" price cuts by individual OPEC member nations. These difficult times have also brought some conflicting interests among the OPEC nations to the surface, notably the diverging needs of those members with large populations and ambitious development plans that desperately need constant revenues from oil exports and other member countries that can afford to take a longer-range view in arriving at output and pricing decisions.

Other Raw Material Cartels

In spite of OPEC's recent problems, the cartel undeniably succeeded in enhancing the wealth and economic power of its member countries. It also won the support and admiration of other Third World nations, that viewed its successes during the 1970s as victories in their common struggle against economic domination by the industrialized nations of the First World. It is not surprising, therefore, that countries that produce and export other primary commodities have tried to organize similar cartels. The commodities that have been involved in such efforts include tin, copper, bauxite, coffee, natural rubber, cocoa, and bananas.

These attempts at cartelization have fallen far short of the OPEC model in terms of their effectiveness in raising the prices of the raw materials produced by the member countries. The lack of success of these "other OPECs" can be explained by reference to the conditions that are necessary for forming and maintaining an effective cartel—conditions that the OPEC producers initially fulfilled, but that the other cartels do not fulfill. The main conditions required for a workable cartel are first, inelastic demand for the product or commodity involved, and second, ability of the cartel members to control a large part of the total output of that product or commodity.

Inelastic demand means that purchasers of the product will be unwilling or unable to reduce their consumption greatly in response to price increases, and such inelasticity generally is associated with an essential product for which there are no close substitutes. Petroleum clearly exhibited these characteristics in the 1970s, especially in a short-run sense, inasmuch as it had become a vital and not easily replaceable source of energy for a vast segment of the world's industries as well as for the tens of millions of consumers who use gasoline in their automobiles and heating oil in their homes. To draw an extreme contrast, the short-term inelasticity of demand for petroleum could be set against the case of a commodity such as bananas, which presumably are not truly essential to anyone and for which other foods can readily be substituted to fill nutritional needs.

Since the export cartels are designed to affect world market prices, the relevant measure of total supply is the output available for marketing internationally. In the early 1970s, the OPEC member countries accounted for more than 80 percent of the crude petroleum being produced for sale in international markets and held an even larger proportion of the world's known petroleum reserves. Again by way of contrast, the countries that have endeavored to cartelize the bauxite and copper markets collectively account for smaller proportions of world production of the raw materials and must also contend with supplies coming from the recycling of the metals made from those raw materials.

The limitations noted above have prevented those cartels that sought to emulate OPEC from matching its impact on the international economy. However, it would be premature, if not foolhardy, to dismiss the cartel movement as a transitory phenomenon. OPEC, for its part, has had a dramatic influence upon the division of wealth, the level of economic activity, and the pace of economic development throughout much of the world, and its decisions have affected the consumption habits and economic well-being of nearly everyone. This demonstration of how concerted action by a few producers of key commodities can alter the course of economic events in our increasingly interdependent world is a lesson that must not be overlooked or disregarded. Unless national governments cooperate in establishing rules for the conduct of trade and in seeking ways to redress the inequalities that permeate the international economy, it is highly likely that some nations will continue to experiment with cartels or similar devices to improve their own economic positions at the expense of other countries.

Summary

1. Economic integration is the joining together of national economies through the reduction or elimination of nationalistic obstacles to trade, investment, or other economic activities. This joining together can be carried to different levels, such as free-trade areas, customs unions, common markets, or economic unions.

2. The modern economic integration movement began in Western
    Europe in the 1950s and spread from there to many other parts
    of the world. The Western European integration effort has been
    the most successful and has had the greatest impact upon inter-
    national trade and investment patterns.

3. Economists have identified a number of effects of regional eco-
    nomic integration. Some of these are defined as static effects,
    whereas others are termed dynamic effects.

4. The major static effects of economic integration are trade crea-
    tion, trade diversion, and the effects on resource productivity as-
    sociated with the mobility of such resources.

5. The principal dynamic effects of economic integration have to do
    with the attainment of economies of scale in production and
    with alterations in competitive relationships.

6. In addition to its effects upon the participating nations, regional
    economic integration can have substantial effects upon countries
    that are not participating in the integration program. These ex-
    ternal effects are associated with trade diversion and with the
    impact of economic integration upon income and demand within
    the integrating region.

7. Empirical studies have shown that regional economic integra-
    tion, especially in Western Europe, has had a substantial effect
    upon U.S. international trade and international investment.

8. Several cartels have been formed in recent years by the nations
    that produce and export raw materials. These organizations are
    designed to give their members greater control over the market-
    ing of such commodities.

9. The most important and successful of the raw material producer
    cartels is the Organization of Petroleum Exporting Countries.
    OPEC's success in dramatically raising the price of oil during the
    1970s resulted in a massive transfer of income and wealth from
    the oil importing nations to OPEC countries.

10. OPEC's successes led the nations that produce other raw mate-
    rials to form similar cartels, but these have been less effective
    than OPEC.

Questions for Review or Discussion

1. Describe the various levels or degrees of economic integration.

2. How did the motivation for economic integration in the indus-
    trialized nations of Western Europe differ from the motivation
    for economic integration among the developing countries?

3. Explain the difference between the "static" and the "dynamic"
    effects of regional economic integration.

4. "A determination of the net efficiency and welfare effect of a re-
    gional economic integration program would entail an assessment

and balancing out of its trade creation and trade diversion effects." Explain.

5.   Differentiate between internal and external economies of scale and explain how each relates to economic integration.

6.   Explain how the trade diversion effect of regional economic integration relates to the economic situation of industries in countries that are not participating in a regional economic integration program.

7.   Describe the income effect of regional economic integration and relate this effect to the impact of regional integration on nonparticipating countries.

8.   What is a cartel? How do the cartels that have emerged during the past 20 years differ from their historical predecessors?

9.   What are the requirements for an effective cartel? How do these requirements explain the success of OPEC relative to the other raw material producer cartels that have been formed?

Case

Philips Gloelampenfabrieken N.V.

The Treaty of Rome, which was signed in 1957, promised to eliminate the economic barriers that divide Europe. In 1985, however, countries belonging to the European Common (EC) Market can't seem to agree on how to take down trade barriers that still divide them. As unemployment has grown, Western European nations have become even less willing to dismantle existing trade barriers. Nevertheless, an agenda of 300 recommendations to remove all trade barriers by 1992 was approved in June 1985 at a European summit conference in Milan. Lord Cockfield, the common market commissioner who wrote the free-trade plan, insists that there is no other way to proceed, especially since a major benefit of removing barriers to trade would be giving European industries a home market that would rival the United States in size.

Some progress is being made. Trade among the Common Market countries is already over $300 billion and is expanding faster than member nations' gross national product (GNP), thus increasing the integration of the European economies. New cooperative agreements in the areas of space, broadcasting, and computer research have been signed in 1985 both among countries and companies. However, significant reductions in tariff and nontariff trade barriers is a slow process because of the conflicting interests of the various members. Each country faces domestic pressures to protect some domestic industry from foreign competition. It is estimated that such trade barriers cost European consumers between $60 and $80 billion annually (*The Wall Street Journal*, August 7, 1985) or about 3 percent of the EC's total output.

Philips is one of the world's largest multinational corporations. It had 1984 sales of $16.81 billion and profits of $347.8 million. It sells only 7 percent of its output in The Netherlands while Europe accounts for about half. Philips discovered the limitations of its home market in Holland when in the early 1900s it had to go to Czar Nicholas II of Russia to sell its annual output of 500 electric light bulbs.

A truck driver on an average Philips trip in Europe carries 35 documents and faces border delays and tariff payments. Because of the fragmented market in Europe, Philips ties up 29 percent of its invested capital in inventories—about a third more than would be necessary in a unified European market. The cost of carrying this extra inventory is estimated at about $175 million (50 percent of its profits). Because of different national standards within the EC, Philips makes 29 different types of electrical outlets, 10 kinds of plugs, 12 kinds of cords, 12 types of irons, 15 types of cake mixers, and 3 kinds of televisions. This variety means shorter production runs and, according to company estimates, its consumer electronics would be 7 to 10 percent cheaper if Europe were truly a single market. Similar situations exist in other product groups. For example, West German "purity" standards exclude other beers as do French standards for windshield wipers.

Common Market governments buy over $400 billion of goods each year but spend only a small percentage of that outside their borders. For example, state-owned telephone companies import only about 2 percent of their requirements. In order to qualify as a "local" firm, Philips has telecommunications plants in five countries even though one plant would be more efficient.

Philips considers its sales and profit prospects for the near future to be sluggish, primarily because of barriers to trade that still exist within the EC. According to Philips, not only do these barriers raise the costs of doing business, but they also prevent the development of European technology, especially in areas where development costs are so high that only a single large market can support them.

In view of the obvious advantages, why is it taking so long for the reduction of trade barriers within the EC? What should Philips do to help the EC?

Sources: Gary Putka, "Philips Finds Obstacles to Intra-Europe Trade Are Costly, Inefficient," *The Wall Street Journal*, August 7, 1985, pp. 1, 14; "Philips in a New Light," *The Economist*, January 5, 1985, pp. 60–61; and Gary Putka, "Common Market More Than Battles," *The Wall Street Journal*, August 7, 1985, p. 22.

Part 3

THE INTERNATIONAL
FINANCIAL SYSTEM

Chapter 10

INTERNATIONAL FINANCIAL MARKETS

Chapter Objectives

- To describe the foreign exchange market and the international money and capital markets
- To explain and illustrate how the foreign exchange market functions to facilitate international business transactions
- To identify the financial instruments that are commonly utilized in international business transactions and to explain the purposes of those instruments
- To trace the expansion of international banking activities in recent years and to establish the reasons for that expansion
- To examine the evolution of international money and capital markets and show how those financial markets support the operations of international business firms
- To describe the principal official financial institutions that operate at international, regional, and national levels and to explain the aims and functions of those institutions

Conducting international business operations or other international economic transactions necessarily entails transfers of money from country to country. The financial aspects of international business include making payments for imported goods or services, receiving payments for exports, transferring capital funds abroad for investment purposes, receiving or paying interest or dividends on such international investments, and a host of other financing activities that may take place in connection with business arrangements among firms or individuals in different countries. In addition to such private international business dealings, governments also engage in overseas purchasing and selling, foreign lending and borrowing, and giving or receiving intergovernmental grants, all of which likewise require international financial flows.

The financing of international business and economic transactions is more complicated and may often prove more hazardous than the financing of comparable transactions that take place within a single nation. This added complexity and risk is due in large measure to the simple but inescapable fact that different countries use different monies or national currencies, so that when the residents of these countries do business with one another, purchasing power must be converted from one currency to another. Since the values of these currencies in relation to each other generally are not fixed or stable, the holding and converting of foreign currencies involves considerable uncertainty and risk. Moreover, national governments often attempt to influence these currency values and to regulate international monetary transactions, so the financing of international business is subject to extensive governmental intervention and legal controls.

The need to finance the vast and rapidly growing volume of international economic transactions in the face of such complications and uncertainties has led to the emergence and expansion of **international financial institutions and markets.** These institutions, and the markets they create, take on many different organizational forms and engage in a wide range of financial activities. But their fundamental and common purpose is to facilitate international trade and investment by arranging and expediting international transfers of funds. Many of these financial intermediaries are privately owned business enterprises, and their operations therefore are predicated on and guided by their own profit motives. But the international financial system also includes numerous public agencies and institutions, whose existence and operations presumably are dedicated to maintaining economic stability and increasing the economic welfare of the nations that they represent or of the world as a whole.

This chapter will examine the nature and functions of the international financial markets. The first portion of the chapter will focus upon the **foreign exchange market,** which is principally concerned with the financing of international trade and other forms of international business that regularly require firms to make and receive payments in different national currencies. The second part of the chapter will concentrate on the **international money and capital markets,** that is, those markets through which funds are loaned and borrowed by business firms, governments, and individual investors for both short and longer periods of time. This separation is somewhat artificial, since, in reality, the foreign exchange market and the money and capital markets are interlinked and directly affect each other, but such a separation is helpful in attempting to describe these complex markets and explain their functions.

The Foreign Exchange Market

The foreign exchange market is a worldwide network of financial institutions that facilitate international business transactions by trading (buying or selling) foreign exchange. Foreign exchange itself consists of several types of financial instruments, all of which represent liquid financial claims on foreign residents. These instruments include **national curren-cies,** that is, the banknotes which circulate as the domestic money or medium of exchange in each of the world's countries. Whenever the currency of one nation is held by a resident of another nation, this constitutes a liquid financial claim that that holder has on the nation which issued the currency, and therefore qualifies as foreign exchange. A second, and quantitatively more important, component of the total stock of foreign exchange consists of **deposits in commercial banks.** Such deposits are claims on the banks in which they reside, and when they are owned by individuals, business firms, or banks from other countries, they constitute foreign exchange. The great bulk of the mon-etary payments that are made in conducting business internationally are actually accomplished by transferring ownership of these bank de-posits from one party to another.

In addition to currencies and bank deposits, foreign exchange in-cludes a variety of short-term debt-type financial instruments that are used in financing international commercial transactions. One such in-strument, which is employed extensively in exporting and importing, is the **bill of exchange.** The features and uses of bills of exchange will be described later in this chapter.

Structure of the Foreign Exchange Market

Like many other markets, the foreign exchange market includes **dealers** and **customers.** The dealers are mostly commercial banks, which hold "inventories" of foreign exchange—consisting mainly of deposit bal-ances in other banks, denominated in different national currencies—and which stand ready to buy or sell this foreign exchange in response to the requests of their customers. Although almost every commercial bank everywhere in the world can and probably does deal in foreign exchange on occasion, what might be regarded as the "nucleus" of the foreign exchange market is made up of a relatively small number of very large banks that are located in the major commercial and financial cities of the world. In the United States, for instance, the foreign exchange market is centered in some 15 to 20 large banks, most of which are headquartered in New York. Some of the important foreign exchange trading centers outside the United States are London, Paris, Tokyo, Zurich, Frankfurt, and Singapore. The large banks in these centers own branches in other countries and also maintain correspondent relation-ships with many other banks both within and outside their own coun-tries. This network makes it possible for all of its member banks to meet the needs of their respective customers, by arranging purchases and sales through the foreign exchange trading departments of the nucleus banks. Thus, the great bulk of foreign exchange transactions, which now amount to billions of dollars each business day, are actually cleared through these few major banks.

Figure 10.1   The Foreign Exchange Market

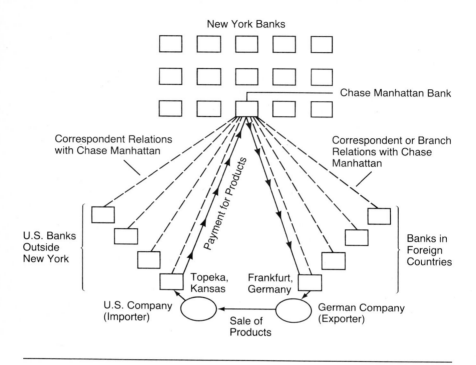

This structure and its workings can be illustrated by the schematic model in Figure 10.1. This is a greatly simplified diagram of a portion of the global foreign exchange market, with its nucleus in New York. The boxes in the center represent the large New York banks that comprise that nucleus, and one of those banks has been identified as the Chase Manhattan Bank. The diagram also shows a few of what, in reality, is a much larger number of other American and foreign banks with which Chase Manhattan has correspondent or branch relationships. Banks that have such relationships perform a variety of services for one another on a reciprocal basis, and, as mentioned previously, the large banks that deal regularly in foreign exchange will also keep deposit balances in their overseas correspondent banks.

Figure 10.1 shows how the financing of a common type of international business transaction would be handled through the foreign exchange market. An American company in Topeka, Kansas is assumed to have imported products from a company in Frankfurt, West Germany. Such a purchase could require the U.S. importer to pay the German exporter in deutschmarks, in which case the American company would have to arrange with its bank in Topeka to make this payment. Since it is not likely that a bank in Topeka, Kansas would get a large number of such requests from its customers, this bank probably would not own deutschmark deposits itself. But, as a correspondent of Chase Manhattan, the Topeka bank could readily fill its customer's need to remit deutschmarks to the German firm by contacting the foreign exchange trading department at Chase (via telex or telephone) and instructing Chase to make this payment. Chase would respond to the Topeka bank's instructions by immediately contacting another of its correspondent banks in Frankfurt and ordering that bank to transfer the required amount of deutschmarks from Chase's deposit account to the account of the German company. Meanwhile, the Topeka bank would have been paid for the marks in dollars by its Topeka customer and, on some prearranged schedule, the Topeka bank would pay Chase Manhattan for those same marks.

Although many international payments might be more complicated than this hypothetical one, and more than two commercial banks may become involved, the example serves to demonstrate the fundamental process through which such payments are effectuated. It might also be worth noting that the sophisticated communications links that now exist among commercial banks allow these payments to be made very quickly— thus, the entire Topeka-to-Frankfurt funds transfer described above could have been carried out in a matter of minutes, or even seconds.

In addition to the so-called "retail" segment of the foreign exchange market, in which commercial banks deal with business firms and individuals wishing to buy or sell foreign exchange, there is a "wholesale" segment, wherein the large banks trade foreign exchange among themselves. These trades frequently are arranged by foreign exchange brokers, which specialize in matching the demands for, and supplies of, foreign currencies among their bank clients. The volume of transactions taking place in this interbank segment actually far exceeds the retail volume, although a considerable part of the interbank dealings are brought about by the banks' desire to replenish foreign currency balances that have been reduced by sales to their nonbank customers or to dispose of what the banks regard as excessive holdings of particular foreign currencies that they have accumulated through purchases from those customers. The interbank market thus makes it possible for the foreign exchange dealer banks to satisfy the requirements of their customers, and at the same time, to maintain whatever portfolio of foreign currency deposit balances they feel is optimal in terms of their own profitability objectives and risk constraints.

The governmentally controlled central banks of many countries are also frequent and important participants in the foreign exchange market. Central banks such as the U.S. Federal Reserve Bank, the Bank of England, the Bank of Japan, and West Germany's Bundesbank (to mention just a few) operate in the market as the banking agents of their respective national governments. In that capacity, they conduct the foreign exchange transactions that are connected with intergovernmental borrowing and lending or the other numerous and varied international economic activities of their governments. But these central banks also *intervene* in the foreign exchange market, buying or selling their own national currencies or foreign currencies in order to influence exchange rates or other market conditions. The purposes and nature of these intervention actions will be explained more fully in the following chapter, but they warrant mentioning here as part of the structural and operational features of the foreign exchange market.

Functions of the Foreign Exchange Market

The foreign exchange market performs a number of functions that are essential to carrying on international business. The performance of these functions occurs principally in the retail segment of the market where, as indicated above, foreign exchange dealers interact directly with business firms that must buy or sell foreign exchange in order to finance their international trading or investing activities. This section will consider how international companies utilize the foreign exchange market in making and receiving international payments, extending credit, and reducing or avoiding some of the risk resulting from transactions that involve the use of different national currencies.

Making and Receiving International Payments.   Figure 10.1 has already illustrated how two business firms in different countries could make use of the foreign exchange market to pay for products that one of those firms had purchased from the other. In this relatively simple but common type of international business deal, the purchaser of the products (a hypothetical American company located in Topeka, Kansas) was able to contact its own bank and arrange—through the network of correspondent banking relationships that forms the foreign exchange market—to have the foreign seller (a company in Frankfurt, Germany) paid immediately for the products. One significant but easily overlooked aspect of that payment procedure was that the American company paid for the goods in its own domestic currency (U.S. dollars, which the company would pay into the bank in Topeka), while the German company received payment in its domestic currency (deutschmarks, which would be transferred into its account in the bank in Frankfurt).[1] The need to convert purchasing power from one currency to another, which was alluded to earlier as one of the complicating features of doing busi-

---

[1]The amount of dollars the U.S. firm would have to pay for the deutschmarks that it owed the German firm would depend upon the exchange rate between the two currencies that the foreign exchange dealers were quoting at the time. The way in which these exchange rates are determined and quoted will be discussed in Chapter 11.

ness internationally, thus was fulfilled routinely through the foreign exchange market, whose major dealer banks are willing to buy and sell from their diverse foreign currency deposits held in branch and correspondent banks around the world.

International payments and collections are, of course, required in all types of international business activities and arrangements. The example that has been used thus far concerned an export–import transaction, but much the same method of transferring funds from one country to another will be used by firms that are acquiring (or selling) real properties or financial assets overseas or receiving (or paying) dividends or interest on such foreign investments. Companies that enter into international licensing arrangements likewise use the foreign exchange market as a means of receiving royalties from (or paying royalties to) their licensing partners.

Facilitating Credit Transactions.   In addition to helping companies make and receive the payments associated with their varied international business operations, the foreign exchange market also facilitates the use of **credit** in those operations. Credit has become a vital element in doing business internationally, so much so that it may be asserted that companies that are unable or unwilling to extend credit to foreign customers or middlemen will find it extremely difficult to compete successfully in world markets. The importance of credit stems partly from the possibility that goods may be "tied up" for long periods of time in transit from country to country, so that buyers are less willing to pay for such goods prior to receiving them. But it also reflects the fact that business firms in many areas of the world—notably the developing countries—often are undercapitalized and perennially short of cash, so that international companies that want to sell to them must offer lenient credit terms.

While credit has become an essential ingredient for an effective international marketing program, extending such credit to foreign customers can be risky. This is not due to any general lack of "credit-worthiness" on the part of foreign business firms or businesspeople. Rather, it has to do with the difficulties of gathering reliable financial and credit information on companies located in countries that may not have well-developed credit rating bureaus or strict financial disclosure regulations, as well as with the likelihood that the laws of different countries will not be uniform in their specifications of the responsibilities of debtors or in the legal processes which are available for collecting debts.

Bills of Exchange.   The foreign exchange market offers international companies several means of coping with this foreign credit dilemma. One of these involves the use of bills of exchange, which are mainly employed in the financing of export–import transactions. A bill of exchange is essentially a written order to pay a sum of money specified by the bill, to someone that is also specified by the bill, at a time that is either specifically stated or established and understood from the standardized form of the bill. In international trade, such bills are ordinarily initiated or drawn by an exporting firm (referred to as the drawer), that is ordering an importer or the importer's bank (referred to as the drawee) to pay whatever amount of money the importer had previously agreed to pay for the exporter's products. For example, an American company that had sold some machinery to a French company for a total price of one million French francs might draw a bill of exchange on the French importer, or that importer's bank, for those million francs.[2] If the French buyer had agreed to pay for the machinery immediately, the bill of exchange would be what is termed a **sight bill,** which specifies that the drawee must pay the amount indicated when the bill is presented. But if the arrangement between the American seller and the French buyer had included credit terms, the bill used would be a **time bill,** which is simply a bill of exchange which specifies that payment is to be made at some future date. In international trade, the most common credit periods are either 30 days, 90 days, or 180 days. Therefore, a "180-day bill" (for instance) would be utilized if the exporter had agreed to allow the importer 6 months in which to pay for the goods.

There are at least two important advantages that an exporting firm can realize by using bills of exchange in credit sales to foreign customers. First, such a bill—once it has been accepted by the party on whom it is drawn—serves as tangible evidence that a debt has been incurred.[3] Returning to the example above, the American company that sold the machinery and drew a bill of exchange on the French company would, if necessary, be able to use the accepted bill as legal evidence that the French company had an obligation to pay the one million francs when the bill became due. Secondly, the American company could "discount the acceptance," which means that it could use the accepted bill of exchange as collateral to borrow money from a commercial bank. The term "discount" indicates that the lender would advance the company less than the full face value of the bill (e.g., the American company might receive 950,000 francs, or the equivalent of that in dollars, for the one-million-franc bill of exchange), with the difference representing the interest the lender is charging for the money being advanced. When the bill of exchange eventually becomes due and is paid by the French company, the proceeds will serve to repay the bank that made the loan and took the bill as collateral.

---

[2]Whether the bill of exchange would be drawn on the importing company or that company's bank would depend on whether the bank had agreed to permit the bill to be drawn upon it. This agreement would occur through the issuance, by the bank, of a *letter of credit,* which will be explained shortly.

[3]A drawee "accepts" a bill by writing "accepted" on it and signing and dating it. That act binds the drawee to pay the bill when it becomes due. Often these bills of exchange will be forwarded to the drawee through commercial banking channels, and certain documents needed to get possession of the goods involved in the export–import transaction will be attached to the bill of exchange. When the importer accepts the bill, he or she will receive those documents and thereby be able to acquire the goods that have been purchased.

Figure 10.2   Use of a Letter of Credit

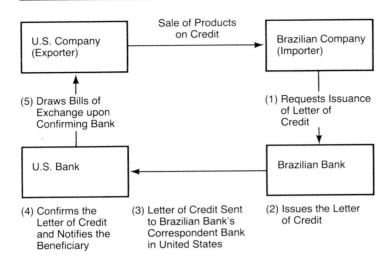

The opportunity to discount bills of exchange enables exporting companies to respond to the credit demands of their customers without actually having to wait to receive cash for the products that they are selling. This capability can be crucial to companies, especially smaller ones, that are trying to compete in export markets, inasmuch as the financial positions and cash flow needs of these companies frequently are such that they cannot afford to tie up large amounts of funds in receivables. The willingness of banks in the foreign exchange market to engage in the discounting of bills of exchange therefore provides a significant service in support of international trading activities.

Letters of Credit.   Another widely used means by which banks in the foreign exchange market assist in providing credit is through **commercial letters of credit.** Although there are many different technical forms of these letters of credit, their basic purpose is to substitute the credit standing of commercial banks for that of nonbank businesses, thereby providing companies that sell on credit greater assurance of receiving full and timely payment. The way this works can be explained most easily by once more considering an example of an American company that is negotiating a sale to a foreign firm, this time one in Brazil. Assuming, as is likely, that the prospective buyer wants to buy on credit, the American company will be seeking a way to meet this credit demand without taking on an excessive amount of risk. A letter of credit might be used in such a situation.

Figure 10.2 identifies the parties that would take part in this letter of credit transaction and indicates the role each might play. Before agreeing to sell on credit to the Brazilian customer, the American company would ask (or insist) that the Brazilian firm arrange for a letter of credit to be issued to cover the shipment of merchandise that the two companies are negotiating. From that juncture, the steps in the process would be as follows (these steps also appear in Figure 10.2):

1. The Brazilian company would contact its bank in Brazil and request that bank to issue the letter of credit.

2. The Brazilian bank would issue the letter of credit, naming the U.S. exporter as the **beneficiary** of the letter. This would allow the American firm to draw bills of exchange (up to the maximum amount specified in the letter of credit) on the Brazilian bank, which would be obligated to accept those bills. Bills of exchange drawn on and accepted by commercial banks generally are regarded as much less subject to the risk of nonpayment than those drawn upon other (nonbank) business firms. Such "bank acceptances" therefore can be discounted more readily and at lower interest charges.

3. The Brazilian bank would forward the letter of credit to a correspondent bank in the United States.

4. The U.S. correspondent might then merely notify the American exporter that the letter of credit had been issued and received. But it is also possible (depending upon the specific agreement that had been reached by the two companies and acceded to by the banks) that the U.S. bank would **confirm** the letter of credit.

5. Confirmation of the letter of credit by the American bank would enable the exporter to draw the bills of exchange on that bank. This confirmation may further enhance the credit rating of the accepted bills. More importantly for the exporter, it avoids the prospect that payment could be delayed due to restrictions that the Brazilian government might impose upon transfers of funds from Brazil to the United States.

6. Eventually, the issuing bank will repay the confirming bank whatever amount has been paid out to the beneficiary and will, in turn, collect that amount (plus a small fee for initiating the letter of credit) from the importing firm.

By issuing and confirming letters of credit, the banks in the foreign exchange market provide valuable services and assurances to both exporting and importing firms. Letters of credit greatly reduce the possibility that exporters will not be paid for their products, as well as the possibility of delays in payment due to government actions. For importing firms, the issuance of letters of credit makes credit purchases feasible. It also gives importers added protection, inasmuch as the banks will make certain that the exporters furnish all the documents that are required to transfer title to the goods involved and to ship those goods from country to country before they accept the exporters' bills of exchange.

The Exchange Rate Risk. There is still another significant way in which the foreign exchange market assists companies that are engaged in international operations. This has to do with the **exchange rate risk,** which can be defined broadly as the risk of unanticipated losses (or gains) in international business transactions due to changes in the prices of national currencies in relation to one another.

The exchange rate risk is a matter of serious concern to international companies, especially under the current international monetary arrangements, in which national governments do not all attempt to maintain a fixed rate of exchange among their currencies.[4] Since the activities of international firms often involve very large sums of money, even small fluctuations in the relative values of the different currencies with which they are dealing can have a substantial impact upon their profits. Indeed, it is not uncommon for such companies to report gains or losses from such exchange rate changes that equal or surpass those resulting from their regular business operations.

The foreign exchange market offers international business firms a means of reducing or avoiding the exchange rate risk. This works mainly through what are known as **forward** foreign exchange transactions. These transactions essentially involve **contracts** between foreign exchange dealers and their business customers, which obligate the dealers to exchange (either buy or sell) a specified amount of one currency for another at a future date that is established in the contract. Most importantly, the dealers agree to exchange the currencies at a price (exchange rate) that is fixed at the time the contract is entered into. Consequently, a business firm that has made such a contract with a foreign exchange dealer will know with certainty what it will have to pay, in its own home currency, for a foreign currency that it has contracted to buy on the set future date; or, alternatively, it will know exactly how much it will receive, in its home currency, for a foreign currency that it has contracted to sell. The risk of unanticipated losses due to exchange rate fluctuations is thereby eliminated.

The way in which these forward transactions can enable a business firm to overcome the exchange rate risk can be demonstrated by once more considering the previous example of an American company that has sold machinery to a French company. By agreeing to make that sale on 180-day credit terms and further agreeing to accept payment in French francs (one million francs in the example), the U.S. firm would have exposed itself to the exchange rate risk. The existence and nature of that risk can be understood by contemplating the potential effects upon the American company of changes in the franc/dollar exchange rate during the 6-month interval between the time at which the sale was

---

[4]The involvement of governments in determining rates of exchange among currencies, and how such governmental involvement has changed over time, will be covered in Chapter 11.

made and the time at which payment would be received. The following hypothetical data point up some of those potential effects:

Transaction: Sale of machinery by a U.S. company to a French company
Price: 1,000,000 French francs   *Credit Terms:* 180 days
Date of Sale: January 7, 1985   *Payment Due:* July 2, 1985

	Franc/Dollar Exchange Rate	Sales Revenue (in Dollars)
January 7, 1985	8.00 Ff = $1.00	$125,000
July 2, 1985	9.50 Ff = $1.00	$105,263
	7.20 Ff = $1.00	$138,889

Although the figures above are imaginary, they serve to show how the sales revenues that a company would realize from a foreign credit sale could be affected by exchange rate fluctuations that occurred during the credit period. In this case, the franc/dollar exchange rate is assumed to have been 8 francs to the dollar when the American company made the sale to the French buyer; in the absence of exchange rate changes, then, the U.S. firm would anticipate receiving $125,000 for the million francs that it would eventually collect from the buyer. However, the rate at which foreign exchange dealers would actually be selling dollars for francs when the company collected its million francs could be quite different than the rate in effect when the sale was made. Only two of the virtually unlimited range of possibilities are postulated above. The first of these possibilities is that the price of the dollar would have risen from 8 francs to 9.5 francs, which would result in the U.S. exporter receiving considerably less revenue than originally anticipated from the sale of its machinery. The second possibility is that the price of the dollar would have fallen to 7.2 francs, in which event the exporting firm would enjoy an unexpected addition to its proceeds from the sale.[5]

Given the situation described above and assuming that the American company did not wish to bear the uncertainty of what its dollar proceeds from the sale would actually turn out to be, a forward contract would provide a solution. In this instance, the U.S. exporter—at the same time that it was closing the sales deal with the French importer—could contract with a foreign exchange dealer to sell one million francs forward, for delivery in 180 days. Inasmuch as the dollar price that it would receive for those francs would be firmly set in the forward contract, the U.S. company would know exactly how much it was going to receive in dollars for the product that it was selling, and those revenues would

---

[5]Since exchange rate changes can result in either gains or losses, international companies may choose to gamble or "speculate" on those changes. Generally, however, such companies prefer to avoid the risks associated with exchange rates, which are outside their sphere of control and expertise.

Box 10.1

Small Companies Deal with Foreign Exchange Problems

The U.S. Farm Raised Fish Trading Co., a catfish firm in Jackson, Mississippi, has developed its own strategy for dealing with foreign exchange problems. It just tells its foreign customers it wants to be paid in dollars. "So far, no problems," says its director of export market development.

Other small firms don't take such a conservative approach. Some try to protect themselves by purchasing currency futures as a hedge against fluctuations, while others attempt to make money by correctly predicting currency trends.

American African Export Co., a New York shoe concern, sometimes enters agreements with its bank. These require the company to pay for delivery of imported shoes at a set dollar price. The bank, for a fee, assumes the risk of fluctuations by paying the foreign supplier at the exchange rate prevailing at delivery time. "Speculation isn't our business," says the company's vice president.

Source: Hank Gilman and Robert Johnson, "Trading Abroad Leaves Small Firms With Host of Currency Complications," *The Wall Street Journal* (September 27, 1984), 14.

be immune from the effects of whatever fluctuations might occur in the franc/dollar rate in the foreign exchange market.[6]

The American company envisioned in the foregoing example had entered into a business arrangement in which it would *receive* future payment in a foreign currency, and it consequently was concerned with averting a loss due to a fall in the value of that currency relative to the dollar. Therefore, the tactic utilized by this firm was to sell that foreign currency forward for a guaranteed price in dollars. Companies operating internationally will, of course, often be in the opposite position, that is,

---

[6]The U.S. company probably would not actually "deliver" the one million francs collected from the French firm to fulfill its forward sales contract with the foreign exchange dealer. It more likely would sell the franc proceeds and close out its forward contract in separate transactions. But the effect, as far as the exchange rate risk is concerned, would be the same, since any loss (or gain) which the firm experienced through its sale of the collected francs would be offset by a gain (or loss) on the forward contract, and the firm would therefore have avoided the exchange rate risk.

they will have undertaken obligations to *make* future payments in foreign currencies. The forward exchange market tactic applicable to such positions obviously would be for the companies to buy the needed foreign currencies forward, in order to avert losses that they would otherwise incur if those currencies rose in value relative to their domestic currency.

The availability of forward contracts has become a well-established feature of the foreign exchange market. The major U.S. foreign exchange dealers, for example, regularly quote the rates at which they stand ready to contract for future purchases or sales of the most widely used foreign currencies, and those quotations are given so as to correspond with the time intervals for which credit is usually extended in international trading transactions.[7] Thus, if a U.S. company wished to contract for the future receipt or delivery of any of the world's principal national currencies (this includes the British pound, the Canadian dollar, the French franc, the Japanese yen, the Swiss franc, and the West German deutschmark), and if the time period involved were either 30, 90, or 180 days, the contract could be effectuated immediately via a call to a foreign exchange dealer. Although setting up forward contracts in other currencies or for longer time periods cannot be done quite so simply, it is nonetheless possible for business firms to negotiate such contracts with foreign exchange dealers on an individualized basis.

By making it possible for firms to reduce the risk of dealing with different national currencies, the foreign exchange market unquestionably helps to encourage international business activity. This section has also pointed out how the market contributes to the continuation and expansion of such activity by making credit more readily available and safer to use and by arranging easy and speedy transfers of funds between countries. These financing functions performed by the foreign exchange market have now become so easily accessible and standardized that international companies may take them for granted. But they are essential to the smooth conduct of international business and their efficient performance relies upon a very intricate and sophisticated set of institutional relationships, communications linkages, and uniform financial instruments and practices.

International Money and Capital Markets

The foreign exchange market has been described above as that part of the international financial system in which national currencies (or, more precisely, financial claims denominated in those currencies) are traded for one another through intermediary organizations known as **foreign**

---

[7] An illustration and further explanation of these forward rate quotations appear in Chapter 11.

exchange dealers. The transactions of international business firms in that market are mainly associated with the foreign payments and collections necessitated by their ongoing business operations.

International companies have another type of financing need, which has to do with acquiring the funds to establish and carry on their business activities and with investing the cash proceeds from those activities. The mammoth corporations that dominate the international business scene, together with their small- and medium-sized counterparts, must raise vast sums of money to build, buy, and expand their worldwide production and marketing installations and to purchase the equipment, materials, and labor services to operate those facilities. These companies also are constantly seeking reasonably safe and profitable places to invest funds for which they may not have an immediate internal use.

These financing needs of international companies are now being met by financial institutions that operate on a global scale and through money and capital markets that stretch across national borders. Although some international marketing of bonds and other securities took place prior to the Second World War, the growth of these international money and capital markets has been most pronounced during the last quarter-century and has paralleled the great expansion of international operations by nonfinancial corporations.

This section will be devoted to a broad survey of some of the more important features of these international financial institutions and markets. It will include a look at the international activities of commercial banks and at the so-called Eurocurrency and Eurobond markets. In addition to examining these privately owned and operated financing entities, it will briefly inspect some of the major official organizations that are involved directly or indirectly in the financing of international business.

International Commercial Banking

As more and more of the large industrial corporations based in the United States, Western Europe, and Japan began doing business throughout the world in the post–World War II period, the commercial banks that had been financing their domestic operations decided to follow their customers overseas. This global spread of commercial banking advanced very rapidly during the 1960s and 1970s, with growth rates of banks' international assets averaging between 25 and 30 percent annually for those two decades.[8]

Commercial banks have utilized a number of different organizational forms and approaches to establish their presence in overseas markets. One of these has been the development of **correspondent relationships** with banks in other countries. These relationships, which were referred

---

[8]Organization for Economic Cooperation and Development, *The Internationalisation of Banking* (Paris, OECD, 1983), 16.

to previously in connection with the foreign exchange market, basically involve agreements among the correspondents to perform various services for one another (e.g., confirming letters of credit) on a reciprocal basis. Such agreements make it possible for the correspondent banks to help their customers make or receive foreign payments and do business in different currencies without the banks having to own and staff banking facilities in more than one country.

Correspondent relationships with foreign banks are useful primarily for financing importing and exporting, and the commercial banks whose corporate customers have undertaken foreign production and other business ventures abroad have usually found it necessary to set up their own foreign offices in order to more fully serve the manifold financing requirements of those customers. Some of these are **representative offices,** which do not engage in normal banking functions, but assist customers in making business contacts in the countries in which they are located and furnish advice and information on business conditions and opportunities in those countries. Others are **agencies,** which usually offer a full range of banking services to business clients, but, either by choice or because of legal restrictions, do not accept deposits from the public.

In addition to such limited-function types of foreign offices, commercial banks have created or otherwise acquired a multitude of foreign **branches** and **subsidiaries,** which generally are full-fledged banking organizations. A foreign branch is an integral extension of its parent bank, whereas a subsidiary is incorporated as a separate company.[9] Despite these legal differences, however, both branches and subsidiaries are under the managerial control of their parent banks. Thus, at the same time that they are doing business in the countries in which they are located and responding to the depository and credit demands of businesses and individuals in those countries, they also are functioning as part of an integrated worldwide banking operation administered by the parent bank.

This geographically dispersed but managerially coordinated structure is the key attribute of contemporary international banking. Such a structure enables the international bank to work effectively with the large industrial corporations that also are doing business through affiliates located in many different nations. Those corporations have come to expect that their banks will be able to provide funding and financial advice to their individual foreign affiliates, but will also be capable of expediting transfers of funds among those affiliates. The international banks, with their far-flung web of branches and subsidiaries, are in a stronger position to fulfill those expectations than are those banks whose offices are confined to a single country.

---

[9]In categorizing these organizational forms, a further distinction is sometimes made between "subsidiaries" and "affiliates," with the former term applied to a foreign bank in which the parent bank holds a controlling interest and the latter applied to a foreign bank in which the parent has a minority interest.

The ability of the large international banks to shift funds easily and quickly from country to country is clearly an important advantage in servicing the needs of their international corporate clientele. But it also gives the banks themselves a broader range of both sources of funds and lending opportunities. The large international banks headquartered in the United States, for example, have often relied on their foreign branches to supply them with money to be loaned to American borrowers, particularly when the Federal Reserve System was curtailing the availability of monetary reserves in the United States. At other times, the American parent banks have used their foreign branches to loan out excess deposits that could not be profitably loaned in the United States itself.

Today's international banks continue to be engaged primarily in the basic, traditional commercial banking functions of gathering funds from depositors and utilizing those deposits as a basis for making short- or medium-term loans. But the growing scope and complexity of international business operations and the increasing sophistication of the firms engaged in such operations have led the banks into many other related areas of activity and service to their customers. Mention has already been made of the importance of moving money across national boundaries, and a number of international banks have collaborated to develop electronic communications facilities and linkages that have enabled them to greatly reduce the time required to transfer funds from country to country. This, in turn, has enabled these banks to assist their corporate clients in implementing efficient international cash management procedures, which minimize the hidden costs of underutilization of funds due to delays in the transfer process.

International banks have also taken up the challenging tasks of exchange rate forecasting and country risk analysis as part of the package of information and advisory services they offer to international companies. The banks' exchange rate forecasts are designed to help those companies avoid losses of income or asset value that might otherwise result from unforeseen variations in the relative prices of different currencies. Their country risk analyses generally deal with the overall economic, political, and social situation of individual countries, with a view toward helping their corporate clients make decisions that give due consideration to the risks inherent in doing business in those countries.

In addition to carrying on basic depository and lending functions and providing a variety of related innovative services such as those described above, international banks have ventured into activities that lie outside the traditional commercial banking sphere. This is especially true of American banks, which are allowed to engage in certain activities abroad from which they have been legally excluded within the United States itself. A provision which was written into U.S. banking law in 1919, commonly referred to as the **Edge Act,** empowers American banks to form so-called Edge Act subsidiaries for the purpose of engaging in international banking *or other international or foreign financial operations.* The Edge Act subsidiaries themselves are chartered under federal law in the United States; but these subsidiaries can then become holding companies for foreign banking offices. Moreover, the Edge Act subsidiaries are able to make direct investments in nonbank business enterprises overseas, engage in investment banking, and operate mutual funds. These are fields of operation which American banks (at least until quite recently) have not been permitted to undertake in their own domestic market, but which they have entered into vigorously as part of their aggressive movement into the more wide-open realm of international banking.

The Eurocurrency Market

The term "Eurocurrency" has come to be used broadly to refer to bank deposits denominated in a currency other than the national currency of the country in which the bank is located. The Eurocurrency market therefore consists of the banks that take in and loan out such deposits, and the communications, interactions, and transactions that occur among these banks and between the banks and their customers. The original Eurocurrency was the Eurodollar (i.e., the U.S. dollar-denominated deposits held in banks in Western Europe), and Eurodollars still constitute the largest single component of total Eurocurrency deposits. But this market has expanded greatly over time, both geographically and in terms of the national currencies involved, so that it now includes Eurosterling (British pounds deposited outside the United Kingdom), Euromarks (deutschmark deposits in non-German banks), Asiadollars (dollar deposits in banks in Southeast Asia, notably Singapore and Hong Kong), as well as several other segments comprised of banks on one country or region that are doing business in an "external" currency.

As Table 10.1 shows, the Eurocurrency market has also increased tremendously in size since its beginnings in Western Europe during the 1950s. The emergence of the market at that time is usually traced to the Soviet Union's wish to have U.S. dollars available to pay for purchases from the West, combined with its politically motivated reluctance to keep deposits in banks in the United States itself. Some commercial banks in Great Britain and France were willing to help resolve that dilemma by accepting and maintaining dollar deposits for the USSR.

The irony of Soviet involvement in the birth of a financial apparatus that might now be regarded as the epitome of "big-money capitalism," is appealing. However, the real growth of the Eurocurrency market occurred after Soviet participation and is attributable to this market's ability to satisfy certain financial needs more effectively than they can be satisfied elsewhere. One of these needs is that of owners of funds who are looking for investment outlets that offer a combination of high yields, safety, liquidity, and—in some instances—anonymity and freedom from government scrutiny. The other basic need is that of organizations (mainly government agencies and large business firms) that wish to borrow sizable amounts of money at the lowest possible interest cost.

Table 10.1   **Size of the Eurocurrency Market***

Year	Deposits (Billions of U.S. Dollars)
1964	$ 15
1965	18
1966	24
1967	31
1968	45
1969	78
1970	115
1971	150
1972	210
1973	315
1974	395
1975	485
1976	595
1977	740
1978	950
1979	1,235
1980	1,525
1981	1,860
1982	2,060
1983	2,153
1984	2,383

Sources: Pre-1970 figures from Organization for Economic Cooperation and Development, *The Internationalisation of Banking* (Paris, OECD, 1983), 133; post-1970 figures from Morgan Guaranty Trust Company, *World Financial Markets,* various issues. Data for the two periods may not be exactly comparable.

*Foreign currency deposit liabilities of Eurocurrency banks.

There are several reasons why the Eurocurrency market has proved capable of fulfilling such needs exceptionally well. First, there is the factor of government control and supervision. By contrast with the domestic banking systems of most countries (the U.S. system in particular), the Eurocurrency market has remained virtually free of government regulation. This absence of regulation has greatly aided the Eurocurrency banks in attracting both depositors and borrowers. Since these banks have not been subject to official limits on the interest they can pay to depositors or saddled with the costs of conforming to regulatory and reporting requirements, they have been able to offer enticing interest yields on deposits. Government regulation has also stimulated the expansion of the Eurocurrency market by turning borrowers toward that market when other funding sources have been foreclosed. There were several periods in the 1960s and 1970s, for example, during which the U.S. and British governments made it very difficult or costly to raise funds in their respective domestic financial markets for transfer abroad.

This caused many borrowers, including U.S.-based international companies, to go to the Eurocurrency market for needed funds.

Other reasons for the Eurocurrency market's efficiency and success are found in the nature of its clientele and operations. The Eurocurrency market caters almost entirely to big industrial corporations, national governments and their central banks and economic agencies, and nonbank financial institutions. The sheer size and financial soundness of these entities eliminates much of the risk that banks serving a more diverse population ordinarily face, and thereby allows Eurocurrency banks to attach lower risk-premiums to the interest they charge. Transactions in this market are also conducted on a large scale, with deposits and loans usually made in millions of dollars or the equivalent in other currencies. These large-volume transactions enable the banks to keep their average transactions costs low and thus to simultaneously offer good returns to depositors and highly competitive interest rates to borrowers.

The Eurocurrency market plays a significant part in the financial operations of many international business firms. By making deposits in the Eurocurrency banks, these firms are able to earn substantial returns on temporarily surplus funds while keeping those funds liquid and readily available. Although Eurocurrency deposits are made for fixed periods of time, those time periods can range from as short as overnight to as long as several months, and firms needing cash quickly can also borrow against their Eurocurrency deposits. In addition to accepting conventional time deposits, Eurocurrency banks also issue and sell negotiable certificates of deposit (CDs). These certificates are essentially promises to pay or "IOUs" from the issuing bank; investors who buy them are assured of a fixed interest return for the period until the CD matures, but they also have the option of reselling the CD for cash at any time through a well-established secondary market.

Besides providing a convenient and profitable depository for excess funds, the Eurocurrency market meets many of the borrowing needs of international companies. Loans are available to such companies for either very short or longer periods—periods of several years in some cases— and in amounts varying from a few hundred thousand dollars to as much as a *billion dollars*. (The largest loans usually are arranged through a syndication of several banks.) The interest charged for these loans has historically been based upon the London Interbank Offer Rate (LIBOR), which is the interest rate which the Eurocurrency banks set on loans to one another. Business firms or other nonbank borrowers pay a "spread," that is, an amount above LIBOR, which can vary from a fraction of 1 percent to several percent, depending upon the credit standing of the borrower, the time period of the loan, or other considerations. The important point is that the cost-efficiency of the Eurocurrency market has kept these interest charges generally below those which the same borrowers would have to pay elsewhere. Even a small interest differential can result in very substantial savings when millions of dollars are being borrowed, and the opportunity to realize such savings has helped

Table 10.2   *Eurobond Issues*

Year	Eurobonds Issued (Billions of U.S. Dollars)
1970	$ 3.0
1971	3.6
1972	6.3
1973	4.2
1974	2.1
1975	8.6
1976	14.3
1977	17.8
1978	14.2
1979	18.7
1980	23.9
1981	31.6
1982	51.6
1983	48.5
1984	79.5
Currency denomination of 1984 issues	
U.S. dollar	$63.6
German mark	4.6
British pound	4.0
Japanese yen	1.2
European composite units	3.0
Other	3.0

Source: Morgan Guaranty Trust, *World Financial Markets,* various issues.

to make the Eurocurrency market a prime source of funding for international corporations.

The Eurobond Market

The Eurocurrency market is essentially a banking or money market, in which funds are deposited in and borrowed from commercial banks. Those deposits and loans often are made for relatively short periods of time. The Eurobond market, by way of contrast, is a bond or capital market, thorugh which funds are raised on a longer-term basis via the marketing of debt securities. Like its Eurocurrency counterpart, the Eurobond market is an international financing mechanism, which makes it possible for organizations based in one country to acquire funds from investors in other parts of the world.

Eurobonds are payable in a currency other than that of the country of the issuer of the bond and are marketed outside the country in which the issuing organization is located. By far the largest portion of these bonds are denominated in U.S. dollars and, as the "Euro" designation indicates, Western Europe has historically been the largest market for such bonds. Table 10.2 shows the volume and growth of sales of Eu-

"But—first—a word about Government bonds!"

robonds and also indicates the mix of currencies in which these bonds were denominated for the latest year covered by the data.

The Eurobond market has emerged and flourished for many of the same reasons as the Eurocurrency market. A good part of the impetus for the development of this market came from the U.S. government which, during the 1960s, imposed taxes and other restrictive measures to curtail foreign borrowing in the United States and transfers of capital

Box 10.2

Tapping the Eurobond Market

Signal Cos. has issued $125 million of Eurodollar bonds, becoming the latest in a growing number of U.S. corporations that are raising funds in that market for the first time.

Apparently, though, it isn't for the money. "We have about $1.2 billion in cash and very little debt," says Gary M. Cypres, chief financial officer of the La Jolla, California technology and engineering company. Signal "wanted access to a large capital market that's separate from the U.S. Next time, we may come to this market for $500 million and we'll know we can do a major offering at a substantial saving" to a comparable U.S. financing, says Mr. Cypres.

Source: "Eurobond Market Lures Another U.S. Concern," *The Wall Street Journal* (January 23, 1985), 34. Reprinted by permission of *The Wall Street Journal,* © Dow Jones & Company, Inc. 1985. All Rights Reserved.

funds out of this country. Those measures caused many borrowers, including American firms and their foreign affiliates, to look for alternative sources of funds, and the sale of dollar-denominated bonds in Europe was devised to provide such an alternative. The ability to escape stringent government regulation has continued to account for much of the appeal of the Eurobond market, as the issuance of such bonds is not subject to the registration and public disclosure requirements that usually apply to bonds issued and sold within a single country. Eurobonds can also be "bearer bonds," which means that the purchasers need not be identified and registered. This is an appealing feature to investors who wish to maintain anonymity and perhaps to avoid the payment of taxes on their investment income. The accompanying illustration offers a humorous commentary on the appeal of government bonds.

The international character of the Eurobond market has also contributed to its continued growth. New issues of Eurobonds can be marketed in several countries simultaneously and thus can tap a wide range of investors. These issues can also be made payable in any one of a number of different national currencies or in a composite "basket" of such currencies. This enables the issuer and the investment bankers that are marketing the bonds to select whatever currency or combination of currencies they think will be most attractive to investors at the time the bonds are issued.

Dealings in the Eurobond market involve the borrowing of impressive sums of money for fairly extended periods of time. Borrowings of $100 million have become commonplace, and the market has easily absorbed a number of single bond issues ranging from $300 million to $1 billion in total value. A few issues sold in this market have maturities of as long as 20 years, but the great bulk of the issues carry maturities in the 6- to 15-year range. The major borrowers in this market include governments (national, state, and local), international financial institutions such as the World Bank, and private industrial and financial corporations. The private corporations as a group have accounted for between 60 and 85 percent of the massive volume of funds that have been borrowed through Eurobond sales in recent years.[10] This is a clear indication that these companies (most of which are operating internationally) have come to rely heavily upon the Eurobond market to fill their medium- and long-term external funding requirements.

Official International Financial Institutions

The period since the Second World War has witnessed the establishment of numerous government-sponsored financial organizations. Many of these have been set up by individual national governments to finance economic development projects and enterprises in their own nations or to provide financing for exports from those nations. But some have been created by multilateral agreements and have been designed to support and encourage international trade and investment and to facilitate intergovernmental lending and related transfers of funds.

These international financial institutions generally are not involved in financing private international business firms in a direct way. Nevertheless, their existence and operations often affect such firms and their activities indirectly. For this reason, it is useful to examine some of the more important of these organizations and to consider their place in the global economic and business systems.

The World Bank Group

The largest and best-known of the international lending institutions is actually a group of three affiliated organizations known as the **World Bank Group.** This group includes the World Bank itself (officially entitled the International Bank for Reconstruction and Development or IBRD), the International Development Association (IDA), and the International Finance Corporation (IFC). The World Bank began operations in 1946, and its establishment at that time was a part of a broad plan and agreement among the United States and its World War II allies for

[10]William H. Baughn and Donald R. Mandich (eds.), *The International Banking Handbook* (Homewood, IL: Dow Jones-Irwin, 1983), 207–210.

reconstructing the war-devastated world economy and creating a supportive environment for the growth of international trade and investment and the development of the poorer nations.[11]

The World Bank technically is part of the United Nations, but the UN has little to do with its management. The Bank is owned by 144 member nations, that have subscribed to its capital stock and are represented on its Board of Governors. That Board has delegated the authority to carry on the Bank's operations to a group of 21 executive directors, each of whom represents either a single large country or a group of smaller countries. The voting power of these directors is proportioned on the basis of their country (or group of countries) contributions to the Bank's capital, which, in turn, is based essentially on the economic wealth of those countries. This arrangement results in the large nations, including the United States, France, Great Britain, and Japan, wielding considerable power over the Bank's policies and activities (the USSR and most of the East European communist countries have not become members of the World Bank).

For the past 30 years, the World Bank has been principally engaged in making long-term (up to 20-year maturity) loans to the developing countries for projects that are expected to contribute to the economic progress of those countries. By the middle of 1983, the Bank had made a total of nearly $90 billion of such loans.[12] Individual loans are typically for several million dollars and are either made directly to national governments or are guaranteed by the government in whose territory the money is to be used. The main project-areas that have been financed by World Bank loans include education, transportation, water supply and sewerage, industry, and—especially in recent years—agriculture and rural development.

The World Bank raises most of the funds that it has available for lending by selling its own bonds or otherwise borrowing in the world's private capital markets. For this reason, and because of requirements in its charter, the Bank has felt obligated to exercise considerable prudence in its choice of projects to be financed and to set repayment terms and interest rates close to those applicable to commercial loans. Those constraints, albeit reasonable in principle, made it difficult for the Bank to respond to the borrowing needs of some of the poorest developing countries. Those countries could not always guarantee the profitability of developmental projects that they needed to undertake nor fulfill the repayment terms that the Bank's policies prescribed.

This problem led to the establishment, in 1960, of the IDA as an affiliate of the World Bank. The IDA is sometimes referred to as the

---

[11]The International Monetary Fund (IMF) was founded during the same period as another institutional component of this strategic plan for restoring and maintaining global economic prosperity and growth. The objectives and functions of the IMF are covered in Chapter 11.

[12]*The World Bank Annual Report 1983* (Washington, DC-The World Bank, 1983), 220.

"soft loan" arm of the World Bank Group, since it extends credits to developing nations on much more lenient terms than those which the Bank itself can offer on its loans. The IDA's credits are available with no interest charge and with as long as 50 years for the borrower to repay. The IDA's funds are provided by the member countries of the World Bank Group, with the amount of each member's contribution determined by its wealth and resultant capacity to pay into this pool of loanable funds. What this means in practial terms is that the IDA functions as a multilateral conduit through which developmental aid is channeled from the richer, industrialized nations to the poorer, developing ones. Slightly over $30 billion of credits had been disbursed by the IDA as of the end of June 1983.[13]

The IFC operates in a different manner than the other two members of the World Bank Group, although its fundamental mission, like theirs, is to spur economic development in the Third World. It does this by providing venture capital, both through loans and stock purchases, to private businesses and by helping to create and expand local capital markets in developing nations. The IFC also supplies technical and managerial assistance to fledgling business firms and organizes syndicates with commercial banks and national development banks to finance such firms. The majority of the businesses that the IFC has supported have been in manufacturing, but it has also assisted in the development of tourist and agriculturally related industries.

Since the IFC concentrates upon the financing of new businesses (rather than large-scale governmental projects) and emphasizes joint participation with other investors, it has functioned with much smaller capital resources than those of the World Bank and the IDA. Those resources come from the paid-in capital of the organization's member nations, borrowings from the World Bank and other sources, and income that the IFC earns from its loans and equity investments. Because the IFC makes a practice of relinquishing its involvement in business ventures as soon as they become profitable enough to induce private investors to take over its ownership shares or replace its loans, it has been able to turn over its investment portfolio regularly and stretch its own capital over numerous projects. This mode of operations has allowed the IFC to successfully fulfill its role as a catalyst for the establishment and growth of privately owned and privately financed business enterprises in the developing countries.

Regional Development Banks

In addition to the World Bank Group, whose membership and activities span virtually the entire globe, there are several official financial institutions whose concerns are limited to particular geographic areas. The

---

[13]*Ibid.*

basic aims and operating procedures of these **regional development banks** are much the same as those of the World Bank Group. They endeavor to foster the economic and social development of their member nations, and do this primarily by making loans and technical assistance available for industrial, agricultural, and infrastructure projects. They also are frequently involved in formulating regional development plans and in trying to encourage private investment from both within and outside their region. Some of these institutions have been established in connection with the regional economic integration programs that were discussed in Chapter 9, and they usually are given responsibility for furthering economic cooperation and balanced development among the nations involved in these integration schemes.

In view of the essentially similar nature of the various regional development banks, the following listing should suffice to identify the more important of their number and to highlight their objectives and activities[14]:

1. The **Inter-American Development Bank (IADB)** was founded in 1959 and is headquartered in Washington, D.C. Its original members were 19 Latin American countries and the United States, but its membership has since been broadened to include most of the Western European countries, Japan, Canada, and several countries in the Caribbean. All of these members contribute to the IADB's capital, but its loans for economic and social development go entirely to Latin America. It raises funds by borrowing in the industrialized nations and uses those funds to finance public infrastructure projects and private industrial and agricultural projects in Latin America. It also furnishes technical assistance to the Latin American countries, both through its own personnel and through sponsorship of facilities to train technicians and skilled workers.

2. The **Asian Development Bank (ADB)** came into existence in 1966. Its headquarters are in Manila, The Philippines. Like the IADB, this organization has member nations from both Asia and elsewhere, but its development financing and technical assistance operations are directed toward the Asian region. The ADB makes some loans at commercial terms and interest rates, but it also operates a special Asian Development Fund, from which "soft" loans or program loans (those unconnected with specific projects) are available.

3. The **African Development Bank (AfDB)** began operations in 1966, with its headquarters in Abidjan, the capital of the Ivory Coast. The existence of the AfDB is designed to reduce the economic dependence of the African nations on their former colonial rulers and to support joint economic projects among those nations.

---

[14]The information included in this listing is taken from Chapters 32 and 33 of William H. Baughn and Donald Mandich (eds.), *The International Banking Handbook* (Homewood, IL: Dow Jones-Irwin, 1983). Chapter 32, Jose D. Epstein, Professor of Economics, Washington, D.C., former Treasurer and Manager, Interamerican Development Bank.

4. The **European Investment Bank (EIB)** was created by the treaty which established the European Economic Community (EEC) in 1958. It is located in Luxembourg, and its membership consists of the ten EEC member countries. The EIB's original aim was to fund investment projects within the territory of the EEC members and to contribute to the balanced economic development of those countries. But its lending activities have since been extended to the many countries that have become associated with the EEC.

5. The **Islamic Development Bank (IDB),** located in Saudi Arabia, was founded in 1975. Its membership and sphere of operations includes the Islamic nations of North Africa, the Middle East, and Asia. The IDB is involved in the financing of foreign trade, as well as the more usual development banking tasks of providing loans, equity funds, and technical assistance for economic projects.

Although the above listing and summary descriptions do not cover all the regional development financing institutions that have sprung up around the world during the last four decades, it is indicative of how widespread such organizations and their activities have become. Moreover, the regional development banks, along with the World Bank Group, comprise only part of the elaborate structure which governments have erected to finance development projects and related economic undertakings. Most of the Third World countries have also set up their own domestic development financing institutions, which often are funded by and work closely with their regional and international counterparts. While there still is disagreement as to its overall effectiveness in accelerating economic growth, this global network of development banks has made vast sums of money available for that purpose.

Given their own economic strength and their ties to the industrialized countries, most international business firms obviously have not been prime candidates for direct financial assistance from this cohort of development financing institutions. However, the existence and operations of these institutions have nonetheless affected international companies in a number of ways. The development banks have been heavily involved in financing and otherwise supporting the creation of what economists call "infrastructure" or, more broadly, "social overhead capital" in the developing nations. These terms include transportation and communications systems, energy generating installations, educational and training establishments, and other facilities and activities that immediately or eventually serve industry and business. The increased availability of such infrastructure components has unquestionably aided international business firms in establishing and conducting modern production and marketing operations in the Third World countries.

International companies have also supplied much of the equipment, materials, and skilled human resources that have been employed in the multitudinous projects financed by the development banks, and have thus benefited from this direct expansion of their markets. Although the secondary market-expansion effects are much more difficult to quantify, there is little doubt that international companies have also reaped very substantial benefits from the higher levels of employment and income and the opportunities to supply new local industries that have resulted from the efforts of the development banks. These official financing institutions therefore warrant inclusion in any study of the international financial system and its impact on international business.

Summary

1. Financing international business transactions is generally more complicated and risky than financing comparable transactions occurring within a single nation. The added complexity and risk is largely due to the use of different currencies and to government interference in the transfer of funds from country to country.

2. The need to finance a growing volume of international business transactions has resulted in the emergence of international financial institutions and markets which facilitate international trade and investment by arranging and expediting international transfers of funds.

3. The foreign exchange market is a worldwide network of financial institutions which buy and sell foreign exchange. Foreign exchange consists of a variety of instruments representing liquid financial claims on foreign residents.

4. The major foreign exchange dealers are large commercial banks located in the principal commercial and financial cities of the world. These banks maintain branch or correspondent relationships with other commercial banks which make it possible for business firms and individuals to buy or sell foreign exchange anywhere in the world.

5. Governmentally controlled central banks frequently intervene in the foreign exchange market in efforts to influence exchange rates.

6. The foreign exchange market performs three main functions in connection with international business operations. These include arranging international payments and collections, supporting the use of credit in international transactions, and making it possible for business firms to avoid the exchange rate risk.

7. Bills of exchange and letters of credit are financial instruments that are extensively utilized in financing international trade and facilitating the use of credit in trade transactions.

8. The forward market in foreign exchange makes it possible for business firms to avoid the exchange rate risk by entering into contracts for future receipt or delivery of foreign currencies at fixed prices.

9. The needs of international companies to acquire funding for their operations and to invest temporarily surplus funds are accommodated through international money and capital markets. These include the international operations of commercial banks, the Eurocurrency market, and the Eurobond market.

10. Commercial banks have greatly expanded their international facilities and services in order to serve the worldwide funding need of their corporate clients.

11. The Eurocurrency market is made up of banks that take in and loan out deposits denominated in currencies other than the currency of the country in which the bank is located. This market has expanded spectacularly in size since the 1950s, as well as in terms of its geographic coverage and the currencies involved.

12. The Eurobond market, which involves the marketing of bonds payable in currencies other than the home currency of the issuer, has become a significant source of medium- and long-term capital for international business firms.

13. A multitude of official financial institutions have been established since the Second World War. These institutions, which operate at international, regional, and national levels, have been principally engaged in funding developmental projects in Third World countries, but their activities have yielded important benefits for private international companies.

Questions for Review or Discussion

1. Explain how the need to deal in different national currencies can increase the complexity and risks of doing business internationally.

2. Define "foreign exchange" and describe the major financial instruments which make up the stock of foreign exchange.

3. What is meant by the description of the foreign exchange market as a worldwide "network" of commercial banks?

4. Assume that a business firm in your locale has purchased goods from a foreign supplier and received a bill payable in the currency of the supplier's country. Explain how the firm in your locale could utilize the foreign exchange market to pay for the goods.

5. What are the circumstances that add to the risk of extending credit to buyers in foreign countries?

6. What are the main advantages that exporters realize by using bills of exchange in connection with sales to foreign customers?

7. Explain *why* and *how* a letter of credit would be employed in an international trade transaction.

8. Describe the forward market in foreign exchange and explain how this market can help business firms avoid the exchange rate risk.

9. Identify and explain the principal factors that have contributed to the establishment and expansion of the Eurocurrency market.
10. Define the following terms and explain how each relates to the international money and capital markets: (a) Eurobonds, (b) LIBOR, (c) Edge Act subsidiaries.
11. Identify the organizations that make up the World Bank Group and explain how the operations of these organizations differ from one another.
12. What are the principal objectives and functions of development banks?

Case

The Toledo Anderson Grain Co.

Michael Masters, the president of Toledo Anderson Grain Co., was considering various alternatives for financing the $100 million in new funds that were needed to complete its acquisition of Champion International Grain Co.

The alternatives being considered included a credit line syndicated by a group of U.S. banks, a bond issue in the United States underwritten by Merril, Smith, and Fenner of New York, and a Eurobond issue underwritten by First Atlantis Trust of London. Each of the alternatives would make the funds available at short notice for a period up to 7 years with no early repayment penalties after the second year.

The credit line would carry an interest rate that would be adjusted every 6 months to 1 percent above the then-prevailing rate for 5-year treasury bonds while the U.S. bond issue will carry a fixed coupon about 120 basis points above the rate for 5-year treasury bonds on the day before the bond issue. All transactions related to both of these loans were to be denominated in U.S. dollars.

The Eurodollar bonds, on the other hand, were to be issued with a fixed coupon about 1 percent above the rate for 5-year A-rated municipal bonds on the day before the bond issue. While the issue currency and the interest was to be denominated in U.S. dollars, the repayment at maturity was to be in terms of French francs with the maturity amount to be fixed at the exchange rate in effect on the day of the issue. Thus, with this Eurobond issue, while it had a lower coupon, Toledo Anderson would face the risk arising from any adverse changes in the U.S. dollar/French franc exchange rate. Moreover, Toledo Anderson faced some additional risks with the proposed Eurobond issue because it had never before raised money in the Eurocurrency market or anywhere outside the United States. Finally, because of the differing nature of interest rate arrangements among the three alternatives, Mr. Masters felt that it was difficult for him to compare the three alternatives. Therefore, he asked the company's treasurer, Bill Folks, to help him to analyze the alternatives.

According to Bill Folks, comparing fixed and floating rate bonds, even in various currencies, had become relatively easy because of the recent expansion of the market for interest rate and currency swaps. Using this very liquid market, Toledo Anderson could easily obtain quotes for interest rate swaps that would exchange its floating rate interest obligations for fixed rate obligations or vice versa. As a matter of fact, based on these quotes, Folks had found that both domestic alternatives were comparably priced.

Similarly, Toledo Anderson could enter into a 7-year forward contract or buy a 7-year option to exchange its French franc obligation (at the maturity of its Eurobond issue) for a fixed U.S. dollar obligation. Folks had found that the lower coupon on the Eurobond issue more than offset the cost of entering into a forward contract for the payment obligation at maturity.

However, Folks pointed out that Toledo Anderson need not worry about the French franc obligation since the company it was acquiring, Champion International, provides a natural hedge since it sells a great deal of grain in African countries that are former French colonies and whose currencies still move in tandem with the French franc. Finally, Folks pointed out, the Eurobond market has been growing very rapidly, and is becoming the major component of the Eurocurrency market. Over $300 billion of Eurobonds were outstanding at the end of 1984 and another $80 billion had already been issued during the first half of 1985. Even though the United States had removed the withholding requirement for foreign purchases of U.S. bonds, the total Eurocurrency market itself had continued to grow. It has become larger than even the U.S. domestic money supply, and, no U.S. company, including Toledo Anderson, could afford not to develop the ability to raise money in this market. Thus, Folks concluded, Toledo Anderson should select the Eurobond issue.

Mike Masters was intrigued by Folks's recommendation. He was tempted to agree, especially since he knew that Philip Morris had raised from overseas sources most of the money it needed for its October 1984 $6 billion acquisition of General Foods, and that Freddie Mac (Federal National Mortgage Corporation) had sold $350 million of its $1 billion November 1985 bond issue in the Eurocurrency market.

What is your assessment of Bill Folks' recommendation?

Source: W. R. Folks and R. Aggarwal, *International Dimensions of Financial Management,* Boston: Kent Publishing Company, 1986.

Chapter 11

EXCHANGE RATES AND INTERNATIONAL MONETARY ARRANGEMENTS

Chapter Objectives

- *To define the foreign exchange rate and point out the significance of the exchange rate relative to international economic transactions*
- *To explain how foreign exchange rates are determined*
- *To show how national governments and the international monetary regimes they have created influence foreign exchange rates*
- *To review the historical development of international monetary regimes and to analyze the strengths and weaknesses of alternative monetary regimes*
- *To illustrate how national governments utilize foreign exchange controls and to point out the problems associated with such controls*

Preceding chapters of this text have made frequent references to the foreign exchange rate and have stressed the significance of exchange rates in shaping international trade and investment patterns. Later chapters will examine the impact of exchange rates and changes in those rates on the operations and the profitability of international business firms. There is no question that exchange rates constitute one of the key variables that influence economic relationships among nations, as well as business decisions and behavior at the level of individual international companies.

This chapter will consider how foreign exchange rates are determined. This will include an examination of various arrangements whereby national governments endeavor to influence rates of exchange, since governments habitually have played an important part in the workings of foreign exchange markets and the setting of exchange rates in those markets.

The Foreign Exchange Rate

Foreign exchange rates are the prices at which different national currencies are traded for one another in the foreign exchange markets. If this is related to a specific nation and its currency, such as the United States and the dollar, the exchange rate can be defined as the price that must be paid, in dollars, to acquire a unit of any other nation's currency. Thus, the exchange rate between the U.S. dollar and the French franc would be the number of dollars (or cents) that would be required to purchase one franc. If one were concerned with the exchange rate between the dollar and the British pound, the rate would be the number of dollars needed to purchase one pound.

It should be apparent that the market relationship between two currencies could actually be expressed in either of two ways. The relationship between the dollar and the French franc could be stated as the price of one franc in dollars, or as the price of a dollar in francs.[1] However, it is customary when exchange rates are being quoted within any particular country to express those rates as the domestic currency price of the various foreign currencies. It follows from this that when reference is made to an **increase** in the exchange rate, this ordinarily indicates that the price of a foreign currency (or foreign currencies generally) is rising in terms of the domestic currency. Conversely, a **decrease** in the exchange rate would indicate that the price of the foreign currency(ies) in question was falling relative to the home currency.

Figure 11.1 reproduces a listing of exchange rates taken from *The Wall Street Journal.* A look at this listing will reveal some important aspects of exchange rates and the manner in which they are quoted. First, it can be seen that certain foreign currencies have more than one price or exchange rate listed. In most of these instances, there are 30-, 90-, and 180-day forward prices, in addition to the initially listed price. This initial price is the **spot rate,** which is the rate being charged for foreign currencies that are to be delivered to buyers immediately (within 2 business days). The other rates are the **forward rates,** which are the prices at which sellers are currently willing to contract with buyers to deliver the foreign currency at the designated time in the future. (The existence and functions of this forward exchange market were discussed in Chapter 10.)

In some cases, more than one rate will be quoted for a particular country's currency because that country maintains more than one market in which its currency is exchanged for foreign currencies. Such arrangements typically include an "official" market, in which residents of the country can purchase the foreign currencies they need to finance those transactions that have been authorized by the government. The

---

[1]Numerically, the two prices are **reciprocals.** If the price of one franc in dollars is (for example) $0.09, then the price of one dollar in francs would be 1.0/0.09 or 11.11 francs.

Figure 11.1   *Foreign Exchange Rates*

FOREIGN EXCHANGE

Thursday, October 31, 1985

The New York foreign exchange selling rates below apply to trading among banks in amounts of $1 million and more, as quoted at 3 p.m. Eastern time by Bankers Trust Co. Retail transactions provide fewer units of foreign currency per dollar.

Country	U.S. $ equiv. Thurs.	Wed.	Currency per U.S. $ Thurs.	Wed.
Argentina (Austral) ...	1.2484	1.2484	.801	.801
Australia (Dollar) ...	.7000	.7017	1.4286	1.4251
Austria (Schilling)	.05464	.05450	18.30	18.35
Belgium (Franc)				
Commercial rate	.01889	.01888	52.93	52.98
Financial rate	.01880	.01876	53.20	53.30
Brazil (Cruzeiro)	.0001217	.0001217	8220.00	8220.00
Britain (Pound)	1.4430	1.4340	.6930	.6974
30-Day Forward ...	1.4389	1.4298	.6950	.6994
90-Day Forward ...	1.4309	1.4215	.6989	.7035
180-Day Forward ...	1.4205	1.4111	.7040	.7087
Canada (Dollar)	.7319	.7316	1.3663	1.3668
30-Day Forward ...	.7316	.7314	1.3668	1.3673
90-Day Forward ...	.7310	.7307	1.3680	1.3685
180-Day Forward ...	.7296	.7295	1.3707	1.3708
Chile (Official rate)	.005672	.005672	176.30	176.30
China (Yuan)	.3131	.3131	3.1935	3.1935
Colombia (Peso)	.006219	.006219	160.79	160.79
Denmark (Krone)	.1059	.1054	9.4400	9.4850
Ecuador (Sucre)				
Official rate	.01504	.01504	66.48	66.48
Floating rate	.008375	.008375	119.40	119.40
Finland (Markka)	.1786	.1783	5.6000	5.6070
France (Franc)	.1255	.1247	7.9700	8.0200
30-Day Forward ...	.1253	.1246	7.9783	8.0270
90-Day Forward ...	.1249	.1241	8.0050	8.0550
180-Day Forward ...	.1239	.1232	8.0690	8.1200
Greece (Drachma) ...	.006532	.006525	153.10	153.25
Hong Kong (Dollar) ...	.1284	.1283	7.7910	7.7920
India (Rupee)	.08313	.08306	12.03	12.04
Indonesia (Rupiah) ...	.0008897	.0008897	1124.00	1124.00
Ireland (Punt)	1.1875	1.1815	.8421	.8464
Israel (Shekel)	.0006775	.0006775	1476.00	1476.00
Italy (Lira)	.0005669	.0005653	1764.00	1769.00
Japan (Yen)	.004729	.004704	211.45	212.60
30-Day Forward ...	.004732	.004705	211.34	212.52
90-Day Forward ...	.004734	.004709	211.23	212.35
180-Day Forward ...	.004745	.004719	210.75	211.90
Jordan (Dinar)	2.7503	2.7503	.3636	.3636
Kuwait (Dinar)	3.3875	3.3875	.2952	.2952
Lebanon (Pound)	.05634	.05634	17.75	17.75
Malaysia (Ringgit) ...	.4090	.4096	2.4450	2.4415
Malta (Lira)	2.2857	2.2857	.4375	.4375
Mexico (Peso)				
Floating rate	.002092	.002128	478.00	470.00
Netherlands (Guilder)	.3391	.3382	2.9490	2.9565
New Zealand (Dollar)	.5850	.5800	1.7094	1.7241
Norway (Krone)	.1276	.1273	7.8350	7.8550
Pakistan (Rupee)	.06329	.06309	15.80	15.85
Peru (Sol)	.00007173	.00007173	13942.00	13942.00
Philippines (Peso)	.05343	.05343	18.715	18.715
Portugal (Escudo)	.006135	.006173	163.00	162.00
Saudi Arabia (Riyal) ..	.2740	.2740	3.6495	3.6495
Singapore (Dollar) ...	.4706	.4690	2.1250	2.1320
South Africa (Rand) ...	.3890	.3925	2.5707	2.5478
South Korea (Won) ...	.001120	.001120	892.90	892.90
Spain (Peseta)	.006246	.006232	160.10	160.45
Sweden (Krona)	.1275	.1273	7.8425	7.8570
Switzerland (Franc) ..	.4655	.4640	2.1480	2.1550
30-Day Forward ...	.4672	.4656	2.1406	2.1476
90-Day Forward ...	.4698	.4683	2.1285	2.1355
180-Day Forward ...	.4737	.4721	2.1110	2.1180
Taiwan (Dollar)	.02497	.02497	40.05	40.05
Thailand (Baht)	.03759	.03759	26.60	26.60
United Arab (Dirham)	.2723	.2723	3.673	3.673
Uruguay (New Peso)				
Financial	.008667	.008667	115.38	115.38
Venezuela (Bolivar)				
Official rate	.1333	.1333	7.50	7.50
Floating rate	.06840	.06840	14.62	14.62
W. Germany (Mark) ..	.3826	.3799	2.6140	2.6325
30-Day Forward ...	.3836	.3809	2.6068	2.6356
90-Day Forward ...	.3855	.3827	2.5939	2.6130
180-Day Forward ...	.3882	.3852	2.5758	2.5960
SDR	1.07165	1.07204	0.933140	0.932805
ECU	0.845708	0.846513	....	....

Special Drawing Rights are based on exchange rates for the U.S., West German, British, French and Japanese currencies. Source: International Monetary Fund.

ECU is based on a basket of community currencies. Source: European Community Commission.

z-Not quoted.

official market usually exists alongside a "free" market, in which residents of the country can buy whatever foreign currencies are available for other, nonauthorized transactions. The prices that must be paid for foreign currencies tend to be lower in the official market, inasmuch as the government is making foreign exchange available there for those international transactions that it deems to be "good" for the nation's economy. These arrangements will be considered further when the topic of exchange control is introduced later in this chapter.

Another aspect worth noting with regard to the exchange rates appearing in Figure 11.1 is that these are the banks' **selling rates,** that is, the prices at which banks that deal regularly in foreign exchange are ready to sell the various foreign currencies. These same banks will, of course, also be willing to buy foreign currencies, at a **buying rate** that is generally slightly less than the selling rate. The small differential or "spread" between the selling and buying rates allows the banks to cover the costs of maintaining foreign exchange departments and may also yield a profit on their foreign exchange dealings. As the notation near the top of Figure 11.1 indicates, the rates listed there actually apply to large transactions that the foreign exchange dealers carry on among themselves. Those transactions occur in what is termed the **interbank** segment of the foreign exchange market, while the dealings the banks have with their nonbank customers take place in the **retail** segment.

One additional factor that conceivably can influence the exchange rates quoted by foreign exchange dealers is the manner in which the funds involved are to be transferred. Chapter 10 explained that there are a number of instruments or methods—including cables, bank drafts, and bills of exchange—that can be used to effectuate a transfer of funds within the foreign exchange market. These methods may differ in the time required for ownership of the funds (usually consisting of bank deposit balances) to pass from the seller to another party. With a cable transfer, the change of ownership would take place almost instantaneously, whereas, with a written draft, several days may elapse between the time at which a dealer sells foreign exchange (and receives payment for it) and the time delivery is accomplished. This lapse is due simply to the time required to send a written document from one country to another.

To the extent that foreign exchange dealers take this time factor into account, they could be expected to quote higher selling rates for foreign currencies when the funds will be transferred immediately (i.e., through cable transfers) and lower rates for delayed transfers (those involving the use of written instruments). This is predicated upon the advantage that delayed transfers would give the dealers, by affording them an opportunity to continue earning interest or other returns on funds that remain at their disposal for a period after they have been sold. As a practical matter, the dealers may not feel compelled to quote differential rates on this basis, and any differentials that did arise would tend to be quite small.

All of these technicalities that are associated with the setting and quoting of exchange rates should not cause one to lose sight of the fundamental nature and significance of those rates. Exchange rates are, in one sense, just the prices of national currencies. However, they are unique and particularly important prices, since they affect a broad gamut of other cost and price relationships among nations.

Thus, the exchange rate between the currencies of two countries, for instance, France and the United States, can be thought of as simply the price of francs in dollars (and vice versa). It should be realized, however, that this franc/dollar exchange rate plays a large part in determining how much it will actually cost Americans to acquire French products and services, or to undertake investment in France. Moreover, the exchange rate is simultaneously exerting the same kind of influence over the cost (to French citizens) of American goods and investment assets, and any change in the exchange rate will alter this entire array of reciprocal costs. If, for example, the price of the franc rises in relation to the dollar, American residents will find that virtually all French products, as well as trips to France and investments in that country, have become more expensive, whereas the French will perceive an across-the-board "cheapening" of American products and services.

Exchange rates thus constitute a very important intermediate link between the economies of different nations. This makes the question of how these rates are determined a critical one, and also creates a strong incentive for governments to become involved in the rate-setting process. The following section will first look at how exchange rates would be determined under theoretical "free market" conditions, and will then consider the purposes and effects of governmental involvement in the exchange markets.

How Exchange Rates Are Determined

The manner in which exchange rates are determined depends upon the nature of the foreign exchange market, with the key variant being the role played by national governments. Political authorities historically have been inclined to regard exchange rates as being much too important to be left outside their sphere of control. Consequently, exchange markets have generally been characterized by the presence of governmental controls.

It would be impossible to detail all the ways in which individual national governments have been involved in the foreign exchange markets and the setting of exchange rates. However, there are certain general approaches that governments have followed in this regard. These can be referred to as alternative **exchange rate regimes,** since what is being described are different systems or sets of rules and procedures that governments have employed in their efforts to influence the behavior of exchange rates. There have been periods during which a majority of the world's nations have subscribed to the same set of rules and employed commonly agreed-upon procedures relative to the exchange markets, so that a single exchange rate regime can be said to have prevailed throughout most of the world.

This section will identify and describe four of these alternative exchange rate regimes, namely, (1) a freely fluctuating rate regime, (2) a stabilized rate regime, (3) a managed floating rate regime, and (4) a controlled rate regime. The distinction among these regimes mainly has to do with the form and the extent of governmental participation in the determination of rates of exchange.

Freely Fluctuating Exchange Rates

The freely fluctuating rate regime, at least in a pure form, is more a theoretical construct than a real-world phenomenon. In a pure free fluctuating exchange rate regime, governments would maintain a complete "hands off" stance with respect to exchange rates and private transactions in the exchange markets, and there has been no extended period in modern times during which governments have actually shown this degree of self-restraint. However, the theoretical construct is helpful, since it can be used to demonstrate how exchange rates would be determined in the absence of government interference, and it thereby provides a benchmark for understanding and assessing the effects of government involvement in the exchange markets.

Under a pure freely fluctuating exchange rate regime, the foreign exchange market would closely approximate the economic model of pure competition. There would be very large numbers of prospective buyers and sellers of each national currency, which could be regarded as a standardized commodity. Moreover, all these buyers and sellers would have unrestricted access to the market itself, as well as to current information pertaining to prices and other market conditions.

Given such conditions, the exchange rate (i.e., the price of any national currency) would be determined by the interaction between the demand for that currency and the available supply. This can be illustrated by using the familiar graphical presentation of demand and supply curves, which all students reading this are sure to have encountered in their basic economics courses. If the analysis is limited to two countries and two currencies (e.g., the French franc and the American dollar) the illustration becomes quite simple and easy to follow.

Figure 11.2 portrays the foreign exchange market (limited, in this instance, to the market for dollars and francs) from the perspective of U.S. residents. These residents would include American individuals, business firms, and perhaps government agencies that have some interest in acquiring French francs. The bases of that interest will be identified shortly. As with all graphical presentations of how prices are determined by the interplay of demand and supply, the vertical axis of the graph measures the price variable (in this case, the price is the dollar/

Figure 11.2   *Foreign Exchange (Francs) Demand and Supply*

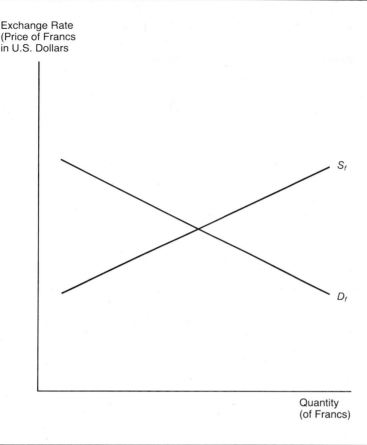

Exchange Rate
(Price of Francs
in U.S. Dollars

S_f

D_f

Quantity
(of Francs)

franc exchange rate, that is, the price of francs in terms of dollars). The variable measured on the horizontal axis is the quantity of francs.

The Demand for Foreign Exchange.   The line D_f represents the combined demand of American residents for francs. It indicates the different quantities of francs that these residents wish to acquire at different exchange rates. Like all well-behaved demand curves, this one slopes downward from left to right, thereby positing an inverse relationship between the price of francs and the quantities that Americans would demand.

This inverse relationship between price and quantity (in addition to being intuitively reasonable and consistent with prior experiences with demand curves) is predicated upon an important characteristic of the demand for foreign exchange. That demand is, for the most part, a **derived demand.** This implies that the residents of one country (in this case, American residents) would not, as a general rule, wish to acquire a foreign currency (the franc) for its own sake. Rather, they are obliged to acquire that currency in order to acquire something else they want or need. Thus, the demand for the foreign currency derives from the demand for other things.

What are these "other things" from which the demand for foreign exchange emanates? In the context of the present example, this question can be addressed in another way, by asking, "Why might Americans need to acquire French francs?" Several reasons should immediately come to mind. One obvious and important reason is that they need the francs in order to pay for **goods or services** that they already have purchased, or wish to purchase, from French suppliers. American companies importing products or materials from France, or American individuals traveling or preparing to travel in France often have to pay for their purchases in the sellers' national currency. These American residents therefore would become "demanders" of French francs in the foreign exchange market, that is, they would be seeking to buy francs from foreign exchange dealers, offering their dollars in exchange.

A second significant source of the U.S. demand for francs would be the desire of Americans to **invest** in France. If an American manufacturing firm wishes to obtain a factory in France, either by buying an existing French factory or building a new facility there, the carrying out of that direct investment project usually would require the American firm to pay out francs to someone (existing owners or builders in France), and this would create a demand for francs by the American firm. Similarly, the purchase of French securities, for example, stocks issued by French companies or French government bonds, by American investors would necessitate the acquisition of French francs by those security purchasers. It is also quite conceivable that American investors might wish to invest in francs per se, if they expected the value of the French currency to rise in relation to the dollar. This sort of investment, which typically would involve the acquisition of franc-denominated bank deposit balances or short-term debt instruments payable in francs by the American investors, could be regarded as an exception to the rule that the demand for foreign currencies is a derived demand (since, in this instance, it is the French currency itself that Americans wish to obtain). But this is still consistent with the idea that the demand for a foreign currency arises from business ventures that require the possession or use of that currency.

There is a third type of economic activity that can engender a demand for foreign exchange. This has to do with what economists call **unilateral transfers,** which may be thought of, in simpler terms, as "gifts." It is by no means uncommon for individuals, organizations, or government agencies residing in one country to make gifts and grants of various kinds to residents of other nations. If these transfers involve money, as they very often do, they will show up in the foreign exchange markets. If, for example, a charitable foundation in the United States decided to make a cash donation to some eleemosynary organization in France, the American donor (or some intermediary) would have to exchange dollars for francs in order to accomplish this gift-type transaction. Any grant of funds by the American governments to French recipients would likewise create a demand for francs in the foreign exchange market.

Once it is perceived that the U.S. demand curve for French francs is derived from the kinds of transactions described above, it becomes clear why that demand curve is downsloping. If Americans are demanding francs because they need them to purchase French economic goods or investment assets (or to make gifts to French residents), it follows that the cheaper the franc is relative to the dollar, the less expensive it would be for Americans to acquire those French goods or assets and the more attractive such purchases would be. Thus, more francs would be demanded by Americans at lower exchange rates, because the lower price of the franc translates into a lower effective price for everything that Americans want to buy from France.

Although the balance of payments and balance of payments accounting will not be dealt with until Chapter 12, the groundwork for that topic can be laid here by pointing out that all the economic activities that have just been referred to in connection with the derivation of the demand curve for foreign exchange would be part of the U.S. (and French) balance of payments for the period in which they occurred. Furthermore, the specific economic acts that were used as examples would all enter the U.S. balance of payments accounts as **debits,** since they would in every case entail **payments** to France by American residents who are either purchasing something (goods, services, or investment assets) from that country or making gifts to French recipients. This establishes an important balance of payments accounting rule, which is that those international economic dealings of a country's residents that create a demand for foreign currencies make up the debit side of that country's balance of payments ledger. Even more important than this accounting truism, however, is recognition of the underlying relationship that exists between the international economic transactions that comprise the balance of payments and the demand and supply forces that are at work in the foreign exchange market. That relationship will be referred to again in Chapter 12.

The Supply of Foreign Exchange.   Figure 11.1 also shows the French franc supply curve S_f, depicting the quantity of francs that would be supplied to American residents through the foreign exchange market at different exchange rates. This supply curve is upward-sloping, which implies that the amounts of francs forthcoming would increase as the price of francs, in dollars, rises. This direct relationship between price and quantity coincides with the usual expectation that the producers or holders of most products, services, or assets would offer more of those things for sale at higher prices than at lower ones. With respect to foreign exchange, the supply curve has much the same "derived" character as the demand curve, in that the willingness of foreign currency owners (French residents in this example) to offer those currencies in the exchange market would be motivated by other economic desires. Thus, French individuals or French business and government organizations would offer their francs in exchange for dollars in order to pay for U.S. imports, to finance investments in the United States, or to make unilateral transfers to Americans, and the more dollars they received for their francs, the cheaper and presumably more appealing these acquisitions or donations would become. The French–American economic dealings just described would all be recorded in the U.S. balance of payments accounts as **credits,** since they would involve **receipts** from abroad. Thus, the supply of foreign exchange available to the residents of a country has its basis in the credit side of that country's balance of payments accounts, just as the demand for foreign exchange is linked to the debit side.

The Equilibrium Exchange Rate.   The intersection of the demand and supply curves D_f and S_f, respectively, establishes the equilibrium exchange rate ER_e (Figure 11.3). This is the price of francs, in terms of dollars, at which the quantities of francs demanded and supplied would be equal. Any higher exchange rate, such as ER_1, would create an excess supply of francs relative to the demand, reflecting the eagerness of French residents to export more of their high-priced goods and capital assets to America (and to obtain more "cheap" American goods and assets) than U.S. residents would be willing to take (and relinquish). This would result in a bidding down of the exchange rate, lowering it from ER_1 to ER_e. By the same reckoning, a rate below equilibrium, such as ER_2, would reflect the opposite set of imbalances between demand and supply, which would bring forces into play that would bid the rate up to ER_e.

It is important to understand and keep in mind that the exchange rate ER_e is the equilibrium rate that results from the interaction between a *particular pair* of demand and supply curves, and that those curves themselves represent a *particular set* of economic circumstances (including production costs, incomes, availabilities and prices of domestic goods, and consumer preferences) that are postulated to exist in the two countries. This means that a change in any of those circumstances would bring about a shift in the related demand or supply curve, which would establish a new and different equilibrium exchange rate.

For purposes of illustrating this, suppose that Americans suddenly developed a craving for French wines. To satisfy this craving, Americans would have to acquire more francs to pay for increased wine imports, and this would require that they offer more dollars per franc. This increased demand for francs (which would be portrayed graphically as an upward shift in the demand curve D_f) would result in a new and higher equilibrium exchange rate. This would be a plausible outcome, since Americans have raised their overall demand for imports from France,

Figure 11.3   Equilibrium and Disequilibrium Rates of Exchange

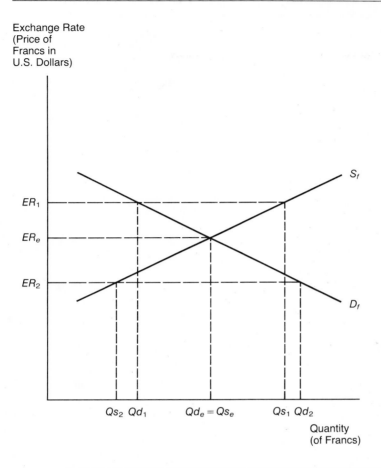

Exchange Rate
(Price of
Francs in
U.S. Dollars)

while the French have experienced no comparable urge to expand their purchases from the United States. French imports in general should therefore become dearer for Americans, and the higher exchange rate would both accomplish and confirm that result.

Assessment of Freely Fluctuating Rates.   Since many factors in the real world can affect a country's demand for foreign goods (not to mention the desires of its residents to carry on other kinds of economic transactions with foreigners) and all these factors are susceptible to change, it should be apparent that a freely fluctuating exchange rate regime would be prone to continuous and conceivably sharp variations in exchange rates. Many influential individuals—including government officials, bankers and other businesspersons, and academic economists—regard this prospect of rate variability as sufficient justification for re-

Box 11.1

Problems of Exchange Rate Instability

Both the size of the foreign exchange market and the volatility of the exchange rates of the world's major currencies have increased greatly in recent years. Transactions in the foreign exchange markets are estimated to average $150 billion per day—about 40 times the average daily volume of transactions on the New York Stock Exchange—and exchange rates fluctuated more wildly during 1985 than at any time since the stabilized rate system was abandoned in the early 1970s.

This has forced companies engaged in international business to devote much more time and effort to activities that are designed to reduce the impact of exchange rate swings. However, neither these multinational companies nor the big international banks have been able to completely eliminate the risks of being caught on the wrong side of sharp exchange rate changes. Morgan Guaranty bank, a highly-experienced foreign exchange dealer, reported currency trading losses in two quarters of 1984, and Fuji Bank of Japan lost 47 million by betting, incorrectly, that the yen was going to strengthen against the dollar. Meanwhile, Rupert Murdoch's Australian holding company, News Corporation, Ltd., said that it realized losses of $102 million dollars "due to a serious misjudgment of the international money markets."

Source: Gary Putka and Michael R. Sesit, "World Currency Prices Become More Volatile, Increase Trading Risks," *The Wall Street Journal* (July 30, 1985), 1, 14.

jecting the installation of such a regime. Their reasoning is that the uncertainty and risk associated with constant and extensive fluctuations in the relative values of national currencies would be a serious deterrent to international trade and investment, and that freely fluctuating rates should therefore be avoided in favor of arrangements that ensure more predictability and stability in currency price relationships.

This reasoning certainly is not without merit. However, there is another consideration that should not be overlooked in reviewing the case for or against a freely fluctuating exchange rate regime. The previous example of trade between the United States and France and the determination of the exchange rate between the dollar and franc illustrated how an increase in the U.S. demand for French imports (specifically, French wine) triggered a rise in the price of francs relative to the dollar, thereby making all French commodities, services, and capital assets more expensive for Americans. By extrapolating from this hypothetical example and its outcome, one can grasp a significant attribute of freely fluctuating rates. This is their tendency to temper a country's demands for foreign goods or foreign investments by "automatically" making those things more expensive, relative to similar domestic goods or investment projects, whenever the country's total imports (foreign expenditures) begin to exceed its total exports (receipts from foreign residents).

This process will be considered in greater detail in Chapter 12, which takes up the subjects of balance of payments disequilibrium and adjustment. But it should now be recognized that whenever exchange rates are permitted to rise or fall freely in response to the demand and supply pressures that emanate from a country's economic transactions with the rest of the world, the rates will naturally move in a manner that serves to maintain a "balance" between that country's total purchases from abroad and its total sales to foreigners. A freely fluctuating rate regime thus helps to prevent serious imbalances in economic transactions among the nations of the world.

Despite this argument for freely fluctuating exchange rates, there have been only a few brief periods in recent history during which national governments have declined to regulate exchange rates and have left the determination of those rates to market forces. Even then, the move toward a freer exchange market has stopped short of the installation of a "pure" freely fluctuating rate regime, and has typically been part of a desperate search for remedies for a deteriorating international monetary situation rather than a calculated choice. The latest episode of this nature occurred in the early 1970s, when a succession of increasingly severe international financial "crises" culminated in the abandonment of the stabilized exchange rate regime that had been established at the end of the Second World War and led to the adoption of arrangements more closely akin to a freely fluctuating rate regime. These arrangements, to which most of the world's major trading nations are now adhering, are usually described as a **managed floating rate system.**

The contemporary managed floating rate system has the basic characteristics associated with a freely fluctuating rate regime, but also includes vestiges of the stabilized rate regime that preceded it. It will be easier to understand this system if the main elements of its predecessor, the stabilized rate Bretton Woods System, are examined first.

Stabilized Exchange Rates: The Bretton Woods System

Before delving into the features of a stabilized exchange rate regime, it may be enlightening to review a bit of history. This will provide a time-frame to which the different exchange rate regimes can be related and may also indicate why the world's governments have opted for one or another regime at particular periods.

During the early 1940s, while the Second World War was still going on, the United States and its allies had already begun to make plans and lay the groundwork for postwar economic recovery. The world had experienced two calamitous eras in succession, first the Great Depression of the 1930s, and then the Second World War, which had left the economies of many nations in ruins and had greatly reduced the volume of international investment and nonmilitary trade. The leaders of the United States and its allies became convinced that the postwar revival of the world economy would require an unprecedented degree of international economic cooperation and that an effective and orderly world financial and exchange rate system would be an essential component of that cooperative effort. Accordingly, a group of high-level government officials and renowned economists representing those countries met at a conference in Bretton Woods, New Hampshire in 1944 and reached agreement on the outlines of a new international monetary system. The rules that nations were to follow in their financial dealings with one another were set forth in a document entitled the **Articles of Agreement of the International Monetary Fund,** and the acceptance of that treaty-like document by the United States and some 40 other nations in 1945 marked the official establishment of the Bretton Woods System.

Characteristics of the Bretton Woods System.   At the heart of the Bretton Woods System was the principle that rates of exchange should ordinarily be kept stable. This thinking was consistent with the basic aim of restoring and expanding international trade, since stable exchange rates were expected to reduce a good deal of the risk that might otherwise discourage businesses from undertaking trade with other countries. It also coincided with the fixity of exchange rates that had existed under the pre-1930s gold standard, before the economic turmoil engendered by the Great Depression and World War II.

The arrangements adopted to secure the stability of exchange rates included first, a requirement that each nation, on accepting the Articles of Agreement, specify a par value for its currency. While this par value was nominally expressed in terms of gold, the nations involved (with one important exception) were not obligated to actually sell gold in exchange for their respective currencies. The one exception was the United States, which did take on the obligation to redeem dollars for gold at a specific rate, providing those dollars were proffered by national **monetary authorities,** that is, central banks or treasury agencies. In this way, the value of the dollar was directly linked to gold and given a fixed value in terms of that metal.

A second major aspect of the Bretton Woods arrangements was the expectation that each nation would endeavor to maintain the par value it had set for its currency in relation to the dollar. The principal method by which this was to be accomplished was **exchange market intervention,** which meant that national monetary authorities would undertake to sell or buy their currencies in the foreign exchange market whenever this was required to prevent the exchange rate from rising or falling more than 1 percent above or below its par value. In effect, the monetary authorities were to offset any imbalances between currency demand and supply arising out of private international economic transactions in order to keep those imbalances from altering the market rate of exchange.

To carry out this stabilization function, it was necessary for the monetary authorities to hold or have ready access to liquid assets they could offer in exchange for currencies. This was not a matter of serious concern for a nation whose currency was increasing in value in the exchange markets, since that nation's central bank could, in essence, "create" the domestic money needed to meet the demand that was driving up the price. But the authorities of a nation whose currency was falling in value faced a more difficult problem, in that they had to be in a position to trade other national currencies (generally U.S. dollars) for their domestic currency. The provisions that were made for this eventuality constituted a third important component of the Bretton Woods arrangements. This had to do with the availability of **international reserve assets** that the monetary authorities could draw upon for purposes of exchange market intervention.

A portion of the reserve assets needed for intervention would be owned by the monetary authorities of each nation. These consisted partly of convertible currencies (actually bank deposit balances denominated in dollars or other major national currencies) that the monetary authorities could accumulate over time by exchanging their home currency for the dollars and other foreign currencies earned by their residents through trade or investment.[2] In addition to these official holdings of convertible currencies, the monetary authorities might have reserves in the form of gold, which could readily be sold to the U.S. Treasury for the dollars needed to intervene in the foreign exchange markets.

To supplement these "owned" reserves and thereby reinforce the intervention capabilities of national monetary authorities, the Bretton Woods System included facilities through which those authorities could, if necessary, borrow the funds needed to conduct exchange rate stabilization efforts. The International Monetary Fund (IMF) was established to serve as a "pool of funds" from which its member nations could borrow dollars or other convertible currencies if their own reserves proved insufficient to counteract destabilizing demand and supply pressures in the exchange markets. The IMF acquires these funds from all its members under an arrangement in which each nation subscribes (i.e., pledges to make available to the IMF) a specified amount of gold and its domestic currency. The amounts subscribed, termed the nation's "quota," are

---

[2]A **convertible** currency is one that can be freely and easily exchanged for other currencies. Full convertibility of a currency would require, first, the absence of legal restrictions on the exchange of that currency, and, second, a sufficient demand for the currency in the foreign exchange markets to make it possible for holders to trade it readily for other currencies.

based upon each nation's economic situation, with the larger and wealthier nations pledging more than the smaller and poorer ones. A nation's quota also determines the total amount it can borrow from the IMF, as well as the voting power it has in setting and administering IMF policies.

A member nation's ability to borrow from the IMF is not entirely "automatic," that is, the institution has considerable discretion as to whether or not (and how much) a member country is permitted to borrow. Over the years, the IMF has used this discretionary power to convince member nations to conform to the rules and the spirit of the Bretton Woods agreement, which included measures designed to reduce government restrictions on international transfers of funds or the convertibility of currencies. It has also required nations wishing to borrow from it to take steps to curb inflation or other internal economic problems. The IMF has thereby taken the role of "disciplinarian" vis-à-vis member nations that are pursuing what it regards as reckless domestic economic policies.

The fourth significant feature of the Bretton Woods System was the allowance it made for changes in the par values of currencies. The Articles of Agreement permitted a member nation to **devalue** its currency (i.e., to lower its par value) in order to correct a condition of "fundamental disequilibrium" in its balance of payments. This condition was not defined in a way that made it possible to establish its existence through precise quantitative measures, but it was generally understood to refer to an imbalance in a country's international economic transactions that was sufficiently severe and chronic as to make it virtually impossible for the par value of the nation's currency to be maintained through intervention by the monetary authorities or internal economic measures. Although this implied that a nation should alter the par value of its currency only as a "last resort," this provision in the Articles of Agreement nevertheless recognized and accepted devaluation or revaluation as a remedy for serious difficulties in a country's international economic situation.

Thus, the overall exchange rate concept embodied in the Bretton Woods System was that those rates basically should be stable, but that they could be changed in response to extraordinary circumstances. This approach (sometimes termed the "adjustable peg" concept) constituted a compromise between a system, such as the pre-1930 gold standard, that dictated that exchange rates be rigidly and permanently fixed, and the other extreme of a pure freely fluctuating rate system. This compromise was designed to provide sufficient exchange rate predictability and certainty to support the expansion of international commerce, without ruling out occasional, discretionary rate changes as a means of dealing with stubborn balance of payments problems.

Operation of the Bretton Woods System.   The period during which the Bretton Woods System was in operation was marked by historically unparalleled rates of growth in international trade and investment, and the System is credited with contributing significantly to this phenomenon. But the Bretton Woods System became a victim of its own success, as it ultimately proved incapable of coping with the dramatic developments that were occurring in the world economy. Those developments revealed flaws in the Bretton Woods System which led to its eventual breakdown.

The most basic of those flaws was the system's very heavy reliance on the strength of the American dollar, which, in turn, was contingent on the continuing health and primacy of the U.S. economy. During the system's formative years, the United States was unquestionably the world's preeminent economic power, and the dollar was the world's strongest and most sought-after currency. Those conditions were assimilated into the Bretton Woods arrangements and became essential for their perpetuation. This occurred by deliberate design, but also evolved over time in an unplanned fashion. The deliberate aspects included the status and obligations that were assigned to the dollar through its unique convertibility into gold and its place as the standard monetary unit to which the values of other currencies were pegged. This made the stability of currency values that the system was striving to provide dependent upon maintaining the dollar's convertibility into gold at a fixed price.

The Bretton Woods System soon came to depend on the dollar and the underlying vitality of the American economy in other ways. The United States was the center of the postwar revival of international trade, as well as the source of most of the private investment capital and government financial assistance that was being transferred internationally in the early postwar period, and the majority of international economic transactions were therefore being financed with dollars. This fact, together with the presumed security and immutability of the dollar's value, encouraged both private businesses and national monetary authorities to accumulate dollar-denominated financial assets. The dollar thus took on two essential and closely-related functions, first, as a "reserve currency" and second, as a source of "liquidity" for the burgeoning global business network.

The American dollar fulfilled all those functions tolerably well through the 1950s and early 1960s, but then a succession of troubles began to emerge. American domination of internationl markets was steadily eroded by the resurgent industries of Western Europe and Japan, and the United States began to register large deficits in its international balance of payments. Under the Bretton Woods arrangements, the monetary authorities of other nations were effectively forced to buy up the excess dollars being generated by the U.S. deficits in order to keep exchange rates stable, and as these superfluous foreign-held dollar balances became larger and larger, foreign nations' confidence in the ability and willingness of the United States to honor its gold-conversion commitment faltered. This problem was aggravated by America's full-scale entry into the Vietnam conflict, which accelerated its balance of payments deficits and placed other national governments in the distasteful position of having to finance (by accumulating the dollars spawned by those deficits) what to many of them was an unpopular war.

Even when it became evident that the dollar was overvalued, many of the foreign nations with balance of payments surpluses proved reluctant to surrender their competitive advantage in export markets by increasing the par values of their currencies. On the other hand, countries that were (like the United States) experiencing chronic balance of payments deficits tended to resist devaluations of their currencies for reasons of "national prestige." Meanwhile, the dollar's fixed link to gold, which was the keystone of the Bretton Woods System, restricted America's options and maneuverability in dealing with its own economic problems.

By the late 1960s, the existing international monetary system was being overwhelmed by economic events and by its own rigidities. A series of financial "crises" erupted, as international business firms and national governments attempted to unload their holdings of dollars and other weak currencies by converting them into stronger currencies or into gold. Currency speculators joined in those melees in order to profit from the exchange market instability which they were sometimes engineering and invariably aggravating. The U.S. Treasury, after having given up more than one-half of its gold reserves, began unofficially refusing to make further conversions of dollars into gold. Finally, in August 1971, the United States formally suspended its obligation to sell gold for dollars, an action that, for all practical purposes, signaled the demise of the stabilized-rate regime that had been founded more than 25 years earlier at Bretton Woods. Despite some subsequent efforts to salvage that regime—efforts that included the convening of international monetary conferences and two official devaluations of the U.S. dollar—more and more nations abandoned their commitment to stabilized exchange rates. Thus, without any global agreement or definite plan, the world drifted into a new monetary order which came to be described as a **managed floating rate regime.**

The Managed Floating Rate Regime

The contemporary managed floating rate regime is essentially the outgrowth of a series of ad hoc decisions and measures by national governments, some of which have received after-the-fact ratification by a majority of the IMF's members and have thereby become legitimate features of the regime. The most basic of these features is that exchange rates are permitted to "float," that is, to move upward or downward in response to market demand and supply forces, to a much greater extent than they could under the Bretton Woods System rules. But this floating of rates is by no means as free and complete as it would be under a "pure" freely fluctuating rate regime.

Characteristics of the Managed Floating Rate System.   In the first place, many countries have chosen to peg the value of their currency to that of another national currency (or several other national currencies) and to keep that relationship fixed. This has created a situation characterized by the existence of a number of "currency blocs," wherein exchange rates between the currencies of the countries within a particular bloc are stabilized, but all those currencies float relative to the currencies of other blocs. Some of these blocs are made up of many small countries that have tied their currencies to that of one major nation. For instance, a large number of the developing countries have pegged their currencies to the U.S. dollar, while another smaller group have tied their currencies to the French franc. Meanwhile, several of the Western European countries have entered into an arrangement known as the European Monetary System (EMS), under which their currencies are linked together on a stabilized-rate basis while floating in relation to the dollar and other non-EMS currencies.

The contemporary regime also departs from the pure model of freely fluctuating rates by having (and sanctioning) occasional government intervention in foreign exchange markets for the purpose of influencing rates of exchange. This constitutes the "managed" feature of the regime, as the intervention of national governments is supposed to occur in order to prevent exchange rate fluctuations from becoming so exaggerated as to be detrimental to international business activity or to the health of national economies. The guiding principle is that national governments can and should take actions, either individually or collectively, to correct "disorderly" exchange market conditions that would otherwise have undesirable economic consequences. While this principle itself is basically sound, there is no clear-cut definition of what, in fact, comprises sufficient "disorder" to justify exchange market intervention. This ambiguity makes it possible for governments to manipulate exchange rates for reasons of their own nationalistic self-interest. Since the inception of the floating-rate regime, many national governments and central banks have been criticized for such manipulative practices, with the most frequent charge being that they have deliberately kept their national currencies undervalued in order to promote exports and discourage imports.

Role of the International Monetary Fund.   Other important features of the managed floating rate regime and issues relating to that regime have to do with the role of the IMF and the appropriate form and use of international reserve assets. While the shift from stabilized to floating exchange rates as the basic modus operandi for the international monetary system reduced the IMF's formal responsibility to help member nations maintain stable values for their currencies, it continues to serve as a source of funds for countries that are experiencing international trade and payments difficulties. The nature of the IMF's lending activities has been changing over time, so that most of its loans now are going to those developing countries with deep-seated external debt problems (those problems were described in Chapter 3), rather than to nations that need temporary financing to carry out exchange stabilization measures.

The IMF also remains deeply concerned with the issues of adequate reserves and liquidity for the international monetary system. In this regard, its efforts have been directed toward reducing the system's dependence on either dollars or gold (a dependence that contributed to the collapse of the Bretton Woods arrangements) and promoting the use of reserve assets that can, in effect, be "created" by the IMF itself. These are the so-called *special drawing rights* (SDRs).

Special drawing rights first appeared on the international monetary scene in the early 1970s, following a decision by a majority of the IMF member countries to create and distribute this new type of reserve asset. As their name indicates, SDRs are essentially rights that member countries have to draw upon (i.e., borrow from) the IMF, and those rights are "special" in that they are not limited by the amounts that the countries have paid into the IMF. This means that the IMF, by making SDRs available, can increase the total supply of reserves and liquidity in the international economy, rather than merely accumulating a "pool" of gold and national currencies contributed by its members from which it then lends to those members in need of financial assistance. The SDRs can serve as a reserve asset or as a component of international liquidity because the IMF's member nations have agreed to transfer and accept them in settlement of debts, in exchange for their respective national currencies, and as collateral for loans.

A major argument in favor of SDRs is that they constitute a liquid asset, the supply of which can be *controlled* by international agreement and in keeping with the liquidity needs of the world economy. By contrast, an international monetary system that relies on gold or a particular national currency (such as the dollar) for its liquidity has no way of assuring that the supply of gold or the national currency will correspond with current needs. The amount of gold available for monetary use is subject to several largely "uncontrollable" factors, including output rates and the proportion of that output that is going into nonmonetary uses (e.g., industry, jewelry-making, or hoarding by private individuals). The amount of a particular national currency that is available for use as an international money is likewise difficult to control, since it depends on the balance of payments situation of the reserve-currency country and the willingness of persons and organizations outside that country to acquire, hold, and utilize its currency. Moreover, these two determinants can work at cross-purposes, in that a reserve-currency country supplies its currency to foreigners by having deficits in its balance of payments, while the persistence of such deficits can undermine the confidence that foreigners have in the value of the reserve currency and therefore their willingness to continue holding and using it.

Notwithstanding the advantages attributed to SDRs as a reserve asset and the efforts of the IMF to promote their utilization, SDRs have not yet won widespread acceptance as a replacement for gold and dollars in international monetary circles. Even though the IMF has officially "demonetized" gold by abolishing its fixed price and eliminating its use in transactions with member countries, both national treasuries and private parties still cling to gold as an intrinsically valuable and presumably "inflation-proof" commodity. Meanwhile, the dollar continues to serve not only as the principal medium of exchange for financing private international business transactions, but also as a substantial part of the total monetary reserves of national governments.

Assessment of the Managed Floating Rate System.   The continuing attempts of the IMF to bring about what it regards as needed improvements in international monetary arrangements reflects the fact that the contemporary managed floating rate regime is by no means universally regarded as ideal. As has been indicated, this regime is largely the product of makeshift measures and agreements among various groups of countries that were adopted as the Bretton Woods System was disintegrating. Consequently, there is a widespread feeling that further refining and strengthening of the contemporary regime is in order. But the consensus ends there, for there are great divergences of opinion as to what kinds of changes should be undertaken. This is partly the result of different theoretical views among professional economists and government leaders as to what constitutes the "best" type of exchange rate regime, but it also reflects more pragmatic differences in the economic positions and concerns of various nations and interest groups. For the present, therefore, international economic transactions continue to be carried out under the managed floating rate arrangements, while the quest for a more perfect international monetary system goes on.

Exchange Controls

In the preceding descriptions of exchange rate regimes, it was implicitly assumed that private parties (i.e., individuals, business firms, and other private organizations) were free to trade national currencies for one another through the foreign exchange markets, and that governments were primarily involved in stabilizing or otherwise influencing exchange rates by intervening in the markets to either offset or reinforce the demand/supply effects of those private transactions. In reality, national governments can and often do affect exchange rates in a much more direct manner, by imposing and enforcing **legal controls** on private dealings in foreign exchange. For the sake of consistency in terminology, a situation characterized by such direct governmental regulation of foreign exchange transactions will be referred to as a **controlled rate regime.** In such a regime, a national government seeks to control the exchange rate for its currency by invoking its sovereign power to control the overall demand for, and/or the supply of, foreign exchange.

Exchange controls have been used extensively by governments throughout this century. They were an integral part of the ubiquitous economic controls that the belligerent nations maintained during the two World Wars, and they were widely used in attempts to deter the massive international flights of capital that accompanied the economic upheavals of the Great Depression. Almost all countries retained tight restrictions on foreign exchange transactions during the economic reconstruction period following the Second World War, but the industrialized Western nations found it feasible to reduce those controls by the end of the 1950s. Thus, exchange controls are now utilized mainly by Third World nations, whose governments look on them as essential components of their economic development programs, and in the Second World countries, where they are part and parcel of the centrally planned national economic systems.

Features of Exchange Control Regimes.   Exchange controls vary greatly among nations, so practicality requires that description of exchange control regimes be limited to some common and general features. One of these is the legal requirement that residents obtain the foreign exchange they need to carry on international transactions from sources (usually the central bank and private commercial banks) that have been designated by the government to operate as part of the exchange-control mechanism. Residents are similarly required by law to sell all the foreign exchange they have earned or otherwise acquired to these official agencies. This makes the government the sole *legal* seller and buyer of foreign exchange and thereby enables it not only to decide the purposes for which foreign exchange will be made available, but also to set the domestic currency price (exchange rate) at which foreign currencies will be purchased and sold.

The government can exercise these powers in a number of ways. It can, for example, allocate the supply of foreign exchange among its residents so as to regulate the volume, composition, and origins of the nation's imports. The government typically would accomplish this by establishing some form of **licensing** requirement, under which residents of the nation have to apply to the exchange control authorities for licenses to import goods and to acquire the foreign exchange needed to pay for those goods. The authorities then decide which imports qualify for such licenses, which means that they make foreign currencies available for purchasing certain imported goods, while refusing to provide those currencies for other imports. The governments of developing countries usually rationalize such allocations by linking them to economic development needs (e.g., priority in the granting of licenses may be given to importers of products or materials that are deemed essential to the country's economic development plan), but other, less laudable, considerations may also influence the granting or withholding of licenses.

Under a strict exchange control regime, the national government in effect assumes a monopoly position in supplying foreign exchange to residents of the nation (as well as a monopsonistic position as the only legitimate buyer of foreign exchange). This obviously gives the government a great deal of influence over both the buying and selling rates, which, among other things, permits the government to use exchange controls as a source of revenue. By requiring residents to surrender their foreign currencies for a lower price (in the domestic currency) than is charged when those same currencies are resold to other residents, the government can realize substantial revenues by exploiting its monopoly–monopsony status.

The ability to control the exchange rate also enables the government to set different rates for the same foreign currency in order to encourage some transactions, while discouraging others. The government of a developing country might, for instance, charge its residents a higher domestic-currency price for dollars that were going to be used to import luxury-type consumer goods from the United States and a lower price for dollars to be used to import capital goods or industrial materials. This so-called "multiple-rate" approach can also be applied to the purchase of foreign currencies, so that the government might pay the country's exporters more for dollars that were earned by selling manufactured goods abroad than for dollars earned from the sale of raw materials, thereby providing an incentive for domestic businesses to expand manufacturing activities and a disincentive to continue producing primary products.

Exchange controls often are applied to international investments as well as to exports and imports of goods. The developing countries have made extensive use of such controls to deter transfers of capital abroad, with the idea that this would preserve more of the scarce supply of capital funds for domestic investments. Many of the more economically advanced countries, including the United States, have also used exchange controls to limit outflows of capital funds that were thought to be contributing to balance of payments problems. The U.S. government maintained various types of legal restrictions on foreign investments by American companies throughout most of the 1960s and early 1970s, in an attempt to mitigate the deficit in the U.S. balance of payments.

Exchange controls clearly can be a powerful tool in the hands of national governments, since the ability to regulate the availability and price of foreign exchange is tantamount to dictating the volume and nature of international economic transactions in which the people and companies of the country can engage. This has made such controls attractive to governments with a predilection for centralized direction of their nation's economy, and to governments contending with problems in their economic relationships with foreign countries. But exchange controls are far from perfect instruments for attaining national economic objectives, and they may create as many difficulties as they resolve.

Box 11.2

Coping with Exchange Controls

In Western France, a Frenchman straps on a money belt loaded with French francs given to him by a multinational company operating in France. He hang glides over the Swiss border so he can get Swiss francs to deposit in a Swiss bank account.

In New Delhi, a major international airline gives a case of Scotch to a government official. The government thereupon permits the airline to convert $18 million worth of rupees into dollars to take to the airline's home country.

Corporations often must go to such lengths to get around foreign-exchange controls. It is one of the oldest games in international finance, and one of the riskiest. It also has become one of the most widely played.

Countries have long limited the holding and purchase of foreign currency within their borders, often as a way to support the value of their own currencies. But since the global debt crisis came to a head two years ago, the controls have spread as developing countries have tried to allocate scarce dollars and other so-called hard currencies to specific imports or to pay interest on foreign debt.

The result is that multinational corporations often can't get their money out of the developing countries. These blocked funds represent everything from uncollected bills and unpaid trade credits to royalties and dividends that companies want to convert to hard currency and ship home.

Source: "Funds Blocked Abroad by Exchange Controls Plague Big Companies," *The Wall Street Journal* (December 3, 1984), 1. Reprinted by permission of *The Wall Street Journal*, © Dow Jones & Company, Inc. 1984. All Rights Reserved.

Problems of Exchange Control Regimes.   First, exchange controls are highly susceptible to being evaded, and the use of these controls to keep a nation's residents from acquiring the imported goods that they want or from transferring money out of the country often stimulates unlawful activities such as smuggling and "black markets" in foreign products or foreign currencies. There are innumerable ways for residents of an exchange-control country to circumvent the rules, particularly if they can enlist the aid of foreigners with whom they are carrying on business transactions, and few if any governments that have endeavored to maintain rigid exchange control regimes have been able to prevent rampant flouting of the restrictions.

Second, even when exchange controls are not being widely evaded, they are apt to distort trade and investment patterns in a manner that leads to suboptimal results. The controls make the currency of the country employing them **inconvertible** in the free-market sense, inasmuch as it can only be exchanged for other currencies under conditions and for purposes specified by the government. Bureaucratic judgments are thus substituted for market forces in determining what, how much, and with whom the residents of the country will trade, and those judgments will not always be based upon efficiency or consumer welfare considerations. Moreover, the complications and delays in making and receiving international payments that frequently are encountered under exchange control regimes can discourage foreign investors and traders from dealing with an exchange-control country, even if they are not legally precluded from doing so. In short, exchange controls are a departure from, and an interference with, free international movements of goods and capital funds, and their usage therefore entails the same potential problems and inefficiencies that have been identified and analyzed in prior discussions of other legal barriers to trade and investment.

Conclusion

This chapter has examined the basic character of exchange rates and the key role they perform in shaping international economic transactions and relationships. It has also considered the question of how exchange rates are determined, first in a theoretical sense, and then with reference to the historical and contemporary actuality of governmental involvement in the foreign exchange markets. It has been shown how the methods employed by national governments to influence exchange rates have altered over time and how they differ among nations. It was noted that these variations reflect the dynamics of world economic conditions, as well as differences of opinion among economists and political leaders regarding the ideal international monetary system.

Since nothing is more certain than the prospect of continuing changes in global economic conditions—except continuing arguments among economists and politicians—it is apparent that the unsettled state of international monetary affairs will persist into the foreseeable future. International business firms and managers must therefore be prepared to cope with the risks and complications (and the exciting opportunities) associated with unpredictable exchange rates. These issues will be discussed in detail in Chapter 16, which deals with financial management in multinational business firms.

Summary

1.   Foreign exchange rates are the prices at which different national currencies are traded for one another in the foreign exchange markets.

2. The exchange rate is a unique and important price, in that the exchange rate between any two national currencies links the cost and price structures of the two nations and thereby greatly affects economic transactions between those nations.

3. The manner in which exchange rates are determined depends upon the nature of the foreign exchange market, with the key variant being the role played by national governments.

4. The rules and procedures that governments utilize in attempting to influence the behavior of exchange rates can be distinguished and categorized by reference to different exchange rate regimes. These regimes may be categorized as freely fluctuating rate regimes, stabilized rate regimes, managed floating rate regimes, or controlled rate regimes.

5. The freely fluctuating rate regime is actually a theoretical construct, rather than a real-world phenomenon. Such a regime would be characterized by the absence of government restrictions on foreign exchange transactions and there would be no governmental efforts to influence exchange rates. Under such conditions, exchange rates would be determined entirely by supply and demand forces emanating from unregulated private international business dealings.

6. The exchange rate regime that existed from the end of the Second World War until the early 1970s involved stabilized exchange rates. These stabilized rates were the main feature of the international monetary arrangements referred to as the Bretton Woods System.

7. The Bretton Woods System collapsed in the early 1970s, and was replaced by a looser set of international monetary arrangements in which exchange rates normally "float" in response to market demand and supply, but remain subject to some management by national monetary authorities.

8. Many nations, notably the Third World countries and the Second World countries, with their system of central economic planning, maintain tight controls over the availability and prices of foreign currencies. Such controls enable the governments to regulate economic transactions between their countries and the rest of the world, but the substitution of official discretion for market-based economic decisions can result in a loss of efficiency and reduced consumer welfare.

Questions for Review or Discussion

1. Define the term *exchange rate* and indicate how exchange rates are usually quoted.

2. If we are considering the exchange rate between the U.S. dollar and the German mark and we find that the price of one mark in

dollars is $0.4132, how could we immediately ascertain the price of one dollar in marks?

3. "Exchange rates are unique and particularly important prices." Explain why this is so.

4. Explain how the equilibrium exchange rate would be determined in a free and competitive foreign exchange market.

5. What is meant by the statement that the demand for foreign exchange is, for the most part, a *derived* demand?

6. How are the demand for, and the supply of, foreign exchange related to the international economic transactions in which the residents of a particular country are engaged?

7. Identify and describe the major features of the Bretton Woods international monetary system.

8. With regard to exchange rates, the Bretton Woods arrangements have been alluded to as an "adjustable peg" system. Explain this terminology.

9. Describe the major features of the contemporary managed floating rate regime and compare these to the Bretton Woods System.

10. What are the methods through which governments maintain an exchange control regime? What are some of the principal purposes of exchange controls?

Case

The Bolivian Peso

In early July 1985, Mr. Miranda, a schoolteacher in La Paz, Bolivia, received his monthly salary of 25 million pesos. While his wife rushed to buy a month's supply of rice and noodles, Mr. Miranda hurried off to change the rest of the pesos to black-market U.S. dollars. Bolivian pesos were dropping in value hourly. The day Mr. Miranda was paid, the U.S. dollar was worth 500,000 pesos, therefore his salary was equivalent to $50, while just a few days later, with the exchange rate at 900,000 pesos, it was worth only $27.

The rapid devaluation of the peso reflects the hyperinflation currently rampant in Bolivia. According to official statistics, the 1984 Bolivian inflation rate was 2,000 percent while the 1985 rate is expected to be 8,000 percent, though other estimates range many times higher. In one 6-month period, prices soared at an inflation rate comparable to 38,000 percent annually. A major cause of this inflation is that governmental revenues cover only 15 percent of national expenditures, and the country's deficit is equivalent to about 25 percent of the Bolivian gross national product.

With the help of unofficial money changers operating on the street, Bolivian merchants quickly convert pesos resulting from sales to black-market U.S. dollars. Merchants monitor the price of the dollar and adjust peso prices upward accordingly to keep pace (they don't drop prices when the dollar drops in value temporarily). Most of the black-market dollars come from the illegal cocaine trade. Bolivian cocaine traffickers earn an estimated $1 billion annually of which $300 to 400 million filters back into Bolivia.

Money changing has expanded greatly. One may see this competitive free market in action by the following example of how one might change $5 to pesos. Driving down the street in a Bolivian city, one has only to lower the car window and shout "What's your price?" to a group of money changers lounging on the curb. The car is immediately surrounded by money changers shouting offers. Within seconds the price of the dollar rises from 800,000 to 850,000 pesos. Later the same day the rate will rise to 950,000 pesos. Interestingly, the official rate at the time of this example was 75,000 pesos to the dollar!

While the interest rate on regulated bank loans is only 110 to 140 percent, interest rates on street loans average 10,000 percent. Naturally, banking has moved to the streets, with total official bank deposits falling from $600 million in the early 1980s to less than $10 million in mid-1985. In spite of this chaos, few companies have collapsed. However, they operate differently. A mining company lost $7 million in mining but made $12 million in financial deals. According to the mine owner, "Bolivians are learning that only a chump tries to make a profit producing something" (*The Wall Street Journal*, August 13, 1985). Miners have to exchange their export dollars at the official rate while their costs soar along with the free-market rate.

Tin production at state mines dropped from 18,000 to 12,000 tons in 1984. Workers smuggled out the best ore in their lunchpails. This ore ended up in neighboring Peru which now exports 4,000 tons a year without possessing a major tin mine. Similarly, 20 percent of Bolivia's gasoline is smuggled into Brazil for sale on the free market because of the low official price in Bolivia. To obtain extra cash, government workers resort widely to petty corruption and bribery. The Bolivian economy is rapidly deteriorating.

What does the situation in Bolivia illustrate about the role of auction markets and inflation in the determination of exchange rates? Should something be done to encourage greater monetary stability? If so, what?

Sources: Everett Martin, "Amid Wild Inflation, Bolivians Concentrate on Swapping Currency," *The Wall Street Journal*, pp. 1, 20; and W. R. Folks and R. Aggarwal, *International Dimensions of Financial Management*, Boston: Kent Publishing Company, 1986.

Chapter 12

THE BALANCE OF PAYMENTS

Chapter Objectives

- *To define the balance of payments and to indicate its significance and the usefulness of the balance of payments accounts*
- *To explain and illustrate the procedures involved in balance of payments accounting*
- *To explain the concept of balance of payments disequilibrium and to show how the presence of disequilibrium can be diagnosed through the balance of payments accounts*
- *To identify the principal causes of balance of payments disequilibrium*
- *To examine the processes of adjustment to balance of payments disequilibrium and to analyze the effects of different adjustment processes*
- *To point out how balance of payments problems and the methods that nations use to correct such problems can affect firms doing business in or with those nations*

International business consists of economic transactions that are carried out by persons, business firms, or governmental entities that are residents of different countries. These transactions take a variety of forms, including (but not limited to), the exchange of goods, the rendering of services, the acquisition of productive assets, or the provision of intangible inputs. Each such transaction is generally the result of a decision, or set of decisions, made by a few individuals (e.g., the managers of a company) who are likely to be unaware of or unconcerned about the great multitude of similar activities that are taking place at the same time. But the *combined effect* of these international economic dealings can become a matter of grave concern for a nation and those responsible for its economic health. Moreover, the responsible authorities may deem it necessary to respond to problems they see in their nation's overall international economic situation by limiting or otherwise interfering with their citizens' freedom to do business with foreigners.

The combined total of the economic transactions that take place between the **residents** of a particular nation and **foreign residents** during some given period of time comprises that nation's **balance of payments.**[1] Virtually all nations, as well as the International Monetary Fund, compile and publish statistical data on these transactions in balance of payments accounts. These accounting records are extremely useful to government officials, since the information contained in the accounts enables those officials to keep track of the nature, magnitude, and direction of the economic dealings between their country and the rest of the world. Also, and perhaps more importantly, analyses of this information can help the governmental authorities to determine whether the existing level and pattern of such dealings can or should be continued, or whether changes are needed. This kind of analysis relates to the very important concept of **balance of payments equilibrium** (and disequilibrium), a concept that will be examined later.

Although business managers may not be as deeply involved with balance of payments considerations as their counterparts in government, they nevertheless may find that such considerations are exerting a substantial influence on their company and their own managerial tasks. It is not uncommon, for example, for national governments to react to balance of payments problems by placing controls on imports, foreign investments, profit remittances, or other international transfers that are essential parts of an international company's activities. The ability of such companies to carry on their normal business operations can thus be seriously hampered by governmental responses to balance of payments conditions. Many basic decisions that international managers must make—such as deciding whether to initiate or expand operations in particular foreign countries, to make loans to foreign affiliates or extend credit to overseas customers, or to import needed components or materials—can likewise become subject to concerns or constraints that are linked to the balance of payments.

An understanding of balance of payments is also imperative for companies and managers that are dealing with different national currencies. Exchange rates, that is, the values national currencies have in relation to one another, will be directly determined by the volume and direction of the economic transactions in which those currencies are being utilized, and it is precisely those transactions that make up, and are recorded in, the balance of payments accounts. Thus, any attempt to comprehend and forecast exchange rate movements will necessarily entail references

---

[1]For balance of payments purposes, the *residents* of a country include all its governmental bodies and those individuals and organizations that reside permanently and have their economic "center of interest" in the country. It is particularly important to note in this regard that a business firm is considered a resident of that country in which it is chartered and doing business, irrespective of the citizenship of its owners or managers. Thus, the French subsidiary of an American corporation would be a resident of France, and transactions between the parent corporation and subsidiary would be international transactions that would enter the balance of payments accounts of both countries.

to the balance of payments situations of the countries whose currencies are involved. Furthermore, the story does not end there, for exchange rate movements also exert an effect on the transactions encompassed in the balance of payments. This circular relationship between exchange rates and the balance of payments will be looked at more closely below.

The Balance of Payments Accounts

In order for government officials and other concerned parties to be able to grasp what is taking place in a nation's economic dealings with the rest of the world, it is necessary that data describing those dealings be gathered and reported in a systematic fashion. Like all other accounting systems, the balance of payments accounts arrange information in a manner intended to help users of that information draw correct inferences regarding the occurrences being reported. With regard to a country's international economic transactions, two kinds of distinctions are especially important. The first has to do with the **nature of the transaction,** and the second with whether the transaction will result (either immediately or subsequently) in the *receipt* of money from foreign residents or will necessitate a *payment* to foreign residents.

Differences in the nature of the transactions involved are shown by recording those transactions in different sections within the overall balance of payments accounts. The three major sections that are utilized for this purpose are the **current account,** the **capital account,** and the **official reserves account.**

The Current Account

The current account actually encompasses two quite different types of economic transactions, and therefore contains two subaccounts. One of these is **purchases (imports) and sales (exports) of goods and services.** Such purchases and sales almost always constitute the largest component of a nation's total international economic activity in quantitative terms, and they also are looked upon as especially important because of their direct effects upon the level of economic output and employment in the nation(s) involved. The "goods" referred to here are all the tangible products and commodities that are being imported and exported, and these are designated in the accounts as **merchandise trade.** The "services" include transportation, financial (banking and insurance) services, and the kinds of services (e.g., lodging, restaurant meals, entertainment) associated with tourist travel. The services rendered via international transfers of capital and technology are also recorded in this segment of the balance of payments accounts. Thus, income in the form of dividends, interest, or royalties that a resident company received from its overseas investments or licensing arrangements would show up here as receipts from the "sale" of the services of capital or technology.

The second type of transaction covered by the current account is **unilateral transfers** (sometimes called **unrequited transfers**). The terms "unilateral" or "unrequited" refer to the one-sided character of these transactions, which involve the giving of something of economic value to foreign residents without receiving or expecting to receive anything of similar value in return. Such gifts often are made by governments, for example, the government of one nation may grant money or goods to another nation as part of an economic or military aid program, and, so long as the government making the grant does not receive any tangible compensation or establish a claim for future payment, this is a unilateral transfer. (In reality, such intergovernmental grants often are designed to secure the friendship, goodwill, or political allegiance of the recipient, but these do not have measurable economic value.) Unilateral transfers also take place among private parties, for example, charitable groups in one country may make donations to needy individuals or organizations in other countries, or persons working outside their native country may send money to their families back home. These "immigrant remittances" can be an item of substantial magnitude in the balance of payments accounts of countries that have large numbers of their citizens working abroad or that have many alien workers in their labor force.

The Capital Account

The capital account records financial flows that are associated with international investments. As pointed out in Chapter 4, international investments can vary in their duration and with regard to the exercise of managerial control by the investors. These variations are recognized by categorizing capital transactions as short- or long-term and (with respect to the long-term transactions) as either direct or portfolio.

The Official Reserves Account

The transactions appearing in the official reserves section of the balance of payments accounts are those that take place among **monetary authorities,** that is, national treasuries and central banks and international financial institutions such as the International Monetary Fund. These transactions entail transfers of monetary gold or changes in foreign-currency-denominated bank deposit balances that are held by the monetary authorities, as well as short-term borrowing and lending among those official entities. Transactions of this sort generally are carried out for the purpose of financing imbalances in other segments of the balance of payments and thereby reducing the fluctuations that would otherwise occur in exchange rates. These so-called "compensatory" transactions will be considered in greater detail later in this chapter.

The Double-Entry System

In addition to categorizing a country's international economic dealings by type, its balance of payments accounts also indicate whether a particular transaction (or, more precisely, one of the two sides of that transaction) will entail *receipts* from foreign residents or *payments* to foreign residents. Technical exactness demands this reference to "sides" of transactions, since balance of payments accounting follows the double-entry convention, in which every transaction is regarded as being two-sided and accordingly is recorded by a debit and a credit entry of equal magnitude. This accounting methodology is perfectly consistent with the real character of most international economic transactions, inasmuch as they involve an *exchange* of something of value for something else of (presumably) equivalent value. For instance, any time a company located in one country exports merchandise to a customer in another country, it either will be paid for that merchandise immediately or will establish a claim on the buyer for future payment. By the same token, an investment by a resident of one country in another country normally involves the exchange of capital funds (money) for capital goods or for securities (e.g., stocks or bonds) that constitute claims on future income. Although unilateral transfers are an exception to this norm of exchange, they too are made to comply with the double-entry convention by the use of entries that represent the making or receiving of a gift. If, for example, the U.S. government were to make a gift of food to a famine-stricken foreign country, the "giving" of that food would be noted in the U.S. balance of payments accounts by a debit entry in the unilateral transfers subaccount of the current account, which would match the credit entry under merchandise trade evidencing the actual export of the food.

Debit Items.   The debit entries in a country's balance of payments accounts record those sides of its international economic transactions that immediately or eventually entail payments to foreign residents. This coincides with the conventional rules of double-entry accounting, in which debit entries indicate either an increase in assets or a decrease in liabilities. Thus, when residents of a country import goods from abroad, this is an increase in the nation's real assets which also necessitates paying for the goods, hence, a debit item in the nation's balance of payments accounts. By the same reckoning, a decision on the part of a resident of a nation (say, a business firm) to reduce its debts to foreign residents (say, a foreign bank from which it had previously borrowed money) would necessitate a payment to that foreign bank, and that payment, which reduces the nation's international liabilities, would also be a debit entry in its balance of payments accounts.

The foregoing examples can be expanded into a list of the more common occurrences that would be recorded by debit entries in the various sections of a nation's balance of payments accounts:

I. Current account
  A. Merchandise imports (purchases of tangible goods from foreign residents)
  B. Imports of services
    1. Purchases of transportation services from foreign residents
    2. Purchases of financial services from foreign residents
    3. Tourist expenditures, that is, purchases by residents of the nation while traveling abroad
    4. Purchases by the nation's government and military personnel stationed abroad
    5. Payments (e.g., fees or royalties) for managerial services or technology acquired from foreign residents
    6. Payments (e.g., interest or dividends) to foreign investors for the "services" of their capital invested in the nation
  C. Unilateral or unrequited transfers to foreign residents
    1. Government grants of money or goods
    2. Charitable gifts
    3. Pension payments to foreign residents
    4. Immigrant remittances to foreign residents
II. Capital account
  A. Short-term investment abroad by residents of the nation
    1. Deposits in foreign banks or savings institutions
    2. Purchases of short-term securities issued by foreign companies or government agencies
  B. Reductions in short-term investments in the nation by foreign residents
    1. Withdrawals of deposits in domestic banks or savings institutions
    2. Liquidation of short-term securities issued by domestic companies or government agencies
  C. Long-term portfolio investment abroad by residents of the nation
    1. Purchases of equity or long-term debt securities issued by foreign companies or government agencies
  D. Reductions in long-term portfolio investments in the nation by foreign residents
    1. Liquidation of equity or long-term debt securities issued by domestic companies or government agencies
  E. Direct investment abroad by residents of the nation
    1. Initial investments or increases in investments (including reinvestment of earnings) in controlled foreign enterprises
  F. Reductions in direct investments in the nation by foreign residents
    1. Liquidation or decreases in foreign investments in controlled domestic enterprises
III. Official reserves account
  A. Purchases of gold by the nation's monetary authorities

B. Increases in the nation's deposits with the International Monetary Fund

C. Loans by the nation's monetary authorities to foreign monetary authorities

Credit Items.   The credit entries in a nation's balance of payments accounts are records of those sides of its international economic transactions that immediately or eventually result in receipts from foreign residents. This is in keeping with standard double-entry accounting principles, wherein credit entries indicate either a decrease in assets or an increase in liabilities. Following is a listing of the usual bases of credit entries in the various sections of a nation's balance of payments accounts:

I. Current account
  A. Merchandise exports (sales of tangible goods to foreign residents)
  B. Exports of services
    1. Sales of transportation services to foreign residents
    2. Sales of financial services to foreign residents
    3. Tourist receipts, that is, sales to foreign residents traveling in the nation
    4. Sales to foreign government or military personnel stationed in the nation
    5. Income (e.g., fees or royalties) for managerial services or technology supplied to foreign residents
    6. Income (e.g., interest or dividends) for the "services" of capital invested in foreign nations
  C. Unilateral or unrequited transfers from foreign residents
    1. Grants of money or goods from foreign governments
    2. Charitable gifts received
    3. Pension receipts from abroad
    4. Immigrant remittances received from citizens working abroad
II. Capital accounts
  A. Short-term investments in the nation by foreign residents
    1. Foreign-owned deposits in domestic banks or savings institutions
    2. Sales to foreign residents of short-term securities issued by domestic companies or government agencies
  B. Reductions in short-term investments abroad by domestic residents
    1. Withdrawals of domestic residents' deposits in foreign banks or savings institutions
    2. Liquidation of short-term securities issued by foreign companies or government agencies
  C. Long-term portfolio investment in the nation by foreign residents

      1. Purchases of equity or long-term debt securities issued by domestic companies or government agencies

  D. Reductions in long-term portfolio investment abroad by domestic residents

      1. Liquidation of equity or long-term debt securities issued by foreign companies or government agencies

  E. Direct investment in the nation by foreign residents

      1. Initial investments or increases in investments (including reinvestment or earnings) in controlled domestic enterprises

  F. Reductions in direct investments abroad by domestic residents

      1. Liquidation or decreases in investments in controlled foreign enterprises

III. Official reserves account

  A. Sales of gold to foreign official agencies by the nation's monetary authorities

  B. Withdrawals of deposits with the International Monetary Fund

  C. Borrowings by the nation's monetary authorities from foreign monetary authorities

Errors and Omissions. Inasmuch as all international transactions engaged in by the residents of a nation are regarded as two-sided in balance of payments accounting, logic dictates that the accounts should balance, that is, that total debits and total credits should be equal for any accounting period. In practice, however, such balance is not likely to occur routinely or automatically. Such disparities between the logic of the accounting system and the results of the actual data gathering and reporting process are attributable to the magnitude and complexity of that process. In theory, a nation's balance of payments accounts should be a complete and precise record of each and every international economic transaction in which its residents were involved during a given time period. However, such precision and comprehensiveness are not, in fact, feasible when dealing with a vast multitude of economic transactions involving many thousands of individuals and business units. Much of the data for balance of payments accounts must, of necessity, be compiled from samples and estimates, and the task is understandably subject to some discrepancies and errors. As a consequence, there is a high probability that the total of all reported debit items will not equal the total of all reported credit items.

    In order to bring about the equality of total debits and total credits that the rules of double-entry accounting demand, an "errors and omissions" entry is utilized. While this is, in one sense, just a device for balancing the accounts, the entry may also have some interpretative usefulness. This derives from the presumption that there are certain kinds of international transactions—particularly short-term private capital movements—that are more apt to "slip through" the data-gathering process and therefore to account for any discrepancies in the recorded totals. Based on this reasoning, the size and position (debit or credit) of the errors and omissions entry is regarded as an indicator of the magnitude and direction of unreported short-term capital flows, and changes in this entry from one accounting period to another may likewise be indicative of shifts in such flows.

Since an equality of total debits and total credits for the accounting period is an inevitable result of the accounting procedures used, it follows that this "balance" in the balance of payments accounts has no analytical or economic significance. In other words, one cannot determine whether a country is or is not facing problems in its economic dealings with the rest of the world by comparing the totals of its recorded foreign payments and receipts, as those will perforce be the same. To make such a determination, it is necessary to delve more deeply into the balance of payments accounts and to look for evidence of what is termed **balance of payments disequilibrium.**

Balance of Payments Disequilibrium

The concepts of equilibrium and disequilibrium are used extensively in economic analyses, as well as in other social and natural sciences. In all these uses, the concepts refer to the same basic set of circumstances. **Equilibrium** can be thought of as a stable state or situation, in which the relevant operational forces are in a sustainable relationship with one another and hence there are no pressures for change. Obviously, then, **disequilibrium** refers to an unstable situation, wherein the existing relationship among the operational forces is not a sustainable one. A common illustration of this, with which all students of economics should already be familiar, is a market situation, in which the "operational forces" are the demand for, and supply of, the product involved. If demand and supply equal one another at the currently established price, the market is said to be in equilibrium. But an inequality between the quantity of the product that buyers wish to acquire at that price and the quantity that producers were willing to sell would be a disequilibrium state, in which the imbalanced demand and supply forces would act in such a way as to change the price.

When these concepts are applied to a nation's balance of international payments, equilibrium denotes that the existing pattern of economic transactions between the nation and the rest of the world is capable of being maintained, whereas disequilibrium connotes the presence of a "problem" in the nation's international economic dealings that is going to require some corrective action. What this often means in practice is that the residents of the nation in question are endeavoring to acquire more goods, services, and investment assets from foreign residents that they can pay for through their collective current sales of goods and services abroad plus current inflows of capital funds associated with longer term foreign investments in the nation. The consequence of such endeavors would be a condition of deficit disequilibrium in the nation's balance of payments—in more commonplace terms, the nation would be attempting to "live beyond its means" in relation to the international economy.

Measuring Balance of Payments Disequilibria

While it is not hard to grasp this commonsense notion of balance of payments disequilibrium, identifying and measuring such disequilibria tend to be somewhat difficult exercises. This is due in part to the lack of preciseness in the concept itself. The presence of disequilibrium infers that the nation cannot continue to carry on the amounts and types of international economic transactions in which it is presently engaging. But this leaves open questions relating to the nature, causes, and seriousness of the situation, as well as the time frame within which the nation needs to alter its international economic behavior. Moreover, different national governments may have quite different attitudes toward problems in their international economic accounts. Some governments might, for example, look on an international payments deficit as an inevitable concomitant of their country's need to develop its domestic economy by importing capital goods or industrial materials from abroad. In such a situation, the deficit might be tolerated so long as the country could find the means to finance it. For other countries, especially those that give high priority to maintaining a stable exchange value for their currency or otherwise projecting an image of financial soundness, a deficit in the balance of payments is apt to be viewed with considerably more alarm.

This absence of definitional precision and attitudinal uniformity relative to balance of payments disequilibria is reflected in the varying ways in which disequilibria are measured and reported. As an example, the United States for many years followed a procedure in which several different measures of balance of payments disequilibrium were regularly reported. That procedure, incidentally, differed in some fundamental ways from those being utilized at the time by most other countries, and it took many years of deliberations by two high-level national commissions to reduce some of the complexities and inconsistencies in the system.

Probably the most fundamental and widely accepted methodology for ascertaining whether a nation is experiencing balance of payments disequilibrium and determining the character and extent of the problem is one that relies on a distinction between international transactions that are "autonomous" in nature and those that are "compensatory." In this context, autonomous transactions are those that take place in response to economic or political motives, and that are independent from other balance of payments transactions and from the overall condition of the nation's balance of payments accounts. The term **autonomous** is synonymous with *independent*, so autonomous balance of payments transactions are the consequence of decisions that have been made independently of the rest of the country's dealings with foreign residents. **Compensatory** transactions, on the other hand, are those that are undertaken in order to "compensate for" or "accommodate" other aspects of the nation's total international dealings.

The distinction between autonomous and compensatory transactions is not totally clear-cut, but there are general guidelines that are fairly well established. Thus, all current international transactions (imports and exports of goods and services, as well as unilateral transfers) usually are treated as autonomous, as are long-term private capital movements. The rationale for this is that the business firms, government bodies, and individuals that undertake transactions of these kinds ordinarily do so for reasons that are unrelated to (independent of) the rest of their nation's international dealings, and their decisions are not conditioned by the overall state of their country's balance of payments. For example, when the managers of a business firm are deciding whether they should export some of their company's output to foreign buyers, or whether they should make direct investments abroad, it seems reasonable to presume that their decisions will be predicated on business considerations and motives and will not be influenced by concerns or circumstances relating to the balance of payments.

Official reserves transactions are treated as compensatory, since, as has been noted previously, such transactions typically are undertaken by national monetary authorities as a means of financing imbalances in other segments of the balance of payments accounts.

This leaves private short-term capital movements as the principal type of transaction that does not fall entirely within one or the other of the two categories. Such capital movements can be either autonomous or compensatory, depending upon the underlying purpose. If, let us say, a corporation based in the United States made a short-term loan to one of its foreign affiliates to help that affiliate finance an inventory buildup, that international transfer of short-term capital would clearly be an autonomous transaction, based strictly upon business considerations. On the other hand, if residents of a country were to engage in short-term borrowing from foreign lenders in order to pay for imported goods, that would be regarded as a compensatory transaction, since the borrowing took place in order to "accommodate" other items in the balance of payments. The designation of short-term capital movements as either compensatory or autonomous thus may entail "judgment calls" by the analysts, who must attempt to surmise the purposes for which the transactions were carried out.

Once the distinction between autonomous and compensatory transactions has been drawn, a determination can be made as to the presence and the dimensions of balance of payments disequilibrium. A net debit imbalance—that is, an excess of debits (payments) relative to credits (receipts)—in the sum of the **autonomous transactions** would indicate a condition of **deficit disequilibrium,** whereas a net credit imbalance—that is, an excess of credits (receipts) relative to debits (payments)—in the autonomous transactions total would indicate a condition of surplus disequilibrium. Such imbalances would mean that the country in question was not achieving a financial parity between external receipts and payments through those transactions that were occurring "for their own sake," and that compensatory transactions would therefore be required. The size of the net imbalance (either debit or credit) in autonomous transactions would be the measure of the magnitude of the disequilibrium condition.

An Illustration of Balance of Payments Disequilibrium

This mode of detecting balance of payments disequilibrium can be understood more easily through the use of an illustration. A hypothetical balance of payments statement for an imaginary country called Constantina can be used for this purpose. This statement, which is a condensed record of the economic transactions of Constantina's residents during the year 1985, is shown in Table 12.1. Following conventional usage, debit entries are preceded by a negative sign (−) and credit entries by a positive sign (+), and the amounts are in "constantines," the mythical country's monetary unit of measurement.

Constantina's balance of payments accounts reveal that the nation's residents exported 800 million constantines worth of goods and services to foreign countries during 1985, while importing 1,100 million worth of goods and services from abroad, thereby registering a deficit of 300 million in those current transactions. However, Constantina residents received 100 million in grants and gifts during the year, while making gifts and grants of 50 million to foreign residents, so the credit balance in those unilateral transfers reduced the net debit imbalance for the current account as a whole to 250 million constantines.

In the capital account, the country realized a **net inflow** of long-term investment capital of 100 million constantines, as foreign residents invested 200 million in the nation during 1985, while residents of Constantina were increasing their long-term investments abroad by 100 million.

If the transactions described above are assumed to represent all of the **autonomous items** in Constantina's balance of payments for 1985, then, in keeping with the previous definition of balance of payments disequilibria, it can be concluded that Constantina was in deficit disequilibrium in its international accounts to the tune of 150 million constantines. In other words, the residents of Constantina, in their autonomous dealings with foreign residents, had spent, "given away," and invested that much more abroad than they had collectively realized from foreign sales of goods and services, gifts from foreign residents, and capital inflows resulting from long-term investments in their country. Stated still an-

Table 12.1   *Constantina—Balance of Payments, 1985*
(Figures in Millions of Constantines)

	Debits (−)	Credits (+)
Current account		
Exports of merchandise and services		+ 800
Imports of merchandise and services	− 1,100	
Unilateral transfers (gifts and grants)		
To foreign residents	− 50	
From foreign residents		+ 100
Current account balance	− 250	
Capital account		
Long-term investment		
Direct and portfolio investment abroad	− 100	
Direct and portfolio investment in		+ 200
Constantina by foreign residents		
Balance on autonomous transactions	− 150	
Short-term investment		
Borrowings from foreign residents		+ 100
Official reserves account		
Gold exports (sales) by Constantina		+ 50
monetary authorities		
Balance on compensatory transactions		+ 150
Account totals	− 1,250	+ 1,250

other way, their payments to foreign residents associated with their autonomous international transactions exceeded their receipts by 150 million constantines.

What made it possible for the residents of Constantina to carry on this pattern of international economic transactions, in which they were, in essence, spending more than they were earning? The residents of a nation collectively accomplish this feat in much the same way that an individual or a single family might, that is, by borrowing or by using "savings" to make up the difference. By going back to Constantina's balance of payments statement and focusing attention on the portion that is below the dashed horizontal line, it can be seen that residents of Constantina also engaged in certain *compensatory* transactions during 1985. First, they borrowed the equivalent of 100 million constantines from abroad on a short-term basis. Those borrowings may have been arranged by private residents (e.g., business firms in Constantina that were acquiring imports on credit) or by governmental authorities. In either event, the borrowings, which increased Constantina's short-term financial liabilities to foreign residents and therefore were recorded as credit entries, provided part of the wherewithal for financing the debit imbalance in the autonomous accounts. Second, the official reserves account shows that Constantina's monetary authorities sold some of the country's gold reserves. That sale, which reduced the nation's assets and therefore created a credit entry in the balance of payments accounts, provided the remaining amount needed to cover the autonomous deficit. (*How* and *why* national monetary authorities actually engage in such activities will be considered later in this chapter.)

When both the compensatory and the autonomous transactions are considered, Constantina's balance of payments accounts for the year 1985 "balance," as the totals of the debit entries and of the credit entries are equal. But the nation is nonetheless confronting a problem that effectively precludes it from continuing to carry on the amounts and kinds of international economic dealings that it conducted during 1985. Constantina cannot reasonably expect to go on compensating for a deficit in its autonomous accounts by borrowing and drawing down previously accumulated assets, since both those sources of compensatory financing have limits. Neither the willingness of foreign creditors to extend credit to Constantina's residents nor the country's reserves of monetary gold or other liquid assets are inexhaustible "funding pools" that can sustain an excess of expenditures, relative to receipts, in the country's autonomous international transactions. Thus, Constantina's balance of payments evinces the "unsustainable condition" which is the essence of disequilibrium.

Consequences of Balance of Payments Disequilibrium

The hypothetical situation that was constructed for Constantina was one of *deficit disequilibrium*, manifested by an excess of debit items (representing payment obligations to foreign residents), relative to credit items (representing current or prospective receipts from foreign residents), in the autonomous components of the country's balance of payments accounts. It should be apparent that a country might equally well be experiencing **surplus disequilibrium** in its balance of payments, which obviously would be manifested in the opposite way (i.e., by an excess of credits, relative to debits, in the autonomous transactions). Indeed, for the "real world," taken as a whole, logic dictates that any balance of payments deficits that some countries are experiencing at any given time will necessarily be offset by surpluses in the international accounts of other nations. Inasmuch as the entire world is a single, closed economic system (we are not, as yet, doing business with any other planets), countries that are importing more things of economic value than they are exporting can only be doing this because other countries are *temporarily* willing and able to export more than they are importing.

As a practical matter, a deficit in a nation's balance of payments generally is viewed as a more serious and pressing problem than a surplus.

A country experiencing a deficit is compelled to find ways of financing the negative imbalance in its autonomous international transactions, either through borrowing or dissaving (i.e., drawing down its international reserve assets). Moreover, a deficit—especially one centered in the trade sector—can be giving off ominous signals relating to the country's international competitive position and its prospects for maintaining acceptable levels of domestic employment. If such a deficit becomes chronic, those portents may turn into actual declines in employment and output, as foreign-produced goods inexorably displace internal production. A deficit also puts downward pressure on the value of the country's currency in the foreign exchange markets, which means that the monetary authorities must either intervene in those markets to "prop up" the currency's value or accept its decline.

Although the manifestations and consequences of surplus disequilibria tend to be regarded with less trepidation than those associated with balance of payments deficits, such surpluses are by no means entirely benign. A country that is recording a surplus in its international accounts may be looked upon with envy by other nations, since it appears to be competing successfully in trade or in attracting investment capital. However, such envy may itself become the source of problems for the surplus nation, to the extent that it spawns policies or actions that are directed toward reducing whatever commercial advantages that nation is presumed to possess. Japan provides a good contemporary example of a country whose continuing balance of payments surpluses have made it a target for harsh criticism and have led other nations to erect a multitude of "defensive" import barriers against its goods.

In addition to engendering complaints and retaliatory measures by other nations, a balance of payments surplus can create or intensify inflationary pressures within the economy of a surplus country. This occurs in part because the excess of monetary receipts from abroad relative to foreign payments will (unless they are offset or "sterilized" by domestic monetary policy measures) expand the nation's money supply, and this expansion can, in turn, raise the level of prices. The actual extent of such inflationary effects will depend upon a number of factors, including the degree to which spending responds to changes in the money supply and whether increases in spending are accommodated by increasing employment and real output, rather than by raising prices. Nevertheless, a country that has a substantial and persistent surplus in its balance of payments accounts must contend with the inflationary threat which that surplus poses.

Causes of Balance of Payments Disequilibria

What causes balance of payments disequilibria? There is no single, simple answer to this question, for disequilibrium in the balance of payments can result from a variety of events or circumstances, which often are intermingled and interactive. Furthermore, no two cases of balance of payments disequilibrium are apt to be exactly alike in terms of causation, that is, the particular confluence of circumstances that brings on disequilibrium in one country at one particular time is not likely to recur in identical form in that country or to be exactly duplicated elsewhere in the world. Perhaps the most practical way to respond to the question is to offer a few generalizations regarding the more common causes of balance of payments disequilibria.

It is possible and not unusual for disequilibrium in the balance of payments to result from sudden, drastic disruptions of a country's productive capacity. Wars, revolutions, or more limited military actions may destroy some or all of a nation's economic infrastructure or industrial facilities and thereby render it incapable of either satisfying the economic needs of its populace through domestic output or producing sufficient exportable goods to pay for needed imports. It may therefore be forced to "borrow" the goods it needs from foreign countries, and its balance of payments would show a trade deficit that was being underwritten by increasing debts to foreigners. Virtually all the Western European nations found themselves in this unhappy condition following the Second World War, and they experienced a long string of balance of payments deficits while they were gradually reconstructing their economies.

Natural disasters or weather-induced variations in agricultural output can also throw a country's balance of payments into disequilibrium. This possibility is especially likely for countries that are highly dependent upon a few products or commodities for their economic livelihood and their export revenues. An interesting example of this kind of development is the case of Peru, which established a strong balance of payments position by exporting fishmeal (a high-protein animal feed derived from anchovies), only to see that position deteriorate when climatic changes dramatically reduced the anchovy population in the country's Pacific Ocean fishing grounds. A similar but more widespread instance occurred in the early 1970s, when successive years of drought in several parts of the world made it necessary for many countries to greatly expand their imports of agricultural commodities.

While dramatic changes in economic output of the sort described above can bring on serious balance of payments problems, such changes often have the virtue of being short-lived and perhaps even self-correcting. At a minimum, the nation or nations involved can readily identify the source of their balance of payments difficulties.

Usually, however, balance of payments disequilibria spring from economic developments of a more complicated type. Shifts in price relationships among countries are a prime example of such developments. A country beset by inflation is apt to find deficits appearing in its international accounts, as relative increases in the prices of its goods and services progressively reduce its ability to export while simultaneously making imported goods more appealing to its residents. Changes in relative interest rates, which essentially are the prices of capital funds, can likewise engender balance of payments disequilibria by moving such funds from countries whose interest rate structures have become "too low" toward nations offering higher interest returns. Even economic prosperity can create imbalances in international transactions, as nations in which output and incomes are rising rapidly in comparison to the rest of the world increase their demand for imported industrial or consumer goods. These price, interest rate, and income changes are often associated with **business cycles** (i.e., recurring upturns and downturns in overall economic activity), and the resulting balance of payments problems therefore are termed "cyclical disequilibria."

Still another general category of causes of balance of payments disequilibria includes economic changes that may occur gradually but are more permanent in nature. Countries may, over time, become more dependent on imports because domestic sources of raw materials have been depleted or population growth has outpaced their ability to expand agricultural output. Unless they can expand exports sufficiently, such import dependency could lead to chronic payments deficits. Conversely, nations may be faced with declining foreign demand for commodities or products that have accounted for a large portion of their export sales, and this could also engender persistent balance of payments problems. This describes the situation of many raw material producing Third World nations during the 1950s and 1960s (see Chapter 3). The inability of countries to adapt their economies to such fundamental alterations in international demand and supply conditions can result in what is termed "structural disequilibria" in the balance of payments.

Adjustment to Balance of Payments Disequilibrium

It was shown in Balance of Payments Disequilibrium, above, that disequilibrium in a country's balance of payments, whether it be deficit or surplus disequilibrium, raises some serious problems for that country. Moreover, disequilibrium is a state incapable of being sustained. It follows, therefore, that whenever disequilibrium exists, some **correction** or **adjustment** must occur. Something must happen that will reduce the imbalance in the country's autonomous international economic transactions.

While it is valid to assert that balance of payments disequilibrium necessarily requires adjustment, it should be pointed out that the urgency of such adjustment can vary greatly from nation to nation. As noted previously, different countries, depending upon their national priorities and their position in the world economy, may hold quite different views as to the seriousness of disequilibrium in their international accounts and may therefore assign greater or lesser importance to adjustment efforts. How quickly adjustment must take place will also depend to a considerable extent upon the ability of a nation to *finance* the imbalance in its autonomous transactions. A country having consider-able international reserves, that is, a large stock of gold or convertible foreign currencies available to its monetary authorities, would be able to engage in compensatory financing activities for an extended period of time. By the same token, a country that could borrow readily from foreign official or private lenders might manage to fund a deficit in its balance of payments for a long period, thereby deferring measures that would eliminate the deficit. The United States, for example, persistently registered a deficit in its balance of payments throughout the 1950s and 1960s, which it was able to finance by dint of its very large gold reserves and the willingness of other nations to accumulate dollar deposits which were, in effect, American "IOUs." But even that unique situation had its limits, and the United States was eventually compelled to take drastic steps to reduce its balance of payments deficits.

Since balance of payments disequilibrium resides in the autonomous components of the affected nation's balance of payments, permanent adjustment will entail fundamental changes in those components. A nation experiencing disequilibrium faces the need to amend its inter-national economic behavior in a manner that will reduce the imbalance in its autonomous transactions to manageable proportions. This con-ceivably could involve realignments in any or all of those transactions, including long-term capital movements and unilateral transfers. But the brunt of the adjustment process is likely to be borne by the merchandise trade and service transactions, since exports and imports of goods and services constitute the largest and most continuous form of international economic activity for most countries.

There are three basic ways in which adjustment to balance of pay-ments disequilibria can occur or be effectuated. These include: (1) changes in exchange rates, (2) changes in prices and incomes, and (3) controls on international trade or monetary transfers. The first two of these are often termed "market adjustments," since they are accomplished through alterations in market conditions or relationships. The third approach is termed "nonmarket adjustment," as it entails governmental interfer-ence with normal market conditions or processes. In fact, even so-called market adjustments often involve government actions to initiate or sup-port the changes needed to restore balance of payments equilibrium.

Adjustment Through Exchange Rate Changes

In order to comprehend how changes in exchange rates can correct balance of payments disequilibria, the relationships between the ex-change rate and the transactions that make up the balance of payments must be understood. It will be easier to accomplish this if attention is focused upon a particular country. Let us therefore return to the myth-ical country of Constantina, and consider how its balance of payments situation will affect, and also be affected by, the exchange rate.

Exchange rates are the prices of national currencies in relation to one another, and it is conventional to define the exchange rate as the domestic currency price of a unit of foreign currency. With regard to Constantina, then, the exchange rate can be thought of as the price, in constantines, of other national currencies. To further simplify the investigation, all foreign currencies will (by assumption) be consolidated, and the dollar alone will represent the currency of the rest of the world. Thus, the **exchange rate** refers to the price, in constantines, of one dollar.

It was learned in Chapter 11 that the exchange rate is fundamentally determined by demand and supply forces interacting in the foreign exchange market. Furthermore, it was pointed out that those demand and supply forces originated in the host of economic transactions that were taking place between the residents of the nation whose currency was being considered and the residents of other nations, that is, by the nation's *balance of payments*. Constantina's *demand* for dollars thus can be said to emanate from the desire of its residents to purchase (import) goods or services from abroad, or to invest in foreign countries, or to make gifts (unilateral transfers) to foreign residents—in other words, all of those economic acts that would entail *payments* to foreign residents and enter its balance of payments accounts as *debit* entries. Conversely, the *supply* of dollars that is available to residents of Constantina through the foreign exchange market comes from their sales (exports) of goods and services, investments in the nation by foreign residents, or gifts received from foreign donors. These, of course, comprise the economic transactions that involve *receipts* from abroad and are recorded as *credits* in Constantina's balance of payments accounts.

Given these relationships between the foreign exchange demand and supply schedules and the underlying balance of payments transactions, it becomes apparent that a state of disequilibrium in a nation's balance of payments will be accompanied by an imbalance between demand and supply in the foreign exchange market. If the total values of those autonomous transactions that are engendering a demand for foreign currencies exceed the total values of the autonomous transactions that are creating a supply of such currencies (or vice versa), the exchange rate will be unstable. With deficit disequilibrium, the excess demand for foreign currencies, relative to the supply that is forthcoming, will put upward pressure on the price(s) of those currencies in terms of the deficit nation's money. By the same reckoning, a surplus in a nation's balance of payments would show up in the foreign exchange market as an excess supply or offering of foreign currencies that would tend to reduce their prices.

These exchange market effects of balance of payments disequilibrium can be perceived by looking once again at Constantina's balance of payments accounts for 1985. Table 12.2 reproduces the balance of payments data that were initially presented in Table 12.1, but goes one step further to indicate how the autonomous transactions undertaken by Constantina's residents would affect the demand/supply relationships in the foreign exchange market.

Table 12.2   *Constantina—Balance of Payments, 1985*
(Figures in Millions of Constantines)

	Debits (−)	Credits (+)	Foreign Exchange Market Effects
Current account			
Exports of merchandise and services		+800	Supplies foreign currency (dollars)
Imports of merchandise and services	−1,100		Demand for foreign currency
Unilateral transfers (gifts and grants)			
To foreign residents	− 50		Demand for foreign currency
From foreign residents		+100	Supplies foreign currency
Current account balance	− 250		
Capital account			
Long-term investment			
Direct and portfolio investment abroad	− 100		Demand for foreign currency
Direct and portfolio investment in Constantina by foreign residents		+200	Supplies foreign currency
Balance on autonomous transactions	− 150		Net (excess) demand for foreign currency

Table 12.2 reveals the problem that would develop in the foreign exchange market as a consequence of the autonomous transactions that Constantina's residents were carrying on with foreign residents during 1985. Those transactions would create an imbalance between the amount of foreign exchange (dollars) required by Constantina's residents and the amount that foreigners would be supplying in connection with their autonomous dealings with Constantina. This imbalance could be described either as an excess demand for dollars or, alternatively, as an excess supply of constantines. But, regardless of how it is described, its natural tendency would be to raise the exchange rate, that is, the price of dollars in terms of constantines.

Whether or not this tendency would actually bring about an increase in the exchange rate would depend upon how the monetary authorities of Constantina or other involved countries responded to the exchange market pressures, and their responses would in turn be conditioned by the exchange rate regime under which they were operating. If the monetary authorities were adhering to what has previously been described as a floating rate regime, they would be inclined to permit the exchange rate to follow the dictates of the market demand and supply forces. In that case, Constantina's residents would find the price of the dollar rising as they attempted to purchase dollars for constantines in order to pay for the goods, services, and investment assets they were acquiring from abroad.

This alteration in the exchange rate could be expected to have a mitigating effect upon the deficit disequilibrium that had set it into motion. The appreciation in the value of the dollar (or depreciation in the value of the constantine) would make foreign goods, services, and investment assets more expensive for residents of Constantina, while simultaneously making that country's products, services, and investment assets cheaper for foreign residents. Such changes in relative prices ordinarily would result in reduced purchases from abroad (imports) by Constantina's residents, and increased sales (exports) to foreign buyers. The extent of these induced changes in exporting and importing behavior would be influenced by various factors, including the elasticities of demand for imports and exports, the time required for the revised prices to be reflected in commercial orders and billings, and the ability of Constantina to shift resources internally to accommodate the new demand and supply patterns. While these factors interject an element of uncertainty into the process, they do not negate the basic tendency for exchange rate changes to counteract balance of payments disequilibria if those rates are permitted to react freely and naturally to market pressures.

A floating exchange rate regime thus contains a sort of "built-in equilibrating mechanism," since balance of payments disequilibria would immediately and automatically bring about exchange rate realignments, and those realignments would, in turn, work toward restoring equilibrium. This mechanism is viewed as one of the principal advantages afforded by such a regime, and proponents of floating rates also point out that this continuous and automatic adjustment of balance of payments problems through exchange rate changes relieves national governments of the need to initiate or alter domestic economic policies in order to deal with such problems. However, floating rate regimes also have some disadvantages (which were identified in Chapter 11) and national governments have seldom been content to allow exchange rates to fluctuate with complete freedom. Balance of payments adjustments therefore may have to take place in a different manner than the one that has just been described.

The adjustment process would differ somewhat if the existing exchange rate regime was characterized by **stabilized** rather than flexible rates. If Constantina was operating under a stabilized rate regime, its monetary authorities would be obligated to prevent the price of the constantine from deviating from its established par value in relation to the dollar. They would therefore have to attempt to contravene the downward pressure that their country's balance of payments deficit would be exerting upon the price of the constantine in the foreign exchange market. That effort would entail **intervention** in the exchange market, that is, Constantina's monetary authorities would have to offer dollars in exchange for constantines in sufficient amounts to satisfy the excess demand for dollars emanating from the unbalanced autonomous transactions. Such offerings would be the basis of the compensatory transactions appearing in Constantina's balance of payments accounts, since the country's monetary authorities would have to either draw upon their accumulated dollar-denominated deposits in foreign banks, borrow dollars from foreign leaders, or sell gold reserves in order to acquire the dollars needed for exchange market intervention. Any of these actions would generate a credit entry in the compensatory section of the balance of payments accounts.

The intervention activities described above would provide a means of financing the deficit for a time, and, if the underlying causes of the deficit were themselves transient or self-correcting, such compensatory actions might buy sufficient time for Constantina's balance of payments to return to equilibrium. However, if the deficit was not amenable to quick correction (as would typically be the case in "real-world" situations), Constantina's monetary authorities would find it increasingly difficult to acquire the wherewithal to continue their support of the constantine's exchange market value, and might eventually have to forsake the effort and establish a new par value for the constantine. In this instance, that would be a *lower value*, which is to say, the constantine would be **devalued** in relation to the dollar. (As was seen in Chapter 11, such a devaluation—or, its opposite, an upward revaluation—of the par value of a nation's currency is permissible within a stabilized rate regime as a means of correcting a condition of fundamental disequilibrium in the nation's balance of payments.)

This official devaluation of the constantine would have adjustment tendencies (and limitations) comparable to those that were previously attributed to the more gradual depreciation that would occur with floating rates. The higher price of the dollar should discourage foreign purchases and foreign investment by Constantina's residents, while making the country's exports more attractive to foreign buyers and encouraging increased investment in the country by foreign companies or individuals. The basic balance of payments adjustment process thus is the same under floating or stabilized rate regimes, although the manner in which the equilibrating exchange rate changes are effectuated, as well as the timing of such changes, differ in the two regimes. It was remarked earlier that, with floating rates, such equilibrating exchange rate changes take place *continuously* and *automatically;* this can be contrasted with the stabilized rate regime, in which those changes would happen only periodically and would be more subject to the **discretion** of the monetary authorities.

Adjustment Through Price and Income Changes

The reduction or elimination of disequilibrium in a nation's balance of payments may occur through alterations in its level of prices of income relative to those of other nations. This means of adjustment may serve in place of exchange rate changes if the latter are precluded or delayed by governmental policies or actions. Otherwise, it may supplement and reinforce the equilibrating effects of exchange rate changes.

The connections and interactions that exist between a country's economy and its balance of payments are readily apparent, but also quite complex. Since the balance of payments represents the international portion of a country's total economic activity, it is evident that the state of its economy, as measured by such variables as prices, employment, incomes, and interest rates, will exert an effect upon its balance of payments. But the international transactions that comprise the balance of payments will simultaneously be affecting those same internal economic conditions. For instance, a country experiencing rapid inflation is apt to find its residents importing more goods from abroad (since foreign goods would become cheaper in relation to home-produced goods as the inflationary trend progressed). This expansion of imports might then exert an influence on domestic prices, either through competitive pressures or through more roundabout effects on the demand for domestic products or the supply of money and credit.

All the complexities of the balance of payments/domestic economy nexus cannot be dealt with here, but the illustrative case of Constantina can again be used to outline the main elements of the price–income adjustment process.

The initial link in that process would be the contractionary effect that Constantina's balance of payments deficit would exert on prices and incomes within the country. Because Constantina's residents were effectively spending more for imports and foreign investment than they were realizing from export sales and investment capital inflows, there would be a net transfer of monetary assets out of the country and thus a reduction in the domestic money supply. In the absence of offsetting money-creating activities by Constantina's central bank, this reduction in money supply would tend to reduce the general price level (or keep prices from rising as much as they otherwise would) in Constantina. The extent of this downward effect on prices would depend on a number of factors, including the velocity of monetary transactions and the flexibility of prices within Constantina's economic system. But it would be reasonable to anticipate some decline, especially in relation to prices in those countries that would be experiencing balance of payments surpluses coinciding with Constantina's deficit.

In addition to its impact upon the money supply and prices, Constantina's balance of payments deficit would have a depressing effect upon incomes in the country. This would be due to the excess of import purchases relative to export sales, which, in simplest terms, means that Constantina's residents are spending a portion of their income for foreign-produced goods and services that is not being matched by receipts from foreign sales. Thus, the country is experiencing a "leakage" from its income-spending stream, equal to the amount by which import spending exceeds export receipts. Those net foreign expenditures could be expected to bring about declines in employment and incomes in Constantina, since spending for goods produced abroad is unlikely to provide as much employment for domestic workers and capital as would spending for goods produced at home. (This is not to imply that import spending creates *no* domestic employment opportunities, since the importation of foreign products does provide jobs for those involved in transporting, processing, and marketing those products.)

As in the case of price changes, the income changes associated with a balance of payments deficit can be affected by other conditions and events and are therefore difficult to predict with exactness. But here again, the basic tendency would be for the deficit country to undergo a contraction of employment and income, while those foreign countries with corresponding balance of payments surpluses would be realizing employment and income gains.[2]

The second link in this balance of payments adjustment process is the effect the shifts in relative price and income levels among the deficit and surplus countries would have upon their economic transactions with one another. Since those shifts ordinarily would be toward lower prices and incomes in the deficit country (Constantina in our example) and higher incomes and prices in surplus countries, Constantina should find the foreign demand for its exports growing, while its own residents would be constrained to curtail their imports of foreign goods and services. Such outcomes would be attributable to the "cheapening" of Constantina's products relative to those produced abroad, as well as to the combination of declining purchasing power among Constantina's residents and increased purchasing power overseas.

If this price/income adjustment process is compared with adjustment through exchange rate changes, the final stages of the two are found to

---

[2]The magnitude of the ultimate change in national income that is caused by a balance of payments deficit or surplus is apt to be considerably greater than the deficit or surplus itself. This is due to the **multiplier effect** which (students of economics should recall) refers to the tendency for any autonomous increase or decrease in spending to trigger a "chain reaction" of further spending changes. In the case of a balance of payments deficit, the spending "leakage" that was noted above has the same effect as an autonomous spending reduction within the economy.

be essentially the same. In both instances, balance of payments problems are eventually mitigated by alterations in imports, exports, or other autonomous transactions. The differences in the adjustment processes themselves have to do with whether those alterations are induced by realignments of currency values or by realignments of price and income levels within and among the nations involved.

These can be very important differences, however, in terms of the impact of balance of payments adjustment on the economies of the countries that are undergoing such adjustment. A point often made in this regard is that adjustment through exchange rate variations is less likely to have extensive effects on a nation's *entire* economy, since the changes necessary to correct a deficit or surplus would mainly take place in the foreign trade sector. By contrast, if exchange rates are fixed and adjustment must therefore occur through the creation of price and income differentials, the whole economy may be affected. Such a possibility would be heightened if the government found it necessary to use monetary or fiscal measures to expedite the adjustment process. If, for instance, Constantina's government officials felt compelled to deflate domestic prices and incomes in order to cure the country's payments deficit, the tight money and contractionary fiscal policies that they would implement would be felt throughout the nation's economy.

Such differences in the economic impact of the two alternative adjustment processes may be reflected in their **political feasibility.** A nation's political leaders might find it distasteful to instigate or tolerate declines in domestic employment and output for the sake of correcting a deficit in the balance of payments. Relying on exchange depreciation to correct the problem is apt to be somewhat more palatable politically, since the rate changes themselves may escape public notice, and their effects on the domestic economy may be hard to detect. When faced with a choice between these two alternatives, then, government officials are wont to view exchange rate variations as the lesser of two evils. But they may also reject both of these adjustment processes in favor of a third option, the imposition of controls on trade or other international transactions.

Adjustment Through Government Controls

National governments frequently employ controls on foreign trade or investment for the purpose of correcting balance of payments disequilibria. Such measures include import duties or quotas, subsidies for exports, or specific limitations on international capital transfers. Exchange controls, which permit governments to manipulate international economic transactions in a somewhat less overt manner, are also widely used as a means of coping with balance of payments disequilibria.

Controls are appealing to governments confronted with balance of payments problems, since they appear to offer a way of striking directly at the causes of those problems without unduly disrupting the domestic economy. If, for example, Constantina's situation is considered again, it is easy to see why that country's government officials might decide that imposing legal curbs on imports or overseas investment would be the simplest and most direct means of eliminating the balance of payments deficit. Not only would such curbs hit the autonomous transactions that appear to be responsible for the deficit, but their effects also would appear to fall only on those economic groups (foreign and domestic) that actually are engaged in export–import trade or international investment.

Despite these superficial attractions, however, controls are not a panacea for balance of payments difficulties. In the first place, government restrictions on trade aimed at reducing balance of payments deficits are subject to the same dangers as those imposed for other purposes. The possibility of retaliation by foreign countries is never completely absent, so a country (such as Constantina) that raises barriers to imports in an attempt to reduce a deficit could find its ability to export similarly curtailed. Limits on outflows of investment capital may also be self-defeating, insofar as they sacrifice future receipts of earnings from abroad for the sake of immediate relief from balance of payments problems.

Economists further point out that trade and investment controls serve mainly to *suppress* the immediate manifestations or symptoms of trouble in a nation's international economic situation, rather than dealing with the causes of such trouble. The gist of this assertion is that controls (e.g., import barriers or restrictions on capital movements) can bring about a temporary improvement in the balance of payments accounts, but such measures do little or nothing to alter the underlying economic circumstances or behavior patterns that affect those accounts. Any relaxation of these controls would therefore be followed by a resurgence of the state of disequilibrium in the balance of payments. Moreover, the conditions that caused that disequilibrium might actually worsen while the palliative measures were in effect.

The Balance of Payments and the International Business Firm

This chapter has mainly considered how the balance of payments and balance of payments disequilibria relate to national economies. But it is also necessary to be aware of how companies doing business internationally can be affected by the balance of payments situation.

International business firms must be on the alert for serious disequilibria in the balance of payments of those countries in or with which they are doing business, since such disequilibria, and the compensatory measures they entail, heighten the risks and difficulties these firms will encounter. Some of these risks and difficulties stem from the exchange rate variability that accompanies imbalances in a nation's international transactions. It has been shown how balance of payments disequilibrium can bring about exchange rate changes, either "automatically" when rates are flexible, or through official devaluations or revaluations under stabilized rate regimes. Firms conducting their operations by using foreign currencies, and holding assets and liabilities valued in those currencies, may find that exchange rate changes can exert a tremendous effect on their profits and net worth. It is not uncommon for international companies to gain or lose as much through exchange rate fluctuations in some accounting periods as they earn or lose as a result of their actual business operations. This close link between exchange rate behavior and the financial health of international business firms means that such firms must be aware of, and responsive to, balance of payments developments affecting the relative prices of different national currencies. (The methods whereby international companies cope with exchange rate fluctuations will be investigated in Chapter 16.)

A second important way in which balance of payments problems can confound the operations of international companies has to do with the measures governments utilize to alleviate such problems. National governments may respond to balance of payments disequilibria (especially deficit disequilibria) either by imposing restraints on foreign trade and monetary transfers, or by undertaking actions to deflate domestic prices and incomes. Both types of corrective measures are almost certain to have adverse consequences for international firms that are doing business with the countries involved. Trade and exchange controls invariably adversely affect these firms' functioning, since the ability to move resources (including money), materials, component parts, and finished products readily from country to country is essential to maintain these companies' efficient and flexible worldwide operational capability. Such controls also debar firms from taking full advantage of changing production and marketing opportunities in different locales. Deflationary measures also erode international firms' profitability by reducing the demand for their products as part of the general economic contraction that the governments are engineering.

In addition to the complications that balance of payments problems can create for international firms that *already* are doing business in the affected nations, many countries now look at the potential effects international firms may have on their balance of payments *before* they allow these firms to set up operations in their territory. More and more nations are now "screening" proposed investments in their economies by foreign-controlled international companies, and one of the tests the prospective investors often must pass relates to the probable effect of the investment project on the host country's balance of payments. Thus, a company may have to show that its operations will strengthen the country's balance of payments position (or, at least, not be detrimental to that position) before it is permitted to enter that country.

These instances of interaction between business enterprises and the balance of payments could easily be expanded, but it should be evident by this time that any firm engaged in business on an international scale must be prepared to contend with a variety of requirements, problems, and risks that are linked to balance of payments conditions. The international manager therefore cannot dismiss the balance of payments as an esoteric subject of concern only to government officials and academicians. Indeed, the balance of payments comprises a nation's overall economic relationship with the remainder of the world, and therefore relates to the life and livelihood of all human beings.

Summary

1. The combined total of the economic transactions that take place between the residents of a particular nation and foreign residents during some given time period comprises that nation's balance of payments. These transactions are recorded in balance of payments accounts.

2. The balance of payments accounts arrange information on a nation's international economic transactions in a systematic fashion. Differences in the nature of transactions are shown by recording them in different sections of the balance of payments accounts, namely, the current, capital, and official reserves accounts.

3. The balance of payments accounts follow the double-entry accounting convention, in which every transaction is regarded as being two-sided and accordingly is recorded by a debit and credit entry of equal magnitude. The debit entries in a country's balance of payments accounts record those sides of its international economic transactions which immediately or eventually entail payments to foreign residents. The credit entries are records of those aspects of international economic transactions that result in receipts from foreign residents.

4. Since every international economic transaction creates equal debit and credit entries in the balance of payments accounts, the accounts should balance, in the sense that total debits should equal total credits for any accounting period. Deficiencies in data-gathering procedures may necessitate the use of an errors and omissions entry to bring about this accounting balance.

5. Disequilibrium in a nation's balance of payments denotes the existence of a problem in the nation's economic dealings with the rest of the world that requires some corrective action. The presence of disequilibrium is diagnosed by separating autonomous from compensatory transactions.

6. A net debit or credit imbalance in the sum of the nation's autonomous transactions indicates a condition of deficit or surplus disequilibrium, and the size of that imbalance measures the magnitude of the disequilibrium condition.

7. Balance of payments disequilibria can have a variety of causes, including sudden disruptions of the nation's productive capabilities, cyclical changes in prices or incomes, or longer-term structural changes in international demand and supply patterns.

8.   Whenever disequilibrium exists, some adjustment or correction must occur. The three basic ways in which adjustment can be effectuated are through exchange rate changes, internal price and income changes, or direct controls on international transactions.

9.   Balance of payments problems and the adjustment measures utilized to correct those problems can cause significant complications and added risks for international business firms doing business in or with the countries involved.

Questions for Review or Discussion

1.   Define the term *balance of payments.*
2.   What are the major types of economic transactions recorded in the balance of payments accounts? How are those transactions categorized in the accounts?
3.   What are the bases for determining whether a particular "side" of an international economic transaction should be recorded as a debit or a credit entry?
4.   "A nation's balance of payments accounts always balance." "Nations often have deficits or surpluses in their balance of payments." Explain how these two seemingly contradictory statements can both be "true" or valid.
5.   Give both a technical and a common-sense explanation of balance of payments disequilibrium.
6.   What kinds of problems in a nation's economy can be caused by balance of payments disequilibrium? How can internal economic problems cause disequilibrium in the balance of payments?
7.   Explain the similarities and the differences in the three basic balance of payments adjustment processes. Indicate why national governments might prefer one or the other of these adjustment processes.
8.   How can balance of payments problems affect the operations of international business firms?

Case

Ace Motor Company

The time was the fall of 1985. Sonia Blackburn, the treasurer of the Ace Motor Co., was trying to determine if she should recommend that the company consolidate its North American engine manufacturing operations at its plant in Mexico. Such a recommendation would mean that all of the company's automobile manufacturing operations in Mexico, the United States, and Canada would use Mexican-made engines.

One factor that Sonia felt was critical in making her recommendation was the exchange rate between the currencies of these three countries over the next 10 to 20 years. While she knew that these relationships would be influenced by the nations' relative rates of inflation, she remembered that in one of her college economics courses, the professor had emphasized the relationship between the exchange rate and the balance of payments (BOP) of a country. However, she also knew that recently the U.S. dollar had continued to increase in value even though the United States had consistently experienced BOP deficits. Consequently, she asked her assistant, Brian Miller, to prepare a report on the relationship between the BOP and the exchange rate of a country.

Brian reported to her that the relationship between the exchange rate of a country and its BOP was fairly complex and had changed over time as the major currencies moved after a quarter of a century from a "fixed" exchange rate system to a floating exchange rate system in the early 1970s. Under the fixed exchange rate system, set up after World War II at a conference held at Bretton Woods in New Hampshire, international differences in domestic economic policies gave rise to deficits or surpluses in a country's BOP account that had to be corrected by changing domestic economic policies or, occasionally, by changing the exchange rate after getting permission to do so from the International Monetary Fund. Thus, under the Bretton Woods System, a country's BOP accounts were an important indication of the pressure faced by a country to change its domestic economic policies. Under the Bretton Woods arrangement, the U.S. dollar was the currency that was to be used to buy or sell excess supply or demand for a currency to keep it at or near its fixed exchange rate. Under the floating exchange rate system, each country could presumably pursue its own domestic economic policies and the exchange rate would adjust automatically and continuously to offset international differences in domestic economic policies. The BOP accounts under this system would not show persistent deficits or surpluses and therefore were no longer an important indication of the pressure to change the value of a given currency. Thus, Brian felt that Ace Motor Co. should ignore the BOP accounts in assessing the strength of a currency.

Sonia, however, felt that the BOP accounts were still an important indication of supply and demand for a particular currency and reasoned that, for an economic good like a currency, the basic forces of demand and supply still determined its price. Furthermore, she had just received a letter from her congressman, Jack Hemp, in which he reported that he is organizing an international summit conference of bankers, economists, and government officials to discuss the possible move back toward some form of a fixed exchange rate system.

What course of action do you recommend for Sonia Blackburn? Should she continue to monitor the BOP accounts of the countries in North America, and how should she analyze the role of these accounts in her decision?

Part 4

MULTINATIONAL BUSINESS ENTERPRISES

Chapter 13

THE MULTINATIONAL CORPORATIONS

Chapter Objectives

- *To delineate the essential characteristics of multinational corporations and to identify the world's major multinationals*
- *To analyze the basis and nature of the conflicts that have existed between multinational firms and national governments*
- *To assess the effects of multinational corporations upon the economies and political systems of their home and host nations*
- *To examine and evaluate the historical development and current status of national, regional, and international policies relating to multinational corporations*

The massive expansion of international business that has taken place over the past quarter-century has been carried out, to a large extent, by a relatively small number of very large business firms. These **multinational corporations** (MNCs) have been the subject of a tremendous amount of attention.[1] Hundreds of studies have been made of their behavior and performance and of their effects on the economies, politics, and cultures of the nations of the world. They have been investigated by many private and public organizations, including the United States Senate and the United Nations (UN), and the UN has established a permanent commission that continuously surveys their activities and their impact upon the world economy.

This concern is attributable to the enormous size of these corporations and their operations. Several of the largest multinationals have sales

---

[1]Such designations as **multinational enterprises** (MNEs), **world companies,** and **global companies** are also frequently applied to these firms, while the term **transnational corporation** (TNC) is favored by many individuals and organizations, especially those associated with the United Nations. Although these various designations are sometimes used to convey differences in the user's concept or definition of the business firms being described, they are employed interchangeably in this text.

revenues exceeding ten billion dollars per year, and their annual output is larger than the gross national product of many of the world's nations. The immense stock of resources, productive assets, and money they control and that they can move quickly and easily from country to country imbues these firms with an aura of power that has caused national governments, international institutions, and many other groups and individuals to regard them with deep apprehension.

This chapter will focus on the MNCs. It will examine their distinctive characteristics and the nature of their operations and will analyze the causes and consequences of the controversy that has surrounded these extraordinary business entities.

The Character of the Multinational Corporation

What are the distinguishing features of a MNC? There is no universally accepted answer to this question, and different definitions and descriptions of the MNC exist. It is possible nonetheless to identify the salient characteristics of such corporations.

Some of those characteristics are organizational and operational. They relate to these firms' structural characteristics and the general nature of their operations. Probably the most obvious characteristic is that these companies conduct business in more than one country.[2] Such multi-country operations are carried on by a **parent** or **headquarters** company that has acquired and subsequently exercises control over **affiliates** located in other countries. The foreign affiliates might conceivably be engaged in a variety of business functions (e.g., marketing the parent company's products or raising funds to finance its operations), but **foreign production** is the usual hallmark of the MNC.

The other features that define the MNC are managerial in nature. The following interrelated characteristics are particularly relevant in this regard:

1. A multinational corporation is an *integrated* worldwide business system. This means that the parent company and its foreign affiliates act in close alliance and cooperation with one another, as distinct from functioning separately and autonomously. Such integration is evidenced through resource transfers, that is, movements of capital, technology, and managerial personnel between parent and affiliates and

---

[2]A quantitative dimension is sometimes applied to this characteristic. For example, a firm may be viewed as having "crossed the multinational threshold" whenever more than 25 percent of its total sales revenues come from operations outside the parent firm's home country. While such quantification may be useful in certain instances, there is no logical way to define the exact point at which a company becomes multinational.

among the affiliates themselves. It also frequently entails a division of responsibility among the affiliates for supplying the various materials or components that go into the MNC's final products. This allows the MNC to acquire materials and produce component parts wherever it is most advantageous to do so. Such advantages often are connected with differences in the cost of labor or other inputs, but proximity to markets or sources of raw materials, or favorable laws and political conditions may also influence the firm's choice and allocation of production sites.

2. A MNC is ultimately controlled by a single managerial authority (typically the top management group of the parent company) which makes the key, strategic decisions relating to the operations of the parent firm and all its affiliates. Such centralization of management is imperative for achieving and maintaining worldwide integration and for attaining the basic objective of profit maximization for the multinational enterprise as a whole. Thus, decisions as to the MNC's overall product mix, the sourcing of inputs (including capital funds), the location of production facilities, and the markets to be served are made centrally in order to take maximum advantage of cost and market opportunities in various parts of the world, to insure smooth interactions among the affiliates, and to avoid detrimental interaffiliate competition for markets or resources.

3. The managers of a MNC, especially the central management group, are presumed to possess a "global perspective." This means that the top managers regard the entire world as the relevant frame-of-reference for making the kinds of resource acquisition, locus of production, and market decisions identified above. It also implies the absence of any preferential emphasis upon the parent country's home market on the part of those managers.[3]

In summary, a MNC is a group of business units located in different countries, whose operations are coordinated by a management "control center" that makes decisions on the basis of global profit opportunities and objectives. Later in this chapter, consideration will be given to how these basic characteristics have brought MNCs into conflict with national governments and other interest groups. Before proceeding to that topic, however, it is useful to look at the actual firms making up the world's MNCs, and to examine their activities.

---

[3]This concept of differing management philosophies and their effects on the orientations of international companies has been emphasized in the works of Howard V. Perlmutter and others. Perlmutter distinguishes between **ethnocentric companies,** which are home-market-oriented, **polycentric companies,** which are oriented toward the individual markets of foreign host countries, and **geocentric companies,** which are world oriented. See Howard V. Perlmutter, "The Tortuous Evolution of the Multinational Corporation," *Columbia Journal of World Business IV* (January–February 1969), 9–18; also see Yoram Wind, Susan P. Douglas, and Howard V. Perlmutter, "Guidelines for Developing International Marketing Strategies," *Journal of Marketing* 37 (April 1973), 14–23.

The Multinationals

No exact count of the total number of MNCs is available. But the UN and other international organizations have estimated that there are more than 10,000 business firms with direct investments in more than one country, and a recent UN study indicated that there were some 98,000 affiliates of such firms operating throughout the world.[4]

Such numbers may be somewhat misleading, however, because a substantial portion of the assets, revenues, and affiliates associated with international companies is actually controlled by relatively few corporations. One frequently cited estimate of this concentration ratio indicates that 430 of the world's largest industrial corporations account for approximately three-fourths of all foreign direct investment and ownership of foreign affiliates.[5]

Who are these multinational corporate giants? Table 13.1 identifies the world's 50 biggest industrial corporations and records their 1984 sales revenues, which totaled more than 1.2 *trillion* dollars for that year.

Table 13.1 also specifies the nationality of the headquarters company of each of these firms. Twenty-two of the 50 biggest MNCs are based in the United States, while another 24 are headquartered in the industrialized nations of Western Europe and Japan, and only four (the national oil monopolies of Kuwait, Venezuela, Brazil and Mexico) represent the developing countries. This mix of national origins coincides with the general pattern for all MNCs. It is estimated that between 75 and 85 percent of the world's foreign direct investment and a like percentage of all foreign affiliates are owned by companies from the United States and a handful of the other Western industrialized nations. Moreover, those affiliates are themselves heavily concentrated in the developed regions; three-fourths of the affiliates are located in developed countries and only one-fourth in the developing nations. This First World domination of multinational business may eventually be lessened, since there has been an upsurge of foreign direct investment activity by Third World companies and the state-owned enterprises of Eastern Europe in the past few years. For the present, however, multinational corporate power continues to reside mainly in the Western industrialized economies.

Table 13.2 lists the 50 largest American MNCs based on their sales revenues for 1983. This group includes financial, retailing, and transportation concerns, as well as industrial corporations. The table also shows the percentage of each firm's 1983 revenues and operating profits that came from foreign operations. The importance of those overseas operations is highlighted by the fact that 17 of these 50 companies earned

[4]United Nations Centre on Transnational Corporations, *Transnational Corporations in World Development*, Third Survey (New York: United Nations, 1983), 32.

[5]John M. Stopford, John H. Dunning, and Klaus Haberich, *The World Directory of Multinational Enterprises* (London: Macmillan, 1980), xiv.

Table 13.1   **The 50 Largest Industrial Corporations Ranked by Sales**

Rank 1984	Rank 1983	Company	Headquarters	Sales (Thousands of Dollars)
1	1	Exxon	New York	90,854,000
2	2	Royal Dutch/Shell Group	The Hague/London	84,864,598
3	3	General Motors	Detroit	83,889,900
4	4	Mobil	New York	56,047,000
5	6	Ford Motor	Dearborn, Mich.	52,366,400
6	5	British Petroleum	London	50,662,063
7	8	Texaco	Harrison, N.Y.	47,334,000
8	7	International Business Machines	Armonk, N.Y.	45,937,000
9	9	E.I. du Pont de Nemours	Wilmington, Del.	35,915,000
10	—	American Tel. & Tel.	New York	33,187,500
11	12	General Electric	Fairfield, Conn.	27,947,000
12	10	Standard Oil (Ind.)	Chicago	26,949,000
13	11	Chevron	San Francisco	26,798,000
14	15	ENI	Rome	25,798,221
15	14	Atlantic Richfield	Los Angeles	24,686,000
16	17	Toyota Motor	Toyota City	24,110,656
17	16	IRI	Rome	23,353,993
18	18	Unilever	London/Rotterdam	21,598,790
19	19	Shell Oil	Houston	20,701,000
20	22	Elf-Aquitaine	Paris	20,662,330
21	24	Matsushita Electric Industrial	Osaka	19,993,170
22	44	Chrysler	Highland Park, Mich.	19,572,700
23	27	Pemex (Petróleos Mexicanos)	Mexico City	19,404,780
24	28	Hitachi	Tokyo	18,485,905
25	23	U.S. Steel	Pittsburgh	18,274,000
26	21	Française des Pétroles	Paris	18,158,752
27	26	Philips' Gloeilampenfabrieken	Eindhoven, Netherlands	17,834,690
28	30	Nissan Motor	Yokohama	17,513,435
29	25	Petrobrás (Petróleo Brasileiro)	Rio de Janeiro	17,087,298
30	29	Siemens	Munich	16,638,012
31	35	United Technologies	Hartford, Conn.	16,331,757
32	31	Volkswagenwerk	Wolfsburg, Germany	16,034,741
33	33	Phillips Petroleum	Bartlesville, Okla.	15,537,000
34	20	Occidental Petroleum	Los Angeles	15,373,000
35	32	Daimler-Benz	Stuttgart	15,274,386
36	36	Bayer	Leverkusen, Germany	15,108,180
37	—	Kuwait Petroleum	Kuwait	14,996,649
38	—	Nippon Oil	Tokyo	14,785,379
39	40	Tenneco	Houston	14,779,000
40	37	Hoechst	Frankfurt	14,555,318
41	34	Sun	Radnor, Pa.	14,466,000
42	43	BASF AG	Ludwigshafen-am-Rhein	14,183,965
43	50	Mitsubishi Heavy Industries	Tokyo	14,057,316
44	41	ITT	New York	14,000,988
45	—	Petróleos de Venezuela	Caracas	13,597,752
46	39	Fiat	Turin, Italy	13,546,932
47	48	BAT Industries	London	13,461,180
48	46	Imperial Chemical Industries	London	13,426,455
49	42	Nestlé	Vevey, Switzerland	13,241,814
50	47	Procter & Gamble	Cincinnati	12,946,000

Source: "The World's Largest Industrial Corporations," FORTUNE (August 19, 1985), p. 179, © 1985 Time Inc. All rights reserved.

Table 13.2 The 50 Largest U.S. Multinationals

Company	Sales Revenues—1983 (Millions of Dollars)	Foreign Revenue (Percentage of total)	Foreign Profits (Percentage of total)
Exxon	88,651	69.7	54.0
Mobil	55,609	58.7	67.2
Texaco	40,068	62.8	73.0
Phibro-Salomon	29,757	67.5	50.0
IBM	40,180	42.5	39.1
Ford Motor	44,455	36.2	18.8
General Motors	74,582	20.0	6.9
Gulf	26,581	43.4	61.8
Standard Oil Calif.	27,342	40.1	47.5
E.I. du Pont de Nemours	35,173	30.8	26.6
Citicorp	17,037	56.6	54.4
ITT	20,249	38.6	57.6
BankAmerica	13,299	44.7	47.4
Dow Chemical	10,951	52.3	74.0
Standard Oil Indiana	27,937	19.2	35.5
Chase Manhattan	8,523	58.0	42.1
General Electric	27,681	17.2	17.7
Occidental Petroleum	19,709	23.1	36.7
Safeway Stores	18,585	24.4	45.9
Sun Co.	14,928	28.7	12.5
Procter & Gamble	12,452	29.6	12.1
J.P. Morgan	5,764	59.8	54.3
Xerox	8,464	40.1	33.7
Eastman Kodak	10,170	32.2	5.7
Sears, Roebuck	35,883	9.0	D/P
Goodyear	9,736	31.5	24.9
United Technologies	14,669	20.8	25.9
Manufacturers Hanover	6,596	44.7	48.7
Phillips Petroleum	15,249	18.7	51.5
Union Carbide	9,001	31.2	38.9
Dart & Kraft	9,714	28.9	35.7
Coca-Cola	6,829	40.4	57.6
Pan Am World Airways	3,789	70.5	72.5
Colgate-Palmolive	4,865	54.6	47.8
CPC International	4,011	62.0	61.7
American Express	9,770	25.2	55.3
Minnesota Mining & Mfg.	7,039	34.7	26.4
Allied Corp.	10,022	24.4	66.7
Tenneco	14,449	16.7	15.3
Johnson & Johnson	5,973	39.5	49.3
Nabisco Brands	5,985	38.9	31.3
F.W. Woolworth	5,456	42.0	40.3
Bankers Trust New York	3,852	54.8	39.8
GTE	12,944	15.9	3.8
Beatrice Foods	9,327	22.1	18.9
American Brands	5,018	37.9	21.5
Chemical New York	4,903	38.4	42.2
Fluor	5,301	34.9	62.4
American International Group	3,997	46.1	64.1
Pfizer	3,750	48.0	45.9

Source: "The 100 Largest U.S. Multinationals," Forbes, July 2, 1984, 129–130. Reprinted with permission.

more than one-half of their total profits outside the United States, while another 17 earned between one-third and one-half of their profits abroad.

Multinational Corporate Conflicts

As noted previously, the evolution of the MNCs has not been universally approved or entirely peaceful. On the contrary, the emergence and growth of these firms have elicited widespread concern over the legitimacy and consequences of their operations, and harsh criticism of their policies and activities.

Disapproval of the multinationals has come from many sources. Leaders of organized labor have seen the expansion of foreign operations by MNCs as a deliberate scheme to subvert the wage and employment standards that the unions have won in the firms' home countries. Bankers and international monetary authorities have viewed the foreign currency dealings and fund transfers of the multinationals as a serious threat to world financial stability. Government officials have looked on the multinationals' transfers of resources and money from country to country as devices for avoiding national taxes and legal constraints. Finally, nationalist leaders and their followers have perceived the spread of multinational business as a threat to the economic and political sovereignty of individual nations. A common thread runs through all these indictments: the notion of *conflict*. At the most fundamental level, conflict is seen to exist between the *global* goals of the multinationals and the *national* objectives of the individual countries from which, or within which, those firms are carrying out their operations. The basic assumption here is that the multinationals, in endeavoring to maximize their profitability on a worldwide basis, are prone to either disregard the needs and aspirations of their home or host nations or (what is worse) to play those nations off against one another.

Whether or not such suspicions are well founded, they have serious implications for MNCs. Although these corporations possess great economic power, political and legal power still resides in nations and their governments, and the policies they put into action can profoundly influence the ease or difficulty of multinational business operations. Perceived conflicts between MNCs and the nations with whom they are involved can thus bring about government policy responses that may undermine the practicability and profitability of a continuing business relationship.

The seriousness of this conflict clearly suggests the need for resolution, but this has proved difficult to achieve. Some conflict may be unavoidable, given the inherently divergent aims of MNCs and national governments. But difficulties also arise because multinationals are, by definition, always engaged in business activities and relationships with more than one country. Therefore they face the virtually impossible task of trying to reconcile their actions with the different and perhaps opposing needs of those separate countries. Still another complicating factor is the multiplicity of effects that any action by a multinational firm is likely to have on its home and/or host countries. This not only makes it hard to evaluate the *net* impact of a particular undertaking, but also stresses that when a multinational firm takes action to achieve a specific goal, this may thwart the achievement of another objective that is important to its home or host nation.

The presence of such conflicts, as well as the difficulties of resolving them, can best be understood by examining some of the problems and disputes that have arisen between multinational corporations and national governments. Among the more important and contentious of these problem areas are those relating to the balance of payments, employment, and economic development effects of multinational corporate investments and operations. These problem areas will be examined in turn, with a view toward revealing the main points at issue, illustrating the complexity of those issues, and identifying some of the obstacles to their resolution.

One point must be clarified before discussing these issues. It must be reiterated that the essence of a MNC's activities (especially its international direct investments) is the transmission of resources from country to country. Multinational corporations have been variously described as "agents" or "vehicles" for such intercountry transfers of capital, technology, and managerial or entrepreneurial skills. This implies that a multinational company will accumulate such resources in certain countries (usually its home country) and subsequently transfer them to other (host) countries for use in production processes there.

The relevance of this concept of the MNC to the current discussion is twofold. First, it brings up the prospect that some nations will "gain" resources and associated economic benefits from the activities of MNCs, whereas other nations stand to "lose" due to those same activities. The second, corollary implication is that the way in which a particular nation views MNCs, as well as the policy responses that its government makes to these firms, is apt to be heavily influenced by whether that nation is a net *contributor* or a net *recipient* of the resources that are being reallocated by the MNCs. Both of these points will be raised again in the following discussion of areas of conflict between MNCs and national governments.

The Balance of Payments Effects of Multinational Corporations

Chapter 12 of this text explained the nature and consequences of balance of payments problems and indicated that many of the world's nations have been plagued with such problems during the past several decades. Inasmuch as the MNCs came into prominence in this same era and have been heavily involved in most international transactions that affect payments balances, it is not surprising that MNCs have frequently been

Table 13.3   Potential Effects of U.S. Firm's Investment in Brazil on the U.S. Balance of Payments

Positive	Negative
Increase in U.S. exports, as U.S. parent firm or other American companies ship equipment, materials, or components to the new production plant in Brazil	Reduction in U.S. exports, as farm implements produced by Brazilian affiliate displace U.S.-made implements in Latin American market
Reduction in U.S. imports, as materials or components previously imported to produce farm implements in the United States are no longer required, since production has been shifted to Brazil	Increase in U.S. imports, as American parent firm imports implements produced in Brazil to be sold in the United States
Increased capital inflows to the United States, as American parent firm receives profits or other income (e.g., fees for technical assistance) from its Brazilian affiliate	Increased capital outflows from the United States, as American parent firm transfers capital funds from the United States to finance the establishment and operations of its Brazilian affiliate

linked to those problems. The multinationals have been blamed, in particular, for causing or aggravating balance of payments deficits, so that there has been a perceived conflict between the MNCs and national efforts to maintain balance of payments equilibrium.

Several studies have been done to determine if such charges against the MNCs are valid, but the results of those inquiries have been mixed and inconclusive. This is understandable, since this is one of those areas referred to above in which MNCs' actions exert several different effects, some of which may counteract others. Consequently, it is extremely difficult to establish and measure the net outcome of those actions.

A hypothetical example may help to underscore this difficulty. Assume that a U.S.-based MNC that produces farm implements decides to set up a new affiliate in Brazil. How might this decision eventually affect the balance of payments of the United States, which, in this instance, is the "contributor" nation from which resources will be transferred by the MNC? Some of the more obvious possibilities are listed in Table 13.3, which designates those potential effects as being either positive or negative. (In this context, positive effects are construed as those that would reduce a deficit disequilibrium in the U.S. balance of payments, whereas negative effects are those that would worsen such a deficit.)

Although Table 13.3 is limited to analyzing the balance of payments impact of just one investment venture by one (hypothetical) multinational company, it still barely scratches the surface of such an analysis. First, it identifies only the more likely *direct* effects of such a decision and does not consider any of the possible *secondary* effects. For example, the new production facility in Brazil presumably would provide additional employment and income to Brazilian workers, who might then conceivably spend more for goods imported from the United States, so that there would be a secondary effect upon the U.S. balance of payments.

Second, Table 13.3 does not take account of the **time factor.** With respect to the movements of capital funds associated with this project, for instance, a substantial period of time might elapse between the initial capital outflow to establish the Brazilian affiliate and any inflows of investment income from that undertaking. Such time lags may be critical to countries that are experiencing immediate and pressing deficit problems in their payments balances, and countries in that position have shown a tendency to place restrictions on capital outflows for foreign direct investments, even though such restrictions can reasonably be expected to reduce the income that would be received from foreign sources in the future.[6]

Third, the effects listed are based on a number of unstated assumptions which may or may not apply to the actual foreign investment decisions of MNCs. One such assumption is that the parent company will use the new Brazilian facility to produce goods destined for markets, both overseas and in the United States itself, that previously had been served by U.S. production. While this is not an implausible assumption, it does overlook the following two possibilities:

1. That the Brazilian production site would enable the MNC in question to develop new markets in Latin America or elsewhere that could not be penetrated by exports from the United States because of transportation costs, import duties, or other factors, so that the Brazilian investment would not displace existing U.S. output but would add to the total world output and sales of the American-owned MNC.

2. That if the parent firm did not shift its production from the United States to Brazil, it would lose out to foreign competitors in both its overseas and domestic (U.S.) market, so that the U.S. exports would decline and imports rise in any case.

The second possibility above relates to the "defensive" motivations that many multinational firms cite as the chief impetus for investing outside their home countries.

The basic lesson to be derived from all the caveats cited above is that

---

[6]This tendency was exhibited by the U.S. government during the 1960s, when it imposed legal limits on foreign direct investments by American companies in an effort to alleviate the U.S. balance of payments deficit.

analyzing the balance of payments effects of MNCs is complicated, even when approached on a hypothetical or theoretical basis. When attempts are made to actually measure and predict such effects for MNCs as a group, the complications are even more formidable. This has not inhibited such attempts, since the complexities also make it possible for those who oppose multinational corporations to produce studies that supposedly demonstrate that MNCs have had a detrimental impact upon payments balances, while simultaneously allowing advocates of the MNCs to turn out studies with opposite findings. Nor has it prevented national governments from drawing their own conclusions regarding this issue and accordingly developing policies to control multinational investments. Thus, in this controversy, as in many others, positions have often been taken and policies made on the basis of dubious "fact finding."

The balance of payments issue illustrates another serious dilemma that confronts MNCs in their relationships with nations and governments. As mentioned previously, these corporations may often be caught in situations in which they cannot reconcile their decisions and actions with the differing interests of the different nations with which they are associated. This dilemma clearly exists in the balance of payments area, since the foreign investment-related activities of MNCs will exert opposing effects on the payments positions of contributor and recipient countries, and virtually anything that an MNC might do to strengthen the balance of payments of contributors will therefore have unfavorable effects upon recipients (and vice versa).

The U.S. firm's investment in Brazil can be used again to demonstrate this problem. Suppose the American parent company decided (perhaps at the urging of the U.S. government) to take some steps to help the U.S. balance of payments situation. Such steps might include a reduction of its imports of farm implements from its Brazilian affiliate, an acceleration of its repatriation of income from that affiliate, or perhaps borrowing more capital funds in Brazil in lieu of transferring funds from the United States to finance the Brazilian operations. While these measures would likely be applauded by the U.S. government because of their positive repercussions on the U.S. payments balance, the government of Brazil might well be dismayed at their negative impact upon that country's balance of payments and foreign currency reserves. This example shows how the efforts of multinational firms to support the goals of one nation or group of nations can lead to conflicts with other nations.

The Employment Effects of Multinational Corporations

The question of how the activities of MNCs have affected employment has probably received more widespread attention and raised more ire than the balance of payments issue. This is not surprising, since jobs, wages, and working conditions are much more immediate and comprehensible concerns to the average citizen than international payments accounts. In fact, however, these two issues are tightly interconnected, since the extent to which overseas investments by MNCs will affect employment depends to a considerable degree on the export and import consequences of those investments.

The employment-related conflicts in which MNCs have been embroiled have mainly involved contributor countries (notably the United States). The crux of these conflicts is the contention that international transfers of capital and technology by the MNCs have shifted employment opportunities from those countries to foreign recipient countries. As noted above, this involves exports and imports, since foreign production by the MNCs is presumed to be displacing exports from the contributor countries or supplying goods that are imported into those countries in competition with domestic output.

Some further charges against the multinationals are that they pay low wages and maintain poor working conditions in foreign countries, thereby exploiting workers in those countries while also undercutting the gains in wage levels and workplace standards that organized labor has won over the years in the more advanced, contributor nations. The MNCs purportedly accomplish this undercutting either directly, by importing cheaper goods from their low-wage production locales abroad, or indirectly, by threatening to move their production facilities to such locales unless concessions are made by their existing workforce.

As with the balance of payments dispute, the controversy over the employment effects of MNCs has raged for many years. A multitude of studies by both critics and supporters of the MNCs have failed to establish definitively what the overall impact of these firms on employment has been.

Certainly there is no question that MNCs have established production facilities outside their home countries in order to benefit from lower labor costs. The hundreds of American-owned manufacturing facilities that are operating just across the U.S. border in Mexico and in other parts of Latin America and the Far East are clear evidence of this tendency. Moreover, it is not just the U.S.-based MNCs that have been seeking out cheaper labor. Western Europe multinationals are deeply involved in this search, and even the giant Japanese firms—long known for their diligent workers, productive efficiency, and resultant cost advantages—have been shifting their manufacturing operations into Southeast Asian nations recently to keep labor costs down. But this evidence, in and of itself, does not substantiate the conclusion that MNCs have, on balance, "destroyed" jobs in contributor countries by transferring capital and technology abroad. A crucial question that must be answered is whether any jobs that are lost due to such transfers would not otherwise have fallen victim to foreign competition. This brings up the same *defensive* motives for overseas investments that were

Box 13.1

Saving Jobs or Exporting Them?

The Hoover Company announced plans to build a plant in Juarez, Mexico to assemble small floor and furniture cleaning appliances for sale in the U.S. The products will be assembled from parts made at the company's facilities in North Canton, Ohio.

Assembling in Mexico will result in the loss of some jobs in Ohio, where the cleaners are currently assembled. However, the company said that even more jobs would disappear because of a loss of sales to low-priced competitors from Asia if it did not begin the Mexican operation.

Source: "Hoover Co. Will Build Plant at Juarez, Mexico to Assemble Products," *The Wall Street Journal,* November 27, 1984, 48.

referred to earlier in relation to the balance of payments issue; whenever the MNCs plead such motives, it becomes virtually impossible to prove that they are to blame for declines in employment.

Indeed, this line of reasoning can even be used to argue that employment in contributor countries is protected and enhanced through foreign investments by multinational firms. For example, an American-based multinational that wanted to acquire production facilities in Mexico might well contend that moving the more labor-intensive portions of its manufacturing processes to that low-wage country would enable it to maintain its competitive position in the U.S. market or elsewhere in the world, and that this would preserve the more highly skilled and higher paying jobs of its American workers.

The dispute over the employment effects of MNCs will probably never be resolved on the basis of empirical evidence, since there is no satisfactory way of answering the question, "What would have happened (to employment levels) if a series of actions (foreign investments by multinational firms) that took place had not taken place?" Furthermore, this "unanswerability factor" becomes even more pronounced if the inquiry is projected into the future. Unfortunately, this lack of definite answers has perpetuated mistrust and adversarial relationships between workers and companies, and has sometimes resulted in government policies being predicated upon emotions and biases rather than cogent factual analyses.

Economic Development Effects of Multinational Corporations

The role of MNCs in the economic development of Third World nations has been extensively studied and hotly debated. Although sweeping historical observations are always hazardous, it is safe to assert that the MNCs were widely regarded as important contributors to the development process during the first two decades of the post–World War II period. The government of the United States (then the source of most foreign direct investment by multinational firms) actively encouraged American companies to expand their operations in the developing countries. That encouragement was based in part on humanitarian concerns for the economic progress of those countries, but there was also a notion that private investment from the United States would strengthen them, both economically and ideologically, against communist influence. Meanwhile, the majority of the developing countries themselves were soliciting and welcoming investment by the multinationals, in the belief that it would help provide the capital, technology, and entrepreneurial stimuli that were considered essential for development and which those countries were unable to generate in sufficient quantities domestically.

Those universally positive views of the multinationals' involvement in the development of the Third World began to change during the 1960s. In the United States, there were rising suspicions that continuing transfers of resources abroad by the MNCs might be impairing domestic capital formation and technological leadership, so that whatever benefits the developing countries were realizing were coming at the expense of economic growth in the United States itself.

The multinationals also began to experience increasing difficulties during the 1960s in their relationships with host countries in the developing regions. This was attributable, in part, to a rising spirit of nationalism, which manifested itself in an emotional resistance to further foreign penetration and control of the economies of those newly independent nations. But it also reflected growing doubts about the contributions that the multinationals were actually making to these nations' economic development.

This reappraisal of the developmental impact of the multinationals involved the broad issue of relative benefits and costs to host countries. The actual calculation of such benefits and costs is highly complex, entailing the identification and measurement of a multitude of direct and indirect effects that the initial transfer of resources, subsequent operations, and eventual remittance of profits or other income by multinational companies would exert upon host nations' economies. The time dimension is also an important factor in such calculations. As a general rule, the benefits to host countries from foreign direct investment by MNCs are greatest and most apparent in the early stages of such investment projects, when productive resources are being received and new jobs are being created. Later on, however, such benefits may ap-

Box 13.2

Mixed Emotions over Multinational Investment

More than a decade ago, the U.S.-based International Paper Company offered to build a $500 million pulp and papermaking facility in Venezuela in return for access to government-owned timber plantations. After four years of negotiations, company officials thought that they had a deal. However, the Venezuelan government imposed a series of conditions at the last minute, including a requirement that would limit the company's ownership to 25% of the project. Those demands caused International Paper to withdraw from the negotiations.

Now Venezuela's huge pine forests are standing uncut and the debt-ridden nation spent $85 million last year to import pulp. The Venezuelan government is trying once again to attract foreign investors to provide the capital and technology for a pulp and papermaking project. The country's external debt is $34 billion, and its finance minister has declared that "it's better to have foreign investment than foreign debt." So far, however, the response from potential investors, who are concerned with Venezuela's red tape and tough investment terms, has been lukewarm.

Source: Art Pine, "Debt-Ridden Nations Impose Many Barriers on Foreign Investors," *The Wall Street Journal*, January 21, 1985, 1.

pear to be outweighed by costs to the host country, which are most visible in the continuing outflows of profits and other payments to the parent company.

The disenchantment with the multinationals among the developing nations during the 1960s and thereafter was related to this cost-benefit issue and was frequently based upon oversimplified assessments of such benefits and costs. However, more specific issues have also been raised by the developing countries regarding the MNCs. One issue is that the presence of multinationals in a developing country tends to deter the establishment of new economic enterprises by local investors and entrepreneurs. This stifling of indigenous enterprises is presumed to result from the competitive threat that the large international companies pose or through the preempting of scarce resources by those companies. This latter criticism presupposes that the multinationals will employ the best managers and the most highly skilled technicians and workers that are available in the countries in which they operate and will finance their operations by securing funds within those countries, thereby denying those essential resources to locally owned businesses.

A second set of concerns has to do with the technology that the multinationals bring to the developing countries as part of their foreign direct investment projects. Here the MNCs have been faulted on two seemingly contradictory counts; first, for supplying technology that is too sophisticated and capital-intensive for the usually low-skilled and underemployed labor forces of the developing countries; and second, for supplying technology that is obsolete and therefore does not help prepare the developing countries to compete effectively in the fastest-growing segments of international markets.

The multinationals have also been criticized for introducing expensive consumer goods to the developing nations. Such criticisms have been based partially on political and cultural considerations, the implication being that this engenders a consumption-oriented value system among the masses in those nations and may lead to political unrest by creating demands that cannot be fulfilled. But economic development might also be retarded, insofar as efforts to import consumer products or produce them domestically interferes with investments deemed more vital to a nation's development program.

All these charges against the MNCs defy verification on an aggregate basis. There unquestionably have been numerous instances in which multinational firms have discouraged native entrepreneurs, introduced inappropriate technology, or supplied nonessential products in developing countries. It is far from clear, however, that these cases have been so widespread or serious as to cancel out the beneficial effects that the resource transfers carried out by the MNCs have had upon the economic growth of Third World nations. In fact, the chief criticism that has been directed toward the multinationals by the UN, the World Bank, and other international institutions concerned with economic development is that the MNCs have not been nearly active enough in making direct investments in Third World nations.

Policy Responses to Multinational Corporations

The preceding section pointed out the difficulties of systematically measuring the many effects of MNCs and thereby arriving at a meaningful evaluation of the net gains or losses that they bring to contributor and recipient nations. However, it was pointed out that those complexities have not deterred governments from instituting new policies or amending existing policies in response to the rapid expansion of the multinationals. The preceding section also touched on the conflicts between the interests of national governments and those of the MNCs.

The specific policy measures applicable to foreign direct investment by multinational firms that have been put into effect by home and host countries are too numerous to describe in detail. This section will be concerned instead with considering the general character of government policies toward MNCs and how the broad thrust of those policies has changed over time. This survey will look first at the United States, as representative of home country policies, then at host country policies, and finally at some international attempts to devise policies relating to the MNCs.

U.S. Policies Toward Multinational Firms

If one were attempting to identify a historical turning point in U.S. policies affecting multinational corporations, the middle years of the 1960s would be a sound choice. From the end of World War II until that time, the U.S. government had been encouraging American companies to invest abroad, especially in the developing nations. That encouragement took tangible form in U.S. laws and government actions. Those included the income tax laws, which accorded favorable treatment to income from foreign investments, a series of treaties that the U.S. negotiated with foreign nations to guarantee American firms the right to do business in those nations and protected them against discriminatory treatment, and the establishment of a program to provide insurance against losses of overseas investments due to political problems.[7]

Governmental encouragement and support for the foreign ventures of U.S. corporations began to lessen in the mid-1960s. Mention has already been made of the emergence of homefront opposition to the ongoing expansion of foreign investment by American companies around that time. One of the strongest voices in that opposition was that of organized labor. American labor unions, which traditionally had been supporters of free international trade, began attacking the multi-nationals for "exporting American jobs" and started lobbying intensely for government action to restrict these firms' foreign investments, transfers of technology, and imports into the United States. A bill that would have imposed stringent limitations upon such activities was introduced into Congress in the early 1970s. This legislation, referred to as the Burke–Hartke Bill in reference to its principal congressional supporters, was reviewed and debated for many months, and a modified but still blatantly protectionist and highly restrictive version came very close to being passed by the U.S. lawmakers.

By the 1960s, U.S. government officials had also become concerned with some aspects and results of the activities of the multinational firms. The main focus of that concern was the balance of payments deficit, which first appeared in the late 1950s and reached severe proportions in succeeding years. Although few in the government went so far as to

---

[7]This political risk insurance program was first put into effect in the late 1940s. Since 1969, it has been administered by a U.S. government agency known as the Overseas Private Investment Corporation (OPIC).

place all blame for the deficit on foreign investments by American corporations, legal limits upon such investments came to be accepted as a means of dealing with the problem. The government imposed so-called "voluntary" restraints upon direct investment in industrialized countries in 1965, and those limits were made mandatory in 1968 and retained until 1974.

The taxation of multinational firms also became a subject of controversy in the 1960s. The U.S. tax codes allowed American corporations to defer tax payments to the U.S. government on profits earned by their foreign subsidiaries until those profits were repatriated by the American parent company. The argument was raised that this deferral privilege was not only contributing to the balance of payments deficit by encouraging U.S. firms to reinvest their income overseas, but was also being abused by those firms. That alleged abuse involved the establishment of "tax haven" affiliates in foreign nations with low tax rates and the subsequent channeling of the multinational enterprises' worldwide profits into those havens. Such arguments led to a sequence of modifications of the tax laws, which progressively reduced the tax advantages U.S. multinationals had previously enjoyed on their overseas income.[8]

The U.S. government's support of overseas expansion by American multinationals was further eroded by a series of revelations of misconduct that surfaced in the early 1970s. Those involved payments that several multinationals had made to various highly placed foreign government officials in connection with business deals that were being negotiated or carried out in their country. Those revelations not only raised serious ethical questions, but also stirred up strong outcries abroad against political meddling and influence-buying by the American MNCs.

The U.S. government reacted to this problem by instituting the Foreign Corrupt Practices Act (FCPA) in 1977. This act makes it unlawful for American companies and managers to make payments to foreign political officials, candidates, or parties for the purpose of obtaining or retaining business, and also required companies to set up accounting systems for tracking down such illicit payments. Many U.S. firms have objected strenuously to this law, first because they contend that it is ambiguous and difficult to comply with, and, second, because they regard it as a competitive handicap in countries in which payoffs are an accepted part of conducting business.

The FCPA actually constitutes just one manifestation of a broader aspect of official U.S. policy that has created serious problems for American MNCs and has caused continuing friction between those firms and the government. This broader issue is the U.S. government's insistence on exercising legal jurisdiction over the acts of American parent com-

---

[8]The taxation of foreign income will be considered again in Chapter 16, which deals with financial management in multinational firms.

panies *and their foreign affiliates,* even when those acts take place outside the boundaries of the United States. The term **extraterritoriality** is used in reference to such attempts by national governments to project their legal power into the territories of other nations, and it is generally agreed that the U.S. government has been particularly inclined toward such behavior.

Extraterritorial extensions of U.S. legal authority have occurred in cases related to several different areas of law, but the major difficulties for multinational firms have involved the antitrust statutes and the several U.S. laws that apply to trade with "unfriendly" foreign nations. In the antitrust realm, the U.S. courts and enforcement agencies have intervened in numerous instances either to prevent American-based MNCs from entering into business agreements abroad that might conceivably have anticompetitive effects in the United States, or to force them to withdraw from such arrangements and to divest themselves of ownership of foreign companies. Since the United States has traditionally interpreted and enforced antitrust prohibitions much more strictly than other national governments, the American multinationals have frequently found themselves in trouble with their own government over agreements, actions, or acquisitions that have been legally permissible in the countries in which they were undertaken.

The extraterritorial enforcement of restrictions on trade with countries deemed to be unfriendly to the United States—a category that includes most of the communist nations of Eastern Europe and Asia, with Cuba thrown in for good measure—has also proved very troublesome for American multinational companies. Here again, the United States generally has been much more adamant about the need for such restrictions and more vigorous in imposing and enforcing them than have most of its traditional allies among the other Western industrialized nations. Consequently, American firms have often been caught in the middle of contentious situations in which the U.S. government was forbidding them (and their overseas affiliates) from selling certain goods to the communist countries, while the governments of the countries in which those affiliates were located were insisting that such sales be made.

One of many such situations developed in the early 1980s, when the U.S. government reacted to the imposition of martial law in Poland by placing an embargo on sales of specified equipment to the Soviet Union. That equipment was to be used in building and operating a huge pipeline to transport natural gas from Siberian fields to Western Europe. The United States attempted to apply the embargo not only to equipment and technology from the U.S. itself, but also to that being provided by the Western European affiliates of American companies, at which point the governments of Great Britain, France, West Germany, and Italy raised strenuous objections and ordered the affiliates to ignore the U.S. government's prohibitions.

This furor eventually subsided, but not before considerable injury had been done both to American companies and to relationships between the United States and Western European governments. The damage included immediate losses of sales by U.S. firms, as alternative sources of supply were found for equipment that was to have been provided by some of those firms; but it also included increased misgivings among foreign businesspeople as to the long-term reliability of American companies as suppliers or as business partners. Meanwhile, many Western European politicians and government officials looked upon the pipeline episode as one more example of the U.S. government's disregard for the political sovereignty and sensitivities of other nations.

The extraterritoriality issue involves many technical points of law, which continue to be debated by legal experts and which cannot and need not be addressed here. However, regardless of the legal "rightness or wrongness" of the U.S. government's stance on this issue, it is clear that the United States has promulgated laws relating to business that are out of harmony with those of most other nations. This, combined with the government's diligent efforts to extend the coverage of those laws to encompass the worldwide activities of U.S.-controlled MNCs, has generated much confusion for those enterprises, as well as placing them in the middle of intergovernmental disputes and causing them to incur both current and future business losses.

Although the United States government has never formulated a comprehensive and coherent policy position vis-à-vis MNCs, the foregoing review indicates that the *direction* of its actions over time has been toward less support and more regulation of those corporations. This is not to say that the American government has become "anti-multinational business," for the United States, by comparison with most other nations, has remained committed to the free movement of goods and resources internationally and has adopted relatively few restrictions upon multinational firms. Nevertheless, the behavior of such firms is more closely scrutinized and readily criticized today than in earlier years, and this has placed a greater burden of responsibility on those firms to perform in a manner consistent with the interests of the American public and the demands of the U.S. government.

Host Country Policies Toward Multinational Corporations

It has been noted previously that nations hosting the affiliates of MNCs have often displayed mixed feelings toward those firms. This ambivalence has been most pronounced in the developing nations. They have been especially in need of and eager to acquire the productive resources and employment opportunities that the multinationals can supply. At the same time, however, they have been particularly sensitive to the threat of economic domination by those gargantuan, foreign-based business enterprises and increasingly dubious about their overall contribution to the development of host country economies.

These conflicting and shifting attitudes are reflected in the policies that the developing nations have fashioned to deal with the MNCs.

Those policies comprise a complex mixture of incentives, performance requirements, and controls, with the proportions of these different and sometimes contradictory elements varying from nation to nation and from one time period to the next. For the sake of brevity and manageability, this policy mix will only be broadly outlined here.[9]

Investment Incentives.   The developing countries have made extensive use of various incentives to induce multinational firms to locate operations within their borders. Some of the most common of these incentives are tax concessions, protection from competition, foreign exchange guarantees, and financial assistance.

Tax Concessions.   Host countries often grant reduced income tax rates to MNCs or exempt them from paying taxes entirely for specified periods of time. Such "tax holidays" can be for as long as 10 years or more. Import duties may also be reduced or waived on materials or components that are being brought into the host country by affiliates of the MNCs.

Protection from Competition.   Host countries frequently promise that multinational affiliates will enjoy an exclusive, protected market, and employ high import tariffs or restraints on domestic production of competing goods to fulfill such promises.

Foreign Exchange Guarantees.   The governments or central banks of host countries may assure multinational affiliates that foreign currency will be made available to pay for needed imports or for remitting profits or other income to parent companies.

Financial Assistance.   Multinational affiliates may be eligible for low-interest loans or other forms of financial assistance from host country governments or financial institutions.

Despite the widespread incidence of these incentive programs, their general effectiveness in attracting multinational investments or influencing choices of investment locales has not been firmly established. Moreover, there is an obvious danger that the too-liberal use of such incentives will cause host countries to forfeit much of their share of the benefits from such investments. This potential becomes especially great whenever the developing countries compete against one another to attract foreign investors.

Although the developing countries have become aware of the uncertain results and potential dangers of these investment incentives, this

---

[9]Much of the following material is based upon information appearing in The United Nations Centre on Transnational Corporations, *Transnational Corporations in World Development: Third Survey* (New York: United Nations, 1983).

has not led to any marked reduction in their usage as yet. However, some of the more advanced developing countries that constitute good market or production opportunities for MNCs have become more sophisticated and selective in their incentive programs in recent years. They have begun to use such incentives to promote investment in certain high-priority sectors or geographic sections of their economies, rather than offering blanket incentives to the multinationals. A few of these countries have also tried to tie the value of the incentives they offer to the contribution that the investment project is expected to make to domestic employment or other economic goals. Finally, there have been some agreements among groups of developing countries to adopt common or collective foreign investment incentives instead of competing among themselves for such investment. All of these movements indicate that the MNCs are not likely to find such a plentiful and easy harvest of investment incentives in the Third World in the future as they have in the past.

Domestic Control Policies.   While the developing countries have continued to give investment incentives to the MNCs, they have simultaneously instituted policies designed to reduce the possibility that such investments will lead to foreign control of their economies. Some of those policies exclude or limit foreign involvement in specific sectors of the host country's economy. More and more of the developing countries have been placing such sectors as transportation, communications, public utilities, raw material extraction, and certain manufacturing industries off-limits to foreign investors. The selection of the sectors to be closed to foreigners may be based on their essentiality to the economy as a whole or on the premise that they can be adequately developed by local investors and entrepreneurs. In other instances (e.g., the extraction of raw materials), the prohibitions placed on foreign ownership may reflect a lingering resentment over the presumed exploitation of such resources or industries by foreigners in the past.

Many developing countries also require local participation in the ownership and management of multinational affiliates although the exact form and level of such participation differs from country to country. A fair number of the Third World nations now demand majority ownership by nationals as a general rule, but exceptions are made if necessary to entice multinationals to invest in critically needed economic ventures or in particularly backward or depressed geographic regions. Other developing nations accept minority participation by nationals in new enterprises, but require that this be increased to a majority position within some set period of years. The principal purpose of all such requirements is to give representatives of host countries a voice in controlling the businesses involved, but they also enable local investors and managers to share in the profits and salaries those businesses generate.

Performance Requirements.   In addition to their efforts to prevent the multinationals from dominating them economically, the host developing countries have been attempting to force those firms to perform in a manner that coincides with their national interests and enhances the benefits they will realize from the presence of multinational affiliates. Some of the more common of these measures are local content requirements, exporting obligations, limits on foreign payments, and technology transfer rules.

Local Content Requirements.   Local or domestic content requirements require multinational affiliates to utilize some specified amount or proportion of domestic inputs in their production processes. Such local inputs may be in the form of labor, materials, or component parts, but the intent in all cases is to bring about a substitution of local resources for imported ones, thereby increasing employment and income within the host country.

Exporting Obligations.   Multinational affiliates are often obligated to export a designated portion of their output, in order to help host countries develop new markets for their products, earn foreign exchange, and overcome balance of payments problems.

Limits on Foreign Payments.   Multinational affiliates are subjected to legal ceilings on the profits they can remit to their parent companies and on what they can pay their parent firms for patent rights, technological know-how, or other resources. Such ceilings are designed to compel the affiliates to reinvest profits domestically, to reduce the costs and increase the returns that accrue to the host nations, and to relieve balance of payments pressures by reducing capital outflows from those nations.

Technology Transfer Rules.   A growing number of host developing countries now monitor technology transfers between multinational parent firms and affiliates, and demand that the affiliates in their countries be given the most up-to-date technology available. The purposes of these procedures and demands are to insure host country access to advanced technology and to maintain the competitiveness of local affiliates in international markets.

The organizational arrangements and methods that the developing countries use to enforce all of the rules and regulations applying to multinational firms are almost as diverse as the laws themselves. Several of those countries have established special, permanent agencies to oversee foreign affiliates, whereas others rely upon their tax and foreign exchange authorities or upon their ministries of finance, industry, or planning and development. In some cases, the granting of investment incentives and the enforcement of investment controls are the responsibility of a single agency, while in other cases these functions are separated. With regard to methods of enforcement, increasing numbers of the developing countries now emphasize **preinvestment screening** procedures, which require prospective foreign investors to demonstrate that the projects they are proposing will yield positive benefits to the host country and will comply with both its laws and its economic development plans before those projects are approved by the host government.

The effectiveness of the policies that the developing countries have applied to MNCs also varies markedly. Those countries with the largest resource endowments, indigenous production capabilities, and large market size have generally instituted the most stringent regulatory and benefit-sharing policies and have been reasonably successful in getting the MNCs to accept and abide by them. By contrast, the smaller and more backward developing countries have found it difficult even to attract multinational firms with incentive programs, much less to impose and enforce strict controls over those firms. This unevenness indicates, not surprisingly, that the effectiveness of host country policies vis-à-vis MNCs is largely a function of the relative strength and bargaining power of the party or parties on each side of those policy confrontations. This realization has prompted great interest among developing nations in the establishment of collective or international policies for dealing with the multinationals.

Collective Policies Toward Multinational Corporations

One of the earliest and most ambitious attempts to establish collective policies toward MNCs was undertaken by the member nations of the Andean Common Market (ANCOM) in 1970. The five countries (Bolivia, Chile, Colombia, Ecuador, and Peru) that made up ANCOM at that time formulated and enacted a far-reaching set of rules governing foreign investments in their combined territories. Those rules excluded foreign investors from a number of economic sectors and activities, placed limits upon profit repatriation and payments for capital funds and technology imported by multinational affiliates, and put pressure on foreign investors to relinquish ownership and managerial control of their affiliates to nationals of the ANCOM member countries within a fixed period of time.

This foreign investment code commanded wide attention and stirred up a substantial amount of controversy when it was put into effect by the Andean nations. Other developing countries looked upon it as an innovative approach to the establishment of a "united front," which could forestall mutually detrimental competition for foreign investment and compel the MNEs to provide more benefits and give more control to host countries. Meanwhile, representatives of the multinationals and their home countries criticized the harsh treatment that it imposed on foreign investors and predicted that it would result in a "drying up" of investment capital flows to the ANCOM countries.

As is frequently the case, ANCOM's experiment has not lived up to the highest hopes of its supporters nor fulfilled the dire predictions of its critics. There has been friction within ANCOM over the alleged laxity of some member countries in enforcing the foreign investment code, and Chile withdrew from the organization in 1976 partly as a protest of its stringency and its unfavorable impact on foreign investment in that nation. On the other hand, there has been no wholesale withholding or withdrawal of foreign direct investment from the Andean region, although there are some indications that the code has discouraged such investment. But even though its direct effects have been less dramatic than originally anticipated, the ANCOM code has provided inspiration and ideas that have influenced the developing nations in their continuing quest for effective policy responses to the MNEs.

A number of other efforts have been made during the past decade to devise common, international policies relating to the activities of MNCs. Some of these have been concerned with specific aspects of such behavior, such as international transfers of technology, restrictive business practices, or illicit payments (extortion and bribery). Others have endeavored to cover virtually all facets of multinational corporate operations and relationships with home and host nations. One example of this broad approach is the **Declaration on International Investment and Multinational Enterprises.** This declaration was adopted in 1976 by the Western industrialized countries that make up the Organization for Economic Cooperation and Development (OECD). The OECD declaration includes a comprehensive set of guidelines pertaining to the business practices of MNCs. Those guidelines only constitute *recommendations*, however, and the declaration calls upon the multinationals to observe them voluntarily.

The second major attempt to institute international standards for regulating the multinationals involves a **Code of Conduct Relating to Transnational Corporations,** which is being formulated by the UN. This proposed UN Code

addresses a broad range of considerations underlying activities of transnational corporations including: respect for national sovereignty and observance of domestic laws, regulations and administrative practices; adherence to the economic goals and development objectives, policies, and priorities of the countries in which they operate; adherence to the socio-cultural objectives and values of those countries; respect for human rights and fundamental freedoms; noninterference in internal political affairs and intergovernmental relations; and abstention from corrupt practices. Specific code provisions pertain to: the ownership and control of transnational corporations; balance of payments and financing; transfer pricing; taxation; competition and restrictive business practices; transfer of technology; employment and labor; environmental protection; consumer protection; and disclosure of information. The code will also consider the treatment of transnational corporations by the countries in which they operate.[10]

---

[10]George W. Coombe, Jr., "Multinational Codes of Conduct and Corporate Accountability: New Opportunities for Corporate Counsel (Appendix)" in *The Multinational Enterprise in Transition,* ed. Phillip D. Grub, Fariborz Ghadar, and Dara Khambata (Princeton, NJ: Darwin Press, 1984), 449.

The above quotation shows that this code is intended to address a very broad range of issues having to do with relations between multinational firms and sovereign nations, as well as numerous practices in which those firms engage. In view of its comprehensive coverage and the controversy that has long surrounded those issues and practices, it is perhaps not surprising that the UN has been struggling to draft this document for *nearly 10 years*. Furthermore, its final form and content, as well as its chances of eventually being ratified and implemented, are still cloudy and uncertain. Draft versions of the code have been severely criticized by spokespersons for the multinationals and their home governments for its negative connotations regarding the activities of MNCs, its potentially restrictive effects on business, its vagueness (particularly with respect to the critical question of how it will be enforced), and what they view as a lack of balance or "fairness" regarding the respective obligations of the MNCs and of host governments.

The prognosis for this particular code of conduct may be less important, however, than the fact that it represents a serious effort on the part of a world organization to construct an international legal framework to govern the actions of business enterprises that operate on an international scale. The need to close the gap between the "global reach" of the multinationals and the national limits of government regulatory power has been emphasized for many years, especially by the developing countries. This demand for multilateral regulation has been received more favorably in recent times by the governments of the MNCs' home countries and even by some of the multinationals themselves, on the grounds that the existence of international "rules of the game" might forestall disputes between the MNCs and individual national governments and make foreign investments and operations more secure against arbitrary or discriminatory governmental treatment.

The difficult challenge in this is to come up with regulations and standards that will fulfill the legitimate need for public oversight of the multinationals without impinging on their legal rights or their ability to operate efficiently. This task continues to be complicated by the intrusion of such emotion-laden concepts as nationalism and national sovereignty on the one side and free enterprise on the other. But a movement is at least under way to resolve the conflicts that the advent of the multinationals has engendered through international cooperation and the application of the rule of law.

Summary

1. The great post–World War II expansion of international business activity has been carried out, in large measure, by giant business firms known as multinational corporations.
2. Multinational corporations are large-scale business enterprises made up of a group of business units located in different coun-

tries, whose operations are coordinated and integrated by a "management control center" consisting of the top management of the parent company.

3. The power and activities of multinational corporations are concentrated in a relatively small number of very large firms headquartered in the Western industrialized nations.

4. The *global* goals and interests of the multinational corporations have brought them into conflict with nations and their governments, whose aims and interests are essentially *national* in scope.

5. The major areas of conflict between multinational firms and national governments have to do with: (a) the effects of multinational firms on the balance of payments, (b) their effects upon employment, and (c) their impact upon economic development.

6. With regard to the balance of payments, the multinationals have been criticized for aggravating payments deficits, but the multiple effects of their decisions and actions has made it exceptionally difficult to determine the validity of such criticisms.

7. The multinationals have also been charged with "exporting jobs" from their home countries by transferring their resources and operations abroad. Such charges have remained unsubstantiated, however, due to the difficulty of determining whether the jobs lost through such transfers would not have been eliminated in any event by international competition.

8. While multinationals were regarded as important positive contributors to the development of Third World nations in the early post–World War II era, there have been growing doubts and criticisms with respect to their net effect upon the economic progress of those nations.

9. There has been a general trend toward greater control over the multinational corporations on the part of both home and host country governments. This is manifest in the institution of policies that have lessened governmental support for the multinationals and imposed greater restraints on their activities.

10. In addition to the tightening of home and host-country controls over the multinationals, efforts have been under way to formulate international rules and standards pertaining to these firms.

Questions for Review or Discussion

1. Identify and describe the principal characteristics that distinguish multinational corporations from other business organizations.

2. Explain what is meant by the description of multinational corporations as "integrated worldwide business systems."

3. "The managers of multinational corporations are presumed to possess and exercise a *global perspective*." Explain the meaning and implications of this statement.

4. What supposedly constitutes the *fundamental conflict* between multinational corporations and individual nations?

5. What is meant by the description of multinational corporations as "transfer agents" between "contributor" and "recipient" countries?

6. Identify some of the principal balance of payments effects that may result from foreign direct investments by multinational corporations and explain why it is difficult to analyze the total or net effect of such investment on a nation's payments balance.

7. It is often asserted that overseas investment by American multinational firms inevitably "destroys" jobs in the United States. Explain why this argument may not be valid in all instances.

8. What are the principal *benefits* and *costs* to host developing countries that are associated with multinational investment in their economies?

9. What major changes have occurred in U.S. government policies toward multinational corporations in recent years?

10. What is the *extraterritoriality* issue with respect to multinational corporations?

11. The policies of developing countries toward multinational corporations have been described as a "complex mixture of incentives, performance requirements, and controls." Give examples of each of these types of policy and explain why developing countries utilize such a policy mix.

12. Why are *international* codes of conduct for multinational corporations regarded by many individuals and organizations as essential? What are the main obstacles to the enactment and implementation of such codes?

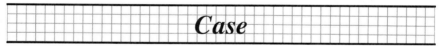

Case

Union Carbide

On August 28, 1985, Union Carbide Corp. announced a massive restructuring that involved closing a number of its plants, resulting in a pretax $990 million charge against income and a dismissal of 4,000 employees, about 15 percent of its workforce. Union Carbide also announced a repurchase of 10 million shares, or 14 percent, of its outstanding common shares. The company also announced that it would commit an additional $100 million to improve the safety of its operations. The company declined to connect these actions with the series of recent problems it had been having involving leaks of hazardous chemicals from its plants. These incidents had resulted in injuries and deaths to many people and massive lawsuit claims filed against the company. The company also declined to connect its actions with the need to fend off a potential takeover of Union Carbide by GAF Corp. which already held 7.1 percent of Union Carbide common stock.

Until December 3, 1984, Union Carbide seemed well on its way to recovery from the recent recession. Profits were up for the most recent quarter, and for 1984 the firm expected to earn about $340 million or about $4.84 per share. The company's stock was selling for $48 per share. Union Carbide was the seventh largest chemical company in the world with over 100,000 employees, 700 plants and other facilities, and annual sales of over $7 billion. It was generally considered to be a large and successful multinational firm.

At 12:30 a.m., December 3, 1984, local time [2:00 p.m. Eastern Standard Time (EST)] there was a major leak of the toxic gas methyl isocyanate (MIC) from a Union Carbide pesticide plant in Bhopal, India. According to official count, this cloud of gas killed 1,754 people and seriously injured over 60,000 people. Other estimates put the death toll at over 2,500 and the number of injured at over 120,000. In any case, it was clear that the leak in Bhopal was the worst recorded industrial accident in history. Union Carbide's stock value plunged by over 30 percent (to $32 per share) within a week. The company faced the problem of how it could discharge its massive legal and moral liabilities and survive as a business. A number of class action lawsuits against Union Carbide were filed immediately in the United States on behalf of the victims, and in India by private lawyers and later by the national government. Since the lawsuits sought damages for up to $20 billion—a figure far greater than the company's net worth—Union Carbide faced possible bankruptcy.

Union Carbide retained management control but only 50.9 percent of the ownership of the Bhopal plant and since 1982 the plant had been operated solely by local Union Carbide personnel. Ironically, the Bhopal plant manufactured agricultural pesticides to help India's Green Revolution that had made the country more than self-sufficient in grain production for food. The lawsuits against Union Carbide charged that the firm was strictly liable for the damages caused by the leak as it had breached its duty to provide for the safe operation of the plant, failed to warn local residents of the dangers of the gas leak, and was negligent in equipping and maintaining the plant with adequate and workable safety measures and evacuation plans. The subsequent investigation showed that the plant's safety equipment was either not in working order due to lack of attention or poor maintenance, or had failed. Part of the maintenance backlog was caused by a reduction in the staffing of the MIC operation from 12 to 6 persons at the money-losing Bhopal plant. A 1982 corporate report and a 7-week 1985 investigation by the *New York Times* after the accident disclosed safety violations at the Bhopal plant. These reports showed that the safety violations were due to misplaced cost-saving measures, negligence, and inappropriateness of the particular safety measures in the context of a developing country.

Immediately after the Bhopal accident, Union Carbide reassured other communities where it processed MIC that they faced no similar danger. However, on August 11, 1985, the Union Carbide plant in Institute, West Virginia, where MIC was also processed, suffered an uncontrolled toxic gas leak which caused more than 130 people to be hospitalized. A few days later, at one of Union Carbide's plants in South Charleston, West Virginia, there was a leak of hydrochloric acid that set off alarm sirens but injured no one. It was later revealed that 16 other toxic chemical leaks had occurred at the South Charleston plant during 1984, while there had been 6 toxic leaks at the Institute plant during the same period. These accidents were not considered important enough to draw media attention before the Bhopal disaster.

This series of leaks seems to indicate that control of hazardous chemicals is technically a most difficult task, especially since Union Carbide had greatly increased its safety efforts after the Bhopal disaster. Furthermore, it appears that these problems with hazardous chemicals are not limited to Union Carbide. According to a report in the *Economist* (February 16, 1985, p. 69), 100,000 people die each year in developing countries from causes related to pesticide production while another 1.5 to 2 million suffer from acute pesticide poisoning. Two weeks before the Bhopal disaster, a tank of liquified gas exploded in Mexico City, killing 452 people.

The experience of Union Carbide raises many important questions regarding the regulation and control of firms' foreign operations. What is the responsibility of a company for protecting the environment and for ensuring the safety of its operations? Should firms exert closer control over their foreign operations? Should host-country governments make their regulation of foreign businesses more stringent? Should host countries discourage or prohibit investment in their economies by foreign firms?

Sources: "Gas Leak is Expected to Reduce Investments in the Third World," *New York Times,* December 12, 1984, p. 8; "Union Carbide Fights for Its Life," *Business Week,* December 24, 1984, pp. 52–56; T. M. Gladwin and I. Walter, "Bhopal and the Multinational," *The Wall Street Journal,* January 16, 1985, p. 28; "Union Carbide Cites Errors in Chemical Leak," *The Wall Street Journal,* August 26, 1985, p. 6; Barry Meier, "Union Carbide to Restructure, Take Write-Off," *The Wall Street Journal,* August 29, 1985, p. 3; "Union Carbide Reports 16 Toxic-Gas Leaks at 1 West Virginia Plant in 1984," *The Blade* (Toledo), August 28, 1985, p. 15; and Barry Meier, "A Year After Bhopal, Union Carbide Faces a Slew of Problems," *The Wall Street Journal,* November 26, 1985, pp. 1, 22.

Chapter 14

MANAGEMENT OF MULTINATIONAL FIRMS: STRATEGY, ORGANIZATION, AND STAFFING

Chapter Objectives

- To emphasize the importance of strategic planning in multinational corporations and to identify the principal aims of such planning
- To describe the strategic planning process and the major components of that process in multinational corporations
- To show the relationship between multinational corporate strategies and the organizational structure of multinational corporations
- To identify the factors that generally determine the organizational structure of multinational firms and to illustrate the most common organizational forms multinationals have adopted
- To examine the purposes and problems of the staffing function in multinational corporations and to analyze the elements involved in performing that staffing function

A multinational corporation (MNC) was described in Chapter 13 as a business enterprise composed of a number of individual units (affiliates) operating in different countries. The activities of those affiliates ordinarily are controlled by a central management group in the parent company, which endeavors to coordinate their operations and to allocate resources, production responsibilities, and markets among them in such a way as to optimize the efficiency and maximize the profitability of the enterprise as a whole.

Chapter 13 was concerned primarily with why those intrinsic characteristics of MNCs create tensions and conflicts between such firms and external institutions, notably national governments. It did not deal with the question of how multinational firms achieve and maintain the internal coherence that enables them to function as integrated business systems and to take maximum advantage of the opportunities that their large size and ability to operate on a worldwide scale afford.

The answer to that question lies in the realm of multinational management. The management of a multinational enterprise entails keeping a massive, integrated global business operation viable and profitable in the face of diverse and changing conditions in the various countries in which portions of that operation are being carried on. Among the most fundamental and essential requisites for success in such a task are the formulation of a strategy for attaining the enterprise's objectives, the creation of an organizational structure that is consistent with and supportive of the strategy, and the development of a managerial staff capable of effectively implementing that strategy. This chapter will concentrate on these three basic and interrelated elements of the multinational management process.

Multinational Management Strategy

Business firms do not always become full-fledged MNCs by deliberate design. On the contrary, expansion into international markets and operations frequently occurs through an uncoordinated sequence of spontaneous actions. Such actions may be undertaken in response to newly perceived sales opportunities abroad or opportunities to exploit innovative products or technology. They may also be prompted by competitive pressures at home or even the urge to emulate competitors that have moved overseas. It is likewise not uncommon for companies to acquire foreign affiliates piecemeal, as separate investments rather than as interlocking components of a global business organization.

Notwithstanding their often haphazard early evolution, such companies usually reach a stage at which they recognize the need to develop a comprehensive strategy to weld their various operations and affiliates together and guide their future course. Many of today's MNCs have been awakened to that need by the greatly intensified competition they have been experiencing, which has made the attainment of organizational coherence and greater efficiency a necessity for survival. The opening of wider, unified markets through trade liberalization and regional economic integration has also increased the requirements for more comprehensive strategies, as has the threat of adverse actions by individual governments and the resultant need to systematically assess political risk and fashion overall corporate strategies to counter such risk.

A basic aim of strategy development in MNCs is to create a synergistic relationship in which all operations become mutually supportive and affiliates begin working together to fulfill common objectives, rather than going their independent ways. The corporate strategy of a multinational firm thus is intended to constitute the overall framework within which the individual affiliates operate. The objectives, policies, and practices of those affiliates must conform to and support the general corporate strategy if the desired integration and synergy are to be achieved and maintained.

These integration and synergy requirements create a special challenge with regard to strategy making in MNCs. On the one hand, the individual affiliates are expected to support one another, as well as the goals and interests of the enterprise as a whole. On the other hand, those affiliates are likely to be operating in very dissimilar national environments, and they must retain the capability to respond effectively to the conditions and constraints existing in their respective locales.

This "global integration versus national responsiveness" dilemma pervades the entire process of developing and implementing multinational corporate strategies and may affect any aspect of those strategies. As an example, the corporate strategy of a multinational firm might dictate that expenditures for modernization or expansion of production facilities should be financed by the individual affiliates themselves. But such a policy could place quite different demands and restraints on the various affiliates, inasmuch as the availability and cost of borrowed funds may vary considerably from country to country. Another example would be a strategy decision to consolidate a MNC's research and development (R&D) activities and to supply the same new technology to all affiliates on a standard-fee basis. While such an approach might yield substantial benefits by lowering R&D costs and protecting technological secrets, it could create serious problems for affiliates in countries for which the standardized technology was not appropriate or in which the host government maintained strict limits on payments for imported technology.

The existence of such complications and incongruities must, as a practical matter, be taken into account in the setting of multinational corporate strategies. This implies that such strategies, if they are to be workable, cannot be so rigid as to rule out exceptions or departures in response to the particular environmental circumstances and pressures with which the separate affiliates must contend. It further implies that those strategies cannot be imposed solely "from the top down" by the parent company. Rather, it is desirable if not essential that managers at all locales and levels of a firm be heavily involved in the development of its corporate strategy. These needs for flexibility and for a combination of "top down" and "bottom up" strategy making have been recognized by most of the MNCs that have become seriously involved with strategic planning.

Elements of Strategy

A multinational corporate strategy is, in essence, a plan that establishes goals and objectives and sets forth the basic approaches that will be taken, as well as the resources that will be committed, to accomplish those goals and objectives. Strategic plans typically have a time horizon extending several years into the future, although provision is usually made for periodic reassessment and, if necessary, revision of those plans.

Multinational corporations do not all accord the same emphasis to strategic planning, nor do they all have the same depth of experience or involvement with it. Moreover, the factors that are taken into account and the planning procedures themselves are not uniform among the multinationals. It is possible, however, to identify certain elements that are found in most multinational corporate strategic plans. Those elements, and the linkages among them, can be presented as a generalized strategic planning model. This model is diagrammed in Figure 14.1, and its constituent elements are explained briefly in the following sections.[1]

Environmental Analysis.   One of the common elements in multinational strategic plans is an analysis of market environments. Such analyses entail the specification of conditions or circumstances that would be expected to have either positive or negative effects on the firm's prospects for doing business profitably, combined with attempts to measure and forecast the existence and dimensions of such conditions. The conditions may be of an economic, political, or cultural nature, or they may have to do with regulatory or technological factors and developments. The extent and nature of competition is also an important subject of such analyses.

The initial step or "first cut" in environmental analyses may be a global screening procedure, in which the firm analytically scans the entire world and either selects or rules out certain countries on the basis of broad criteria. A firm might, for instance, establish some minimum standards, in terms of population size, per capita income, political stability, or stage of industrialization, that it regards as indispensable for successful operations and exclude regions or countries that did not meet those standards from further consideration. Those regions or countries that "passed" such preliminary screening tests would then be analyzed in greater depth.

The results of environmental analyses can contribute to the setting of strategy in many ways. They may be used to target new markets that the firm is not presently serving, but they can also aid in deciding whether existing marketing or production activities should be expanded or contracted. They often provide valuable guidance in determining which mode of operations should be used by the firm in particular areas. Certain combinations of political instability and competitive intensity, for example, might indicate that exporting would be preferable to the acquisition of production facilities.

---

[1]The discussion in the remainder of this section is based upon models and descriptions of international corporate planning from the following sources: William A. Dymsza, "Global Strategic Planning: A Model and Recent Developments," *Journal of International Business Studies* (Fall 1984): 169–183; S. B. Prasad and Y. Krishna Shetty, *An Introduction to Multinational Management* (Englewood Cliffs, NJ: Prentice-Hall, 1976), 67–82; Arvind P. Phatak, *International Dimensions of Management* (Boston: Kent Publishing, 1983), 39–62.

Figure 14.1   ***The Multinational Strategic Planning Process***

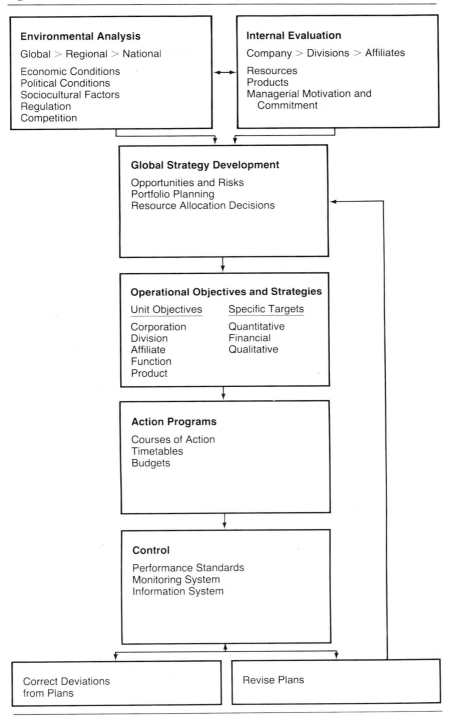

Environmental Analysis

Global > Regional > National

Economic Conditions
Political Conditions
Sociocultural Factors
Regulation
Competition

Internal Evaluation

Company > Divisions > Affiliates

Resources
Products
Managerial Motivation and
    Commitment

Global Strategy Development

Opportunities and Risks
Portfolio Planning
Resource Allocation Decisions

Operational Objectives and Strategies

Unit Objectives   Specific Targets

Corporation   Quantitative
Division   Financial
Affiliate   Qualitative
Function
Product

Action Programs

Courses of Action
Timetables
Budgets

Control

Performance Standards
Monitoring System
Information System

Correct Deviations
from Plans

Revise Plans

Internal Evaluation.   A second element of multinational corporate strategic planning is an inward-looking evaluation of the firm itself. Such
evaluations consider the MNC as an entity, but they are also refined to
the level of individual divisions and affiliates. An inventory of the firm's
real resources (i.e., its material, financial, technological, and managerial
assets and capabilities) and a realistic appraisal of the market strength
of its products are principal components of these internal evaluations,
but they may also be concerned with less tangible factors, such as managerial motivation or commitment to international operations.

These internal evaluations are closely linked to the environmental
analyses. By comparing the firm's resources and capabilities with the
conditions the environmental analyses find to be present or emerging
in global, regional, or national markets, the firm can assess its own
strengths and weaknesses against the requirements for operating successfully and profitably in those markets.

Developing Strategies.   Bringing together the results of environmental
analyses and internal evaluations allows MNCs to identify those business opportunities it is feasible for them to pursue. It also helps them
to weigh such opportunities against the associated problems and risks.
This, in turn, serves as a guide to the critical task of deciding how
resources should be allocated among alternative new business ventures
or ongoing operations, and developing strategies to carry out those
decisions.

One approach to this strategic resource-allocation task that is utilized
by many MNCs is **portfolio planning.** The precise techniques employed
in portfolio planning differ from company to company, but they typically involve some variation of the following steps[2]:

1. Delineating the strategic business units (SBUs) that make up the
firm's portfolio. This entails the segmentation of the firm's overall operations into discrete units, each of which is regarded as constituting a
separate business. The segmentation may be by country, by product,
by a combination of country and product, or by other criteria.

2. Evaluating the existing portfolio in terms of the current position of
the various SBUs in relation to selected variables. Some of the variables
that are frequently employed for this purpose are degree of risk, return
on investment or sales, market share, market growth, and cash flow.

A matrix is often used to establish the position of the SBUs and the
distribution of the total portfolio. Figure 14.2 is a well-known example
of a portfolio matrix, which was developed by the Boston Consulting
Group. This matrix utilizes market growth and relative market share as
the pertinent analytical variables, and SBUs are categorized as either
"stars," "cash cows," "problem children," or "dogs," depending on
their position in the matrix.

---

[2]Phillipe Haspeslagh, "Portfolio Planning: Uses and Limits," *Harvard Business Review*
(January–February 1982):58–73.

Figure 14.2   Portfolio Planning Matrix Indicating Distribution of Strategic Business Units (SBUs)

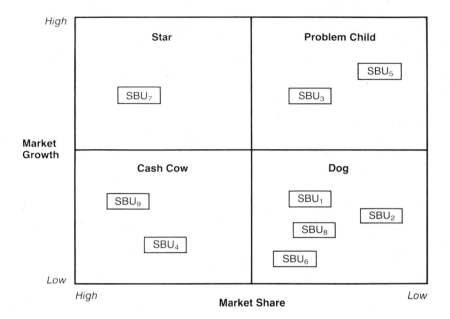

3. Determining the need for realignments of the SBUs in order to attain a better balance of the portfolio. For example, the analysis in step 2 might show that a high proportion of a firm's SBUs (defined by country location) are in low-growth markets. This situation, which is illustrated in Figure 14.2, would indicate a need for the firm to seriously consider a redeployment toward markets with higher growth potential.

4. Developing strategies for allocating or reallocating resources in order to accomplish needed portfolio realignments. This might entail shifting resources among existing SBUs or possibly creating new SBUs. For instance, profits generated by "cash cows" might be used to expand the market shares of "problem children" or to set up new businesses in high-growth markets where they would have the potential to become "stars." It might also entail the development of new products or other means of diversifying the firm's operations.

Setting Specific Objectives and Action Programs.   Analyses and evaluations of the types described above can help a multinational firm in determining its global objectives and developing general strategies. However, those broad objectives and strategies must be "operationalized." This involves the specification of objectives for the various affiliates or other subunits, which, as emphasized previously, should conform to the overall corporate objectives while also recognizing the need for each unit to respond to its own environmental circumstances. It also involves restating the global objectives and strategies in terms that provide practical guidance for managerial decisions and actions, as well as a basis for measuring the results of those decisions and actions. Moreover, the objectives must be related to the activities in which the individual affiliates are actually engaged.

Thus, an operational statement of objectives ordinarily will include financial targets, such as a desired rate of return on assets or sales or a desired year-by-year rate of growth in such financial measures. It will also specify, in either quantitative or qualitative terms, what the affiliate or other subunit wishes to accomplish in production, marketing, finance, research and development and personnel matters, as well as in its relationships with customers, employees, and government agencies.

Once a multinational corporate strategic plan has been refined to this extent, it provides a concrete basis for designing action programs. This requires that managers consider the alternative means by which they can implement the strategies and fulfill the objectives for which they are responsible and then to select those alternatives which they judge to be the most promising. It also requires that they develop timetables for activating the selected courses of action and budgets for financing them. All this must be accomplished in accordance with the constraints the strategic plan imposes on them, with regard to the resources they will have available and the policies to which they must adhere.

Control.   The detailed plans, timetables, and budgets drawn up by the affiliates or other subunits not only constitute an action program for implementing the multinational corporate strategy. They also provide a framework for monitoring and controlling the activities and performance of the subunits.

A control mechanism is an essential component of any strategic plan. But it assumes special importance in MNCs, inasmuch as the plan is to be carried out in many different locales that are geographically distant from the top management headquarters. Moreover, its implementation will be in the hands of managers who will be subjected to diverse and dynamic pressures emanating for their individual operating environments. This makes it imperative for top management to have a means of ascertaining when deviations from the corporate plan are occurring and the reasons for such deviations.

Plans and budgets provide the documentary basis for a multinational control system, as well as the standards against which actual performance and accomplishments can be measured. An effective control system also requires a continuous flow of information throughout the organization. Managerial personnel within each affiliate should be reporting on a regular schedule and in standardized form to their immediate superiors, and the reporting process should extend from the affiliates to any intermediate managerial control centers which the firm maintains, and, ultimately, to the corporation's world headquarters. These reporting procedures ordinarily will be supplemented and reinforced by less formal contacts and communications, such as visits to affiliates by headquarters personnel and periodic meetings of the firm's entire managerial group.

The principal purpose of a control system and the management information system associated with it is to keep the multinational organization functioning in conformity with its strategic plan and objectives. These control and informational systems allow those responsible for the fulfillment of the strategic plan to perceive problems as they arise and take steps to correct them in a timely manner. However, the control process may also reveal that the plan itself has shortcomings or that it has become inconsistent with changed environmental conditions and will therefore have to be reviewed and possibly revised.

The foregoing abbreviated description of strategic planning in MNCs should make it evident that such planning processes tend to be difficult and time-consuming. Some multinational firms have expressed disappointment with what they have determined to be insufficient benefits from such planning in relation to the man-hours of managerial time and effort which have been devoted to it. However, the great majority of such firms have decided that comprehensive, long-range plans are essential for keeping their widespread operations intact and profitable in view of the environmental diversity and uncertainties they face.[3]

Multinational Management Organization

The organization of MNCs and decisions relating to those organizations usually are closely intertwined with the strategic planning function. Indeed, the old "chicken or egg" riddle may apply to this relationship since (as noted in the preceding section) effective strategic planning assumes the involvement of a managerial organization; however, the strategic plans adopted by multinational firms also influence the kind of managerial organization created to implement those plans. The resolution of this riddle lies in the realization that neither strategies nor organizational arrangements are static, but are continually evolving in an interactive fashion.

Thus, the type of managerial organization found in a multinational firm depends partly on the extent and duration of the firm's involvement in international operations. These unquestionably are important determinants of organizational structure, but other factors also play a significant role. The additional determinants include the characteristics

---

[3]Noel Capon, John W. Farley, and James Hubert, "International Diffusion of Corporate and Strategic Planning Practices," *Columbia Journal of World Business* (Fall 1980): 5–6.

of the firm's products and markets, and the attitudes of its top managers toward the decentralization of managerial authority and responsibility.

The remainder of this section will examine how each of the variables identified above may affect the organizational and managerial structures of MNCs. It will also describe some of the different organizational forms that grow out of those variables. Such descriptions are only general characterizations of multinational corporate structures, however, since each individual MNC has its unique managerial organization, and all such organizations change (gradually or quickly) over time.

International Involvement and Experience

There are close parallels between the development of a business firm's organizational and managerial framework and the changes that occur in the nature and dimensions of its international activities. These activities often begin with exporting operations, and the initial small scale of those operations, together with the firm's inexperience, logically dictate the use of independent exporting middlemen.

So long as a firm's international involvement is limited to such indirect exporting, its need for an internal managerial structure to supervise such activity is likewise limited. It is not unusual for firms in this stage of their international evolution to simply assign responsibility for exporting to the existing managerial personnel in the areas of production, marketing, and finance, thereby creating a **"built-in" export management group.** An individual may also be hired or appointed from within to coordinate the exporting operation and to establish and maintain liaison with the middlemen that are marketing the firm's products overseas.

As the volume of foreign sales increases, companies frequently find such small-scale, informal management structures inadequate. The next step often is to establish a **separate exporting department,** staffed with managerial personnel who have expertise in foreign marketing and who are responsible solely for the exporting portion of the firm's total operations. This is likely to coincide with a shift from indirect to more direct exporting, which involves the replacement of independent export middlemen by the firm's own facilities and personnel.

Business firms enter a distinct new stage in their international evolution when exporting is either replaced or supplemented by foreign production and/or foreign licensing. These forms of overseas business activity (especially foreign production) involve a greater commitment of resources on the part of the firm and place heavier demands on management. Whereas exporting mainly requires marketing and some financial expertise, establishing and operating production facilities abroad entails the exercise of managerial skills and discretion in those functional areas *plus* such fields as personnel, procurement, manufacturing, inventory control, and labor relations.

Figure 14.3   ***International Division Structure***

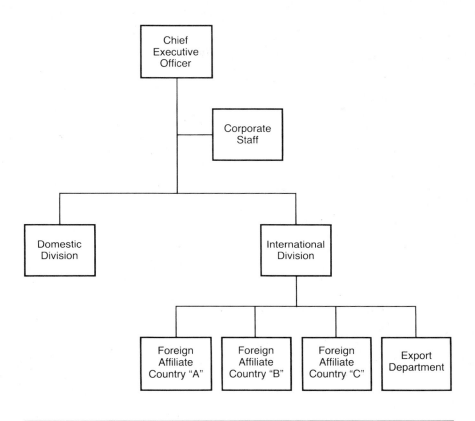

Historically, the establishment of an **international division** has been a prevalent mode of response to such expanded managerial demands. Such divisions have been set up alongside one or more existing domestic divisions and accorded parallel status in the managerial hierarchy. The international division then assumes responsibility for supervising and coordinating all business operations outside the company's home country, and the managers of foreign affiliates report to the head of the international division. This type of management structure is portrayed in Figure 14.3.

The creation of an international division constitutes a definite, tangible expression of a company's intent to continue the development of foreign operations. It consolidates the management of all overseas activities and establishes clearer relationships and lines of authority between foreign affiliates and the parent company . It also brings together those line and staff managers who share international expertise and interests.

On the negative side, however, the creation of an international division effectively splits a firm into two largely autonomous and perhaps even rival segments and tends to perpetuate the segregation of domestic and foreign operations. This may result in unnecessary duplication of functions and personnel, and, more importantly, may interfere with the formulation of overall corporate objectives and strategies for attaining them.

The recognition of such counterproductive tendencies has led many companies to abandon the domestic division/international division dichotomy in favor of a **global management structure.** Such a structure eliminates the separation of foreign from domestic operations, at least at the top of the firm's managerial pyramid where basic strategy and policy decisions are made. The institution of this type of managerial structure is intended to enable a company to attain the worldwide integration of operations and global market orientation that characterizes the "true" multinational corporation.

Product and Market Influences

Regardless of whether a company retains an international division or moves to a global management structure, it must assign managerial authority and responsibility. The kinds of products the firm produces and the character of its markets frequently play a decisive part in determining how such assignments are made.

Many multinational companies have adopted a **product-based approach,** in which managerial responsibility is divided on the basis of products or product groups. Those firms ordinarily set up a number of different product divisions, each of which plans, organizes, and controls most of the functions involved in producing and distributing its particular products throughout the world. Those divisions may receive some support from staff groups that operate at the corporate level, especially in areas such as personnel, research, and product development where aggregate efforts are more economical than individual divisional efforts.

The product-based approach is appropriate for firms that make a number of related but dissimilar products that are directed toward different end-use markets. It becomes even more appropriate if those products are technologically distinctive and complex. In such cases, it is essential that managers be thoroughly familiar with the technical makeup and performance capabilities of the products they are handling and able to communicate with knowledgeable buyers; however, it may be almost impossible for any one management team to gain such in-depth knowledge of more than one product or product group. It is rational, therefore, to establish a separate management team to handle each of the firm's diverse product categories. Companies in the capital goods, chemical, and electronics industries tend to fulfill the criteria, in terms of products and type of markets, that make a product-based structure the logical choice.

A second widely used means of allocating managerial responsibility is the **geographic-based approach,** wherein a firm establishes divisions associated with different geographic areas of the world. The managers in each division are in charge of the functions involved in producing and distributing all the products that the firm is marketing in that region, and affiliates located in that part of the world are under the direction of the region's division head in the parent company. Figure 14.4 provides a diagrammatic comparison of the product-based and geographic-based organizational approaches.

The geographic approach is well suited to companies with relatively simple and homogeneous products which are sensitive to local market conditions. These circumstances mean that knowledge of the economy and culture of the specific locales in which the firm operates is more important for managerial success than detailed product knowledge. Firms that produce foods and beverages, cosmetics, and other consumer staples have used the geographic structure to good advantage.

A third approach followed by MNCs in organizing their operations is the **functional approach.** This involves the division of managerial responsibility and authority along functional lines. Thus, one top executive of the corporation is in charge of worldwide manufacturing, while another is responsible for global marketing. This approach is often criticized for being overly rigid and for its tendency to retard communication and coordination of activities, thus it is less prevalent than the product- and geographic-based structures.

All the approaches described above are unidimensional, in that they emphasize a single dimension (product, geographic area, or function) as the basis for allocating managerial control. While this provides a clear line of command, in which each individual manager reports to his or her superior, it may result in inattention or insensitivity to other important dimensions of the firm's operations or situation. For instance, a company whose management structure and orientation is based entirely on products may fail to take proper account of environmental developments or regional pressures.

This possibility has induced a number of MNCs to adopt a **matrix structure,** in which managerial authority and responsibility are assigned according to more than one dimension. The most frequent combination involves the product-based and geographic-based approaches. The top management group then includes both product executives and regional executives, and the managers of affiliates are often required to report to more than one superior.

Although confusion and conflict may arise in such dual-responsibility structures, they enhance the likelihood that both product and regional concerns will be considered in managerial decisions. Also, both technical and area expertise are utilized in resolving problems and responding to opportunities.

The variety of organizational structures existing among MNCs illustrates the fact that there is no one "best" way to organize for the effec-

Figure 14.4   **Product and Geographic Alternatives in a Global Management Structure**

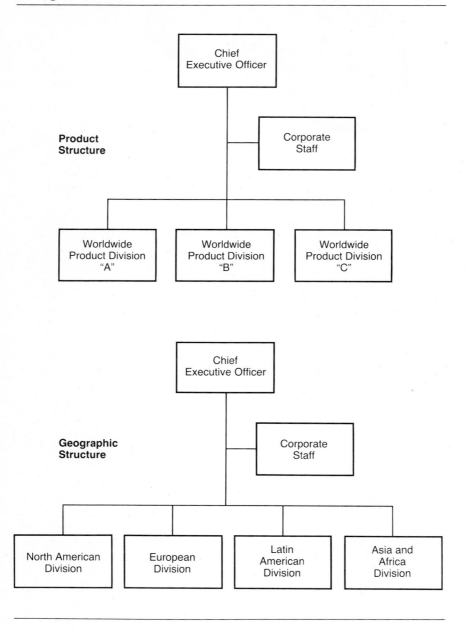

tive management of international business operations. Each company has to design an organization for its particular aims, needs, and circumstances and must be prepared to adapt that structure as those variables change over time.

Centralization Versus Decentralization

The extent to which managerial authority and responsibility should be centralized or decentralized is another key issue in the organization of MNCs. This issue must be addressed in any enterprise that attains a scale of operations that is too large or too diversified to be administered effectively by one or a few persons. But it takes on an added twist in multinational firms, since it entails the division of power between the managers of a parent company based in one country and the managers of affiliates that are operating in many diverse locations throughout the world.

On the one hand, such diversity of operating environments, together with the far-flung nature of a MNC's activities, make a strong case for decentralizing management. Headquarters personnel are unlikely to be familiar with the economic and cultural milieu in each and every country in which the firm is doing business, or capable of quickly discerning and reacting to environmental changes. Such deficiencies may be overcome by giving more discretion and autonomy to the managers of individual foreign affiliates, who are better able to comprehend and respond to local developments. By entrusting more authority to national managers, a firm may also engender a favorable image as a "local" concern and thus avoid political problems. Still another advantage associated with decentralization is that it may reduce the need for an elaborate (and expensive) intracorporate communications and management information system.

On the other hand, there are persuasive arguments for centralizing managerial authority in a multinational firm. The most basic of these grows out of the global integration concept, which stresses the benefits of close cooperation and interdependence among parent firm and affiliates. As noted previously, a substantial degree of central control by managers who are able to perceive business opportunities on a worldwide basis is essential for the development and maintenance of such integration. The centralization of management decision making is also conducive to the development and implementation of uniform policies, as well as standardized products and business practices, and such uniformity and standardization can yield substantial benefits in both cost savings and the perpetuation of high-quality performance throughout the firm.

The choice between centralization and decentralization is a matter of general orientation rather than a strict either/or proposition. This means that MNCs can adopt combinations of these two approaches and are able to shift from one to another as their business expands or as environmental circumstances change. Thus, many MNCs have centralized the management of certain functions, notably research, finance, and product development, while decentralizing others such as marketing and procurement. They have also altered their approach over time, and often exhibit a tendency toward greater centralization as they become more experienced in international operations and more cognizant of the opportunities afforded by worldwide integration.

The existence of these "hybrid" arrangements and the changes occurring in them underscore the need for flexibility in the organizational design of MNCs. The management of a giant business enterprise, whose operations span great physical distances and reach into many diverse markets, cannot be accomplished successfully with a rigid managerial organization. Variety and change will therefore continue to occur in the organization of multinational firms as they evolve and strive to adapt to dynamic environmental conditions and demands.

Multinational Management Staffing

No aspect of multinational management is more essential to a firm's success than the staffing function. Regardless of the soundness of its strategic plans or the appropriateness of its organizational structure, a company cannot hope to cope effectively with the complexities of the global business environment and multinational operations without a talented, dedicated, and well-trained managerial group.

The multinational management staffing function encompasses all the related activities that are required to establish, develop, and maintain such a group. It includes planning and forecasting needs for managerial personnel, recruiting and selecting individuals to fill those needs, training those individuals, and placing them in positions in which their particular capabilities will yield optimal results for the organization. It also includes the development of a system of tangible and intangible rewards and creation of an atmosphere that will motivate managers to put forth their best efforts. These staffing activities will now be considered briefly.

Personnel Planning

The determination of past and future needs for managerial personnel is an indispensable part of a MNC's strategic planning process. As indicated earlier, such planning involves an appraisal of the firm's resources in reference to its market opportunities, and management is one of the most crucial resources that must be considered in such assessments. Comparing its existing managerial staff with what would be required to take full advantage of its worldwide market and profit potential aids the firm in ascertaining any staffing deficiencies and making plans to overcome them.

Those plans should deal not only with the number of managers required, but also with requisite qualifications. They also should include a breakdown of staffing requirements by division, region, affiliate, and business function, as well as a time schedule for responding to those requirements. This type of personnel planning provides a clear guide for the recruitment and selection component of the staffing function.

Recruitment and Selection

Multinational companies can recruit managerial personnel from several different sources, and the emphasis given to each of those sources varies from one company to another and from time to time within individual companies. One of these sources is the home country of the parent organization. Some multinationals rely heavily upon home-country citizens in staffing their worldwide operations, placing these **expatriates** in the top managerial positions of foreign affiliates. The advantages associated with this approach include the opportunity to train managers in domestic operations and headquarters policies and practices before deploying them to foreign assignments. Communication between the parent firm and its foreign affiliates may be easier and less susceptible to misunderstandings when the managers involved share a common background and language, and this approach also ensures that overseas managers will be loyal to the goals of the parent organization.

A second important source of multinational managers is the country in which each affiliate is located. The use of host-country nationals in management positions offers some signficant benefits. One of the most obvious of these is the manager's inherent familiarity with the local language and culture, which eases the task of interacting effectively with workers, customers, and government officials. Political problems may also be avoided or reduced if a multinational firm places indigenous nationals in positions of authority, rather than utilizing expatriates from the firm's home country and thereby perpetuating an image of "foreign control." In fact, many countries now have laws requiring that a specified proportion of the management staff of foreign-owned firms be made up of local residents.

In addition to such cultural and political considerations, staffing with host-country nationals is apt to be much less costly then sending home-country executives and their families overseas. Multinational companies have found it quite expensive to transfer managers abroad, especially from the United States or one of the other industrialized countries to a developing country. The cost of transporting the manager's family and its household belongings and of providing suitable living accommodations, health care, and education for children can amount to a sizable sum in such transfers. Moreover, the salaries, "hardship allowances," and benefit packages that expatriate managers from the First World countries have become accustomed to receiving often far exceed what the firm would have to pay a local manager. It is not surprising, therefore, that many multinational firms prefer to staff their foreign affiliates with local citizens and to use expatriate managers only for short-term assignments, such as starting a new operation, training local personnel, or dealing with a specific problem.

A third alternative available to multinational firms in recruiting and selecting managers is one that essentially overlooks national origins and emphasizes the development of a "cosmopolitan" managerial group. A

Box 14.1

Competing for Managerial Talent in Japan

Foreign companies operating in Japan have faced many handicaps in competing for managerial talent. They usually lack the personal connections that Japanese firms rely upon when they recruit. Moreover, most of the thousand or so foreign subsidiaries are relatively small, which is a drawback in the highly status-conscious Japanese society. American companies in particular have also had a reputation for being quick to fire employees, whereas Japanese firms still stress lifelong job security.

European and American companies nevertheless have begun to have more success in recruiting Japanese managers after years of struggling to find good employees. These companies now are able to attract some graduates from respectable colleges and are hiring experienced managers away from Japanese corporations.

There are several reasons for this increased success in recruiting. The American and European firms are enticing Japanese managers by offering big salaries and promises of Western-style managerial autonomy. Executive recruiters are also learning more effective techniques, such as the use of Japanese go-betweens, for locating Japanese managerial candidates.

Source: Bernard Wysocki, Jr., "Foreign Companies Are Having More Success Recruiting Employees in Japan, Although Some Key Obstacles Remain," *The Wall Street Journal*, January 2, 1985, 8.

firm using such an approach might recruit or select individuals in Western Europe to staff its Latin American operations, while assigning Latin Americans to managerial positions in the United States or the Far East, and sending U.S. citizens to manage European or Middle Eastern affiliates.

This alternative is consistent with the concept of the MNC as a business enterprise that ignores national boundaries in seeking out and acquiring the best resources available and in utilizing those resources wherever their potential productivity is greatest. With respect to managerial resources, this approach presumably could result in the creation of an elite corps of managers, skilled and experienced in international operations, whose loyalties would lie entirely with the firm and who would be prepared to undertake assignments anywhere in the world.

Notwithstanding these conceptual advantages, relatively few MNCs have actually implemented this kind of managerial recruitment and selection program. Practical difficulties account for this, not the least of which is the difficulty of finding individuals with managerial talents who can function effectively in a variety of cultural environments, are fluent in native languages, and who also are sufficiently flexible, in terms of their career paths and life-styles, to willingly accept varied international assignments. This staffing method is also susceptible to the same high costs and political problems that are encountered in the utilization of expatriate managers from a multinational's home country.

Apart from the nationality issue, the recruitment and selection process entails the specification of qualifications that the firm considers necessary for multinational management, combined with continuous efforts to identify individuals with such qualifications either within or outside the firm. Many studies have been made of the criteria companies use in selecting personnel for overseas assignments, and proven managerial competence and/or technical expertise consistently rank at or near the top of those criteria. Such personal qualities as integrity, flexibility, and adaptability are also important selection criteria, as is the willingness of an individual (and his or her family) to live and work abroad.[4]

Studies also indicate that multinational companies generally prefer to recruit from within for international management positions. Foreign assignments almost always go to managers who have extensive experience and solid track records in the company itself or in similar companies, although many multinational firms do recruit recent college graduates and others with limited business experience for staff positions or as line management trainees in their international divisions. Foreign students studying in a firm's home country or students who have gained international exposure in other ways comprise an attractive pool of candidates for such positions, as they are likely to have a good background of knowledge and sensitivity to foreign cultures. Such backgrounds can then be expanded on and developed through the firm's management training program.

Training and Development

The training of multinational managers is similar to management training in general. Managerial personnel must be trained in the specific function and job for which they will be assigned, and must be indoctrinated in the policies and operating procedures of the company, regardless of whether they are to be involved in international or domestic

---

[4]Some examples of these studies of selection criteria for overseas assignments include: John M. Ivancevich, "Selection of American Managers for Overseas Assignments," *Personnel Journal* (March 1969): 189–193; Edwin L. Miller, "The Selection Decision for an International Assignment: A Study of the Decision Maker's Behavior," *Journal of International Business Studies* (Fall 1972): 49–65; Rosalie L. Tung, "Selection and Training of Personnel for Overseas Assignments," *Columbia Journal of World Business* (Spring 1981): 68–78.

operations. However, properly preparing managers for positions over-seas or even for home-office positions related to a firm's international activities requires training beyond that which is ordinarily devoted to the domestic staff.

One area in which there is a need for such additional training pertains to culture and cultural sensitivity. It seems apparent that managers who are being sent to foreign countries, especially for extended stays, could benefit from gaining prior knowledge of the culture and language of those countries. But an appreciation of cultural diversity and its impli-cations for business firms operating in a multitude of countries and societies is also important for international managers even if they are based in the home country.

While surveys have shown that the majority of MNCs are aware of the usefulness of such cross-cultural training, many corporations still do not provide formal programs of this nature. One recent study found that only 32 percent of a sample of U.S.-based multinationals had for-malized training programs to prepare candidates for overseas work, although 69 percent of European companies and 57 percent of Japanese companies provided such training.[5]

Managers involved in the international aspects of a company's busi-ness also require additional training to prepare them for problems that are unique to the international field. For example, international financial managers must be trained to deal with foreign exchange risks and with the methods involved in transferring funds from country to country; international marketing managers must be trained to interact effectively with foreign middlemen, whose organizations and ways of doing busi-ness are apt to differ greatly from those found in the firm's home coun-try; and production managers may need special training in labor relations or in designing production techniques that are compatible with the skills of foreign labor.

Much of the training of multinational managers is done internally by the companies themselves, either through special instructional pro-grams, on-the-job training, or both. In addition, there are organizations in the United States and elsewhere that offer both individualized and group programs to train international management personnel. Many university business schools provide international management educa-tion as a part of their academic curriculum, and some specialize in this area. Private organizations exist that will design programs to fit the training needs of a particular multinational firm or that offer more stand-ardized training and orientation programs, especially for managers and their families who have received overseas assignments.

---

[5]Rosalie L. Tung, "Selection and Training Procedures of U.S., European, and Japanese Multinationals," *California Management Review* (Fall 1982): 57–71.

Compensation Systems

Designing and sustaining a workable compensation system can be a complicated project for MNCs. Such systems must attract and retain competent managers who are willing to adapt to foreign assignments, without making those international managers a "privileged class" and thereby creating dissension within the company. Compensation systems must reflect differences in the cost of living and other special costs that managers are likely to incur in overseas posts, without overcompensating managers and thereby placing undue cost burdens on the firm. In addition, an acceptable balance must be reached between the compensation received by expatriate managers from the company's home country and the compensation received by host-country or third-country nationals who have similar duties.

The compensation system adopted by many U.S.-based multinationals involves a three-part compensation package for expatriate managers. This includes, first, a base salary, which is derived from the company's overall managerial salary scale. Managers at comparable levels within the company presumably will receive equivalent base salaries, regardless of whether they are working in domestic operations or abroad.

The second component of the expatriate manger's compensation consists of premiums. These premiums are intended to compensate managers for any hardships they must endure in living and working in unfamiliar and perhaps undesirable foreign locations. They are also intended to encourage and reward mobility, that is, the willingness of managers to leave their home offices for overseas positions. Implicit in this mobility concept is the idea that overseas positions often will entail more responsibilities than the manager would have in a similar domestic post and that the manager may have to shoulder those responsibilities without immediate or direct support from the headquarters staff.

The third part of the expatriate manager compensation package is made up of various allowances. The basic purpose of these allowances is to allow the manager and his or her family to maintain their accustomed style of living. The allowances usually reflect differences in housing and other living costs, differences in tax liabilities, and the costs of acceptable education for the manager's children.

In addition to its financial components, a MNC's compensation system should recognize other managerial concerns and aspirations. Managers are likely to be as much concerned with their status and prospects for advancement within the firm as they are with salaries and other monetary returns. Their enthusiasm for and performance in international assignments may therefore depend heavily upon how those assignments are viewed and treated in terms of promotions and related considerations.

It is not always possible or desirable for a company to have specific, formal policies pertaining to such issues. However, managers should be given a fairly clear indication of how overseas positions or international posts will affect their career paths. Otherwise, they may be reluctant to accept foreign assignments that might remove them from the "center of action" in the firm's home office, or, conversely, they may push for such assignments simply because they regard them as essential for upward mobility in the corporation. Either of these responses to ambiguity in the managerial reward system could lead to suboptimal results in the multinational management staffing function.

Summary

1. Effective global operations by multinational corporations requires the development of strategies for attaining the enterprise's objectives, the creation of an organizational structure that is consistent with those strategies, and the development of a managerial staff that is capable of implementing them.

2. A basic aim of multinational corporate strategy is to create a synergistic relationship, in which the operations of affiliates in different countries become mutually supportive and directed toward common goals.

3. A multinational corporate strategy is essentially a long-range plan that establishes objectives and commits resources to their fulfillment.

4. The elements found in virtually all multinational strategic plans include: an analysis of the world market environment; an evaluation of the firm's own resources and capabilities relative to world market opportunities; the development of global strategies; setting specific objectives and action programs; and establishing a mechanism for monitoring and controlling the implementation of the strategies and action programs.

5. The organization of multinational corporations is closely interconnected with strategic planning, and strategies and organizational structures tend to continually evolve in an interactive fashion.

6. The factors that determine the nature of a multinational corporation's organizational structure include: the nature, dimensions, and duration of its international involvement; the characteristics of its products and end-user markets; and management attitudes toward centralization or decentralization of authority and responsibility.

7. The multinational management staffing function encompasses all the activities required to establish, develop, and retain a talented, well-trained, and dedicated management group.

8. The managerial staffing function includes personnel planning, recruitment and selection, training and development activities, and the design and maintenance of an effective compensation system.

Questions for Review or Discussion

1.   What is the basic aim of strategy development in multinational corporations?
2.   What conditions or developments have made it imperative for multinationals to develop long-range strategies?
3.   Why are the formulation and implementation of corporate strategies in a multinational firm likely to be more difficult than in a domestic firm?
4.   What is meant by the "global integration versus national responsiveness" dilemma with respect to strategy making in a multinational firm?
5.   What is portfolio planning and how does it apply to the development of multinational corporate strategies?
6.   At what stage in the evolution of their international operations have companies usually found it necessary to establish an international division? What are the principal advantages and problems associated with establishing an international division?
7.   Compare a product-based management structure with a geographic-based structure and indicate the circumstances which tend to make one or the other of these alternative structures more appropriate for an international company.
8.   Discuss the benefits of decentralization of managerial authority and responsibility in a multinational corporation.
9.   What are the chief arguments for the centralization of managerial control in a multinational corporation?
10. What are the principal alternative sources from which multinationals can recruit managers? What are the main advantages and disadvantages associated with each of these sources?
11. What kinds of "special" training do international managers require?

Case

Unilever PLC

Unilever wants to become a truly global company. It already owned three major U.S. companies, Lipton, National Starch, and Lever Brothers when in mid-1985 it made an aggressive takeover bid ($60/share) for Richardson-Vicks, Inc. Unfortunately, it lost out to a higher ($69/share for a total of $1.24 billion) and friendly bid by Procter & Gamble (P&G)—its major rival in the United States and globally. History seemed to be repeating itself, since it was P&G that introduced Tide in the 1940s and clobbered Unilever's dominance in laundry detergents.

Unilever is the world's largest consumer goods company, with annual sales of nearly $23 billion, and the United States is one of the largest and most profitable markets for consumer products. However, until recently, Lever Bros. in the United States was running at a loss. On U.S. detergent sales, Unilever earns 5 percent, compared to P&G's 22 percent. During the last 5 years, Unilever's net income was 3.8 percent of sales compared to P&G's 7.7 percent.

Growth in the United States market has become a priority for Unilever, especially since it does better elsewhere in the world. Even with the largest market, the United States accounts for less than a fifth of Unilever's sales while Europe accounts for more than half. Many of Unilever's brands in the United States are not doing as well as it would like them to do. For example, its toothpaste, Aim, is in a low fourth place in U.S. sales.

Under a new management, Unilever is pumping more money into product advertising and is ruthlessly shedding marginal business. With $1.13 billion in cash (as of June 30, 1985), it is looking for acquisitions. It recently closed its aging but large and costly margarine plant in the United States and replaced it with more modern plants bought from Beatrice Foods. Unilever boosted U.S. promotional spending to $254 million in 1984. Its liquid detergent, Wisk, is doing better (with a 8.8 percent market share) than P&G's Liquid Tide (with 6.5 percent). Unilever's Lipton (tea, soups, and Sunkist orange juice) and National Starch divisions continue to do well and make money. As an aftermath of its failure to acquire Richardson-Vicks, Unilever faces a number of questions. Should it continue to try and expand its presence in the United States where it faces stiff competition from P&G, Colgate-Palmolive, Philip Morris/General Foods, Beatrice/Esmark, R.J. Reynolds/Nabisco, and other recently merged consumer product companies?

Due to the high expense of creating a well-known brand name, buying a brand may be the only alternative. In addition, a merger may lead to savings in advertising and distribution. However, mergers often do not work out and can often slow down a company's efforts to improve its existing businesses. They may also deplete a company's financial resources and add a heavy debt burden. Therefore, should Unilever expand by mergers and acquisitions?

Observers note that Unilever is trying to become a more aggressive, "lean and mean" company. However, Unilever's organizational structure is unusual and may make it sluggish and slow. It has two parent firms, one British and one Dutch, that must agree on strategy. This tends to prolong decision making. Nevertheless, Unilever has become less bureaucratic in the last few years under the "troika" management of Sir Kenneth Durham, chairman of the British board, F.A. Maljers, chairman of the Dutch board, and Michael Angus, vice-chairman of the British board. This "troika" has encouraged less formal and quicker decision making, but questions remain about the effectiveness of the company's organizational structure in a rapidly changing business environment.

Proponents of the current "two-parent" structure argue that the firm's dual headquarters structure has been useful in reducing the influence of any one government on the company and may actually have ensured the survival of the company during politically unstable times such as World War II. In addition, it has helped make Unilever a truly international company.

Should Unilever continue to try and expand in the United States by means of mergers or acquisitions or should it concentrate on expanding its existing businesses in America and elsewhere? Should it abandon its "dual-parent" form and consolidate headquarters in either Great Britain or the Netherlands?

Sources: L. Ingrassia and M. M. Nelson, "Unilever—Despite Failed Bids for Vicks—Shows Signs That The Giant Is Awakening," *The Wall Street Journal,* October 10, 1985, p. 37; and "Why Unilever Wants to Buy American," *Business Week,* October 21, 1985, p. 116.

Chapter 15

MULTINATIONAL MARKETING MANAGEMENT

Chapter Objectives

- *To explain why marketing becomes more complex and demanding when a business firm is engaged in international operations*
- *To identify and consider the basic marketing strategy decisions that must be made by international firms and their managers*
- *To analyze the problems that international companies will encounter in connection with each of the major elements of their marketing programs.*
- *To describe alternative ways in which international firms have dealt with the complications of marketing in foreign countries*

The marketing program of a business firm consists of a number of interrelated functions, all of which are involved with delivering the firm's product to users. The term "delivering" has a very broad meaning here, for it refers not just to the physical movement of the product from where it is produced to where it is used, but encompasses a variety of other activities. These have to do with the following areas:

1. Identifying prospective users that the firm hopes will become customers for its product (marketing research)
2. Informing those prospective users of the product's availability and its ability to satisfy their needs (advertising and personal selling)
3. Improving the product, or, if necessary, creating new products to better meet the customers' needs (product development)
4. Setting prices that are consistent both with the firm's own production costs and profit requirements and with the customers' purchasing power and the competitive situation (pricing)
5. Establishing and overseeing a system of organizations and facilities that can make the product available to customers when and where and in the manner that they want it (development and management of distribution channels)

This list is neither innovative nor exhaustive, but it does identify the principal functions that a firm must perform, or arrange to have performed by others, in its marketing program. The effective performance of these functions is, of course, vital to a business firm's survival, since only those companies that satisfy the demands of their customers can hope to cover their costs of doing business and to realize sufficient profits to justify the continuing use of capital and other resources provided by their owners.

Neither the marketing functions nor the importance of carrying them out effectively and profitably are altered in any substantive way when a business firm begins to operate internationally. Nevertheless, the tasks and challenges confronting the firm's marketing managers will almost certainly be expanded and complicated due to the greater number and diversity of environmental factors with which the managers must contend. Marketing is often regarded as the most "environmentally sensitive" component of the total business process, since it is in its marketing activities that the business firm interfaces most directly and completely with "society" or the public-at-large. It follows from this that the **variations** in environmental conditions—including those conditions that are economic, political, and cultural in character—that the firm will invariably run into as it extends its operations across national boundaries are apt to have an especially weighty impact upon its marketing efforts.

Perhaps the most basic issue that an international firm must address with regard to its marketing program is the extent to which it should *adapt* that program to these divergent environmental circumstances. On one side of this issue is the realization that a successful marketing venture requires that the manner in which the product is presented and delivered, as well as the product itself, be compatible with the characteristics of the target market and the preferences of the consumers in that market. This pushes the firm to adapt or "tailor" its products and marketing techniques to fit each particular market it is endeavoring to service. On the other side of the issue is the equally important realization that adaptation is, almost without exception, a costly undertaking. The efficiencies and resultant cost savings attainable through standardization of products and production processes are well recognized, as are the penalties—in lowered efficiency and higher costs—that tend to arise whenever the **standardization** formula is breached. Often these costs show up as real monetary outlays, but they can also take more subtle forms, such as loss of scale economies in production and distribution, or depreciation of the firm's reputation for consistent quality.

This tradeoff between the possible **benefits** of adapting to the market (such benefits generally would consist of enhanced customer acceptance of the product, which would translate into higher sales and profits) and the **costs** associated with such adaptation applies to every functional aspect of the marketing program. The marketing managers of international companies therefore find themselves deciding whether and how their operating policies and methods need to be changed to better conform with the idiosyncrasies of each national market, and whatever inclinations they have toward such changes must be tempered by recognition of the disadvantages of departing from a standardized approach.

The tasks and concerns of international marketing managers will be examined in greater depth in the remainder of this chapter. This can best be done by treating each major element of the marketing process in turn. This makes it easier to see how these marketing functions are affected by the environmental peculiarities of the international marketplace and the markets of individual foreign countries and to contemplate some of the alternative ways in which marketing managers might respond to this environmental diversity. The aforementioned adaptation versus standardization issue will be referred to frequently throughout this investigation, as will the related issue of how managerial control of an international firm's marketing program should be divided between the parent organization and its affiliates in various foreign markets.

Product Strategy for International Marketing

As soon as the managers of a business firm begin to give serious thought to marketing outside their home country, they come face to face with the adaptation versus standardization issue with regard to product decisions. At the most basic level, the question they must answer is, "What product(s) shall we try to market overseas?" It is conceivable that the answer to this query might be "exactly the same product(s) that we have been marketing here at home."

Such a response might appear naive at first glance, since it appears to overlook environmental dissimilarites among markets in different countries, or at least to downplay their significance in terms of product acceptability. But there may, in fact, be numerous products or product groups for which this approach—which is often referred to as a **worldwide product extension strategy**—could be quite practical and viable. If the uses to be made of the product, the physical conditions under which it would be used, and the characteristics of the users were thought to be much the same everywhere in the world, a pure or perhaps slightly modified product extension strategy would make good sense. This set of similarities may often be found in the marketing of industrial goods, especially capital goods of the high-technology type. A powerful computer, for example, would presumably have comparable applications, and would be acquired and operated by persons with similar training regardless of the country in which it was to be utilized.

It is also conceivable that a company with an interest in international marketing might conclude that its existing products simply could not win acceptance in foreign markets. This could become the basis for what is called a **product invention strategy,** in which the firm sets out to develop entirely new products for overseas markets. Although this has not been a common international product strategy among American companies, there have been a number of instances in which U.S. manufacturers have radically altered the designs of their products in order to make them affordable to lower-income consumers abroad or to increase their serviceability under harsh physical conditions. Meanwhile, the Japanese have made this product invention concept a key part of their aggressive (and highly successful) worldwide marketing campaign, as they have proved eager and able to begin producing new products whenever they perceive an unfilled demand in a foreign market.

Between the opposite extremes of product extension and product invention lies the great middleground in which most international companies tend to settle. The strategy followed by these companies can be termed **rational product adaptation.** This term denotes an awareness and acceptance of the need for *some* modification of products that are being offered in dissimilar foreign market environments, but it also stresses the need to keep such modifications within economical limits and to base them on carefully delineated differences in market characteristics.

In order to successfully implement this strategy, a company must ascertain what changes in its product appear to be dictated by the unique characteristics of each of its foreign target markets, and it must then determine whether the anticipated benefits of such changes justify the costs of making them. An analytical process that management might employ to accomplish these purposes would consist of three phases: (1) A market analysis—the aim of this phase would be to identify those features of the foreign market environment that might make it necessary or desirable to modify the product. Those market features could be of a physical or institutional nature, but they could also relate to the characteristics of prospective consumers or to laws and regulations of the foreign government. (2) A product analysis—in this phase, the firm would essentially be analyzing its own product, with a view toward uncovering any features of that product that might prevent or delay its acceptance by foreign consumers. (3) A cost analysis—this final phase would be concerned with calculating the costs that would result if the product were actually modified so as to fit the market requirements or overcome the obstacles to its acceptance that were identified in the first two phases of the overall analysis.

The application of this sort of analytical process certainly does not guarantee that marketing managers will make exactly the right decisions with respect to adapting their company's products to its varied overseas markets. But it can help them to focus on the relevant factors, including those that are indigenous to the foreign environment and those that reside in the product itself, and it may thereby enable them to achieve a reasonable accommodation between the product and its target market. It also forces the marketing managers to give due consideration to the

Box 15.1

On the Need for Product Adaptation

General Motors of Canada has had nothing but trouble from a $200 million deal to sell cars to Iraq for use by Iraqi military personnel. The first 13,500 cars shipped to Iraq were unfit for the desert climate. The air filters on the Chevrolet Malibus choked on the dust and their transmissions labored in the heat and heavy traffic of Baghdad's streets.

Iraq has refused to accept any more cars until those already delivered are fixed, so GM has tripled its staff of engineers and mechanics in Baghdad, where they are installing supplementary air filters and changing clutches. Meanwhile, 12,000 cars are still sitting on acres of rented space in Canada, and GM is not certain that it will earn a profit even if Iraq accepts and pays for those automobiles.

Source: Peggy Berkowitz, "GM Runs Into a Middle East Crisis: It's Too Hot and Dusty in Baghdad," *The Wall Street Journal,* February 23, 1982, 37.

costs of product adaptation, even though precise estimates of such costs might eventually have to be made by the firm's engineers or production managers.

Inasmuch as the product is only one of several elements in a business firm's total marketing program or "marketing mix," it is quite possible for marketing managers to respond to dissimilarities among their overseas markets by altering something other than the product. They might, for example, choose to keep their product the same and to utilize different promotional messages or methods in order to overcome any cultural resistance to their wares that they encountered in a foreign country. Here the managers would, in essence, be attempting to adapt the foreign culture to their product, rather than adapting the product to the culture. Although this might at first appear to be an exceptionally ambitious undertaking, the fact is that advertising and other promotional activities conducted by international corporations have had an enormous impact upon consumer tastes and preferences around the world and have often been cited, by both critics and admirers, as a powerful instrument for bringing about cultural change. The use of advertising by international marketing managers will be considered in the next section.

Advertising in International Markets

Advertising is one of several promotional or communications efforts that business firms undertake in order to inform consumers and to influence their purchasing decisions. Promotion also includes the more direct communication between the company and its customers that is accomplished through personal selling, as well as a host of other activities—such as exhibits, distribution of samples, and the use of money-saving coupons—that are referred to collectively as *sales promotion*. This discussion will concentrate on advertising, as this aspect of promotion has received the most attention in relation to international marketing, and much of what has been stated with regard to international advertising is also applicable to other forms of promotion.

A company that is trying to sell in many different national markets has to make the same primary choice in advertising that it confronts with respect to its product. Should it develop a single "message" and employ the same methods for transmitting that message for all those markets, or should it devise separate themes and vary its communications media whenever this seems warranted by local market traits? The principal arguments for the first option of worldwide standardization include the familiar ones of minimizing costs (in this case, the costs of creating and producing advertisements) and maximizing the parent organization's control over the manner in which its product is promoted around the world. The case for standardization may also be strengthened by the argument that the motives for buying many products are essentially the same everywhere, and that a single advertising concept should therefore suffice to appeal to all consumers regardless of their nationalities.

Although these points in favor of standardizing international advertising (with necessary allowances for such obvious problems as language differences) can be quite persuasive, there are some compelling reasons why a high degree of standardization may either be impractical or may lessen the effectiveness of the advertising. Probably the most basic of these reasons rises out of the fact that advertising is essentially a communications process, through which someone (the advertiser) is endeavoring to convey information and ideas to someone else (potential customers), usually with the hope of eliciting some positive behavior (purchasing the advertiser's product) from the recipient of the information. The fundamental difficulty with a standardized international advertising program, which typically is devised and controlled by the advertising staff of the parent organization, is that the source of the advertising message resides in one cultural milieu, while the intended receivers of the message come from entirely different and dissimilar cultural backgrounds. The advertising message consequently may have to penetrate a multitude of cultural differences that separate the sender from the receivers, and there is thus a high probability that its meaning will be distorted or its intended effect lost.

Box 15.2

A Beer-Maker's International Advertising Strategy

Peter de Lange, Heineken, N.V.'s corporate advertising manager, is viewing one of the Dutch beer company's French commercials. On the screen, a middle-aged actor with an air of savoir-faire about him holds a glass of Heineken to the light, as if it were a fine wine. He coos about its "finesse," its refined taste.

This is a beer commercial?

Mais oui, the tongue-in-cheek commercial, Mr. de Lange explains, was the opening salvo of an ad campaign to entice the French, a nation of wine drinkers, to buy more beer. He translates the slogan roughly: "Heineken's going to make you love beer." Sipping a glass of Heineken, Mr. de Lange adds, "It's a very good example of how one should approach the French market."

With beer sales in many countries flattening, Heineken is trying to increase its share of existing markets and targeting new markets for growth. But instead of adopting a single multinational ad campaign—which has become fashionable in the advertising world— Heineken is tailoring its advertising to each market.

Heineken beer is brewed to look the same and taste the same nearly everywhere. And, with a few exceptions, Heineken sells itself as a high-class beer worth the extra cost. Otherwise, Heineken tailors its sales pitch to each market. Beer, more than most products, has cultural idiosyncrasies, Heineken says. "In beer drinking, emotion plays a role," says Mr. de Lange.

In developing separate ad campaigns for countries as diverse as Italy, Japan, and Greece, Heineken is displaying the strategy that has made the once-obscure Dutch brewer the biggest beer maker based in Europe and the brewer with the most extensive international operation. "They are very good marketers," says an executive at a major competitor.

Source: Richard L. Hudson, "Competition Gets Scrappy in Heineken's Beer Markets," *The Wall Street Journal*, August 24, 1984, 20. Represented by permission of *The Wall Street Journal*, © Dow Jones & Company, Inc. 1984. All Rights Reserved.

Much of the potential for such distortion or loss of effectiveness is attributable to variations in the meanings and connotations of the symbols that are used to convey the advertising message. Advertisers make use of various symbols, including words, pictures, and colors, to transmit the message that they are attempting to impart to their audience. However, the same symbol is likely to connote very different things or to invoke dissimilar images among people from different cultural backgrounds. The literature on international marketing is replete with examples of advertising "blunders," in which advertisers based in one country (notably the United States) have naively used familiar words, expressions, pictures, or colors in ads designed for other countries and have subsequently discovered that those ads have appeared ridiculous or offensive due to cultural differences in the interpretations of the words or other symbols employed.

One means of avoiding or minimizing such problems is to "localize" advertising, by having those ads that are to be used in each national market produced within that market, or, at least, prepared by persons who are thoroughly familiar with the indigenous culture. This eliminates the aforementioned cultural barrier that separates the source from the recipients in a standardized international advertising program, but may simultaneously wipe out some or all the cost savings and centralized control that come from such standardization.

Cultural incongruities among markets are by no means the only deterrent to a standardized worldwide advertising program. A company's efforts to implement such a program may also be frustrated by considerations relating to **advertising media.**

Both the actual presence of media such as television, radio, magazines, and their availability for use by advertisers vary greatly from country to country. These divergences frequently are a function of differences in the level of economic development or the state of technology—for instance, one would logically expect a lower incidence of television ownership and usage in a poor, developing country than in a wealthy, economically advanced country. However, the availability of media for advertising may also be affected by legal factors. Almost all nations have laws that apply to the use of communications media for advertising purposes, and such laws are far from uniform. The advertising managers of an international firm therefore are likely to find that they are unable to schedule comparable media presentations in all their national markets due to regulatory anomalies.

Even when the same media are physically and legally available, the advertising managers must contend with intercountry variations in the **coverage** provided by each medium and in the *cost* associated with that coverage. The detailed audience analyses that are provided by various media rating bureaus in the United States generally are less available in other countries, so it is difficult for advertisers to ascertain the exact amount and type of coverage that would be obtained from ads placed in particular foreign media. But even a cursory examination of available data pertaining to television and radio ownership, newspaper readership, magazine circulation, and literacy rates reveals sharp divergences in these indicators of media coverage from one nation to another. This clearly implies that a company could not realistically expect to reach the

"How about it, Don Pedro—a thousand pesetas just to shout an endorsement of Rodriguez' Wine during the 'moment of truth'?"

Source: © 1957, Sports Illustrated. Reprinted by permission of Ed Fisher.

same number and kind of potential customers in all national markets by simply duplicating its pattern of media usage in advertising, nor could it count on obtaining its desired coverage by allocating its media budget in the same manner everywhere. In short, a completely standardized approach to the use of advertising media would stand little chance of yielding satisfactory coverage at an acceptable cost in the face of the great differences that exist in media audiences around the world.

Since there are solid economic and organizational advantages to be gained from standardized international advertising, but there is sufficient diversity among national market environments to raise doubts about the practicability and effectiveness of standardization, it is not surprising that there has been a long-standing controversy among members of the advertising profession over the standardization versus localization question. In the meantime, international corporations have had to move ahead with their advertising programs, and have usually worked out pragmatic compromises between the two poles of world-wide uniformity and total conformity to the specific conditions of individual markets.

International Pricing Strategies

Deciding what prices to charge for its products, when to change those prices, and whether or not to grant discounts or rebates to certain customers are crucial decisions for any business firm, and are seldom arrived at easily. As is true of the other elements of a marketing program, pricing tends to become even more complicated when the company involved is offering its products to buyers in more than one national market. Marketing theory asserts that a business firm's market objectives—that is, what it is trying to accomplish in that market—should be the fundamental basis for determining what pricing strategy it should follow. But an international company may often be pursuing different objectives in each of the national markets that it is serving, and may therefore need to develop distinct pricing policies for those individual markets.

As a simple hypothetical example, an American company might be attempting to build a permanent market position in one foreign country in order to gain long-term profits from the anticipated growth of that country's economy. At the same time, this company could be looking for quick, short-term profits in another foreign country that it did not regard as a viable locale for a continuing commitment. These differing market objectives could well result in the firm's choosing quite different pricing methods, perhaps setting a moderate price in order to establish its products solidly in the first country for the long haul, while using higher prices to "skim the cream" from the market of the second country.

The pursuit of differing market objectives is only part of the explanation for the complications that an international company encounters in its pricing practices. The prices a firm can charge are also affected by the environmental conditions and constraints of the marketplace, and international firms must cope with all of the variables that normally influence pricing in their home markets, plus some that are unique to foreign marketing operations. These variables impose definite limits on the discretion and flexibility that marketing managers have in setting prices for their products.

Certain market forces typically operate at the upper end or "ceiling" of a firm's pricing structure, that is, they restrict the firm's ability to charge high prices or to raise prices above their present level. Meanwhile, other factors set a lower limit or "floor" on prices. The combined effect of these variables therefore is to create a kind of "box" within which prices must lie if the company is to have a reasonable chance of success in selling its products.

This concept is illustrated diagrammatically in Figure 15.1, which points out that pricing strategies should be based on the firm's market objectives. But it also indicates that the managers of a firm enjoy only a limited range of discretion in pricing, with the upper and lower limits (ceiling and floor) of that range being imposed by a variety of factors.

The lists of "limiting factors" appearing in Figure 15.1 includes many (but not necessarily all) of the economic, institutional, and legal factors with which international managers must deal as they fashion pricing strategies for foreign markets. As mentioned previously, these phenomena are not encountered only in foreign countries; however, they frequently exert a greater impact on the pricing process there than they would in the company's domestic market. This concept can be dem-

---

Figure 15.1   **Factors Affecting Pricing Decisions**

	Limiting Factors:	Demand (Purchasing Power)
		Competition
		Government Price Controls
		Middlemen
		Exchange rates

| **Market Objectives** ⟶ | Pricing Strategy | Range of Managerial Discretion |

	Limiting Factors:	Cost of Operations
		Government Regulations
		Middlemen
		Inflation
		Competition

---

onstrated by briefly considering how these various factors might affect the pricing decisions of an international company.

Purchasing Power

Purchasing power is always a major consideration in pricing decisions. But international companies must pay particular heed to the necessity of maintaining a realistic relationship between their prices and the purchasing power of their prospective customers, due to the vast disparities in consumer incomes that exist around the world. American companies and their managers may be especially prone to pricing errors resulting from overestimating the purchasing power of foreign buyers, since their usual frame of reference for price making has been the American economy, where the levels of personal income and wealth are among the highest in the world.

Price Controls

Government controls on prices constitute another common feature of foreign markets that act as constraints on the pricing flexibility of international firms. These often take the form of price ceilings that are applied to essential services or widely used consumer staples. In addition to such direct controls, governments can also restrict the freedom of international companies to charge high prices by setting legal limits on the amounts of profits those firms can earn or the amount they are permitted to transfer out of the host country.

The government regulations with which international companies must contend relate not only to the upper end of the pricing range, but also to the lower end. One very widespread and significant group of pricing controls of this latter type consists of the **antidumping laws** which are found in almost every important trading nation of the world. Although the specifics of these laws vary, their common aim is to prevent foreign-made products from being priced so low as to pose a severe competitive threat to domestic producers. A country's antidumping laws prohibit imported goods from being offered for sale at prices lower than those which would be charged for the same goods in the exporting firm's home market. If the government discovers that such pricing practices are being employed and that those practices are causing economic injury to local producers, it can order the prices raised and assess heavy penalties against the offending companies.

The economic rationality of these antidumping laws continues to be a subject of debate among economists and others that are involved in developing and enforcing international trade policies. Whatever their economic merits, however, such laws are a fact of life that international business firms must recognize in formulating their prices. Furthermore, the incidence and scope of these laws, and the strictness with which they are enforced, all have been increasing as international competition has intensified and industrialists in many countries have called on their governments for more protection against imports.

Middlemen

A company that produces goods to be marketed overseas is likely to find that its discretion with regard to pricing becomes subject to the policies and wishes of the middlemen that are handling those goods. The necessity to share pricing authority with middlemen is often more acute in foreign markets, simply because the producing firm has fewer choices with respect to the marketing intermediaries that it can utilize to distribute its products. This problem of availability of marketing channels will be discussed further in the next section. But it is relevant to the current consideration of pricing strategies, since the great majority of international companies must rely upon the services and facilities of independent middlemen for at least part of the widespread market coverage they are seeking.

In Figure 15.1, middlemen appear as limiting factors on both sides of the pricing range. This is intended to point out the possibility that foreign middlemen might pressure a company to hold down prices on the products which they are handling in order to help them achieve or maintain the sales volume they consider necessary for profitable operations. On the other hand, middlemen might resist any efforts on the part of the producing firm to set low prices, insofar as that could reduce their own markups and profit margins on the products involved.

Competition

As is the case with foreign middlemen, the competitors a company meets in its overseas markets are capable of imposing both upper and lower limits on its prices. The top-side limitations are relatively easy to comprehend, since it is obvious that companies generally cannot charge prices that exceed those of their competitors by a greater amount than is justified by quality differences or other aspects of product differentiation. Any company that prices too far above its competition is almost sure to experience grievous declines in its sales volume and market share.

The ways in which competitive considerations curb the ability of an international firm to set prices as low as it might otherwise choose to do are a bit less obvious, but can be as compelling as those that restrain high pricing. One such consideration is the ill-will an international company might generate if it blatantly undercuts the prices of local competitors in its foreign markets. Such pricing practices may arouse nationalistic feelings and public resentment, and thereby lead to punitive actions against the firm by the political authorities. In addition to this element of political risk, pricing below local competitors may lead some prospective customers to believe that the international company is attempting to market an inferior or low-quality product.

Costs of Operations

If a business enterprise is to survive over the long term, the prices it sets for its products must be high enough to cover its costs of operations and to provide an acceptable return (profit) to its owners. These costs and profit requirements thus establish a lower limit to the firm's prices in the long run. There can be many occasions or situations, however, in which a firm finds it necessary or beneficial to price *some* of its output below the *full cost* of producing and distributing it. At such times, the firm may turn to what the economists call variable-cost (or marginal-cost) pricing. This entails setting prices that will defray the additional direct costs incurred in producing a certain quantity of output, but that may not completely cover the fixed costs or "overhead" that ordinarily would be charged against that output.

Variable-cost pricing clearly merits consideration in the development of an international company's pricing strategies, since such a company will be directing portions of its total output to several separate national markets, with dissimilar demand and competitive conditions. The use of variable-cost pricing in some of those markets might enable the firm to overcome competition or to gain quick acceptance of its products, while its prices and revenues in other markets are kept high enough to defray all of its fixed costs. Variable-cost pricing must be used with discretion, inasmuch as prices that appear too low may raise suspicions of dumping, and no company can afford to neglect its fixed costs entirely or indefinitely. But it does provide an option for international managers who might find it difficult to establish a foothold in many foreign markets if they had to price strictly on a full-cost basis.

Trying to maintain a rational relationship between operating costs and prices becomes more difficult for a firm when it is marketing internationally because it then must take account of "new" or higher costs resulting from foreign operations. Inasmuch as products usually must be transported over greater distances and be handled by more middlemen than would be the case in domestic marketing, the costs of the distribution process consequently rise. In addition, products are likely to be subject to import duties or other taxes that would not be levied if they were being manufactured and marketed in a single country, and those taxes must be treated as costs that have to be recovered in the prices of the products. These are only a few of many **incremental** costs associated with international marketing.

Such incremental costs create a pricing dilemma for an international firm. If it tries to pass all these costs along to buyers in its overseas markets, the prices that it must charge are apt to escalate so sharply as to jeopardize sales. But if the firm decides to absorb some of these costs itself, its profit margins will be correspondingly reduced. There is no general solution for this dilemma. Each firm must deal with it by searching for ways to cut incremental costs when feasible, while simultaneously studying the demand characteristics in its various foreign markets to ascertain whether and how much it can permit prices to escalate before sales volumes would be reduced by unacceptable amounts.

Inflation

Individual business firms that are operating in a nation where prices in general are rising rapidly and continuously must employ pricing tactics that take account of that inflationary trend. Inasmuch as inflation is almost certain to include increases in what businesses must pay for the labor, materials, capital goods, and other inputs that they utilize, any company that fails to keep its own prices abreast of those cost increases may soon experience serious financial problems. A fundamental principle that applies to such situations is that the firm should base the prices of its products on **replacement cost,** that is, what it will cost to replace the output that is currently being sold, rather than on **historical cost,** which is what the firm actually paid for the inputs that were used to produce that output.

The United States has experienced persistent inflation since the late 1960s, and American companies consequently have become somewhat used to pricing under inflationary conditions. But the lessons learned from the U.S. experience, where inflation has been relatively moderate, may not fully prepare American companies that are operating internationally for the extreme rates of inflation that are found in some foreign countries. In certain Latin American nations, for example, it is not unusual for the general price level to double, or even triple, during a single year. Such hyperinflationary conditions make it imperative that managers be constantly alert to the impact of spiraling prices on their companies' costs and financial positions, and that they continuously adjust their own prices upward in order to keep their sales revenues rising in concert with the increase in their operating costs. Inflation can thus become the dominant consideration in developing and implementing pricing policies, and it may occupy the bulk of the time and attention of the managers who are responsible for those policies.

Exchange Rates

The prices at which national currencies are exchanged for one another affect the calculations and decisions of interntional companies in a multitude of ways, many of which have been explored in Chapters 10 and 11 of this text. Exchange rates also enter into the pricing decisions of such firms. A company that is selling its products for currencies other than its own "home" currency must, of necessity, be sensitive to the impact that exchange rate changes can have on the foreign market demand for those products and on its own sales revenues, even though it usually cannot control that impact completely.

With regard to exchange rates and pricing policies, perhaps the most basic and critical decision an international company must make is how it will react to exchange rate changes in the pricing of its products. This is often a tough decision, since it usually would be impractical for a company to alter its prices in response to each and every fluctuation in rates of exchange. But it would be irresponsible—and possibly disastrous—for the company to ignore such fluctuations altogether.

This sort of quandary can be exemplified by considering a hypothetical American company that might have been caught up in some actual recent developments in exchange rate relationships. Assume that this company was producing a product in the United States for sale in Mexico, and that the cost of producing that product was $2.00 per unit. If it cost an additional $1.00 per unit to ship the product into Mexico and to provide an acceptable markup or profit margin for the company, the total price, in dollars, that the company would have to realize for each unit of the product sold would be $3.00. For many years prior to 1982, the exchange rate between the Mexican peso and the U.S. dollar was approximately 25 pesos to the dollar. At that rate, the price at which the company's product could be sold in Mexico would have been roughly 75 pesos per unit.

During 1982, serious internal economic problems and foreign trade deficits results in massive devaluation of the Mexican peso. Its value fell as low as 155 pesos to the dollar at one time, and a new official rate was eventually set at 95 pesos to the dollar. Thus, the price of the dollar in terms of pesos almost quadrupled in the space of a few months.

What should the (hypothetical) American company's reaction be to an exchange rate change of this magnitude? If the company continued to offer its product for sale in Mexico for 75 pesos, its peso revenues obviously would not convert into nearly enough dollars to cover its costs of production and transportation, much less return any profit. But if, on the other hand, the company decided to respond to the sharp devaluation of the peso by raising the price of its product in Mexico sufficiently to continue earning $3.00 per unit in U.S. currency, it would have to increase the price from 75 pesos to nearly 300 pesos per unit! Such a drastic price increase might very well eliminate the demand for the product in the Mexican market.

The preceding example may be somewhat extreme, inasmuch as currency values ordinarily do not change as rapidly and dramatically as the value of the Mexican peso did during 1982. Nevertheless, the example serves to illustrate the sort of pricing problems that can result from exchange rate changes, as well as the kinds of difficult decisions that international firms and their managers may face as a consequence of such changes. The volatility of exchange rates thus occupies a prominent place in the list of factors that add to the complexity of formulating and implementing an effective international pricing strategy.

International Channels of Distribution

International companies must develop a system of marketing intermediaries and facilities to deliver their products to overseas markets and distribute them within those markets. These channels of distribution are not only essential for the physical movement of products; they must also help to ensure that the products will be available at the time and place, and in the form and quantities desired by customers. In addition, the institutions making up the marketing channels are directly involved in arranging for transfer of title to the products on terms that are satisfactory to everyone involved in such transactions.

As a general rule, the channels of distribution needed for marketing internationally tend to be lengthier and more intricate than those required for a domestic marketing operation. This is partly due to the greater geographic distances involved in transporting products between countries. But economic, legal, and cultural factors often add to the complexity of international and foreign channel structures. In many foreign countries, for example, distribution channels are made up of numerous small-scale marketing organizations, which frequently are family enterprises that provide employment to many family members. Although such miniature marketing organizations may appear to be grossly overstaffed, undercapitalized, and inefficient from the perspective of large international corporations, such corporations often find that custom, social considerations, and even political pressures make it necessary to deal with these cumbersome distribution systems.

Channels of distribution can be developed by creating new marketing organizations or by utilizing the services of already existing marketing middlemen. Thus, each company must decide whether it should set up and operate its own distribution channels, rely upon independent middlemen, or combine the two approaches. Once this basic decision has been made, the firm still faces the task of determining exactly what kind of marketing facilities it should establish or which middlemen it should select to handle its products.

Channel Selection Criteria

A number of different factors will affect these international channel decisions. Not the least of these is the **availability** of acceptable marketing middlemen. Business firms that have enjoyed the luxury of being able to choose from many available marketing organizations to distribute their products in their home markets frequently find their choices much more limited in foreign countries. Such scarcity of marketing intermediaries is apt to be most acute in developing countries, where modern distribution systems have not yet emerged, and this can be a particularly troublesome problem for companies that are attempting to market products that—because of their newness or technical complexity—require a strong marketing push or extensive support facilities.

Closely related to the availability factor is the question of what specific *functions* a company expects its marketing middlemen to perform. The contributions of middlemen can range from merely keeping a company's products on hand for sale to customers who seek those products out, to actively participating in every phase of the marketing program from product development to aftersales servicing. Each company has to determine what role it wants its channel members to play and then attempt to locate middlemen that are able and willing to fill such a role. This can be a formidable task when a company is trying to develop international distribution channels, since foreign middlemen may not view the marketing process in the same way that the company does and may be used to operating in ways that are not consistent with the company's policies and procedures. Moreover, foreign marketing organizations often are too small and poorly equipped to perform a wide range of marketing functions. International companies therefore frequently find it necessary to provide financing or other forms of assistance to these middlemen in order to ensure that the marketing job will be completely and properly done.

In addition to considering the marketing functions that need to be performed by its overseas distribution channels, a company must also define the amount of market **coverage** that those channels should provide. Coverage may be conceptualized in geographic terms, that is, a company might wish to have its products available to customers in certain geographic portions of a foreign country. But coverage might also refer to the absolute volume of sales that the firm needs to attain in a foreign country in order to make marketing in that country profitable, or to a percentage share of the existing or potential market that the company wants to gain. Regardless of which of these measures of market coverage a company is emphasizing, it will have to set up a distribution system that will be capable of fulfilling these coverage plans.

At least two other factors figure prominently in the choice of international distribution channels. One of these is **control,** specifically the question of who will control the various activities and procedures that make up the marketing program. Since most international companies must rely to some extent on independent marketing middlemen, they must confront this question and decide how much influence they want to maintain over the manner in which their products are marketed abroad. Those companies that are unwilling to simply relinquish their managerial authority—and it probably is safe to assert that the vast majority of international firms would fall into this category—have to work out either formal agreements or informal understandings with their middlemen that clearly delineate the scope and boundaries of each party's managerial discretion. Sharing managerial control is seldom easy, so it is essential that companies choose middlemen with whom they stand a good chance of establishing and sustaining mutually acceptable and effective relationships.

Finally, there is the always-important consideration of **costs;** in this case, the costs of establishing and operating channels of distribution.

Companies must endeavor to get their products distributed at the lowest possible cost, while maintaining the level of distribution services that their customers and their own standards demand. This requires careful comparisons of the relative costs of alternative distribution structures and methods, with a view toward minimizing costs without damaging the quality of the distribution process or relations with customers.

Attempts to hold down the costs of distribution very often entail the sacrifice of other channel goals. Channel costs might be reduced, for example, if a company were willing to accept limitations on the market coverage provided by its middlemen or on the functions that those middlemen perform. Costs might also be lower if the company did not try to exercise close control over the actions of the middlemen that are handling its products. Thus, in developing their channels of distribution, international firms are constantly striving to strike a practical balance between costs and their other channel objectives.

International Channel Structures

As noted above, the distribution channels utilized to market internationally generally are lengthier and more complex than those associated with marketing within a single country. This results naturally from the fact that international marketing, particularly exporting, involves movements of products between, as well as within, different countries. Not only do such products traverse great physical distances, but they also tend to pass through the hands of numerous middlemen in their route from producer to ultimate consumer.

There are many different types of these export marketing middlemen. Indeed, a company that is selecting middlemen for its export marketing channels may find the variety of such organizations bewildering. Moreover, these organizations tend to be nonspecialized and opportunistic, since they attempt to perform whatever marketing functions or services their client companies need. This makes it difficult to draw sharp distinctions among exporting middlemen or to precisely delineate alternative international channel structures. It is possible, however, to describe some of the channel options that are available for carrying on export marketing operations.

Figure 15.2 illustrates one such option. It represents the channel structure that a hypothetical U.S. manufacturing company might utilize to get its products to buyers (those buyers could conceivably be either business firms, government agencies, or individual consumers) in a foreign country. In this illustration, the firm is presumed to prefer **direct exporting,** that is, utilizing its own marketing facilities and personnel to the greatest practical extent.[1]

The American manufacturing firm in this model has established a **foreign sales subsidiary.** This term refers to a company, owned entirely

---

[1]Direct and indirect exporting were described more fully in Chapter 1 of this text.

Figure 15.2   Channel of Distribution Model—Direct Exporting

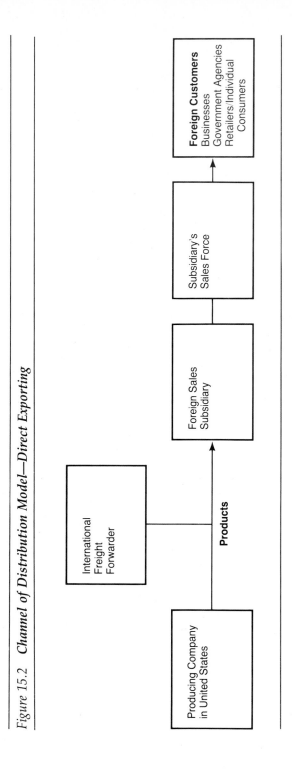

or partially by the manufacturer, that is set up to assist in marketing the manufacturer's products in the foreign country (or, perhaps, in a larger region). The range of marketing activities that are actually performed by such foreign subsidiaries varies greatly from company to company, as do the sizes of their personnel staffs and physical facilities. In all instances, however, these subsidiaries give their parent firms a tangible "presence" in their overseas markets, as well as proximity to their foreign customers, both of which can be highly beneficial in conducting a foreign marketing program.

This model also shows the firm utilizing the services of an **international freight forwarder.** These are organizations that specialize in arranging and expediting the physical movement of products from country to country. Their services usually include selecting economical transportation routes and carriers, consolidating shipments so as to qualify for lower transportation charges, securing and preparing the many documents that are required when goods are being shipped from country to country, and clearing such shipments through the customs agencies of the exporting and importing countries. The knowledge and experience provided by freight forwarders, together with their ability to spread the costs of their transportation-related functions among a number of clients, often makes it cheaper and more efficient for companies to employ these organizations than to try to perform such functions for themselves.

The direct exporting approach exemplified in this channel model involves the use of a sales force employed by the foreign subsidiary. If the customers in the foreign market were business firms or government agencies, the subsidiary's sales personnel probably would be selling to them directly; if the final customers were individuals or households, the subsidiary's sales would more likely be made to retail establishments that would resell to those final customers.

Figure 15.3 illustrates alternative channel arrangements that might be employed by a company that had decided upon a more indirect form of exporting operation. Indirect exporting basically entails the use of middlemen that are not owned by the company whose products are being marketed abroad. These may be either **merchant** middlemen (those which take legal title to the products involved) or **agent** middlemen (those which do not take title, but market the products under a contractual relationship with the producer). Figure 15.3 also lists a few representative examples of the many different types of marketing institutions that actually comprise these two categories of exporting middlemen.[2] The following brief description highlights some of the distinguishing features of these organizations.

---

[2]More detailed descriptions of international marketing intermediaries can be found in standard texts on international marketing. See, for example, Philip R. Cateora, *International Marketing,* 5th ed. (Homewood, IL: Irwin, 1983), Chapter 18.

Figure 15.3   Channel of Distribution Model—Indirect Exporting

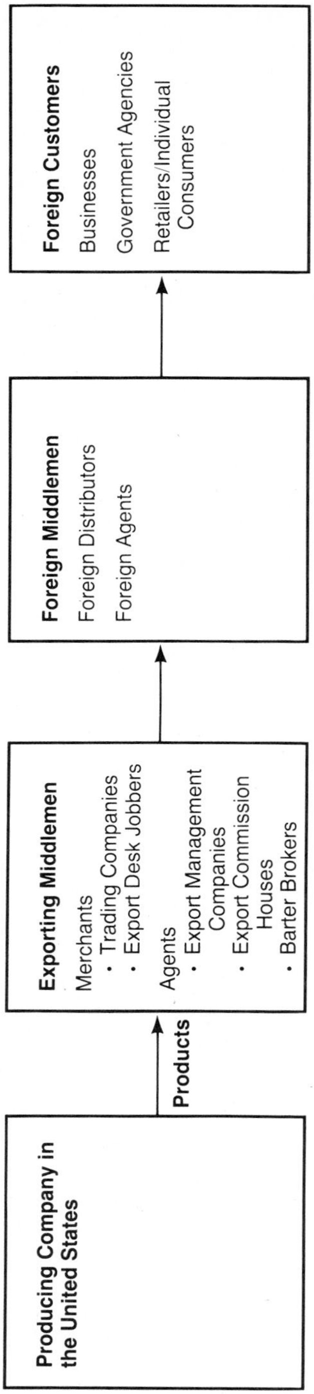

Producing Company in the United States

→ **Products** →

Exporting Middlemen

Merchants
· Trading Companies
· Export Desk Jobbers

Agents
· Export Management Companies
· Export Commission Houses
· Barter Brokers

Foreign Middlemen

Foreign Distributors

Foreign Agents

Foreign Customers

Businesses

Government Agencies

Retailers/Individual Consumers

1. Trading companies. These concerns typically purchase manufactured products from numerous producing firms and subsequently market those products in foreign areas, often through wholesaling and retailing facilities operated by the trading company. Many trading companies are large-scale organizations, and frequently become involved in shipping and financing in addition to their marketing operations. The earliest trading companies included such historically important enterprises as the British and Dutch East India Companies and the Hudson's Bay Company, and the contemporary version includes the giant conglomerates that dominate the Japanese economy and have spearheaded Japan's post–World War II development as a major force in international markets.

2. Export desk jobbers. These merchant middlemen specialize in marketing staple commodities, such as agricultural goods, raw materials, lumber, and basic metals. They purchase such goods for resale and they generally aim to match those purchases with orders that they already have in hand. They do not ordinarily take physical possession of the bulky commodities in which they deal.

3. Export management companies. These agents (also referred to as combination export managers) essentially act as external exporting departments for companies whose exporting volume or experience may be too limited to justify the establishment of such departments internally. Although their basic functions are to locate foreign markets for their clients' products and arrange sales in those markets, they may also carry out promotional and financing activities and arrange transportation for overseas shipments.

4. Export commission houses. These are actually purchasing agents for single buyers or groups of buyers, who place orders that the commission houses attempt to fill from suppliers in the countries in which their offices are located. As an example, a commission house in the United States might be engaged in buying products from American manufacturers in response to orders that the commission house had received from retail stores in Europe.

5. Barter brokers. During the past several years, there has been a striking revival of barter transactions in international commerce, as many nations have attempted to conserve their scarce foreign exchange reserves and dispose of hard-to-sell domestic products by offering such products in direct trade for foreign goods. Such barter deals have created a need for intermediaries that could assist companies to sell goods that they have accepted in trade, and this kind of specialized service is the forte of organizations known as either barter brokers or intermerchants.

The marketing organizations described above are oftentimes referred to as **domestic** exporting middlemen, since they usually are located in the same country as the firms whose products they are handling. They can also be thought of as constituting the portion of the international

---

Box 15.3

Big U.S. Exporters: Japanese Trading Companies

Some of the biggest exporters of American products are the giant Japanese trading companies, which buy U.S. products for resale in Japan and around the world. It is estimated that the American subsidiaries of such firms as Mitsui & Company and Mitsubishi Corporation account for about 10 percent of all U.S. exports. They are among the largest exporters of grain, minerals, chemicals, and machinery from the U.S.

These companies are helping to market products for medium-sized U.S. manufacturers and have been emphasizing their positive contribution to the U.S. trade balance. They also are gradually winning the acceptance of American businessmen and are moving American personnel up in their managerial ranks.

Source: Eduardo Lachica, "Unlikely U.S. Exporter: Japan," *The Wall Street Journal*, November 11, 1981, 31.

---

marketing channel that is primarily concerned with transferring products *between* countries. The remaining portion of a complete international channel structure is made up of marketing intermediaries involved in distributing the products *within* foreign countries.

In Figure 15.3, these foreign middlemen are identified simply as foreign distributors or foreign agents. In reality, there are a multitude of types of marketing institutions that can be used to distribute a company's products in foreign markets, and both the functions and the local designations of such organizations vary greatly from country to country. Thus, the terms that appear in the channel model presented in Figure 15.3 refer very broadly to any of this assortment of merchant or agent middlemen that a producing firm relies on to market its products in foreign countries.

Such middlemen are very important links in an international distribution chain. They not only supply the physical facilities and selling efforts that are required for marketing successfully in foreign countries, but they can also give the companies that utilize their service the benefits of established customer contacts, intimate knowledge of local market conditions, and experience in dealing with those conditions. The careful selection of these middlemen, and the maintenance of sound working relationships with them, therefore are a crucial part of the job of developing effective international channels of distribution.

Conclusion

This chapter has examined the marketing process from the perspective of a business firm that is marketing on an international scale. It has emphasized that a firm undertaking international marketing will experience many problems that might not be encountered in a domestic marketing program, and it has identified some of the more significant of those problems as they affect different elements of the marketing mix. It has also pointed out certain ways in which these difficulties can be dealt with. Although the chapter has stressed the complications of international marketing, it is important to keep in mind that international markets offer rich opportunities for those companies whose managers are sufficiently farsighted to perceive such opportunities and sufficiently adaptable and innovative to cope with the challenges they pose.

Summary

1.   Although the functions involved in marketing a business firm's products do not change in any substantive way when the firm begins to market them internationally, the marketing task will be expanded and complicated due to the greater number and diversity of the environmental factors with which marketing managers must contend.

2.   The most fundamental decision that an international firm must make with respect to its international marketing program has to do with the extent to which it should adapt that program to the divergent environmental conditions that exist in its various foreign markets.

3.   The anticipated benefits of "tailoring" products and marketing techniques to fit the needs of individual foreign markets must be weighed against the costs that invariably result from such modifications.

4.   With regard to the product(s) to be marketed abroad, international companies must choose from among alternative strategies of product extension, product invention, or rational product adaptation. This choice entails analyses of environmental conditions in the foreign markets, of the product(s) themselves, and of the costs of product modification.

5.   The development and implementation of an international advertising program also involves a basic choice between standardizing or localizing the advertising message itself and the media utilized to deliver that message. Cultural differences among national markets constitute a strong argument for localized advertising, whereas considerations of cost and control support standardization.

6.   Different objectives in foreign markets often make it necessary
      for a company to adopt different pricing policies in each of those
      markets, but a company's range of discretion in setting prices is
      typically constrained by a number of conditions or forces that
      limit pricing flexibility.

7.   The channels of distribution that are needed to effectively mar-
      ket products internationally tend to be lengthier and more com-
      plex than those associated with domestic marketing. A firm must
      consider many factors—including the availability of middlemen
      and the functions they should perform, the extent of market
      coverage desired, and the degree of control the firm wishes to
      maintain over the marketing of its products—in developing its
      international distribution channels.

Questions for Review or Discussion

1.   Why might the environmental differences that exist in different
      foreign countries be expected to have an especially strong effect
      on a company's *marketing* operations?

2.   Why is it usually costly for a business firm to depart from a
      standardized marketing program in order to respond to the diver-
      gent conditions found in foreign markets? List some of the addi-
      tional costs that a firm might incur as a result of: (a) product
      modifications and (b) changes in its advertising program.

3.   What is meant by a worldwide product extension strategy? What
      circumstances or product characteristics might make such a strat-
      egy practical?

4.   What is meant by a *rational* product adaptation strategy? How
      can a firm determine how much product adaptation and what
      kind of adaptation is required for a particular foreign market and
      whether or not such adaptation is "rational"?

5.   Explain the following statement: "The fundamental difficulty
      with a standardized international advertising program is that the
      source of the advertising message resides in one cultural milieu,
      while the intended receivers of the message come from entirely
      different and dissimilar cultural backgrounds."

6.   What kinds of media considerations might make it difficult or
      impractical for a company to carry out a standardized interna-
      tional advertising program?

7.   Explain the difference between full-cost pricing and variable-cost
      pricing and indicate some of the circumstances that might make
      variable-cost pricing the best approach for a foreign market.

8.   What are antidumping laws? How can such laws affect the pric-
      ing policies of international companies?

9.   Explain how *inflation* and *exchange rate fluctuations* can influence
      the pricing strategies of companies that are marketing interna-
      tionally.

10. "Attempts to hold down the costs of distribution often entail the sacrifice of other channel goals." Explain this statement and give examples of the possible conflict between cost savings and the realization of other channel goals.

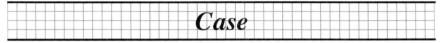

Case

Sunshine Products, Inc.

Joseph Cotton, vice-president for worldwide marketing of Sunshine Products, was considering his options for the advertising campaign to introduce the company's most recent product, a new toothpaste, Shine, that fights tooth decay and plaque significantly better than its existing toothpaste, Smile. Sunshine's advertising agency, Johnny Appleseed, Inc., suggested developing a series of advertising campaigns, each customized to reflect the local customs and practices in each of the 24 countries in which Sunshine wants to sell the new toothpaste Shine. However, a rival agency, Ryan McCann, Inc., made an impressive presentation strongly recommending a standardized international ad campaign for Shine.

Ryan McCann pointed out that a standardized international ad campaign has many advantages over a segmented, national market-by-national market, ad campaign. First, there is likely to be considerable savings in ad production costs since producing the local ads would require only translation and minor modifications of the main ad with a global theme. This global ad could therefore have a much larger production budget than could any of the individual-country ads, making possible a more sophisticated production using media stars with global followings. Second, such a global ad theme will help identify Shine with the upscale high-income professionals in each country who are thinking and shopping alike thanks to cheaper air travel and the new global telecommunications technology. They cite a number of very successful examples of global advertising. For example, "Madge the manicurist" is pitching Palmolive Liquid for Colgate in 22 countries, "Dallas" star Victoria Principal sells Jhirmack shampoo globally, Victor Kiam of Remington sells shavers in 15 languages, and "Mean Joe Green" commercials for Coca-Cola run in 14 countries. Companies like Eastman Kodak, Levi-Strauss, Gillette, and Timex have also been using global advertising for decades.

Johnny Appleseed, on the other hand, points to the need for customizing the ad campaign for the tastes and values in each market. They cite major cultural differences among nations as well as differences in government regulations. For example, because of government regulations, Philip Morris, maker of Marlboro cigarettes, had to eliminate the cowboy from its British commericals. Similarly, because of national cultural differences, Nestle customizes its coffee commercials for each market.

However, Cotton also noticed that most advertising agencies are now expanding their global capabilities and are themselves becoming multinational companies. For example, Ted Bates Worldwide, Inc. now gets half of its $2.6 billion in annual billings from overseas. By stressing the international theme, Saatchi and Saatchi, the aggressive new British ad agency, has become one of the largest and fastest growing major ad agencies.

What should Cotton do? He has to decide between the global and country-by-country ad campaign for Shine and make a final recommendation to Sunshine's president, Ann Miller, within a week.

Source: "Delicate Massage Job," *Forbes,* March 12, 1984, p. 196; and Anne B. Fisher, "The Ad Biz Gloms Onto 'Global'," FORTUNE, November 12, 1984, pp. 77–80.

Chapter 16

MULTINATIONAL FINANCIAL MANAGEMENT

Chapter Objectives

- *To point out and explain the particular financial opportunities and problems that affect international companies*
- *To describe the principal managerial strategies and tactics that multinational companies have utilized to take advantage of their financing opportunities and contend with their financing problems*
- *To analyze the concept of foreign exchange risk and the various ways in which exposure to that risk is defined and measured*
- *To illustrate the methods that multinational companies employ to reduce or avoid foreign exchange risk*
- *To consider the effects of taxation on multinational corporate decisions and operations*

Multinational corporations (MNCs), like all business firms, engage in a multitude of financing activities. They must raise funds, either from their stockholders or external sources, to pay for the fixed assets (e.g., land, buildings, equipment) they need to carry on production and related business operations. They must also earn or otherwise acquire funds to pay their workers and suppliers for the labor, materials, and energy that are utilized in those operations. Their managers must continually make choices among investment projects or other uses of the funds available to them in an effort to maximize the yield from those monetary assets while, at the same time, keeping the risk of loss within acceptable bounds and maintaining sufficient liquidity to meet current cash expenses. Finally, if all these financing functions have been performed well and managers have made sound financial choices, decisions must be made with regard to how profits should be allocated between payouts to shareholders and retention by the firm for reinvestment or as reserves for future contingencies.

Multinational firms enjoy some important financing advantages and opportunities that are not readily available to purely domestic firms. Their global scale of operations provides access to financial markets throughout the world, including the international money and capital markets (described in Chapter 10) and those of the individual countries in which the firms have affiliates. Meanwhile, their integrated organizational structures facilitate the moving of money or monetary assets from country to country. This gives the MNCs a wide range of options for both acquiring and investing funds, while enabling them to spread their financial dependency and risk by diversifying their funding sources and investment portfolios.

But multinational companies also face troublesome financing problems from which their domestic counterparts are largely immune. These grow out of a number of causes including: the necessity of dealing in many different national currencies with fluctuating relative values; the variations in financial conditions, such as the cost and availability of loanable funds and rates of inflation, that are found in the various nations in which operations are being conducted; the divergent financial systems, financing practices, and tax laws among those nations; and the existence of government controls on the transfer of funds from country to country.

Some of the financial aspects of doing business internationally have been examined previously in this text, especially in Chapters 10 and 11, which covered exchange rates and the financing of international trade through the foreign exchange markets. However, full consideration has not yet been given to how multinational firms respond to their unique financing opportunities and difficulties. This chapter will pursue that topic, by looking at the organization, practices, and problems of financial management in MNCs.

Multinational Financial Organization and Practices

Mention was made earlier of a tendency toward centralization of financial management among MNCs. This tendency becomes stronger as firms gain more experience in international operations and the size of those operations expands. Such centralization is typically effectuated either by having almost all financial decisions for the entire firm made by financial specialists in the parent company or international division, or by having those specialists develop policies and guidelines that individual affiliates must follow in making their financial decisions.

The basic aim of this centralization is to optimize financing activities and results for the entire multinational enterprise. Thus, by acquiring funds on a worldwide basis, an MNC presumably will be able to *minimize the overall cost* of the funding which the parent and affiliates collectively require. This is done by raising debt or equity capital wherever interest rates or the yields demanded by stock purchasers are lowest and then allocating those capital funds throughout the corporation. The firm may also realize some significant scale economies by employing this method of financing, inasmuch as the effective interest cost, as well as the administrative and clerical costs of borrowing, tend to be less per dollar raised when money is borrowed in large amounts. Moreover, lenders are apt to be more willing to lend and to charge lower interest when the loans are being solicited and guaranteed by a multinational parent company, rather than by a single affiliate.

Much the same approach can be applied to internal financing. Here decisions are made centrally with respect to how much of a multinational firm's total profits should be retained for reinvestment and how those retained earnings should be distributed among the affiliates for their use.

Multinationals also use centralized financial planning and management to *optimize the returns* from the investment of their available funds. Relying on a headquarters group of financial experts to identify and analyze investment opportunities around the globe is expected to result in the selection of investments with the highest anticipated rates of return.

Capital Budgeting

Such analyses involve capital budgeting, that is, the comparative assessment of alternative long-term investment projects. Capital budgeting becomes quite complicated in a multinational corporate setting, since such factors as the variability of exchange rates, differing levels of environmental risk among countries, unequal national tax burdens, and the possibility of governmental interference with the repatriation of investment income make it exceptionally difficult to calculate the net returns that the company can realistically expect to realize from projects that its affiliates are proposing to undertake in their various host countries. Notwithstanding these difficulties, the goal of global maximization of financial returns demands that multinational firms make such comparisons and allocate their investible funds accordingly.

Cash Management

Centralization of financial decisions and functions can benefit multinational companies in managing their short-term financing, as well as in their medium- and long-term sourcing and investing activities. International cash (or working capital) management, which involves a systematic, corporate-wide approach to the management of cash, accounts receivable and payable, and other liquid assets and liabilities, has become very widespread among multinational firms.

The objectives of these international cash management systems include: (1) reducing the costs that the firm incurs in acquiring and holding liquid assets. Those costs can be either explicit (e.g., the interest that has to be paid for obtaining cash through a short-term loan from a commercial bank) or implicit (e.g., the opportunity cost of having idle, excessive cash that could have been profitably invested); (2) protecting the value of those assets from depreciation due to inflation, exchange rate changes, and other eventualities; (3) making cash or short-term financing more readily available to all units of the firm; and (4) enhancing the returns the firm obtains from the liquid assets in its possession.

Pooling.   Although the design and mode of operation of international cash management systems vary from company to company, certain basic techniques are employed in virtually all such systems. One of these is **pooling,** which entails the accumulation of those liquid assets which exceed current needs into a single, central "pool." Contributions to such pools may come from all the affiliates of an MNC, or they may be accumulated on a regional or other subcorporate basis. Moreover, the notion of pooling of excess funds does not necessarily mean that those funds will actually be transferred to some central depository. It means, instead, that they will be brought under the *control* of one management group, which will decide how they can best be utilized.

That utilization will often involve intracorporate loans, in which affiliates or operating units that are short of cash borrow from a pool that is "stocked" with the unneeded cash of other affiliates or units. Such internal lending benefits all the participating affiliates, and therefore the company as a whole, insofar as the interest saved by the borrowing unit(s) exceeds any interest losses to the lending unit(s). If, for example, one affiliate of a particular MNC needed to borrow $5 million, for which commercial banks in its host country would charge 14 percent interest, while a second affiliate of the same company had $5 million of temporarily excess cash which it could earn only 10 percent by investing externally, a loan through the corporate pool with interest set at 11 percent would be advantageous to both affiliates and would reduce the *net* cost of short-term funding for the entire MNC.

It follows from this that intracorporate lending may not always constitute the optimum use of a firm's pooled excess cash. Analysis of alternative investment opportunities may indicate that the firm would realize a greater net return by investing such funds externally. Nevertheless, the existence of the pool and the centralization of its management would still be beneficial, as it would broaden the range of alternatives being evaluated and might enable the firm to increase its interest earnings by consolidating its funds to make large-volume loans or other investments. This approach also shifts responsibility for short-term investment decisions from the managers of individual affiliates to a team of financial specialists, who are apt to be better equipped to comprehend and deal with the effects which national taxes, inflation, and exchange rates would have on their company's investments.

Netting.   A second technique commonly used in international cash management is **netting.** This is designed to minimize the incidence of fund transfers within a multinational company by establishing a central clearing mechanism, which keeps track of all transactions that are taking place among the affiliates and determines the net payments that must be made and received in settlement of those transactions. Such a procedure can greatly reduce the number and volume of monetary transfers that have to be made as a consequence of purchases and sales of capital goods, technology, materials and components, or other interaffiliate transactions. Since it is costly to send money from one country to another via bank drafts or cable transfers, the elimination of unnecessary payments can bring substantial savings. Furthermore, netting can decrease exchange rate risks, by reducing the amount of foreign currencies that affiliates must acquire to make payments to their sister affiliates.

Leading and Lagging.   The establishment of a central clearing office to monitor and direct interaffiliate payments and receipts also makes it easier for a multinational firm to employ **leading and lagging** as a cash management technique. This technique relates to the timing of fund transfers, either within a multinational firm or between the firm and external parties. By deliberately delaying (lagging) some payments and accelerating (leading) others, a MNC can mitigate the adverse effects of inflation or exchange rate instability on the value of its liquid assets or even profit from such conditions.

One of the general "rules" of leading and lagging is that affiliates located in countries with high rates of inflation or depreciating currencies (which frequently go hand in hand) should accelerate the payment of their debts. This will reduce their holdings of cash or other liquid assets whose real values would be eroded by inflation or a fall in the value of the currency in which they are denominated. The early payment of foreign currency debts by such affiliates also avoids their having to trade more units of their local currency to settle those debts at a later time. The obvious companion rule is that affiliates operating in countries with low rates of inflation and appreciating currencies should defer the payment of their foreign debts and build up their holdings of monetary assets to take advantage of the rising value of their local currency.

The effective application of these rules requires an ability to forecast price level and exchange rate changes, as well as the capability to delay debt payments without incurring serious penalties. These requirements can be fulfilled by a centralized cash management organization in a multinational firm, whose personnel have the facilities and expertise to study and forecast price and exchange rate developments throughout the world and whose managers have the authority to reschedule intra-corporate financial settlements.

Transfer Pricing. In addition to controlling the timing of fund movements within their global corporate organizations, multinational firms are able to exert substantial control over the direction and magnitude of those movements. This is done through the adjustment of **transfer prices,** which is the term used to refer to the prices which are set and recorded for the transactions that take place between parent and affiliates and among the affiliates themselves. The setting of these transfer prices is another important, albeit controversial, technique through which multinational firms attempt to attain their international cash management objectives.

As noted on many previous occasions, there are a great number of business transactions occurring continuously among the affiliated units of MNCs. These include transfers of resources (capital goods, technology, managerial talent, capital funds) and transfers of materials and components for producing products, as well as finished products and services. Inasmuch as the prices to be applied to such transfers are determined internally by the managers of the multinational involved, they can be used as a means of "positioning" funds, that is, shifting the corporation's funds from country to country.

The ability to position funds through transfer pricing opens numerous avenues through which a MNC can protect the value of those funds and enhance its profitability. The reduction or deferral of tax liabilities is one of those avenues. By setting "artificially" high prices (that is, prices higher than would be charged on an "arms-length" sale to a customer outside the corporation) on intracorporate sales to affiliates in countries with high corporate tax rates, the multinational effectively reduces the taxable profits of those affiliates. Conversely, artificially low transfer prices can be charged on sales to affiliates in low-tax countries, thereby increasing the portion of the MNC's total profits that are subject to lower tax rates. The amount of import duties that the firm has to pay on materials or products shipped from one affiliate to another can also be manipulated by transfer pricing, for example, by applying low prices to shipments to countries with high duties that are based on the invoice price of the products being imported.

As with leading and lagging, transfer pricing can be used to shift funds out of weak-currency countries and into countries with strong, stable currencies. This is done by setting high prices on sales to affiliates in countries with depreciating currencies, thereby enabling those affiliates to transfer funds out in the guise of payments for imports from their parent or sister affiliates. This device may allow a MNC to circumvent some of the foreign exchange controls that are frequently imposed by nations whose currencies are falling in value.

Multinational corporations have devised several others ways of utilizing transfer pricing to improve their financial positions. However,

---

Box 16.1

Cutting Taxes By Transfer Pricing?

The U.S. Internal Revenue Service has been conducting an investigation to determine whether several major Japanese auto makers underpaid their U.S. income taxes during the 1970s. At issue is whether Toyota Motor Corp., Nissan Motor Co., and Honda Motors Co. charged their U.S. sales subsidiaries unreasonably high prices for cars, thereby reducing the profits which those subsidiaries reported when the cars were sold to American buyers.

Automotive News, a trade publication, recently reported that the IRS might claim $300 million from Toyota, $200 million from Nissan, and $100 million from Honda. However, a spokeswoman for Honda said that the IRS has stipulated that there is no deficiency in the income tax due from that company.

Source: "Honda Says IRS Dropped It From Tax Investigation," *The Wall Street Journal,* January 9, 1985, 4.

---

governments have become increasingly critical of such pricing schemes in recent years, and have been tightening their tax laws and other regulations in order to prevent what they regard as the deliberate flouting of their national interests and policies through manipulative transfer pricing by the MNCs. The code of conduct for MNCs that is being developed by the United Nations (see Chapter 13) also contains provisions applying specifically to transfer prices. Such official measures have not entirely foreclosed the potential for MNCs to use transfer prices as a financial management tool, but they have curtailed the options that multinational managers have in this area and required them to exercise greater caution in pricing intracorporate transactions.

The foregoing survey of financial management practices in MNCs indicates that these firms have been making determined efforts to increase the productivity of their investments and the efficiency of their utilization of cash and other monetary assets. It also makes reference to the kinds of risks and problems with which the multinationals must contend in pursuing those financial goals. The following section will consider more intensively some of the more prominent of these problems and risks, together with methods multinational firms employ in dealing with them.

Multinational Corporate Financial Problems and Risks

Foreign Exchange Exposure

There is little doubt that the management of foreign exchange and exchange rate risks ranks very high, if not foremost, among the concerns of multinational corporate financial executives. The nature of the exchange rate risk and some means of countering it were discussed earlier (in Chapter 10) in the context of export–import operations. However, the effects of exchange rates and their fluctuations on multinational companies extend far beyond the trade sphere. Virtually the entire range of operating decisions, from the choice of entry strategies for foreign markets to the repatriation of income from those markets, are apt to be influenced by exchange rate considerations. Moreover, the profitability and even the net worth of a multinational firm can be substantially altered by changing relative values of the currencies in which those profits are realized and the firm's assets and liabilities are denominated.

In order for financial managers to deal effectively with exchange rate changes and the risks associated with them, they must first determine the extent to which their firm is actually vulnerable to such risks. **Foreign exchange risk exposure** is the basic measure of how and how much a firm will be affected, in terms of the value of its assets and liabilities and its current and future income, by exchange rate changes.

Such changes can affect a firm in several different ways, and there are different types of exposure. Three major types are translation exposure, transaction exposure, and economic exposure.

Translation Exposure. *Translation exposure* is a measure of how exchange rate changes would affect the financial position of a company as that position is recorded and reported in accounting statements. Translation exposure is therefore also referred to as *accounting exposure.* It results mainly from the consolidation of the financial statements of a multinational parent company and its overseas affiliates, which necessitates restating (translating) the values of assets and liabilities denominated in foreign currencies, as well as revenues and expenses denominated in those currencies, in the parent company's home currency. Inasmuch as the necessity of such translation arises out of national laws or accounting requirements, rather than the need for the firm to actually convert the values reported from one currency to another, any gains or losses recorded through the translation process can be thought of as *unrealized* gains or losses.

Table 16.1 provides an illustration of translation exposure and its effects from the perspective of a U.S. parent company with a subsidiary in West Germany. For purposes of simplification, it shows only the current asset and liability portion of the subsidiary's balance sheet, which is consolidated with that of the parent company at the end of each calendar quarter. It also assumes that the value of those current assets

Table 16.1   *Translation Effect of Exchange Rate Change on*
Consolidated Balance Sheet of U.S. Multinational Corporation

German Subsidiary's Balance Sheet		Dollar Values Recorded on Parent Company's Consolidated Balance Sheet	
		March 31, 1984 (1 DM = $0.36)	June 30, 1984 (1 DM = $0.33)
Current Assets (in DMs)			
Cash	100,000	$ 36,000	$ 33,000
Accounts receivable	160,000	57,000	52,800
Inventory	300,000	108,000	99,000
Total current assets	560,000	201,600	184,800
Current liabilities (in DMs)			
Accounts payable	80,000	28,800	26,400
Bank loans	120,000	43,200	39,600
Total current liabilities	200,000	72,000	66,000
Current assets less current liabilities	360,000	129,600	118,800

and liabilities, expressed in deutschemarks (DMs), remained constant over the quarter covered, but that the dollar value of the DM declined from $0.36 to $0.33 during that time period. In this example, the U.S. company's financial accounts would show a translation loss of $10,800 for the quarter, representing the decline in the dollar value of the German subsidiary's current assets less the decline in the dollar value of its current liabilities. Again, this would be an unrealized loss, since the German subsidiary's current assets and liabilities actually remained intact. It should also be noted that the depreciation of the DM resulted in a translation *loss* because DM-dominated assets exceeded the DM-denominated liabilities. Had the liabilities exceeded the assets, the DM's depreciation would have shown up as a translation *gain* on the parent firm's balance sheet.

Even though translation losses or gains are not realized, they are nevertheless meaningful. By altering a firm's reported net worth, they can influence the perceptions of investors and creditors regarding its financial situation and thereby have an effect upon the availability and cost of capital to the firm. Furthermore, if stockholders and investors are not fully cognizant of the true nature and causes of translation losses, they may look on them as indications of poor performance by management. For these reasons, the managers of multinational companies must be concerned with translation exposure and methods of avoiding or reducing it.

Transaction Exposure.   *Transaction exposure* measures the amount of losses or gains that exchange rate changes would cause a firm to incur in settling obligations or receiving payments in foreign currencies. Such exposure arises out of business transactions (usually of a relatively short-term nature) in which the firm has made a commitment to make or to receive payment in a foreign currency.

Purchases from abroad on credit or credit sales to foreign buyers are frequently the basis of transaction exposure. If, for example, an American company were to buy steel from a Belgian mill and agree to pay for that steel in Belgian francs 6 months after delivery, the U.S. firm would be exposed to a transaction loss or gain. If the price of the Belgian franc rose relative to the dollar during the time in which the debt was outstanding, the U.S. firm would have to pay more dollars for the steel than it had anticipated paying when the purchase was negotiated. Conversely, of course, a decline in the franc's value in terms of dollars would result in a transaction gain for the U.S. company.

Foreign loans are another common source of transaction exposure. If a U.S. company were to borrow funds, from a commercial bank or other lenders, that had to be repaid in a foreign currency, the company would experience a loss if the dollar value of that currency had risen by the time the loan came due for payment. The company would gain, in that it could repay the loan with fewer dollars than it had anticipated when the funds were borrowed, should the price of the foreign currency decline in relation to the dollar. In a sense, transaction gains or losses are more "real" than translation gains or losses, since they affect the amounts of a firm's actual cash inflows and outflows, rather than its financial situation as reported in accounting statements.

Economic Exposure.   *Economic exposure* is concerned with the total impact of future exchange rate changes on a firm's profitability. It is a broader and more subjective concept of exposure than either translation or transaction exposure, as it encompasses the potential effects of such changes on *all facets* of a firm's operations. By the same token, however, economic exposure may be more significant than the others, inasmuch as it relates to the long-term profit performance, and hence to the value, of the firm as a business enterprise.

A comprehensive assessment of economic exposure would include such diverse considerations as how possible variations in exchange rates would affect a company's sales prospects in foreign markets, the costs of labor and other inputs to be utilized in overseas production, or the desirability of acquiring new affiliates abroad. It would entail forecasts of rate changes over an extended period of time, together with calculations of how those changes would affect the net present value of future cash flows from the firm's overseas operations.

Exposure Management

Since economic exposure relates to the broad, long-term effects of exchange rate changes on a multinational company's business activities and financial health, coping with such exposure is a responsibility that is shared by virtually all the company's managers in every operating area. For instance, marketing managers must take account of how exchange rate variations might affect their foreign prices and competitive positions and try to make provision for such contingencies in their marketing plans and programs. Production managers likewise must be cognizant of the potential consequences of such changes in terms of their production costs and the real value of their inventories; while engineers and product development specialists need to be concerned with how exchange rate fluctuations could alter the costs of building and equipping new production facilities abroad or manufacturing new products in foreign locales. Thus, reacting effectively to economic exposure is a continuing task that cannot be handled through standardized responses or assigned to financial managers alone.

On the other hand, there are certain conventional financing techniques that multinational firms can employ to reduce the risks associated with transaction or translation exposure. Some of these, including leading and lagging in foreign payments or collections and netting procedures (which reduce the need for affiliates to acquire or hold foreign currencies in the course of their transactions with one another), have already been described. The other widely used methods all involve some form of **hedging.**

In general, hedging refers to deliberately taking two opposite or offsetting financial positions with the aim of compensating for any losses on one of these positions with gains on the other. There are several ways in which this can be applied to the foreign exchange exposure risk of multinational companies.

Forward Exchange Contracts.   One means of effectuating a hedge is through the use of *forward contracts in foreign exchange.* These contracts and their use in relation to international trade activities were described in Chapter 10. But a multinational company can utilize the forward market to deal with other forms and sources of exchange rate risk.

For instance, the imaginary U.S. firm which (in the example just above) had bought steel from Belgium had taken a "short position" in Belgian currency by agreeing to make payment in that currency 6 months later. The firm could hedge that position by entering into a forward contract with a foreign exchange dealer, through which the firm would contract to buy the amount of francs needed to pay for the steel. Such a contract would specify delivery of the francs 6 months from the contract date, but the price of those francs in dollars would be fixed when the contract was entered into. This agreement would put the firm in a "long posi-

Box 16.2

Losing Sleep over Foreign Exchange Exposure

On a recent cold morning in Honeoye Fall, N.Y., a hamlet 20 miles south of Rochester, Eric R. Nelson crawled out of bed a few minutes after 5 a.m., fed two cats, put on an overcoat over his pajamas and went down to his unheated basement.

For 30 minutes he read news reports from a rented newswire hooked into a video screen, while waiting for his routine 5:30 a.m. phone call from a London bank. When it came, Mr. Nelson bought $6.3 million in yen, $5.1 million in West German marks, and $2.1 million in French francs. It was a normal morning for Mr. Nelson, who is neither an insomniac nor an eccentric millionaire. Over the course of a year, he manages $1.5 billion in foreign currencies for Eastman Kodak Co., based here.

Of Kodak's $10.6 billion in revenue last year, $3.71 billion came from sales outside the U.S. and about half of that came from products exported from the U.S. Because the photographic products company bills its subsidiaries in their own currencies and sells its goods mostly in foreign currencies, Kodak has a "long" position in foreign currencies and a "short" position in dollars. Thus, a rising dollar can produce losses, because Kodak's foreign receivables are worth less when converted to dollars. Conversely, a falling dollar makes the company's foreign sales more valuable in the U.S.

Mr. Nelson's team of seven people is responsible for protecting imports, receivables, royalties, dividends, service fees, and processing costs in 16 currencies. It actively manages about $300 million at any one time.

Source: Michael R. Sesit, "By Trading Currencies, Kodak's Eric R. Nelson Saves the Firm Millions," *The Wall Street Journal,* March 5, 1985, p. 1. Reprinted by permission of *The Wall Street Journal,* © Dow Jones & Company., Inc. 1985. All Rights Reserved.

tion" in Belgian francs, that would offset the short position resulting from its commitment to pay for the steel in francs. This forward contract would complete the hedge, inasmuch as whatever the firm might lose on its payment for the steel as a consequence of an increase in the dollar value of the Belgian franc would be counterbalanced by a gain in its forward contract.

Forward contracts can equally well be used to hedge the transaction exposure resulting from short-term borrowing or lending abroad. For example, an American firm that borrowed Swiss francs from a European commercial bank to be repaid in 6 months would be "short" in francs as a consequence of that borrowing. The firm could reduce the exchange rate risk associated with that short position by "buying francs forward," that is, entering into a forward contract to receive the amount of francs needed to repay the loan when it fell due. Here again, any loss (or gain) realized on the loan transaction as a consequence of changes in the franc/dollar exchange rate would be offset by a gain (or loss) on the forward exchange contract.

Although forward contracts are versatile instruments, there are some limits on their availability. The large commercial banks that deal regularly and heavily in foreign exchange are willing to enter into such contracts routinely, so long as the currencies involved are among the major world currencies for which there is a strong and continuing market demand and supply. But a firm that needed to hedge its exposure in some other national currency might experience difficulty in negotiating a forward contract for that purpose. Moreover, the forward contracts offered by foreign exchange dealers ordinarily do not extend beyond 6 months into the future.

Swap Arrangements.   Another form of hedging that can be employed in situations in which forward contracts are not available or applicable is the so-called **swap arrangement.** This term refers to arrangements between companies, or between companies and banks, in which the parties agree to exchange currencies for one another at one point in time and to reverse that exchange at a predetermined future date. This can best be clarified through some examples.

One simple example of a swap would be an arrangement between a U.S. multinational parent company with a subsidiary in Japan, and a Japanese parent company with an American subsidiary. Assuming that both these subsidiaries were in need of local-currency funding, a swap agreement between the two parents could provide such funding while avoiding exchange rate risks. The U.S. parent firm would loan dollars to the Japanese subsidiary in the United States, while the Japanese parent firm would loan an equivalent amount of yen to the American subsidiary in Japan. The two parents are thus, in effect, "swapping" dollars for yen. Both the loans would be repaid at an agreed-upon future date, with each of the two lenders receiving repayment in their own home currencies. The swap is thereby reversed, in that the American MNC is returning the borrowed yen and the Japanese MNC is returning borrowed dollars.

Another of the many varieties of swap arrangements that have been devised by multinational companies is the *credit swap*. These arrangements typically involve a company and a foreign bank, which may be either a private commercial bank or the central bank of the foreign country. As an example, a U.S. multinational parent company might have a subsidiary in Mexico that needed to acquire Mexican pesos to finance the purchase of equipment in that country. If the U.S. parent firm were to convert dollars into pesos in the foreign exchange market and loan those pesos to its Mexican affiliate, it would be taking the risk that the dollar value of the peso would subsequently decline, resulting in a loss to the firm. Problems might also arise if the Mexican government restricted the conversion of pesos into dollars; such restrictions could make it difficult, if not impossible, for the Mexican subsidiary to repay the loan to its U.S. parent company in dollars, even if the peso/dollar exchange rate had not changed significantly.

Such risks could be avoided through a credit swap between the American company and a Mexican bank. The American parent company could deposit dollars in the Mexican bank's account in one of its branches or correspondents in the United States, while the Mexican bank loaned an equivalent amount of pesos to the Mexican subsidiary. It would be understood that the swap was to be reversed on a specified future date; at that time, the Mexican bank would repay the U.S. parent firm the amount of dollars that had previously been deposited to its account, and the U.S. subsidiary in Mexico would repay the peso loan to the Mexican bank.

Since the amounts of dollars and pesos to be loaned and repaid had been agreed to in the swap arrangement, they would be unaffected by exchange rate changes that occurred while the arrangement was in effect. And, since the subsidiary in Mexico does not have to exchange pesos for dollars to repay its loan or transfer funds from Mexico to the United States, government exchange controls would not be a factor in the repayments.

This credit swap would benefit the U.S. company by alleviating the exchange rate risk and potential exchange control problems. The Mexican bank would benefit by having more dollars available for use in the United States. It is also common practice in these agreements for the banks to acquire the deposits on an interest-free basis, while charging interest on the loans that they advance in their home countries. Thus, the companies that negotiate credit swaps normally incur costs; but those costs are known and certain, as opposed to the uncertain and open-ended prospect of losses that might be incurred in the absence of such arrangements.

Balance Sheet Hedges.   It is also possible for multinational firms to reduce their foreign exchange risk exposure through a **balance sheet hedge.** A hedge of this sort is accomplished by equalizing the amounts of assets and liabilities that are exposed to the effects of fluctuations in the exchange rates of particular pairs of currencies.

The use of a balance sheet hedge can be demonstrated by referring to Table 16.1, which illustrates the translation exposure of an American company with an affiliate in West Germany. Because the affiliate's DM-denominated assets (560,000) exceeded its DM-denominated liabilities (200,000), the U.S. parent firm was exposed to the possibility of a translation loss or gain from a change in the dollar/DM exchange rate.

A balance sheet hedge could be attained in this situation by either increasing the subsidiary's DM liabilities or decreasing its DM assets so as to equate the total assets and liabilities. The subsidiary might, for instance, borrow more funds from German banks or draw down its cash balances and use the funds made available from those sources to buy dollars. The dollars could be held by the German affiliate or remitted to the American parent firm for dividend or other payments. If equality of assets and liabilities were achieved through such methods, the parent company would no longer be exposed to any net translation loss or gain from changes in the exchange rate between the mark and the dollar. Any reduction in the dollar value of DM-denominated assets on the parent's accounting statements would be matched by a reduction in the dollar value of its DM-denominated liabilities, and vice versa.

Limitations and Costs of Hedging.   There are still other hedging techniques used by multinational firms, and there are almost infinite possibilities for varying those techniques to fit the particular needs and circumstances of individual MNCs. One might therefore conclude that such firms have ample means at their disposal to overcome the problems and risks that arise from their holdings of foreign assets and liabilities and dealings in different national currencies.

While such a conclusion is not entirely unwarranted, it is important to keep in mind that the hedging and other foreign exchange management techniques that are available to multinational companies are by no means a total solution to such risks and problems. First, there may be situations in which none of the conventional methods of exposure management would be feasible. Second, firms often encounter conflicts in attempting to protect themselves against the different types of foreign exchange exposure. For example, a firm that was endeavoring to reduce its translation exposure by converting foreign currency-dominated assets into its home currency might well incur a transaction loss in that conversion.

Third, these protective actions invariably have costs attached to them. In some instances, there are obvious monetary costs, for example, the interest costs associated with credit swaps or the premiums that must be paid in forward foreign exchange contracts. In other cases, the costs may be less immediate or apparent. But such "hidden" costs, especially the cost of the managerial time and effort that must be given over to analyzing foreign exchange risks and developing and implementing measures to reduce or avoid them, can be very great.

It follows, therefore, that the financial managers of multinational firms must continuously weigh the relative costs of alternative methods of countering exchange rate exposure in order to minimize the cost of obtaining the protection needed. Moreover, they must decide whether the benefits of such protection justify that cost.

This is a complicated procedure. It entails not only the measurement of a firm's exposed position, but also forecasts of future exchange rate fluctuations. Unfortunately, exchange rate forecasting still is a very imperfect science, notwithstanding the growing number of individuals and organizations involved in it and the seemingly sophisticated predictive models they have developed. Despite their questionable accuracy, however, exchange rate forecasts are indispensable to any rational calculation of the relative costs and benefits of exposure management efforts.

In summary, then, foreign exchange exposure management continues to pose a serious and difficult challenge to MNCs and their managers. Even though numerous ingenious techniques and arrangements have been devised for reducing exposure, and MNCs are able to enlist the aid of commercial banks and other organizations in this task, every multinational firm and its executives must remain constantly alert to the many ways in which their profitability can be affected by exchange rate variations and must be prepared to accept the frustrations and costs of contending with those variations.

Taxation

Taxes present another set of problems for multinational firms. Those problems arise out of the dissimilarities in tax laws, methods or forms of taxation, and effective tax rates that are found among the nations of the world. However, those differences also provide opportunities for astute financial managers to bolster the aftertax profitability of their companies.

Choice of Organizational Form.   The tax variables noted above affect the decisions of multinational corporations in several ways. One of these has to do with *the form of organization* selected by such corporations. For example, under U.S. tax law, the income of foreign **branches** of an American parent company is treated differently than the income of foreign **subsidiaries.** Inasmuch as a foreign branch is legally regarded as an integral extension of the parent, its profits (or losses) are automatically unified with those of the parent company and taxed by the U.S. government in the period in which they are earned. A subsidiary, by contrast, is viewed as a separate legal entity, and its profits therefore are generally not taxable by the U.S. until they are repatriated to the parent as dividends.

These differences can greatly influence a company's choice between these two organizational alternatives. For instance, establishing a new foreign affiliate as a branch might have beneficial tax effects if the company expects that affiliate to record losses in its early years of operation, since those losses will directly and immediately reduce the parent firm's taxable income. On the other hand, a subsidiary arrangement allows the parent firm to defer the payment of U.S. taxes on foreign profits, and that deferral privilege can be very attractive insofar as the U.S. tax rate exceeds that of the country in which the subsidiary is located. (This deferral advantage will be discussed more fully later in this section.)

Tax Haven Affiliates.   Multinational corporations also frequently create affiliates for the sole purpose of reducing or deferring tax payments. Reference has been made previously to **tax haven affiliates.** These are nonoperating or "dummy" organizations that are established in nations (such as the Netherlands Antilles, the Bahamas, the Cayman Islands, Liechtenstein, Panama, and Bermuda) that have very low rates of taxes on business income. The MNCs then use various devices to channel income into those subsidiaries, where it is insulated from the higher taxes of the MNCs' home countries or the host countries in which operating affiliates are located.

Such tax haven subsidiaries often are part of a MNC's transfer pricing strategy. Thus, a multinational firm might set up a subsidiary in a tax-haven country and route its interaffiliate sales through that subsidiary. The actual physical transfer of the goods involved in those sales would continue to take place among the operating affiliates. But the company's accounting records would show that those goods were first being sold to the tax-haven subsidiary and then resold to another affiliate. By combining these "paper" transactions with the proper mix of transfer prices, the MNC might be able to shelter a large portion of its profits from taxation.[1]

As this discussion of tax havens indicates, there are substantial variations in the taxes that different nations levy on business income. The countries listed above represent a group of nations that have deliberately kept their taxes exceptionally low in order to entice multinational firms to set up affiliated offices there. These countries all are quite small and resource-poor, so that the employment and tax revenues that are generated by those corporate offices, and by the banking and other financial facilities that accompany them, are a boon to their economies.

Apart from the tax haven countries, many developing countries use moderate rates of taxation and various special tax incentives as a means of attracting direct investment by multinational firms. Meanwhile, the Western industrialized nations, together with the newly industrializing developing nations, have higher tax rates. Those rates still diverge to some extent among these more advanced nations, although there has been a tendency for those divergences to narrow over time.

Such variations in tax rates can influence the **locational** decisions of MNCs. Whenever those firms are deciding where to locate new production or distribution facilities or determining which existing facilities should be expanded or contracted, differences in the effective rates of taxation that would be applied to the income from those facilities are likely to be one of the critical factors that are taken into account.

---

[1]The U.S. government has attempted to combat this practice by adopting tax provisions (notably Subpart F of the U.S. Internal Revenue Code) that make the income of tax-haven subsidiaries taxable by the U.S. whether repatriated or not. These provisions constitute exceptions to the general rule that the income of foreign subsidiaries is subject to U.S. taxes only when it is repatriated to the United States as dividends.

It is important to recognize, however, that the advantage that a multi-national firm realizes from operating in low-tax countries depends to a great extent on the tax laws of its own *home* country. Again, there are substantial differences in the way in which the major home countries treat the foreign-source income of their MNCs, but the U.S. case can be used to explain how home country tax laws can affect foreign investment decisions, including locational choices.

Tax Treatment of Foreign Business Income.   One of the basic principles of U.S. tax law is that the income of U.S. citizens or residents (including American corporations) is subject to taxation by the U.S. government regardless of where it is earned. The strict application of this principle would eliminate any tax advantage that a U.S.-based MNC would enjoy on profits earned by its foreign affiliates. However, there are additional provisions in U.S. tax policy that can preserve such advantages.

The first of these, which already has been alluded to briefly, is the **deferral** provision. This essentially allows American MNCs to postpone the payment of taxes to the U.S. government on foreign-source income until such time as that income is repatriated, that is, "brought back" to the United States in the form of dividends or other distributions to the parent organization. This makes it possible for the multinationals to keep billions of dollars of income free of U.S. taxes indefinitely, by holding and reinvesting it outside the United States. Inasmuch as the amount of money that is thereby "freed up" is determined by the difference between the taxes that must be paid immediately to the governments of the countries in which foreign income is earned and the taxes that the U.S. government would levy on that income in the absence of the deferral privilege, American companies reap the greatest benefit from that privilege by investing in foreign countries with the lowest rates of taxation.

A second important provision of U.S. tax law relating to income from overseas investments is the **foreign tax credit.** This basically permits American companies to claim taxes paid to foreign governments as a credit against their tax liabilities to the U.S. government. The main aim of this provision is to prevent double taxation, that is, the taxing of the same income by both the government of the country in which it is earned and the government of the country to which it is repatriated. The availability of the tax credit is what makes foreign investment in general feasible, since it removes the possibility that the income from such investment would be taxed more heavily than income from domestic investment. But tax credit considerations can also enter into decisions regarding the types and locations of overseas investments to be undertaken, since there are some intricacies in the foreign tax credit provisions of the U.S. law that may make it more advantageous for American MNCs to invest in certain foreign countries (notably the developing countries) or types of economic activity.

In addition to influencing the organizational structures and the foreign investment decisions of multinational firms, taxes also affect the volume and timing of their international transfers of funds. It is here that financial managers become most directly involved, as they attempt to plan fund transfers so as to minimize the negative effects of taxes on the firm's profits and take advantage of opportunities for tax savings.

To carry out those efforts effectively, financial managers must be knowledgeable with regard to the tax laws and practices of the countries in which their firm is operating, and they must also be aware of recent or impending changes in those laws and practices. If, for instance, a nation in which one of a firm's affiliates is located is contemplating an increase in its business taxes, this may serve as a signal to accelerate dividend remittances from that country or to shift working capital balances to other lower-tax countries.

It is, of course, very difficult for financial managers to be familiar with all the relevant tax provisions of numerous foreign countries and to keep abreast of revisions in those provisions. For this reason, it is virtually imperative that multinational firms use the services of international accounting and legal firms and other tax specialists. However, it remains the responsibility of the multinational corporate financial managers to translate the information and advice provided by these outside experts into decisions and actions that will optimize the financial situation and returns of their companies.

Summary

1. Multinational firms enjoy some financing advantages relative to companies that are operating in a single country. These include their access to international financial markets as sources of funds and their ability to invest throughout the world.
2. However, the multinationals also face many unique financing problems, growing out of the need to deal in many different currencies and national financial environments, as well as governmental controls on international transfers of funds.
3. Multinational firms have exhibited a tendency to centralize their financial functions. This permits them to minimize the overall costs of the funding that they require and to optimize the returns from their investments.
4. The multinationals must apply capital budgeting procedures in making long-term investment decisions, even though comparative assessments of investment opportunities become more difficult in an international setting.
5. International cash management systems, which involve a systematic, corporate-wide approach to the management of liquid assets and liabilities, have become very widely used by multinational firms.

6. Several cash management techniques have become standard practice among multinational corporations. These include the pooling of liquid assets, the netting of intracorporate receipts and payables, leading and lagging in making and receiving payments, and the adoption of transfer pricing strategies that can help the firm position its funds in an optimum manner.

7. The management of foreign exchange risk is one of the principal concerns of financial managers in multinational corporations.

8. Dealing with foreign exchange risk effectively entails constant assessments of the firm's exposure to such risks. There are various types of exposure, including economic, translation, and transaction exposure.

9. Economic exposure is related to virtually all of a multinational firm's operations and dealing with such exposure therefore is a responsibility shared by the entire management team.

10. The principal means of countering translation and transaction exposure is through hedging, which involves the deliberate taking of opposing financial positions in order to compensate for losses on one position with gains from the other.

11. Hedging can be accomplished in a variety of ways, including the use of forward foreign exchange contracts, swap arrangements, and balance sheet hedges.

12. The dissimilarities that are present in the tax laws, tax rates, and taxing methods of the countries of the world create both difficulties and opportunities for multinational financial managers. Multinational firms respond to this tax situation by varying their organizational structures, their investment decisions, and the timing of their international transfers of funds.

Questions for Review or Discussion

1. What advantages do multinational firms enjoy, relative to domestic firms, in the financing area?

2. Identify the nature and basis of the unique financing problems that are faced by multinational corporations.

3. What is the rationale for the trend toward centralization of the finance function in multinational corporations?

4. Why does capital budgeting tend to be more complicated in multinational companies than in domestic firms?

5. What are the objectives of international cash management systems in multinational corporations? How does the centralization of liquid asset management help to attain those objectives?

6. What advantages are associated with the *pooling* of liquid assets in multinational companies? How is such pooling accomplished?

7. How does the process of *netting* work in a multinational firm? What are the advantages of the netting process?

8. Give some examples of how a multinational firm might employ *leads and lags* to improve its financial position or accomplish other cash managment objectives.

9. What is meant by *transfer pricing* in relation to multinational corporations? Describe some ways in which transfer prices could be used to further the financial aims of a multinational corporation.

10. Why are national governments critical of the transfer pricing methods utilized by multinational corporations?

11. Define *foreign exchange risk exposure* and explain how such exposure is measured in a multinational corporation.

12. What is meant by the statement that the losses or gains associated with translation exposure may be *unrealized* losses or gains?

13. What is the relationship between translation exposure and transaction exposure?

14. In what sense might economic exposure be considered more "significant" than either translation or transaction exposure?

15. Define the procedure of *hedging* and explain how it can be used to reduce the foreign exchange risk in multinational corporations.

16. What are the costs that are invariably incurred in responding to foreign exchange risk? How do such costs enter into the risk-management decisions and processes of multinational firms?

17. Explain the *deferral provision* as it relates to the taxation of multinational corporate income and explain how that provision might affect the financial decisions of such corporations.

Case

The Toronto Blue Jays

The Toronto Blue Jays have the best win–loss record in major league baseball. However, in the currency leagues they are nearly at the bottom. They are budgeting a foreign exchange loss of about $2 million for 1985 even though attendance and ticket prices are up.*

The Blue Jays get most of their revenues in Canadian dollars but pay most of their bills in U.S. dollars. Revenues of approximately $21 million will almost all be in Canadian dollars except for income from the U.S. television rights package and 20 percent of the gate receipts from Jays games in U.S. ballparks. Expenses, on the other hand, will be $19 million in U.S. dollars and about $4.5 million in the Canadian currency. Expenses include about $10 million in players' salaries this year (1.5

*As cited in *The Wall Street Journal*, July 15, 1985.

Figure 16.1   Canadian Exchange Rates—Forecasted Versus Actual

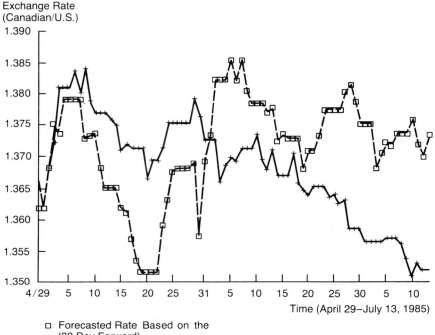

million for relief pitcher Bill Caudill alone) while salaries were $850,000 in 1977, the Jays' first season. All major league salaries are paid in U.S. dollars and anyhow, none of the Jays' players are Canadian.

Mr. Paul Beeston, the Blue Jays executive vice-president for business, estimates that the Jays' expenses rise about $135,000 each season for each 1-cent drop in the value of the Canadian dollar. The Canadian dollar is now at 73 cents U.S. in contrast to the $1.04 value it had in 1976 when the Toronto franchise was created! Ironically, the Blue Jays would be one of the very few profitable major league teams if it weren't for the currency problem (only 8 of the 26 major league teams were profitable in 1984). While Mr. Beeston does not expect the Canadian dollar to rise much soon, he hopes the Jays' success this season with a possible pennant or even a world series win would result in higher attendance, especially at away games when the Jays get 20 percent of the gate receipts in U.S. dollars. The Jays are owned 10 percent by the

Canadian Imperial Bank of Commerce, 45 percent by the large Canadian brewing company, John Labatt, Ltd., and 45 percent by Canadian industrialist R. Howard Webster.

In order to protect themselves from foreign exchange losses, the Jays routinely make forward purchases of U.S. dollars. The team relies on advice on foreign exchange transactions from the economists working for the Canadian Imperial Bank of Commerce. Last year the Jays contracted to buy forward 80 percent of the team's needs for U.S. dollars at about 75 cents per Canadian dollar, and therefore the team is currently slightly ahead. In addition to forward contracts, two new instruments, futures and options, have recently become widely available for hedging against foreign exchange losses. In response to a query from Mr. Beeston, the Bank of Commerce economists have suggested that the Jays consider taking a position in some futures contracts and call options for purchasing U.S. dollars, in addition to their purchases of forward contracts for U.S. dollars. They point out that while normally the forward rate for the Canadian dollar is an unbiased forecast of the future spot rate, they also presented a chart showing that there are often considerable differences between the forward rate and the future spot rate. For the next year, they suggest a mix of 60 percent in forward contracts, 20 percent in futures contracts, and 10 percent in call options for a total of 90 percent of the Jays' projected needs for U.S. dollars.

What should the Jays do? Should they diversify their purchases of U.S. dollars?

Sources: John Mortisugu, "Toronto First in the American League, But Blue Jays Last in Foreign Exchange," *The Wall Street Journal,* July 5, 1985, p. 10; and "Foreign Exchange," *The Wall Street Journal,* March 28–July 31, 1985, various pages.

Appendix

Acronyms and Initials

ANCOM Andean Common Market. Economic integration arrangement among the Andean countries of South America.

ASEAN Association of Southeast Asian Nations. Economic integration program involving six nations in southeast Asia.

CACM Central American Common Market. Economic integration arrangement among the five nations of Central America.

CAP Common Agricultural Policy. Common policies relating to agricultural production and marketing instituted by the member nations of the European Economic Community.

CFIUS Committee on Foreign Investment in the United States. U.S. government committee charged with analyzing foreign investment in the United States and considering proposals for regulating such investment.

COMECON (or CMEA) Council for Mutual Economic Assistance. Economic integration arrangement among the communist countries.

ECLA Economic Commission for Latin America. A United Nations agency that has been instrumental in analyzing the economic problems of the developing countries and formulating proposals for dealing with those problems.

ECSC European Coal and Steel Community. Agreement established in 1952 to allow free trade in coal, steel, and iron ore among the Western European nations.

EEC European Economic Community. Organization of Western European countries that have carried out an extensive program of economic integration. The EEC originally consisted of six nations and now is made up of 12 full members.

EFTA European Free Trade Association. Association of Western European countries that have progressively reduced tariffs and other barriers to trade within their group.

EMS   European Monetary System. Arrangement in which several Western European countries maintain fixed exchange rates among their own currencies while permitting those rates to fluctuate in relation to other currencies.

FCPA   Foreign Corrupt Practices Act. U.S. law which makes it illegal for American companies and managers to make payments to foreign political officials, candidates, or parties for the purpose of obtaining business.

FTOs   Foreign Trade Organizations. Government organizations that conduct the foreign trade of communist countries.

GATT   General Agreement on Tariffs and Trade. An international agreement designed to encourage and support international trade by reducing tariffs and other trade barriers.

GSP   Generalized System of Preferences. Arrangements through which industrialized countries grant preferential import duty rates to products from developing countries.

IBRD   International Bank for Reconstruction and Development (more commonly called the World Bank). International financial institution whose principal purpose is to provide loans to developing nations for projects that are expected to contribute to their economic progress.

IDA   International Development Association. An affiliate of the World Bank which makes very long-term, low-interest loans to developing countries.

IFC   International Finance Corporation. An affiliate of the World Bank which provides venture capital to private firms in developing countries.

ITO   International Trade Organization. Organization that was to be established after World War II to encourage and oversee world trade. This organization never came into being, but many of its intended functions were undertaken through the GATT.

LAFTA   Latin American Free Trade Association. Economic integration arrangement involving the South American countries and Mexico.

LDCs   Less-developed countries (also referred to as developing or Third World countries). Countries characterized by relatively low levels of economic output and income per capita, limited industrial activity, and lack of adequate health, educational, and other social services.

LIBOR   London Interbank Offer Rate. Interest rate that banks in the Eurocurrency market set on loans to one another. This rate forms the basis of interest charges on loans to nonbank borrowers.

MFN   Most favored nation. Provision in international trade laws and agreements which effectively extends tariff reductions and other trade concessions to nations other than those which actually negotiate such concessions.

MNCs (or TNCs)   Multinational (or transnational) corporations. Companies that conduct business operations in several countries. They typically consist of a "parent" firm and a number of affiliates, which, while located in different countries, function as an integrated business enterprise.

NIEO   New International Economic Order. Set of proposals designed to improve the position of the developing countries in the world economy through basic changes in international trade policies and relationships.

NOEDCs   Non-oil-exporting developing countries. Those developing countries that do not produce or export petroleum.

OECD   Organization for Economic Cooperation and Development. Organization made up of the Western industrialized nations which encourages cooperative efforts among those nations in economic studies, economic policy formulation, and the provision of economic aid to developing nations.

OEEC   Organization for European Economic Cooperation. Organization established in 1948 to allocate U.S. economic aid among the Western European nations.

OPEC   Organization of Petroleum Exporting Countries. Group of 13 oil-producing countries which has endeavored to establish and maintain high prices for petroleum by regulating the supply of that commodity.

OPIC   Overseas Private Investment Corporation. U.S. government agency which provides political risk insurance and other forms of assistance to U.S. companies with investments in developing countries.

RTA   Reciprocal Trade Agreements (Act). Legislation enacted in the United States in 1934 which formed the basis for subsequent U.S. initiatives to liberalize international trade.

SBUs   Strategic business units. Constituent units of a business firm's organization, each of which is considered a separate business for portfolio planning purposes.

SDRs   Special drawing rights. An international reserve asset which is created by the International Monetary Fund and allocated among the member countries of the fund.

TEA   Trade Expansion Act. Legislation enacted in the United States in 1962 which gave the president broad authority to negotiate with other nations for the mutual reduction of tariffs and other trade barriers.

UNCTAD   United Nations Conference (Commission) on Trade and Development. This acronym refers both to a series of conferences that focussed on the international trade problems of the developing countries, and to a permanent commission that has been established to study those problems and advocate means of resolving them.

Name Index

The letter *t* indicates a text reference; others are footnote or source note references.

Subject Index

The letter *n* indicates footnote references.